Engendering Development

A World Bank Policy Research Report

Engendering Development

Through Gender Equality in Rights, Resources, and Voice

A copublication of the World Bank
and Oxford University Press

Oxford University Press

OXFORD   NEW YORK   ATHENS   AUCKLAND   BANGKOK   BOGOTA   BUENOS AIRES
CALCUTTA   CAPE TOWN   CHENNAI   DAR ES SALAAM   DELHI   FLORENCE   HONG
KONG   ISTANBUL   KARACHI   KUALA LUMPUR   MADRID   MELBOURNE   MEXICO CITY
MUMBAI   NAIROBI   PARIS   SÃO PAULO   SINGAPORE   TAIPEI   TOKYO   TORONTO
WARSAW

and associated companies in

BERLIN   IBADAN

Published by Oxford University Press, Inc.
198 Madison Avenue, New York, N.Y. 10016

Cover credits: design, Joyce C. Petruzzelli and The Report Team; illustration, Tilly
Northedge (Grundy & Northedge, London).

Manufactured in the United States of America
First printing January 2001

1 2 3 4 5 04 03 02 01

The findings, interpretations, and conclusions expressed in this study are entirely those of
the authors and should not be attributed in any manner to the World Bank, to its affiliated
organizations, or to members of its Board of Executive Directors or the countries they
represent. The boundaries, colors, denominations, and other information shown on any
map in this volume do not imply on the part of the World Bank Group any judgment on
the legal status of any territory or the endorsement or acceptance of such boundaries.

Library of Congress Cataloging-in-Publication Data

Engendering development: through gender equality in rights, resources, and voice.
        p. cm. -- (World Bank policy research report)
      Includes bibliographical references.
      ISBN 0-19-521596-6
      1. Sex role--Developing countries. 2. Women in development--Developing
countries.
      I. World Bank. II. Series.

      HQ1075.5.D44 E55 2001
      305.42'09172'4--dc21

⊗ *Text printed on paper that conforms to the American National Standard
for Permanence of Paper for Printed Library Materials, Z39.48-1984*

Contents

Boxes

Figures

Tables

Foreword

T HE WORLD BANK IS COMMITTED TO A WORLD FREE FROM
poverty. And it is clear that efforts to achieve this must address
gender inequalities. Large gender disparities in basic human
rights, in resources and economic opportunity, and in political voice are
pervasive around the world—in spite of recent gains. And these disparities
are inextricably linked to poverty.

On one level, poverty exacerbates gender disparities. Inequalities
between girls and boys in access to schooling or adequate health care
are more acute among the poor than among those with higher incomes. Whether measured in terms of command over such productive resources as land or credit, or in terms of power to influence the
development process, poor men tend to have less than do nonpoor
men—and poor women generally have least of all. These disparities
disadvantage women and girls and limit their capacity to participate
in and benefit from development.

On another level, gender inequalities hinder development. While disparities in basic rights; in schooling, credit, and jobs; or in the ability to
participate in public life take their most direct toll on women and girls,
the full costs of gender inequality ultimately harm everyone. Evidence
brought together in this report shows this unambiguously. A central
message is clear: ignoring gender disparities comes at great cost—to
people's well-being and to countries' abilities to grow sustainably, to govern
effectively, and thus to reduce poverty.

This conclusion presents an important challenge to us in the development community. What types of policies and strategies promote gender equality and foster more effective development? This report examines extensive evidence on the effects of institutional reforms, economic
policies, and active policy measures to promote greater equality between

women and men. The evidence sends a second important message: policymakers have a number of policy instruments to promote gender equality and development effectiveness.

But effective action requires also that policymakers take account of local realities when designing and implementing policies and programs. There can be no one-size-fits-all formula for promoting gender equality. Identifying what works requires consultations with stakeholders—both women and men—on key issues and actions. This points to a third important message of the report: to enhance development effectiveness, gender issues must be an integral part of policy analysis, design, and implementation.

Engendering Development provides policymakers, development specialists, and civil society members many valuable lessons and tools for integrating gender into development work. The wealth of evidence and analysis presented in the report can inform the design of effective strategies to promote equality between women and men in development. In doing so, it helps us—as policymakers and as members of the development community—to realize our commitment to a world without poverty.

James D. Wolfensohn
President
The World Bank

Preface

GENDER INEQUALITIES UNDERMINE THE EFFECTIVENESS OF development policies in fundamental ways. Yet this is an issue that often lies only at the periphery of policy dialogue and decisionmaking, both in national and international arenas. Part of the neglect comes from policymakers' reluctance to deal with topics that they deem inextricably associated with societal norms, religion, or cultural traditions. Part comes from a belief that gender gaps should be addressed by advocacy, not policy. And part comes from real (or feigned) ignorance about the nature of gender disparities and the costs of those disparities to people's well-being and countries' prospects for development. However, as this report shows, the costs of this reluctance, apathy, or ignorance are high.

The report aims to improve understanding of the links among gender issues, public policy, and development, and in so doing to foster a wider interest in and a stronger commitment to promoting gender equality. This report is written for a broad audience of students and practitioners of development, and especially for those who want to know why gender-related issues matter to development policy and practice. It focuses on evidence from developing countries, but when empirical research on key aspects is thin or missing in these countries, we present findings from industrial countries. Indeed, there are many lessons to be learned and shared across countries that take different approaches and are at different stages of development.

The report has benefited greatly from a large multidisciplinary literature on gender issues as they relate to development. It draws on research from economics, law, demography, sociology, and other disciplines. However, the report does not—indeed, cannot—cover the available literature comprehensively. To narrow the report's scope to manageable limits we have focused on the most recent policy research, and particularly on those studies that use rigorous empirical methods. In making this choice we have omitted some important older work on this topic, as well as more recent case studies based on qualitative information or very small sample sizes. In citing research findings we have applied standards generally accepted in the social sciences, relying largely on published sources in professional journals or books and, for newer research, on studies based on survey data and sound statistical analyses. In a few areas where there are important gaps in the policy literature, we have commissioned new research. These papers have been peer reviewed and have been available for comment at www.worldbank.org/gender/prr.

Finally, the report could have been organized in several different ways. We have chosen to organize it around the principal pathways through which gender disparities are generated and persist. Thus, the report focuses on the role of societal institutions, such as norms and laws, and of economic institutions, such as markets; the role of household power relations, resources, and decisionmaking; and the role of economic change and development policy. Much of the policy literature on gender issues in developing countries prescribes policies and programs with little attention to the factors that might explain gender inequalities. In our view, careful examination of the factors that explain gender disparities can help identify the most effective policy levers for promoting equality between women and men.

Elizabeth M. King
Andrew D. Mason

The Report Team

THIS POLICY RESEARCH REPORT WAS WRITTEN BY ELIZABETH M. King of the Development Research Group and Andrew D. Mason of the Gender and Development Group of the Poverty Reduction and Economic Management Network. They were ably assisted by team members Ananya Basu, Tai Lui Tan, Claudio E. Montenegro, and Lihong Wang, who conducted background research, compiled and analyzed data, prepared tables and graphs, wrote many of the boxes and appendixes, and generally helped in the development of the report. Branko Jovanovic, Cristina Estrada, and Owen Haaga provided additional research assistance. Jane Sweeney and Anna Marie Marañon provided excellent administrative support and production assistance. Bruce Ross-Larson and Molly Lohman edited the report and Mark Ingebretsen managed its production. The report was prepared under the general direction of Karen O. Mason and Lyn Squire.

Acknowledgments

WE ARE INDEBTED TO A LARGE NUMBER OF PEOPLE FOR their support in the preparation of this report. The report benefited greatly from the research findings of background papers written by Dang Nguyen Anh, Raquel Artecona, Lubia Begum, Jere Behrman, Sudharshan Canagarajah, Jennifer Clement, Alejandra Cox-Edwards, Maureen L. Cropper, Wendy Cunningham, Monica Das Gupta, David Dollar, Deon Filmer, Raymond Fisman, Maria Floro, Marito Garcia, Roberta Gatti, Elena Glinskaya, Anne Tierney Goldstein, Hameeda Hossain, Sara Hossain, Le Ngoc Hung, Vu Tuan Huy, Nadeem Ilahi, Nusrat Jahan, Estelle James, Karin Kapadia, Shahidur R. Khandker, Stephan Klasen, Julian Lampietti, Sunhwa Lee, Vu Manh Loi, Michael Lokshin, Lynellyn Long, Margaret Lycette, Le Thi Phuong Mai, Pratima Paul Majumdar, John Maluccio, Nilufar Matin, Nguyen Huu Minh, Haile Mitiku, Claudio Montenegro, Deepa Narayan, Constance Newman, Christine Poulos, Agnes Quisumbing, Rocio Ribero, Patricia Rice, Yana van der Muelen Rodgers, Sidney Ruth Schuler, Stephanie Seguino, Samita Sen, Talat Shah, Linda Stalker, Tania Sultana, Aysit Tansel, Allison Truitt, Patricia Uberoi, Danning Wang, Lihong Wang, Dale Whittington, and Xiaodan Zhang. We are also grateful to Monica Fong, Estelle James, Mead Over, and A. Waafas Ofosu-Amaah who provided us with key inputs for specific boxes.

We thank a group of peer reviewers who generously gave us detailed and useful comments at different stages. Diane Elson, Naila Kabeer, Charlotte Koren, Oystein Kravdal, Marnia Lazreg, Ruvimbo Mabeza-Chimedza, Karen Mason, the Honorable Lady Justice Effie Owour (Kenya), Lyn Squire, Christopher R. Udry, and Martin Weale provided helpful comments on early drafts of the background papers. Several background paper authors also commented on other background papers.

Nisha Agrawal, Harold Alderman, Jere Behrman, Mark Blackden, Gillian Brown, Paul Collier, Maria Correia, Wendy Cunningham, Monica Das Gupta, Jerri Dell, Kemal Dervis, Annette Dixon, William Easterly, Maria Floro, Nancy Folbre, Louise Fox, Indermit Gill, Anne Tierney Goldstein, Jeffrey Hammer, Roumeen Islam, Emmanuel Jimenez, Roger Key, Stephan Klasen, Reidar Kvam, Mustapha Nabli, Lant Pritchett, Agnes Quisumbing, Vijayendra Rao, Susan Razzaz, Jo Ritzen, Shaha Riza, Yana van der Muelen Rodgers, Wendy Wakeman, and Michael Woolcock commented on drafts of the full report.

A wide range of consultations with researchers, policymakers, grassroots leaders, nongovernmental organization staff, private sector representatives, and donor agency staff was undertaken for this report, and we thank all who participated for their time and comments. Members of the World Bank External Gender Consultative Group, the Gender and Development Board, and the Gender and Development Anchor Team provided early inputs into the study. Consultations with groups of donors, activists, researchers, and policymakers in Bangladesh, the Philippines, and Vietnam; at the International Center for Research on Women; and at several workshops and seminars at World Bank headquarters in Washington, D.C. informed our discussion of a number of issues in the report. In-country consultations were organized by Nilufar Ahmad in Bangladesh, Rina Jimenez-David in the Philippines, and Tosca Bruno-van Vijfeijken in Vietnam. Ahmad and Bruno-van Vijfeijken helped commission background papers in Bangladesh and Vietnam.

We thank the many participants of two international electronic discussions on the report. The first was an extensive email discussion of the report's concept note, coordinated by a group of civil society counterparts: Peggy Antrobus, Eva Charkiewicz, Pat Morris, Ruth Rempel, and Gita Sen. The second was an electronic web discussion sponsored by the World Bank Development Forum and coordinated by Susan Razzaz and Lihong Wang, with assistance from Ronald Kim. We are deeply grateful to Leah Gutierrez, Michael Kevane, Stephanie Seguino, Gale Summerfield, and Mona Zulficar, who ably led the electronic discussions of each chapter.

We thank Minister for Development Cooperation Eveline Herfkens (Netherlands), Irene Santiago, and Mona Zulficar, who discussed aspects of the report at a consultative workshop in the Women 2000 Conference ("Beijing + 5") at the United Nations, New York. We also thank workshop participants, who gave us important feedback on how the international community views gender issues in development.

Liliana Longo and Patricia Sader gave generous help in monitoring the budget and contracts. Dawn Ballantyne, Polly Means, Kayoko Shibata, and Qinghua Zhao provided valuable administrative and technical support at various stages of the report's preparation. Lawrence MacDonald gave help and advice on the consultation process for the report. Helene Carlsson assisted in organizing a series of consultative meetings. Roberta Gatti, Masako Hiraga, and Sulekha Patel provided us data for some of our analysis. Fiona Blackshaw, Meta de Coquereaumont, Paul Holtz, Allison Smith, and Alison Strong, of Communications Development, provided editorial support. Paola Scalabrin and Heather Worley in the World Bank's Office of the Publisher gave valuable guidance and assistance at various stages of the report's production.

We also thank Masood Ahmed, Kemal Dervis, Emmanuel Jimenez, Jo Ritzen, Joanne Salop, and Joseph Stiglitz for their encouragement and institutional support for writing this report. The financial assistance of the World Bank Research Committee and the governments of the Netherlands and Norway is gratefully acknowledged.

The opinions and conclusions expressed in this report are those of its authors and do not necessarily reflect positions of the World Bank or its member governments.

Summary

GENDER DISCRIMINATION REMAINS PERVASIVE IN many dimensions of life—worldwide. This is so despite considerable advances in gender equality in recent decades. The nature and extent of the discrimination vary considerably across countries and regions. But the patterns are striking. In no region of the developing world are women equal to men in legal, social, and economic rights. Gender gaps are widespread in access to and control of resources, in economic opportunities, in power, and political voice. Women and girls bear the largest and most direct costs of these inequalities—but the costs cut more broadly across society, ultimately harming everyone.

For these reasons, gender equality is a core development issue—a development objective in its own right. It strengthens countries' abilities to grow, to reduce poverty, and to govern effectively. Promoting gender equality is thus an important part of a development strategy that seeks to enable *all people*—women and men alike—to escape poverty and improve their standard of living.

Economic development opens many avenues for increasing gender equality in the long run. A considerable body of evidence around the world supports this assertion. But growth alone will not deliver the desired results. Also needed are an institutional environment that provides equal rights and opportunities for women and men and policy measures that address persistent inequalities. This report argues for a three-part strategy for promoting gender equality:

- *Reform institutions to establish equal rights and opportunities for women and men.* Reforming legal and economic institutions is necessary to establish a foundation of equal rights and equal opportunities for women and men. Because the law in many countries continues to

Gender equality is a core development issue—a development objective in its own right

1

This report argues for a three-part strategy for promoting gender equality

give unequal rights to women and men, legal reforms are needed, particularly in family law, protection against violence, land rights, employment, and political rights.

- *Foster economic development to strengthen incentives for more equal resources and participation.* Rising income and falling poverty levels tend to reduce gender disparities in education, health, and nutrition. Higher productivity and new job opportunities often reduce gender inequalities in employment. And investments in basic water, energy, and transportation infrastructure help reduce gender disparities in workloads.
- *Take active measures to redress persistent disparities in command over resources and political voice.* Because institutional reforms and economic development may not be sufficient—or forthcoming—active measures are needed to redress persistent gender disparities in the short to medium term.

Gender Equality—in Rights, Resources, and Voice

G*ENDER* REFERS TO SOCIALLY CONSTRUCTED ROLES AND socially learned behaviors and expectations associated with females and males. Women and men are different biologically—but all cultures interpret and elaborate these innate biological differences into a set of social expectations about what behaviors and activities are appropriate, and what rights, resources, and power they possess. While these expectations vary considerably among societies, there are also some striking similarities. For example, nearly all societies give the primary responsibility for the care of infants and young children to women and girls, and that for military service and national defense to men.

Like race, ethnicity, and class, gender is a social category that largely establishes one's life chances, shaping one's participation in society and in the economy. Some societies do not experience racial or ethnic divides, but all societies experience gender asymmetries—differences and disparities—to varying degrees. Often these asymmetries take time to change, but they are far from static. In fact, they can at times change quite rapidly in response to policy and changing socioeconomic conditions.

The term *gender equality* has been defined in a variety of ways in the context of development. This report defines gender equality in terms of equality under the law, equality of opportunity (including equality of rewards for work and equality in access to human capital and other productive resources that enable opportunity), and equality of voice (the ability to influence and contribute to the development process). It stops short of defining gender equality as equality of outcomes for two reasons. First, different cultures and societies can follow different paths in their pursuit of gender equality. Second, equality implies that women and men are free to choose different (or similar) roles and different (or similar) outcomes in accordance with their preferences and goals.

This report uses a variety of types of data and analyses to discuss issues related to gender inequality across the developing world. But measuring and assessing the many dimensions of gender inequality are tricky and difficult, and the lack of gender-differentiated data and analyses in several important aspects of gender equality is a real obstacle. Since empirical evidence is often richer and more available for more developed countries than for less developed countries, the report also reviews the experience of industrialized countries. It presents a combination of micro, country-level, and cross-country analyses, and reviews empirical work from several social science disciplines.

Despite Progress, Gender Disparities Remain in All Countries

T HE LAST HALF OF THE 20TH CENTURY SAW GREAT improvement in the absolute status of women and in gender equality in most developing countries.

- With few exceptions female education levels improved considerably. The primary enrollment rates of girls about doubled in South Asia, Sub-Saharan Africa, and the Middle East and North Africa, rising faster than boys' enrollment rates. This substantially reduced large gender gaps in schooling.
- Women's life expectancy increased by 15–20 years in developing countries. With greater investments in girls and women and better access to health care, the expected biological pattern in female and male longevity has emerged in all developing regions; for the first time, in the 1990s, women in South Asia are living longer than men, on average.
- More women have joined the labor force. Since 1970 women's labor force participation has risen on average by 15 percentage points in East Asia and Latin America. This growth was larger than for men, thus narrowing the gender gap in employment. Gender gaps in wages have also narrowed.

Gender inequalities in schooling and health have decreased substantially— but important gaps persist

3

Despite the progress significant gender inequalities in rights, resources, and voice persist in all developing countries—and in many areas the progress has been slow and uneven. Moreover, socioeconomic shocks in some countries have brought setbacks, jeopardizing hard-won gains.

Rights

In no region do women and men have equal social, economic, and legal rights (figure 1).[1] In a number of countries women still lack independent rights to own land, manage property, conduct business, or even travel without their husband's consent. In much of Sub-Saharan Africa, women obtain land rights chiefly through their husband as long as the marriage endures, and they often lose those rights when they are divorced or widowed. Gender disparities in rights constrain the sets of choices available to women in many aspects of life—often profoundly limiting their ability to participate in or benefit from development.

Figure 1   Gender Inequalities in Basic Rights Persist in All Regions

Index of gender equality

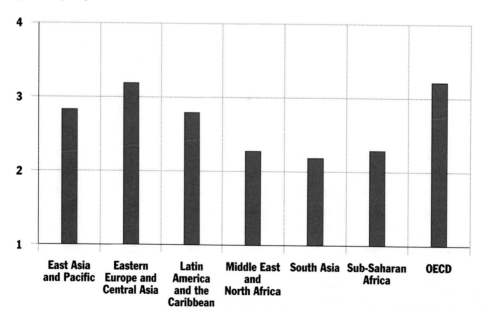

Note: A value of 1 indicates low gender equality in rights, a value of 4 high equality (see note 1 at the end of the summary for more information).
Source: Rights data from Humana (1992); population weights from World Bank (1999d).

Resources

Women continue to have systematically poorer command over a range of productive resources, including education, land, information, and financial resources. In South Asia women have only about half as many years of schooling as men, on average, and girls' enrollment rates at the secondary level are still only two-thirds of boys'. Many women cannot own land, and those who do generally command smaller landholdings than men. And in most developing regions female-run enterprises tend to be undercapitalized, having poorer access to machinery, fertilizer, extension information, and credit than male-run enterprises. Such disparities, whether in education or other productive resources, hurt women's ability to participate in development and to contribute to higher living standards for their families. Those disparities also translate into greater risk and vulnerability in the face of personal or family crises, in old age, and during economic shocks.

Despite recent increases in women's educational attainment, women continue to earn less than men in the labor market—even when they have the same education and years of work experience as men. Women are often limited to certain occupations in developing countries and are largely excluded from management positions in the formal sector. In industrial countries women in the wage sector earn an average of 77 percent of what men earn; in developing countries, 73 percent. And only about a fifth of the wage gap can be explained by gender differences in education, work experience, or job characteristics.

Limited access to resources and weaker ability to generate income constrain women's power to influence resource allocation and investment decisions in the home

Voice

Limited access to resources and weaker ability to generate income—whether in self-employed activities or in wage employment—constrain women's power to influence resource allocation and investment decisions in the home. Unequal rights and poor socioeconomic status relative to men also limit their ability to influence decisions in their communities and at the national level. Women remain vastly underrepresented in national and local assemblies, accounting for less than 10 percent of the seats in parliament, on average (except in East Asia where the figure is 18-19 percent). And in no developing region do women hold more than 8 percent of ministerial positions. Moreover, progress has been negligible in most regions since the

5

1970s. And in Eastern Europe female representation has fallen from about 25 to 7 percent since the beginning of economic and political transition there.

Gender Disparities Tend to Be Greatest among the Poor

GENDER DISPARITIES IN EDUCATION AND HEALTH ARE OFTEN greatest among the poor. A recent study of boys' and girls' school enrollments in 41 countries indicates that within countries gender disparities in school enrollment rates are commonly greater among the poor than among the nonpoor (figure 2). Similar patterns across poor and nonpoor households are seen with respect to boys' and girls' mortality rates for children under 5.

Figure 2 Gender Disparities Tend to Be Greater among the Poor than the Rich

Male to female enrollment ratio among the poor

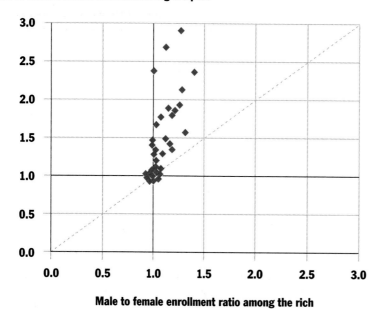

Male to female enrollment ratio among the rich

Note: The enrollment ratio pertains to the proportion of children ages 6–14 enrolled in school, regardless of education level. Poor households are defined as those in the bottom 40 percent of a "wealth" distribution; rich households, those in the top 20 percent. The diagonal line signifies equal gender gaps among the poor and among the rich. See appendix 1 for included countries and years.

Source: Filmer (1999).

Similar patterns also emerge when comparing poor and nonpoor countries. While gender equality in education and health has increased noticeably over the past 30 years in today's low-income countries, disparities between females and males in school enrollments are still greater in those countries than in middle-income and high-income countries (figure 3). And despite the links between economic development and gender equality, women's representation in parliaments remains minimal. A few low-income countries, such as China and Uganda, have made special efforts to open parliamentary seats to women, achieving levels of female representation even higher than those in high-income countries. They demonstrate the potential impact of a social mandate for gender equality.

Figure 3 Gender Equality Has Increased over Time in Low- and Middle-Income Countries—Except in Political Participation

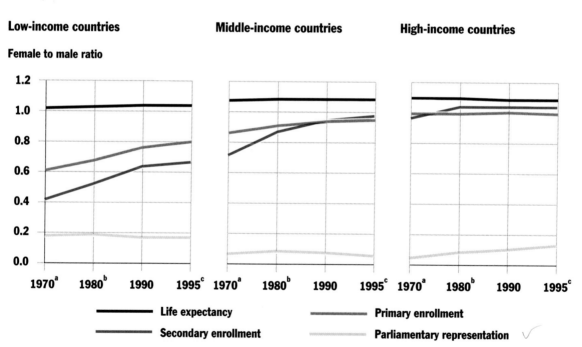

Low-income countries   **Middle-income countries**   **High-income countries**

Female to male ratio

Life expectancy   Primary enrollment
Secondary enrollment   Parliamentary representation

Note: The gross enrollment rate is total enrollment in a school level, regardless of students' age, expressed as a percentage of the official school-age population corresponding to that level in a given school year. The female to male enrollment ratio is the female gross enrollment ratio divided by the male gross enrollment ratio. For parliamentary representation the ratio is seats held by women to seats held by men. All values are population-weighted averages.

a. Parliamentary data are from 1975.
b. Parliamentary data are from 1985.
c. Life expectancy data are from 1997.
Source: Parliamentary data from WISTAT (1998); income data from World Bank (1999d).

It is important to note that these indicators are only a few measurable markers of gender equality. More systematic information is needed on other dimensions—from control of physical and financial assets to autonomy—to better understand how much has been accomplished and how far there is to go.

Gender Inequalities Harm Well-Being, Hinder Development

GENDER INEQUALITIES IMPOSE LARGE COSTS ON THE HEALTH and well-being of men, women, and children, and affect their ability to improve their lives. In addition to these personal costs, gender inequalities reduce productivity in farms and enterprises and thus lower prospects for reducing poverty and ensuring economic progress. Gender inequalities also weaken a country's governance—and thus the effectiveness of its development policies.

Foremost among the costs of gender inequality is its toll on human lives and the quality of those lives

Well-Being

Foremost among the costs of gender inequality is its toll on human lives and the quality of those lives. Identifying and measuring the full extent of these costs are difficult—but a wealth of evidence from countries around the world demonstrates that societies with large, persistent gender inequalities pay the price of more poverty, malnutrition, illness, and other deprivations.

- China, Korea, and South Asia have excessively high female mortality. Why? Social norms that favor sons, plus China's one-child policy, have led to child mortality rates that are higher for girls than for boys. Some estimates indicate that there are 60–100 million fewer women alive today than there would be in the absence of gender discrimination.
- Mothers' illiteracy and lack of schooling directly disadvantage their young children. Low schooling translates into poor quality of care for children and then higher infant and child mortality and malnutrition. Mothers with more education are more likely to adopt appropriate health-promoting behaviors, such as having young children immunized (figure 4). Supporting these conclusions are careful

Figure 4 Child Immunization Rates Rise with Mother's Education

Share of children 12–23 months who had been immunized, by mother's educational level

Percent

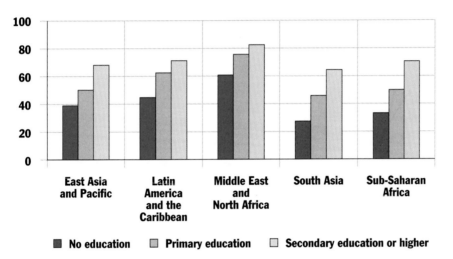

■ No education   **▨** Primary education   **□** Secondary education or higher

Note: All regional values are population-weighted averages. See appendix 1 for general notes and included countries.
Source: Education and immunization data from latest Demographic and Health Surveys; population weights from World Bank (1999d).

analyses of household survey data that account for other factors that might improve care practices and related health outcomes.

- As with mothers' schooling, higher household income is associated with higher child survival rates and better nutrition. And putting additional incomes in the hands of women within the household tends to have a larger positive impact than putting that income in the hands of men, as studies of Bangladesh, Brazil, and Côte d'Ivoire show. Unfortunately, rigid social norms about the appropriate gender division of labor and limited paid employment for women restrict women's ability to earn income.

- Gender inequalities in schooling and urban jobs accelerate the spread of HIV (figure 5). The AIDS epidemic will spread rapidly over the next decade—until up to one in four women and one in five men become HIV infected, already the case in several countries in Sub-Saharan Africa.

- While women and girls, especially the poor, often bear the brunt of gender disparities, gender norms and stereotypes impose costs on males, too. In the transition economies of Eastern Europe men have experienced absolute declines in life expectancies in recent

Figure 5   HIV Infection Rates are Higher Where Gender Gaps in Literacy are Larger

Urban adult HIV prevalence rate

Percent (log scale)

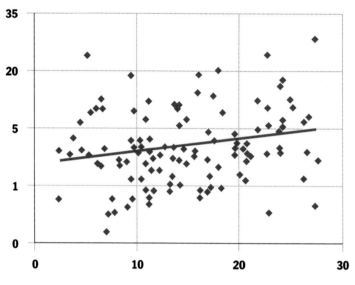

Gap between male and female literacy rates (percentage points)

Note: The plot includes 72 countries (32 in Sub-Saharan Africa, 20 in Latin America and the Caribbean, 15 in Asia, 4 in the Middle East, and 1 industrial country). The vertical axis measuring the percentage of urban population infected with HIV has been transformed into a logarithmic scale. Points on the plot represent data for individual countries after removing the effects of other societal variables used in the regression analysis (including GNP per capita, an income inequality index, religion, and proportion of population foreign born).
   Source: Over (1998).

years. Increases in male mortality rates—the largest registered in peacetime—are associated with growing stress and anxiety due to rapidly worsening unemployment among men.

Productivity and Economic Growth

   The toll on human lives is a toll on development—since improving the quality of people's lives is development's ultimate goal. But gender inequalities also impose costs on productivity, efficiency, and economic progress. By hindering the accumulation of human capital in the home and the labor market, and by systematically excluding women or men from access to resources, public services, or productive activities, gender discrimination diminishes an economy's capacity to grow and to raise living standards.

- Losses in output result from inefficiencies in the allocation of productive resources between men and women within households. In households in Burkina Faso, Cameroon, and Kenya more equal control of inputs and farm income by women and men could raise farm yields by as much as a fifth of current output.
- Low investment in female education also reduces a country's overall output. One study estimates that if the countries in South Asia, Sub-Saharan Africa, and the Middle East and North Africa had started with the gender gap in average years of schooling that East Asia had in 1960 and had closed that gender gap at the rate achieved by East Asia from 1960 to 1992, their income per capita could have grown by 0.5–0.9 percentage point higher per year—substantial increases over actual growth rates (figure 6). Another study estimates that even for middle- and high-income countries with higher initial

Figure 6   Faster Progress in Closing Gender Gaps in Schooling Would Accelerate Economic Growth

Average annual growth in per capita GNP, 1960–92

Percent

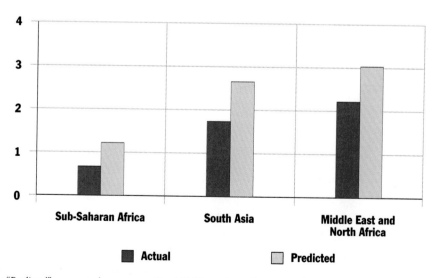

Note: "Predicted" represents the average predicted GNP growth rate for a region if its gender gap in education had started at East Asia's level in 1960 and had narrowed as fast as East Asia's did from 1960 to 1992.

Source: Simulations based on regression results from Klasen (1999a).

education levels, an increase of 1 percentage point in the share of women with secondary education is associated with an increase in per capita income of 0.3 percentage point. Both studies control for other variables commonly found in the growth literature.

Governance

Greater women's rights and more equal participation in public life by women and men are associated with cleaner business and government and better governance. Where the influence of women in public life is greater, the level of corruption is lower. This holds even when comparing countries with the same income (figure 7), civil liberties, education, and legal institutions. Although still only suggestive, these

Figure 7   More Equal Rights, Less Corruption

Corruption index

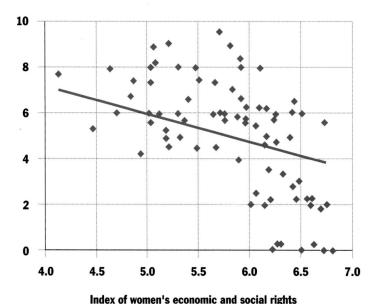

Index of women's economic and social rights

Note: The corruption index uses data from the International Country Risk Guide (ICRG) and transforms it: corruption index = 10 − (ICRG Index − 1) x 2. A value of 0 indicates low levels of corruption; a value of 10 indicates high levels. The women's rights variable is the Women's Economic and Social Human Rights (WESHR) Indicator developed by Purdue University's Global Studies Program. A score of 7 is interpreted as gender equality in economic and social rights. The figure controls for per capita GDP in each country. See appendix 1 for included countries.
Source: World Bank staff estimates; see also Kaufmann (1998).

findings lend additional support for having more women in the labor force and in politics—since women can be an effective force for rule of law and good government.

Women in business are less likely to pay bribes to government officials, perhaps because women have higher standards of ethical behavior or greater risk aversion. A study of 350 firms in the republic of Georgia concludes that firms owned or managed by men are 10 percent more likely to make unofficial payments to government officials than those owned or managed by women. This result holds regardless of the characteristics of the firm, such as the sector in which it operates and firm size, and the characteristics of the owner or manager, such as education. Without controlling for these factors, firms managed by men are twice as likely to pay bribes.

Why Do Gender Disparities Persist?

I F GENDER INEQUALITIES HARM PEOPLE'S WELL-BEING AND A country's prospects for development, why do harmful gender disparities persist in so many countries? Why are some gender inequalities much more difficult to eliminate than others? For example, improvements have been rapid in such dimensions as health and access to schooling, but much slower in political participation and equal rights to property. What factors stand in the way of transforming gender relations and eliminating gender inequalities? Institutions, households, and the economy.

Societal institutions—social norms, customs, rights, laws—as well as economic institutions, such as markets, shape roles and relation-ships between men and women and influence what resources women and men have access to, what activities they can or cannot undertake, and in what forms they can participate in the economy and in society. They embody incentives that can encourage or discourage prejudice. Even when formal and informal institutions do not distinguish explic-itly between males and females, they are generally informed (either explicitly or implicitly) by social norms relating to appropriate gender roles. These societal institutions have their own inertia and can be slow and difficult to change—but they are far from static.

Like institutions, households play a fundamental role in shaping gender relations from early in life and in transmitting these from one generation to the next. People make many of life's most basic decisions

Gender disparities embodied in institutions, household decisions, and economic policy stand in the way of transforming relations between females and males

within their households—about having and raising children, engaging in work and leisure, and investing in the future. How tasks and productive resources are allocated among sons and daughters, how much autonomy they are given, whether expectations differ among them—all this creates, reinforces, or mitigates gender disparities. But families do not make decisions in a vacuum. They make them in the context of communities and in ways that reflect the influence of incentives established by the larger institutional and policy environment.

And because the economy determines many of the opportunities people have to improve their standard of living, economic policy and development critically affect gender inequality. Higher incomes mean fewer resource constraints within the household that force parents to choose between investing in sons or in daughters. But how precisely women and men are affected by economic development depends on what income-generating activities are available, how they are organized, how effort and skills are rewarded, and whether women and men are equally able to participate.

Indeed, even apparently gender-neutral development policies can have gender-differentiated outcomes—in part because of the ways in which institutions and household decisions combine to shape gender roles and relations. The gender division of labor in the home, social norms and prejudice, and unequal resources prevent women and men from taking equal advantage of economic opportunities—or from coping equally with risk or economic shocks. Failure to recognize these gender-differentiated constraints when designing policies can compromise the effectiveness of those policies, both from equity and efficiency perspectives.

So, societal institutions, households, and the broader economy together determine people's opportunities and life prospects, by gender. They also represent important entry points for public policy to address persistent gender inequalities.

Even apparently gender-neutral development policies can have gender-differentiated outcomes

A Three-Part Strategy to Promote Gender Equality

THAT GENDER INEQUALITIES EXACT HIGH HUMAN COSTS AND constrain countries' development prospects provides a compelling case for public and private action to promote gender equality. The state has a critical role in improving the well-being of both women and men and, by so doing, in capturing the substantial social benefits associated with improving the absolute and relative status of women and girls. Public action is particularly important since social and legal institutions that perpetuate gender inequalities are extremely difficult, if not impossible, for individuals alone to change. Market failures, too, mean insufficient information about women's productivity in the labor market (because they spend a greater part of their work hours in nonmarket activities or because labor markets are absent or undeveloped) and are clear obstacles.

Improving the effectiveness of societal institutions and achieving economic growth are widely accepted as key elements of any long-term development strategy. But successful implementation of this strategy does not guarantee gender equality. To promote gender equality, policies for institutional change and economic development need to consider and address prevailing gender inequalities in rights, resources, and voice. And active policies and programs are needed to redress long-standing disparities between women and men. The evidence argues for a three-part strategy for promoting gender equality.

1. Reforming Institutions to Establish Equal Rights and Opportunities for Women and Men

Because social, legal, and economic institutions shape women's and men's access to resources, their opportunities, and their relative power, a critical element in promoting gender equality is establishing a level institutional "playing field" for women and men.

Ensuring equality in basic rights. Gender equality in rights is an important development goal in its own right. Legal, social, and economic rights provide an enabling environment in which women and men can participate productively in society, attain a basic quality of life, and take advantage of the new opportunities that development affords. Greater equality in rights is also consistently and systematically associated with greater gender equality in education, health, and political participation—effects independent of income (figure 8).

If countries in South Asia, Sub-Saharan Africa, and the Middle East and North Africa were to increase gender equality in rights to the level of the "most equal" country in their respective regions, the ratio of women to men in parliament would more than double in the Middle East and North Africa and would increase by more than 60 percent in the other two regions. Although increasing gender equality in rights would have more modest impacts (at the margin) on gender equality

> A critical element in promoting gender equality is establishing a level institutional "playing field" for women and men

15

Figure 8 More Equal Rights—More Equal Resources and Voice

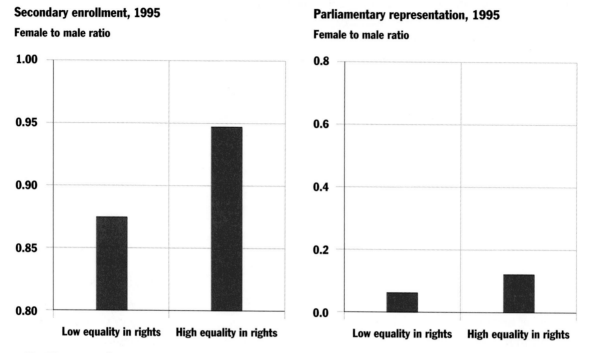

Secondary enrollment, 1995
Female to male ratio

Parliamentary representation, 1995
Female to male ratio

Note: The gross enrollment rate is total enrollment in a school level, regardless of students' age, expressed as a percentage of the official school-age population corresponding to that level in a given school year. The female to male enrollment ratio is the female gross enrollment ratio divided by the male gross enrollment ratio. For parliamentary representation the ratio is seats held by women to seats held by men. An average score of 2.33 or less represents low equality in rights, an average score of 2.67 or greater represents high equality (see note 1 at the end of the summary for more details about the rights index.

Source: Equality in rights' data from Humana (1992); parliamentary data from WISTAT (1998); population weights from World Bank (1999d).

in education, significant rights improvements could go far toward achieving parity between boys and girls in school enrollments. Only in South Asia would sizable gender gaps in enrollments be expected to persist in the face of large improvements in rights. There is thus a critical role for legal reforms that accord equal rights and equal protection to women and men.

But statutory reform is seldom enough. In many developing countries the capacity to implement legal reforms remains weak, complicated by multiple—and inconsistent—legal systems. For example, civil law in Uganda provides for equal rights in divorce—but customary law prevails in the division of conjugal property, and divorced women are unable to retain access to land. In cases of gender-based violence, heavy evidentiary requirements and other procedural barriers (as well as the attitudes of enforcers) stand in the way of justice in a number of countries. In such contexts efforts to strengthen the enforcement capabilities of the country's judicial and administrative agencies are critical to achieving greater gender equality in basic rights. In almost all cases political leadership is decisive.

Establishing incentives that discourage discrimination by gender. The structure of economic institutions also affects gender equality in important ways. Markets embody a powerful set of incentives that influence decisions and actions for work, saving, investment, and consumption. The relative wages of men and women, the returns to productive assets, and the prices of goods and services are all largely determined by the structure of markets. Evidence from Mexico and the United States suggests that firms operating in competitive environments discriminate less against women in hiring and pay practices than do firms with significant market power in protected environments. Similarly, in both urban and rural China, women face greater wage discrimination in jobs that have been administratively assigned to them than in jobs obtained through competitive channels.

More broadly, policies and investments that deepen markets and redress gender disparities in access to information—combined with sanctions against those who discriminate—all help strengthen incentives for gender equality in the labor market. In China and Vietnam, for example, the deepening of rural labor markets has brought with it substantial increases in demand for female labor in nonfarm enterprises, opening up new employment and earnings opportunities for women.

Designing service delivery to facilitate equal access. The design of program delivery—such as school systems, health care centers, financial organizations, and agricultural extension programs—can facilitate or inhibit equitable access for females and males. Moreover, involving the community in the design of service delivery helps to address specific demands within local contexts, often with positive effects on female access and use.

In Bangladesh, Kenya, and Pakistan, for example, girls' enrollments are more sensitive than boys' to school quality and to specific delivery attributes—such as the presence of female teachers, sex-segregated schools and facilities, and safe transport to and from the school. Addressing such considerations can significantly increase parents' demand for educating daughters. In parts of West Africa "mobile bankers" (known as *susu* collectors in Ghana) bring financial services to local markets, workplaces, and homes, eliminating the need for women to travel long distances to save or borrow. And in Bangladesh, group-based lending programs use

Policies and investments that deepen markets and redress gender disparities in access to information strengthen incentives for gender equality in economic participation

17

support groups and peer pressure as a substitute for traditional bank collateral to ensure repayment. Both designs have increased women's access to financial resources.

2. Fostering Economic Development to Strengthen Incentives for More Equal Resources and Participation

In most settings economic development is associated with improved circumstances for women and girls and with greater gender equality—through several channels:

- Households decide about work, consumption, and investments partly in response to price levels and other market signals. Shifts in these signals tend to bring about reallocation of resources. When economic development improves the availability and quality of public services, such as health clinics and schools, it lowers the cost of investments in human capital for the household. If costs decline more for females than for males, or if investments in females are more sensitive to price changes than investments in males as evidence suggests, females benefit more.

- When economic development raises incomes and reduces poverty, gender inequalities often narrow. Since low-income families are forced to ration spending on education, health care, and nutrition, with women and girls bearing much of the costs, as household incomes rise, gender disparities in human capital tend to fall.

Economic development expands opportunities and resources and relaxes constraints—especially among women and girls

As with basic rights, higher incomes generally translate into greater gender equality in resources, whether in health or in education (figure 9). In education, simulations suggest that the largest improvements from income growth are likely to occur in the poorest regions: South Asia and Sub-Saharan Africa. Moreover, the effects of income appear particularly strong at the secondary level. But simulation analysis also suggests that very large increases in income—say, to average OECD levels—would be required to reach equality or near-equality in secondary enrollments in these regions. Such increases are not realistic in the short or medium term. Very large increases in income also would be necessary to induce noticeable gains in gender equality in parliamentary representation.

- When economic development expands work opportunities, it raises the expected rate of return to human capital, strengthening the

18

Figure 9   Gender Equality in Education Improves as Income Rises

Secondary enrollment, 1995

Female to male ratio

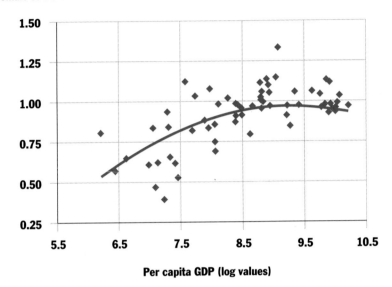

Per capita GDP (log values)

Note: The gross enrollment rate is total enrollment in a school level, regardless of students' age, expressed as a percentage of the official school-age population corresponding to that level in a given school year. The female to male enrollment ratio is the female gross enrollment ratio divided by the male gross enrollment ratio.

Source: World Bank (1999d).

incentives for families to invest in girls' health and education and for women to participate in the labor force. By changing incentives for work, economic development affects gender equality.

- Economic development leads to the emergence of labor markets where none has existed. In so doing, it not only creates or strengthens market signals about the returns to labor but also eliminates some economic inefficiencies. For example, where active labor markets exist, hired labor provides a substitute for female family labor, whether on farms or in household maintenance and care activities. This allows households to use time more efficiently, perhaps reducing women's workload. Where labor markets are absent or do not function well, such substitution is not possible.

- Economic growth is typically accompanied by an expansion of investments in infrastructure—for safe water, roads, transport, and fuel. This too tends to reduce the time women and girls need to dedicate to household maintenance and care activities. In Burkina Faso,

Uganda, and Zambia, for example, women and girls could save hundreds of hours a year if walking times to sources of fuel and potable water were reduced to 30 minutes or less (figure 10). The development of economic infrastructure significantly reduces females' time on domestic chores, with potential benefits for their health, their participation in income-generating activities, and for girls, in schooling.

Although economic development tends to promote gender equality, its impact is neither sufficient nor immediate. Nor is it automatic. The impact of economic development on gender equality depends in large part on the state of rights, access to and control of productive resources (such as land and credit), and political voice. And social policies that combat labor market discrimination or support child care supplement what economic development alone cannot achieve in reducing gender inequalities—as experience shows in the transition economies, the high-growth countries in East Asia, and the adjusting countries in Latin America and Sub-Saharan Africa. Social

Figure 10   Investments in Water and Fuel Infrastructure Can Significantly Reduce the Time Cost of Collection Activities

Average potential time savings per household per year

Hours

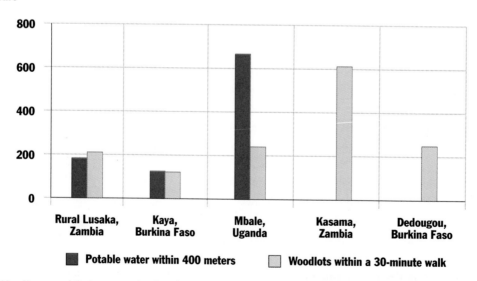

■ **Potable water within 400 meters**   ☐ **Woodlots within a 30-minute walk**

Note: Kasama and Dedougou are already within the 400-meter target for potable water. In parts of Sub-Saharan Africa women account for two-thirds or more of household time for water and fuel collection, while children, mostly girls, account for another 5–28 percent.
    Source: Barwell (1996).

20

protection policies that recognize gender differences in market-based and household work and in risks are also important to protect women (and men) from economic shocks or prolonged economic downturns.

Recent debates on gender and development have tended to pit growth-oriented approaches to development against rights-based or institutional approaches. But the evidence suggests that both economic development and institutional change are key elements of a long-term strategy to promote gender equality. For example, where per capita income and gender equality in rights are low, increasing either equality in rights or incomes would raise gender equality in education levels. Improving both rights and incomes would yield even greater gain (figure 11).

Institutional reforms that strengthen basic rights and policies that foster economic development can be mutually reinforcing. In Sub-Saharan Africa

Figure 11 Gender Equality in Rights and Income Growth Promote Gender Equality in Many Dimensions—From Education to Political Representation

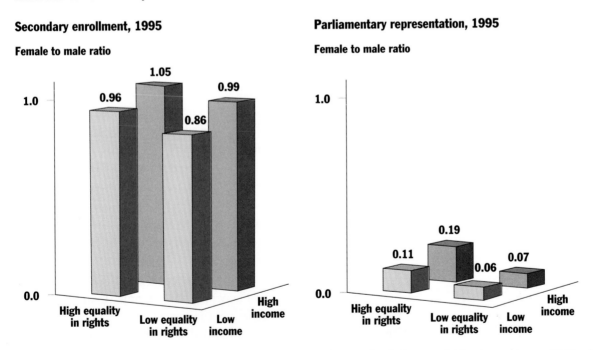

Secondary enrollment, 1995

Female to male ratio

Parliamentary representation, 1995

Female to male ratio

Note: Figures are based on simulations derived from multiple regression results, controlling for income and rights. An average score of 2.33 or less represents low equality in rights, an average score of 2.67 or greater high equality (see note 1 at the end of the summary for more details on the rights index). Low- and high-income countries are grouped according to the median value of per capita GDP. All values are population-weighted averages for each category. See appendix 1 for general notes and included countries, appendix 2 for underlying regression results, and the glossary for definitions of ratios.

Source: Rights data from Humana (1992); parliamentary data from WISTAT (1998); all other data from World Bank (1999d).

establishing land rights for women raises productivity on female-managed plots—increasing women's as well as their families' incomes. Similarly, providing women greater access to savings institutions and credit enhances their economic status and security and helps improve household welfare. In Bangladesh, as women's abilities to borrow capital in microcredit programs increase, their status and bargaining power in the family rise, as does household consumption (income).

3. Taking Active Policy Measures to Redress Persistent Gender Disparities in Command over Resources and Political Voice

Because the combined effects of institutional reform and economic development usually take time to be realized, active measures are often warranted in the short to medium term. Active measures are concrete steps aimed at redressing specific forms of gender discrimination and exclusion—whether in the home, the community, or the workplace. Such measures accelerate progress in redressing persistent gender inequalities— and they are useful in targeting specific subpopulations, such as the poor, for whom gender disparities can be particularly acute.

Since the nature and extent of gender inequality differ considerably across countries, the interventions that will be most relevant will also differ across contexts. Decisions on whether the state should intervene and which active measures should be adopted must be based on an understanding and analysis of local realities. Since active measures have real resource costs, policymakers will need to be selective about which measures to undertake, focusing strategically on where government intervention has the largest social benefits. This implies focusing on areas where market failure and spillover effects are likely to be greatest. This also implies focusing on areas that the private sector is unlikely to take on independently—or to take on well.

Policymakers need to be selective, focusing strategically on where government intervention has the largest social benefits

Beyond assessing whether particular interventions are warranted, choices need to be made on how precisely the state should intervene. For example, is direct public provision of goods or services required? Or can similar objectives be fulfilled more cost effectively through greater availability of information, regulatory and enforcement efforts, or through public subsidies to private providers?

The report focuses on four key areas of active policy.

Promoting gender equality in access to productive resources and earnings capacity. Efforts to promote greater equality of access to and control of productive resources—whether education, financial resources, or land—and to ensure fair and equal access to employment opportunities can advance gender equality as well as enhance economic efficiency. Policymakers have a number of potential entry points for intervention:

- Reducing the costs of schooling, addressing parental concerns about female modesty or safety, and increasing returns to families from investing in female schooling through improvements in school quality can overcome social and economic barriers to girls' education, even in highly gender-stratified societies.
- Designing financial institutions in ways that account for gender-specific constraints—whether by using peer presure to substitute for traditional forms of collateral, by simplifying banking procedures, or by delivering financial services closer to homes, markets, and workplaces—can increase female access to savings and credit.
- Land reforms that provide for joint titling of husband and wife or that enable women to hold independent land titles can increase women's control of land where statutory law predominates. Where customary and statutory laws operate side-by-side, their interactions must be taken into account if efforts to strengthen female access to land are to succeed.
- In countries with relatively developed labor markets and law enforcement capabilities, affirmative action employment programs can increase female access to formal sector jobs. Where there is serious discrimination in hiring and promotions, affirmative action can also raise productivity in firms and in the economy.

Reducing the personal costs to women of their household roles. In almost all societies gender norms dictate that women and girls take primary responsibility for household maintenance and care activities. In developing countries household responsibilities often require long hours of work that limit girls' ability to continue their education and constrain mothers' capacity to participate in market work. Several types of interventions can reduce the personal costs of household roles to women and girls.

- Interventions that increase education, wages, and labor market participation—coupled with adequate access to basic reproductive health and family planning services—all strengthen women's role in making reproductive decisions. But since women and men may have different preferences for family size and contraceptive use, family planning services need to target men as well as women.

Fair and equal access to productive resources and employment opportunities can advance gender equality and enhance economic efficiency

23

- Providing public support for out-of-home child care services can reduce the costs of care, enabling greater economic participation for women and more schooling for adolescent girls. In Kenya reducing the price of child care significantly increases mothers' wage employment and older girls' schooling (figure 12).
- Protective labor market legislation is often a two-edged sword, generating costs as well as benefits for women working in the formal sector. For example, when firms bear all the costs of maternity leave, they may bias hiring decisions against women. When women bear all the costs, the incentives for women to continue work are weakened. Measures that help spread the costs of maternity and other care provisions across employers, workers, and even the state can raise the benefits relative to costs for women and their families.
- Selected investments in water, fuel, transport, and other time-saving infrastructure can hasten reductions in women's and girls' domestic workloads, particularly in poor, rural areas—freeing girls

Figure 12   Low-Cost Child Care Means More Women in the Labor Market, More Girls in School

Increase in mothers' labor force participation and children's (ages 8–16) school enrollment in Kenya due to a 10 percent decline in the price of out-of-home child care

Percent

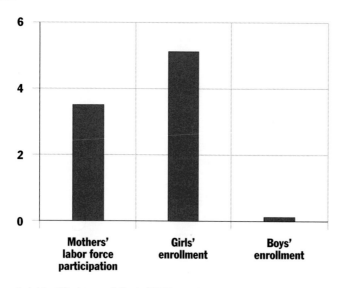

Source: Lokshin, Glinskaya, and Garcia (2000).

to attend school and women to undertake other activities, whether related to income generation or community affairs.

Providing gender-appropriate social protection. Women and men face gender-specific risks during economic shocks or policy reforms. Women command fewer resources with which to cushion shocks—while men, as the traditional breadwinners, are particularly vulnerable to stress associated with large changes in, or uncertain, employment. Taking gender differences in risk and vulnerability into account in designing social protection is particularly important because women and men in the same household may not pool risk.

- To protect both women and men social protection programs need to account for factors that can result in gender bias in participation and benefits. For example, safety net programs have frequently (if inadvertently) excluded women by failing to account for gender differences in labor supply behavior, information access, or the types of work that women and men consider appropriate.
- Old-age security programs that do not account for gender differences in employment, earnings, and life expectancy risk leaving women—especially widows—particularly vulnerable to poverty in old age. A recent study of Chile shows that women's pension benefits relative to men's are highly sensitive to the specific design features of the old-age security system (figure 13).

Taking gender differences in risk and vulnerability into account is important to designing effective social protection

Strengthening women's political voice and participation. Institutional changes that establish gender equality in basic rights are the cornerstone of greater equality in political participation and voice. Similarly, policies and programs that promote equality in education and access to information (including legal literacy) can strengthen women's agency and thus their capacity to participate in the political arena. But like the impact of economic development more broadly, these approaches take time to reap observable benefits.

Recent experience from more than 30 countries, including Argentina, Ecuador, India, the Philippines, and Uganda, suggests that political "reservation" can be effective in increasing political participation and representation in local and national assemblies in a relatively short period of time. "Reservation" legislation takes different forms in different countries, but generally stipulates that a minimum number

Figure 13   Pension Design Affects the Relative Benefits to Elderly Women and Men

Monthly pension income for female and male workers with incomplete primary education in Chile
(female to male ratio in parentheses)

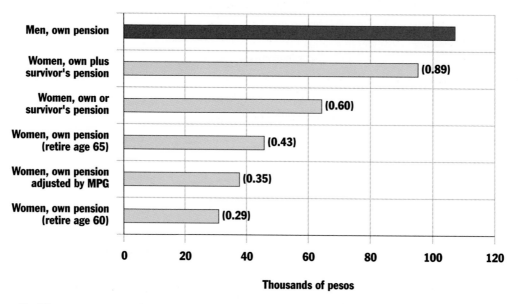

Note: These estimates assume that men retire at 65, women at 60—the statutory retirement ages for men and women—unless otherwise noted. *MPG* stands for the government-supported minimum pension guarantee. The figures are calculated as monthly annuities to urban contributors, assuming a 5 percent rate of return with 2 percent secular wage growth. Males are assumed to survive for 15 years after retirement (at 65) and to make provisions for a survivor's pension for 6 years at 60 percent of their own annuity. If females retire at 60, they are assumed to survive for 23 years, and if they retire at 65, they are assumed to survive for 19 years.

Source: Adapted from Cox-Edwards (2000).

(or proportion) of political parties' candidates or of electoral seats in national or local assemblies be reserved for women.

Challenges for the Future—the Way Forward

THE EVIDENCE PRESENTED IN THIS REPORT MAKES A compelling case for the state to intervene in promoting gender equality. Indeed, the state, civil society groups, and the international community all have critical roles to play in fighting gender discrimination, thus enabling societies to reap considerable benefits. But there remain several important challenges.

Sharpening Policy through Gender Analysis

How to deepen understanding of the links between gender equality and development and how to reflect these links in policy decisions are key challenges for the present and the future. This report brings together extensive evidence on these links, but much remains to be discovered and understood, implying the need for collecting more and better data and for analyses disaggregated by gender. Two areas for more analysis:

- What are the gender impacts of specific macro and sectoral policies? And how do public expenditure choices promote or inhibit gender equality and economic efficiency? Policymakers face numerous competing demands for public resources and attention, with tight fiscal and administrative budgets. Under these constraints, information and analysis help governments achieve the maximum social gains from the gender-related interventions they choose. Moreover, because the nature of gender disparities differ among societies, effective policy needs to be grounded in analysis that integrates local and national gender concerns.
- Increasingly, it will be important to look beyond how policies and programs affect our usual development markers (such as education, health, or labor force indicators) to how specific interventions improve female autonomy, leadership, and voice—both within the household and in society more broadly. Understanding which interventions are most effective in achieving this requires more gender analysis.

How to deepen understanding of the links between gender equality and development and how to reflect these links in policy are key challenges

Addressing Emerging Issues

A related challenge is for policymakers to be forward-looking in the face of rapidly changing circumstances. Indeed, many emerging issues require greater attention by policymakers and policy researchers from a gender perspective, including globalization, decentralization in government, the spread of HIV/AIDS, and the aging of the world's population. For example:

- With birth rates declining and people living longer, the world's population is aging. Among other things, this will result in a substantial rise in the number of widows worldwide during the 21st century. What does this demographic shift imply for social protection, health, and other areas of public policy? Understanding the policy implications of this demographic trend will be an important challenge for research in the coming years.

- Similarly, globalization and new information technologies are transforming the way that production is organized and information shared around the world. Will these changes accelerate progress toward gender equality or widen gender gaps in economic opportunity? Better understanding of the opportunities and risks associated with these forces represents another challenge for researchers and policymakers.

Broadening Partnerships

Another challenge for policymakers is to broaden their partnerships with civil society groups, donors, and others in the international community

A third critical challenge is for policymakers—in their efforts to promote gender equality—to broaden their partnerships with civil society groups, donors, and others in the international community. While policymakers have an important leadership role to play, efforts to combat gender inequalities can be enhanced by active collaboration with civic and international organizations. The donor community can contribute by supporting the collection and analysis of gender-disaggregated data, by incorporating gender analysis into their dialogues with national policymakers, and by sharing "good practice" based on international experience. Similarly, civic groups and local researchers can contribute critical information and analysis based on local knowledge that will enrich the government's policy dialogue.

Fostering broader participation and transparency in policymaking has the potential for tremendous payoffs, both for gender equality and for national development as a whole. Opening public deliberations and policymaking to greater participation by women's groups can directly empower women—and can enhance the impact of policies and programs. The research findings on the links between greater female participation in public life and lower levels of corruption are intriguing. They suggest that facilitating broader exchanges of ideas and greater transparency in policymaking—and enabling greater female participation in the public domain—can strengthen a country's governance and the effectiveness of its development policy. The world cannot forgo salutary effects as remarkable as these.

Note

1. The rights indicator used in figures 1, 8, and 11 is an average of three indexes of gender equality in rights collected for more than 100 countries by Humana (1992). The individual rights indexes focus on gender equality of political and legal rights, social and economic rights, and rights in marriage and in divorce proceedings. The indexes are constructed using a consistent methodology across countries in which the extent of rights is evaluated (on a scale from 1 to 4) against rights as specified in several human rights instruments of the United Nations.

See box 1.1 for details on the rights indexes. See appendix 1 for included countries for figures 1, 2, 3, 4, 7, 8, 9, and 11. See appendix 2 for underlying regression results for figures 3, 8, 9, and 11.

CHAPTER 1

Gender Inequality at the Start of the 21st Century

THE WORLD IS A BETTER PLACE THAN IT WAS AT THE start of the 20th century. While illiteracy, hunger, illness, and violence continue to plague too many of the world's people, there have been many advances—the spread of education and literacy, progress in science and medicine to eliminate or control disease, a freer exchange of information worldwide that makes oppression more costly for the oppressors.

Another advance has been the greater voice of women in their private and public lives. In the 20th century women earned the rights to vote and to hold elected positions in most countries—even if only in principle. They won legislation for special protection as workers when such laws were thought to be beneficial. They have increased their access to health services and education. They have organized effectively both locally and internationally to frame women's rights as human rights and have raised gender issues in development policymaking. International women's conferences—such as those in Mexico City (1975), Nairobi (1985), and Beijing (1995)—are themselves a measure of women's empowerment.

Over the past three decades women's issues—and more recently gender issues—have gained prominence on the development platform. Attention goes not only to the plight of poor and disenfranchised women in developing countries, but also to the unfinished gender agenda in more developed countries. Many issues elicit intense reactions and receive much public attention—female genital mutilation and the AIDS epidemic in Sub-Saharan Africa, exploitation of women sex workers in East Asia, trafficking in women in Asia and Eastern Europe, dowry deaths and "honor killings" in South Asia, unnecessary deaths due to unsafe abortions in Latin America and the industrial countries. Many other gender issues are more mundane but profoundly important to the well-being of millions of women and girls around the world:

- In no developing region do women enjoy equal rights with men. In many countries women still lack independent rights to own land, manage property, or conduct business. In much of Sub-Saharan Africa, for example, women obtain land rights chiefly through their husband, losing these rights when they are divorced or widowed. In some South Asian and Middle Eastern countries women cannot travel without their husband's consent.

- Gender discrimination has raised female mortality rates in some regions, depriving the world of 60–100 million women (Sen 1989, 1992; Coale 1991; Klasen 1994). This reflects gender bias in the provision of food and health care, as well as violence against females, especially in early childhood. In China selective abortion of female fetuses and other son-selection methods have further skewed the male to female birth ratios—from 1.07 in 1980 to 1.14 in 1993. In India the sex ratio at birth is as high as 1.18 in Punjab.

- Across developing regions female-run enterprises tend to be less well capitalized than those run by males. Throughout Sub-Saharan Africa female farmers have poorer access than male farmers to machinery, fertilizer, and extension information. And with a few noteworthy exceptions, female-managed enterprises—farm and nonfarm—continue to have poorer access to credit and related financial services.

- Despite increases in women's educational attainment relative to men's, large gender wage gaps remain. On average, female employees earn about three-quarters of what men earn—but gender differences in education, work experience, and job characteristics explain only about a fifth of the gap. Moreover, women remain greatly underrepresented in higher paying jobs, including administrative and managerial jobs.

- Women are vastly underrepresented at all levels of government, limiting their power to influence governance and public policy. They hold less than 10 percent of seats in parliament in all regions except East Asia. And in no developing region do women hold more than 8 percent of ministerial positions.

While systemic female disadvantages are far more widespread than male disadvantages, gender norms and stereotypes affect men as well as women, often with important impacts on their well-being. For example, in the transition economies of Eastern Europe, increases in women's life expectancies relative to men's in the 1990s were the result not of improvements in female longevity but of increases in male mortality. These increases reflect biological and social factors, including high work-related stress and rising rates of unemployment, smoking, and alcohol consumption. Such phenomena affect the well-being not only of men but of their families and society.

Despite the greater prominence of gender issues in the development debate, the importance of bringing a gender perspective to policy analysis and design is still not widely recognized, nor have the lessons for development been fully integrated by policymakers or the donor community. This report examines the links among gender, public policy, and development to help clarify the value of taking a gender perspective in development policymaking—the value to women and men as individuals and to societies. To do this the report brings together empirical research from many countries and several disciplines, including law, economics, and related social sciences.

The report begins by reviewing gender inequality in developing countries as we enter the 21st century. It then examines the implications of allowing gender disparities to persist—for individuals, communities, and societies. While there clearly are high costs to individuals from gender inequality, a growing body of empirical evidence shows that persistent gender inequalities impose significant costs on societies—on their ability to grow, to reduce poverty, to govern effectively. These human and development costs make a strong case for public action to reduce gender disparities and, in so doing, capture the social benefits associated with greater equality between females and males.

After examining the costs to development of persistent gender inequalities, the report focuses on pathways for transmitting gender inequalities—through institutions, households, and the economy. It also examines the evidence on policies and programs available to redress disparities between women and men. The report concludes by proposing a three-part strategy for promoting gender equality in development.

This chapter focuses on the state of gender inequality in developing countries. It defines gender equality, then examines patterns of gender inequalities in basic rights, command over resources, and political participation and "voice" (the ability to influence and contribute to development)—across and within regions. It also examines the relationship between poverty and gender inequality within countries.

33

The main message from the evidence: despite considerable progress, women and girls remain disadvantaged relative to men and boys in many ways. These disadvantages reduce women's well-being and limit their ability to participate in and benefit from development. The evidence highlights considerable diversity in the nature and extent of gender disparities both across and within regions. It also indicates an important relationship between poverty and gender inequality within countries. Gender disparities, particularly in education and health, tend to be greater among the poor than the nonpoor.

Defining Gender Equality

GENDER REFERS TO SOCIALLY CONSTRUCTED ROLES AND socially learned behaviors and expectations associated with females and males. Women and men are different biologically. Women can give birth to and breast-feed children; men cannot. In much of the world adult men are physically larger than adult women. And women and men experience a number of different biologically based health risks that require different medical responses. All cultures interpret and elaborate these innate biological differences into social expectations about what behaviors and activities are appropriate for males and females and what rights, resources, and power they possess.

Like race, ethnicity, and class, gender is a social category that largely establishes one's life chances, shaping one's participation in society and in the economy. Although some societies do not have racial or ethnic divides, all societies have gender asymmetries—differences and disparities—to varying degrees. Gender roles and relations can vary considerably across societies. But there are also some striking similarities. For example, nearly all societies give the primary responsibility for the care of infants and young children to women and girls, and that for military service and national security to men.

Gender roles and relationships evolve out of interactions among biological, technological, economic, and other societal constraints. Some social scientists argue that gender roles originally reflected efficient survival strategies and sexual divisions of labor, but that as societies have advanced technically and economically these gender asymmetries have become both inefficient and limiting—as gender norms have changed more slowly than the factors that created them. A significant body of evidence presented in this report supports the view that in addition to being inequitable, rigid gender roles and associated gender disparities are often inefficient, imposing significant costs on societies and on development. But evidence also shows that while gender norms may take time to change, they are far from static. In fact, they can change quite rapidly in response to socioeconomic conditions.

Equality is another term that merits clarification. It has been used in a number of ways, referring at different times to equality under the law, equality of opportunity, or equality of outcomes or results (Coleman 1987). In this report we define *gender equality* in terms of equality under the law, equality of opportunity—including equality in access to human capital and other productive resources and equality of rewards for work— and equality of voice.[1] We stop short of defining gender equality in terms of equality of outcomes, however, for two reasons. One is that different societies can follow different paths in their pursuit of gender equality. The second is that an intrinsic aspect of equality is letting women and men choose different (or similar) roles and different (or similar) outcomes according to their preferences and goals.[2]

There are other reasons to be cautious about interpreting gender equality as equality in outcomes. For example, medical research indicates that females have some biological "advantage" over males in life expectancy, both in infancy and later in life. Social norms and practices that affect gender roles and the relative treatment of females and males can either reduce or extend women's advantage in life expectancy. Thus, in contexts where male and female life expectancies are numerically equivalent, this may imply female disadvantage, not gender equality. Similarly, females and males have different epidemiological risks and health care needs. Here again, numerical equivalence in particular health indicators would not necessarily imply gender equality.

That is why this report concentrates on what the familiar markers of gender equality tell us about relative rights, opportunities, and voice for women and men. For example, gender inequalities in education, access to other productive assets, employment, or earnings affect power relations between women and men—and thus their relative ability to influence decisions within their households. These inequalities also translate into disparities in women's and men's capacity to take advantage of economic and other opportunities. Inequalities in political representation, whether at the local or national levels reflect the extent to which women and men have voice in public policy debates and formulation.

The gender and development literature sometimes refers to the absolute status of females ("Have girls' school enrollment rates risen?") and sometimes to the relative status of females ("Has gender equality in school enrollments increased?"). This report addresses both. Focusing on absolute status is important because absolute improvements are fundamental to ensuring that development enhances the well-being of both women and men. For example, increased gender equality in schooling that results from increases in both female and male enrollment rates is clearly preferable to increased gender equality that results from either static or declining male enrollment rates.

But focusing on changes in absolute status alone is not sufficient. Whether in rights or command over resources, status is an important determinant of women's and men's relative power which, in turn, affects their abilities to participate in, contribute to, and benefit from development. And as we discuss in chapter 2, both the absolute and the relative status of women affect development in ways that are relevant to policymakers.

Regional Patterns of Gender Inequality in Rights, Resources, and Voice

DESPITE RECENT PROGRESS, GENDER INEQUALITIES ARE pervasive, persisting across many dimensions of life, turning up in households, social institutions, and the economy. Here the focus is on the key manifestations of exclusion and discrimination by gender: disparities in basic rights, in access to and control of resources, in employment and earnings, and in political voice. The analysis concentrates largely on data available across countries and over time to examine the recent trends and current status of gender inequalities for major developing regions.

Rights

The story of gender inequality is in many ways a story of asymmetrical rights and privileges for men and women. Asymmetries in rights are pervasive—in legal statutes, in customary laws, and in practices in communities, families, and households. These asymmetries exist in the rights to marry, to divorce, to determine family size, to inherit and manage property, to allocate one's labor to household enterprises, to undertake income-earning activities outside the home, to travel independently. Gender disparities in rights constrain the choices available to women in many aspects of life—often profoundly limiting the opportunities they have in the economy and in society.

In Botswana, Chile, Lesotho, Namibia, and Swaziland women are under the permanent guardianship of their husband and have no independent right to manage property (UNDP 1995). In several African countries married women do not own land but instead obtain usufruct rights through marriage (Gray and Kevane 1996). Moreover, in parts of Sub-Saharan Africa men have the right to make claims on their wife's labor, but women do not have that right to their husband's (Dey Abbas 1997). In Bolivia, Guatemala, and Syria men can restrict their wife's employment outside the home. In Egypt and Jordan women need their husband's permission to travel. In some Arab countries women must have their husband's consent to obtain a passport, whereas the reverse is not true (UNDP 1995).

Drawing on several human rights instruments of the United Nations, Humana (1986, 1992) assembled data on political, ethnic, and gender-based rights for more than 100 countries in 1985 and 1990 (box 1.1). The data provide indexes of human rights—with scores from 1 (consistent pattern of violations of rights) to 4 (unqualified respect for freedoms and rights).[3] Of the 40 rights indexes collected, several pertain to gender equality in rights, including indexes capturing political and legal equality, social and economic equality, and equality of rights in marriage and in divorce proceedings.[4]

Cross-country data show what country case evidence suggests: in no region of the developing world do women have equal rights with men in any of these dimensions (figure 1.1).[5] But there are noteworthy differences in women's relative rights status across regions. On average, women in Europe and Central Asia have the greatest (relative) equality of rights—women in South Asia, Sub-Saharan Africa, and the Middle East and North Africa the least.

Political and legal rights. For political and legal rights, all developing regions score between 2 (frequent violations of the rights) and 3 (occasional breaches of respect for rights) on the Humana index. So even where women enjoy political and legal equality under their national constitutions or statutory codes, they do not fully enjoy them in practice.

Box 1.1   Measuring Gender Equality in Rights

THE *WORLD HUMAN RIGHTS GUIDE* (HUMANA 1986, 1992) provides data on the human rights performance of roughly 100 countries with populations of more than 1 million. While there are well understood limits to assigning quantitative rankings to human rights levels, the 1986 edition of the guide served as the basis for the Human Freedom Index, a classification of countries by their human rights performance, in the United Nations Development Programme's *Human Development Report 1991.*

The guides' rights data are obtained using a questionnaire of 40 questions (or indicators) drawn from various articles of three United Nations instruments: the Universal Declaration of Human Rights; the International Covenant on Economic, Social, and Cultural Rights; and the International Covenant on Civil and Political Rights. The evaluation of a country's performance against this checklist of 40 indicators is carried out in two stages.

The first stage is to collect human rights information from the United Nations and other international institutions, government organizations, nongovernmental organizations (Amnesty International, Human Rights Watch), research institutions, newspapers and journals, and rights monitors and researchers in different countries. The second stage is to assign a grade, based on a 0–3 scale, to the assembled evidence on each indicator. A 0 represents a constant pattern of violations of the freedoms, rights, or guarantees of the article or indicator in the questionnaire. A 3 represents unqualified respect for the freedoms, rights, or guarantees referred to in the article or indicator.

This report focuses on three indicators that attempt to measure gender equality in rights:

- Political and legal equality for women (question 21).
- Social and economic equality for women (question 22).
- Equality of the sexes in marriage and in divorce proceedings (question 37).

In this report we use the values 1–4 to correspond to the 0–3 scale Humana uses.

A few other databases provide information on human rights, including the Freedom House Country Ratings and The Women's Economic and Social Human Rights (WESHR) Indicator from Purdue University's Global Studies program. Every year Freedom House compiles ratings for a number of countries on both political rights and civil liberties, but does not provide information on gender equality. The WESHR Indicator focuses exclusively on women's rights, but lacks time series data for many countries. To enable comparison of the greatest number of countries over time, this report uses the *World Human Rights Guide.*

Between 1985 and 1990 gender equality in political and legal rights appears to have improved slightly in most regions, except in Europe and Central Asia, where it declined, and in South Asia, where it seems to have stayed the same.[6]

Social and economic rights. Except in Europe and Central Asia and East Asia and Pacific, women experience lower equality in social and economic rights than in legal and political rights—a pattern most notable in South Asia and Sub-Saharan Africa. Moreover, there was little if any improvement in gender equality in these rights between 1985 and 1990.

Figure 1.1   Women Lack Equal Rights with Men

Political and legal rights, 1985 and 1990

Index of gender equality

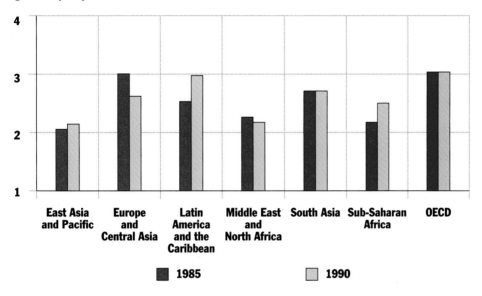

Social and economic rights, 1985 and 1990

Index of gender equality

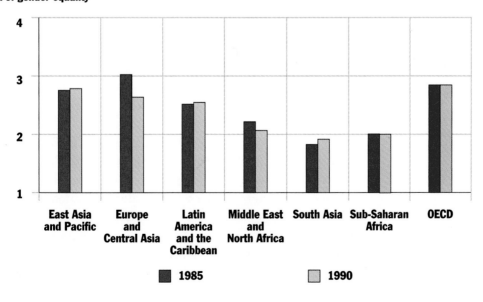

(figure continues on following page)

Figure 1.1 continued

Marriage and divorce rights, 1985 and 1990

Index of gender equality

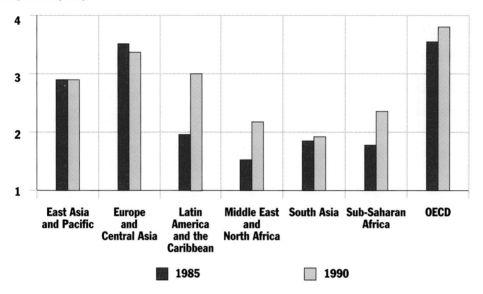

Note: See box 1.1 for gender equality in rights indexes, appendix 1 for general notes and included countries.
Sources: Equality in rights data from Humana (1992); population weights from World Bank (1999c).

Rights in marriage and in divorce proceedings. It is in rights in marriage and divorce that gender inequalities vary most across regions. Again, women in Europe and Central Asia experience the greatest relative equality—women in South Asia, Sub-Saharan Africa, and the Middle East and North Africa the least. Equality of rights in marriage has improved for women in South Asia, Sub-Saharan Africa, Latin America, and the Middle East and North Africa between 1985 and 1990. But for women in Europe and Central Asia it appears to have declined slightly.

Consistent cross-country data on gender equality in rights have not been compiled after 1990, but available information suggests that women's relative rights may have improved since then—especially following the 1995 Fourth World Conference on Women in Beijing, when women's rights became a major focal point in international efforts to promote gender equality. Since the Beijing Conference progress has been observable in women's legal rights, both internationally and nationally (UN 2000). For example, 16 additional states have since ratified the United Nations Convention on the Elimination of All

Forms of Discrimination against Women (CEDAW), bringing the total to 165.[7] A few countries have incorporated gender equality into their constitutions. Others have amended their criminal codes to include domestic violence.

Several countries have revised their labor codes to establish equal treatment of—and equal opportunities for—men and women in work and employment. And according to the Inter-Parliamentary Union,[8] only two countries still do not recognize women's right to vote or stand in elections. Moreover, countries in all regions have affirmative action policies for decisionmaking positions, including quotas for governmental bodies, parliaments, and political parties. As chapter 3 shows, changes in statutory law do not guarantee that gender equality in rights will be fully realized in practice. But these changes do lay the groundwork for greater realization of gender equality in rights.

In sum, while there appears to have been an overall tendency toward greater gender equality in rights in most regions since 1985, women continue to be disadvantaged relative to men in basic rights and associated status—both in statute and in practice. These gender disparities in rights constrain women's choices in many aspects of life—often profoundly limiting their ability to participate in development and reducing their quality of life.

Resources

As with basic rights, women and girls tend to have systematically poorer access than men and boys to a range of resources. This limits their opportunities and—as with rights—circumscribes their ability to participate in and enjoy the fruits of development. The story of unequal access to resources has many dimensions, involving access to human resources, social capital, physical and financial capital, employment, and earnings. Such disparities limit women's ability to participate in development and to contribute to higher living standards for their families. They also translate into greater risk and vulnerability in the face of personal or family crises, in old age, and during economic shocks.

Education. Education is central to one's ability to respond to the opportunities that development presents, but significant disparities remain in several regions (figure 1.2). Disparities persist both in enrollment rates, which capture education flows, and in average years of schooling, which represent the stock of education in the population.

Figure 1.2 Despite Improvements, Gender Disparities Persist in Schooling in Some Regions

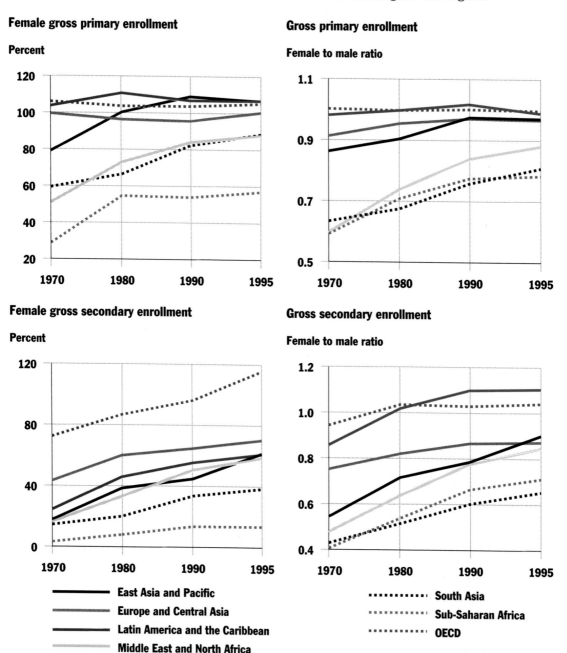

Female gross primary enrollment

Percent

Gross primary enrollment

Female to male ratio

Female gross secondary enrollment

Percent

Gross secondary enrollment

Female to male ratio

East Asia and Pacific
Europe and Central Asia
Latin America and the Caribbean
Middle East and North Africa

South Asia
Sub-Saharan Africa
OECD

(figure continues on following page)

Figure 1.2 continued

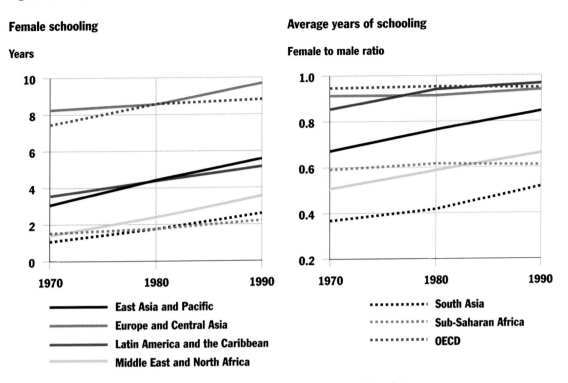

Female schooling

Years

Average years of schooling

Female to male ratio

East Asia and Pacific
Europe and Central Asia
Latin America and the Caribbean
Middle East and North Africa
South Asia
Sub-Saharan Africa
OECD

Note: See appendix 1 for general notes and included countries and the glossary for variable definitions.
Sources: Years of schooling data from Barro and Lee (1994); population weights from World Bank (1999d).

Female primary and secondary enrollment rates and average years of female schooling have generally risen over time. In several regions primary enrollment rates have flattened out at high levels—as in East Asia and Pacific, Latin America and the Caribbean, and Europe and Central Asia, where gross enrollment rates for females have reached or surpassed 100 percent.[9] Girls' primary enrollment rates have also leveled off in Sub-Saharan Africa—but at much lower levels. In Sub-Saharan Africa girls experienced strong gains in primary enrollment rates between 1970 and 1980, but those rates have since flattened out at 54 percent. Absolute levels of female enrollment and schooling remain lower in Sub-Saharan Africa than in other developing regions. Female secondary enrollment rates were just 14 percent in 1995, and average schooling attainment was just 2.2 years in 1990.

How do these trends compare with those for boys? Gender equality in school enrollments and average years of schooling has improved since

1970, as girls' schooling has generally increased faster than boys'. But the gender disparity and the speed in closing gender gaps have varied. As with rights, East Asia, Latin America, and Europe and Central Asia have the highest gender equality in education. In Europe and Central Asia and Latin America average female secondary enrollment rates now exceed male rates, and women have on average about 90 percent as many years of schooling as men.

Starting from lower initial levels of gender equality, South Asia, Sub-Saharan Africa, and the Middle East and North Africa have all registered noteworthy declines in gender disparities in primary and secondary enrollments between 1970 and 1995. Nonetheless, South Asia continues to have the lowest gender equality in education. Women in South Asia have on average only about half as many years of education as men, and female enrollment rates at the secondary level are still only two-thirds of male rates. Moreover, South Asia has larger gender inequalities in education than other developing regions where absolute levels of female education are lower (Filmer, King, and Pritchett 1998).

In Sub-Saharan Africa gender equality in enrollment rates has increased—although at the primary level improvements between 1980 and 1990 tended to reflect absolute declines in boys' enrollment rates rather than improvements in girls'. Moreover, in contrast to South Asia and the Middle East and North Africa, Sub-Saharan Africa made no real progress in closing the gender gap in average years of schooling between 1970 and 1990.

So, while there has been a clear trend toward gender equality in education since 1970, the gains have been slow and uneven for the poorest regions. Closing gender gaps in education—and closing them more quickly—are thus still important development challenges to policymakers, especially in South Asia, Sub-Saharan Africa, and some countries in the Middle East and North Africa. The challenges are particularly important as the world moves into the information age and knowledge-intensive output displaces traditional modes of production. Basic education is the foundation for developing the flexible skills needed to participate in knowledge-intensive economic activity. Those who lack access to basic education are likely to be excluded from the new opportunities, and where long-standing gender gaps in education persist, women will be at increasing risk of falling behind men in their ability to participate in development.

Health. Good health is critical for well-being and, like education, an important resource that enables people to take part in and enjoy the fruits of development. The focus here is largely on life expectancy at birth and the burden of disease, among the few measures of health available by gender for a large number of countries. Gender differences in life expectancy at birth combine the effects of gender disparities in child and adult mortality rates, with early childhood mortality dominating. Gender differences in both life expectancy and burden of disease partly reflect biological differences. But they also reflect important differences in gender roles and in society's treatment of women and men.

This section also reviews evidence on gender-related violence and HIV/AIDS. While fewer data are available on these issues, both have gender dimensions that critically affect the well-being of women and men and their ability to participate in development.

Life expectancy and mortality. In the developing regions life expectancy at birth has risen dramatically for both men and women over the past several decades. Better diets, safer water, and control of communicable diseases have improved health and longevity in much of the world. Since 1970 average life expectancies have increased by at least 15 years in the Middle East and North Africa and in South Asia. Life expectancies across regions have also been converging—except in Sub-Saharan Africa, where improvements have been slower.

Women tend to live longer than men—in part because of biological differences. Medical research shows that in all societies more male fetuses are spontaneously aborted or stillborn; and in most societies male mortality rates are higher for the first six months of life (Waldron 1986). These patterns originate in boys' chromosomal structures and the slower maturing of their lungs due to the effects of testosterone. Later in life women appear to have another biological advantage: at least until menopause, their hormones protect them from ischemic heart disease. Given this biological edge, women's life expectancy will generally exceed men's in the absence of deprivation and discrimination.

Where women and men have the same life expectancy or where men are expected to live longer than women, these outcomes reflect a range of societal factors that work against women and girls. Gender disparities in nutrition and health care that favor males, frequent and complicated pregnancies, and inadequate prenatal and obstetric care can all reduce women's life expectancy relative to men's. Conversely, social and environmental factors that reinforce male gender roles can widen the biological advantage of females in life expectancy. The incidence of premature deaths among males from heart disease, for example, reflects not only their greater biological vulnerability but also the effects of greater work-related stress, higher rates of smoking, and greater exposure to carcinogens in the workplace (WHO 1998).

By 1990 female life expectancy exceeded male life expectancy in all developing regions (figure 1.3). From 1970 to 1997 the greatest improvements in women's relative life expectancies were in South Asia—although the region started from female disadvantage. And despite these improvements, the female to male life expectancy ratios in South Asia remain the lowest in the world. Other regions experienced either slight increases or little change in this ratio between 1970 and 1997. But in Sub-Saharan Africa the ratio declined: even though women's life expectancies rose, men's rose

Figure 1.3   Women Now Outlive Men in All Regions

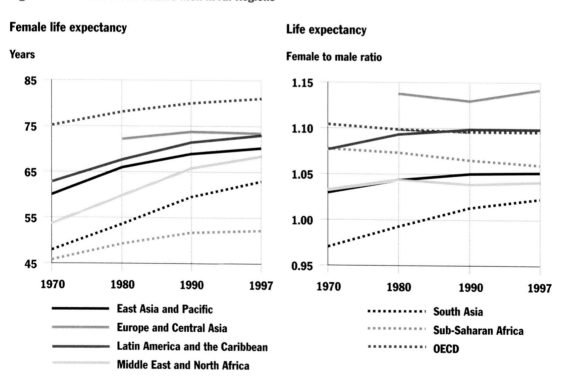

Note: See appendix 1 for general notes and included countries and the glossary for variable definitions.
Source: World Bank (1999c).

even more. In Europe and Central Asia the female to male life expectancy ratio changed little, with the small increases fueled not by absolute increases in female life expectancy but by declines in male life expectancy.

Given female biological advantage at birth, male mortality rates are expected to be higher than female rates. The sex ratio in a country is thus a first indicator of gender discrimination. Several recent studies estimate the number of girls and women that are "missing" in the world as a result of excess female mortality in Asia (mostly China, the Republic of Korea, and India) and, to less extent, in the Middle East and North Africa. Between 60 and 100 million fewer women are alive today than would be in the absence of gender discrimination (Sen 1989, 1992; Coale 1991; Klasen 1994). These estimates are based on comparisons of the actual sex ratio with the sex ratio that theoretically would exist without gender discrimination.

Much of the gender bias appears concentrated among younger age groups. In India gender differences in the food intake of young children help account for higher female mortality; one study found that girls receive not less food but poorer quality food (Das Gupta 1987). Poorer access to health care—particularly for girls born later in the birth order and girls born to rural families—is another reason for the large number of "missing" women (Quibiria 1995; Das Gupta 1987).

Discrimination against girls may be affected not only by cultural preferences, institutional factors, and economic considerations, but also by public policy. In such developing countries as Sri Lanka, the sex ratio (male to female) has declined significantly over the past three decades, thanks to public provision of health care, education, and food, reducing families' tendencies to discriminate against daughters (Bardhan and Klasen 1998). But in China the sex ratio at birth has increased since the 1960s—rising from 1.07 in 1980 to 1.14 in 1993—due to a decline in subsidized health services and to the one-child policy (Li and Zhang 1998). The one-child policy has led parents, who often prefer a male child, to abandon female children, choose sex-selective abortions, or neglect their daughters (Banister and Coale 1994). Globally the number of missing women will increase if current trends in excess female mortality continue—particularly in China (World Bank 1993; Bardhan and Klasen 1998).

Burden of disease. Beyond gross differences in mortality rates and life expectancy, the causes of illness and death differ by gender. A World Health Organization (WHO) study estimates Disability-Adjusted Life

Years (DALYs) lost for females and males in developed and developing countries, by cause (Murray and Lopez 1996). DALYs express years of life lost to premature death and years lived with a disability, adjusted for the severity of the disability.[10] While the 10 leading causes of DALYs are similar for boys and girls under 5, there are noteworthy differences between men and women ages 15–44 (table 1.1). Alcohol use, road traffic accidents, and violence together account for about 27 percent of men's DALYs in developed countries and 16 percent in developing countries. None of these three is in the top 10 for women in developing

Table 1.1 Ten Leading Causes of Disability-Adjusted Life Years Lost for Women and Men, Ages 15–44, 1990

Women		Men	
Disease or injury	**Percentage of total**	**Disease or injury**	**Percentage of total**
Developing regions		*Developing regions*	
Unipolar major depression	12.8	Unipolar major depression	7.0
Tuberculosis	4.9	Road traffic accidents	6.3
Iron-deficiency anemia	4.0	Tuberculosis	6.0
Self-inflicted injuries	3.7	Violence	5.5
Obstructed labor	3.4	Alcohol use	4.7
Chlamydia	3.0	War	4.1
Bipolar disorder	3.0	Bipolar disorder	3.1
Maternal sepsis	2.9	Self-inflicted injuries	3.0
War	2.8	Schizophrenia	2.8
Abortion	2.7	Iron-deficiency anemia	2.7
Developed regions		*Developed regions*	
Unipolar major depression	19.8	Alcohol use	12.7
Schizophrenia	5.9	Road traffic accidents	11.3
Road traffic accidents	4.6	Unipolar major depression	7.2
Bipolar disorder	4.5	Self-inflicted injuries	5.6
Obsessive-compulsive disorders	3.8	Schizophrenia	4.3
Alcohol use	3.2	Drug use	3.8
Osteoarthritis	3.2	Violence	3.2
Chlamydia	2.4	Ischemic heart disease	3.1
Self-inflicted injuries	2.3	Bipolar disorder	3.1
Rheumatoid arthritis	2.2	HIV	2.5

Note: For each disorder in a given population, Disability-Adjusted Life Years lost are calculated by combining: losses from premature death (defined as the difference between actual age at death and life expectancy at that age in a low-mortality population), and loss of healthy life resulting from disability.

Source: Murray and Lopez (1996).

countries—although road accidents and alcohol use are on the list for women in developed countries, accounting for 8 percent of their DALYs.

In both developed and developing countries women lose more DALYs from sexually transmitted diseases (specifically, chlamydia) than men do. Maternal sepsis and abortion are among the top 10 causes of DALYs for women in developing countries—but not for women in developed countries, for whom maternal health care is likely to be more accessible. In fact, maternal mortality varies considerably across developed and developing regions. Whereas average maternal mortality rates are 8 deaths per 100,000 live births in OECD countries and 49 in Eastern Europe and Central Asia, they reach as high as 410 in South Asia and 571 in Sub-Saharan Africa (UNICEF 1999a).

Differences in the burden of disease for women and men translate into gender differences in life expectancy and quality of life that are not captured in standard life expectancy figures. While there is no perfect single measure for summing up the health of a population, a new WHO study computes a measure of life expectancy that adjusts for the impact of illness and disability (WHO 2000).[11] The measure indicates that women tend to lose more healthy life years to disability than men do. Thus, when gender differences in the impact of illness and disability are taken into account, female advantage in life expectancy tends to be smaller than what the standard life expectancy data would suggest.

Violence. Women face gender-specific health risks that conventional data sources may not capture. They are particularly susceptible, for example, to gender-related violence and domestic abuse. Results from more than 50 surveys from across the world estimate that 16–50 percent of women have been victims of physical violence at some time in their life. The greatest risk of gender-related violence comes not from strangers but from spouses and other male family members (Heise, Elsberg, and Gottemoeller 1999). Intimate partner abuse is associated with social norms that grant males control of female behavior and that accept violence as a way to exert power in relationships or to resolve conflict. It is also associated with poverty, male unemployment, and patriarchal control of household financial resources and decisionmaking.

Gender-related violence has direct effects on women's physical and emotional health and well-being, but also has important indirect impacts. For example, women with a history of physical or sexual abuse face greater risk of gynecological disorders, unintended pregnancies, unsafe abortions, sexually transmitted infections, and adverse pregnancy outcomes, including pregnancy complications, miscarriage, low-birthweight deliveries, and pelvic inflammatory disease (Heise, Ellsberg, and Gottemoeller 1999).

HIV/AIDS. While not reflected in table 1.1, AIDS has become a critical issue in developing countries. The United Nations AIDS program estimated that at the end of 1999 more than 33 million people worldwide were infected with HIV and that more than 16 million had already died (UNAIDS 1999). More than 95 percent of all adult HIV infections are in developing and transition economies. Countries in Sub-Saharan Africa have the highest infection rates, while Asian and Eastern European countries have the highest growth rates of infection.

Despite recent medical advances in AIDS treatment, people infected with HIV in the developing world almost always contract AIDS within 2–20 years and die of opportunistic illnesses within a year thereafter. To blame for about 9 percent of adult deaths from infectious diseases in developing countries in 1990, HIV will account directly or indirectly for more than half such deaths in 2020 (World Bank 1999a). In several countries AIDS has already reduced life expectancy by more than 10 years, reversing substantial gains since 1950.

In many countries the AIDS epidemic will spread rapidly over the next decade until up to one in four women and one in five men become infected, the case today in several Sub-Saharan countries. AIDS can be transmitted only by unprotected sex, by blood (either by transfusion or through sharing contaminated injection equipment), or from mother to child. While national epidemics frequently begin within groups of intravenous drug users or commercial sex workers, they spread to the sex partners of the drug users and sex workers—and from infected women to their children. Infection rates are often higher for women than for men for three reasons: three-quarters of all sexual transmission outside developed countries is heterosexual, most commercial sex workers are female, and the infectiousness of HIV is greater from males to females. In Sub-Saharan Africa 55 percent of the 22 million infected adults are women. And among 15- to 19-year-olds there are four or five infected young women for every infected young man (UNAIDS 1999). As chapter 2 discusses, gender disparities in power and command over resources contribute to the spread of HIV worldwide.

The gender differences in the causes of illness and death—produced by a combination of biological, social, and cultural factors—imply that improving the health of females and males requires an awareness not only of the biological aspects of diagnosis and treatment, but also of the social factors that promote or reduce good health. The scientific and medical community—as well as public policymakers—are only beginning to realize the importance of this more comprehensive approach.

Productive assets—land, information, technology, and financial resources. Gender disparities in access to and control of such productive assets as land, information, technology, and financial capital hinder women's ability to participate in and take advantage of the opportunities afforded by development. No consistent cross-country data by gender are available on access to productive resources. But the fact that women generally own fewer assets than men and have poorer access to credit, to other intermediate inputs, and to extension services has been extensively documented.

According to household surveys in Bangladesh, Ethiopia, Indonesia, and South Africa women bring far fewer assets into marriage (Quisumbing and Maluccio 1999). In Bangladesh men's assets at marriage averaged about 82,000 taka in 1996—women's only about 6,500.[12] In Ethiopia total assets, including land and livestock, brought into a marriage by men averaged 4,200 birr in 1997—that by women just under 1,000. These asymmetries in asset ownership persist throughout the life cycle, closely mirroring those at marriage, and affect women's autonomy, their ability to influence household decisions, and their economic status.

In many developing countries titles to land are most often vested in men. In much of Sub-Saharan Africa women obtain land rights through marriage, but these rights are secure only as long as the marriage lasts (Gray and Kevane 1996). Divorced or widowed women lose their control of land (and other productive assets). And when women do own land, their plots are typically smaller than those owned by men (Kumar 1994).

While female-headed households form about a third of all households in Zambia, they are underrepresented among the larger farms, with only a fourth of farms larger than two hectares owned by women. In Nigeria female-headed farms are only a third the size of male-headed farms—0.8 hectare compared with 2.4 hectares—and are generally on inferior land (Saito, Mekonnen, and Spurling 1994). Even when men and women in the same household cultivate separate plots, as in much of Africa, women often control smaller land parcels (Udry 1996). Similar patterns of landholding can be found in Latin America and in South and East Asia (Deere and Leon 1997; Agarwal 1994).

Female-run farms—and more generally, female-run enterprises—are less well capitalized than those run by males. In Kenya female-headed households own less than half the farming equipment that male-headed households own (Saito, Mekonnen, and Spurling 1994). Survey data show that 92 percent of women use hand cultivation methods only, while 38 percent of men use mechanized technology or oxen. In Malawi farms owned by female-headed households use only about half as much fertilizer as the farms of male-headed households (Due and Gladwin 1991). In Burkina Faso male-managed plots are allocated significantly more fertilizer and labor per hectare than female-managed plots for the same crop cultivated by the same household (Udry 1996). Among those owning nonfarm enterprises in Vietnam, women earn less than men—not because of their schooling or age or region, but because they have smaller capital stocks, own less inventory, operate in lower-income industries, and receive less apprenticeship training (Vijverberg 1998).

Women farmers generally receive less technical support for agriculture from extension services (Quisumbing 1994; Chi and others 1998). Data from several Sub-Saharan countries in the 1980s show that extension workers visited 12–70 percent of male-headed households but only 9–58 percent of female-headed households (Quisumbing 1994). Women farmers have less access to these services because they have less education and smaller farms and because extension workers, mostly men, tend to direct services to farms where men are present (Staudt 1978). Only 7 percent of field extension staff in Africa are women (Quisumbing 1994). Similarly, a recent study of the impact of pest management training for rice farmers in Vietnam shows that while 55 percent of male farmers consulted extension service workers, only 23 percent of female farmers did (Chi and others 1998).

With specific exceptions—the result of recent microenterprise initiatives—women continue to have poorer access than men to financial services. It is estimated that women in Africa receive less than 10 percent of all credit going to small farmers and 1 percent of the total credit to the agricultural sector (UNDP 1995). One important reason for this is women's low ownership of land, a critical source of collateral to secure loans. In addition, women have smaller social and business networks that might facilitate access to financial services. Having less "social network capital" explains why female entrepreneurs in Kenya and Zimbabwe have poorer access to supplier credit than male entrepreneurs with similar characteristics (Fafchamps 2000). And when female entrepreneurs do obtain credit, their loans tend to be smaller (Saito, Mekonnen, and Spurling 1994; Vijverberg 1998; Sanchez 1998).

Employment and earnings. Historically, men have had higher rates of participation in the labor force than women—a pattern that continues. But female labor force participation varies considerably across developing regions, with women's share of the labor force ranging from 25 percent in the Middle East and North Africa in 1995 to about 45 percent in Europe and Central Asia and in East Asia and Pacific (figure 1.4). Regional trends also vary. Between 1970 and 1995 women's share of the labor force increased slightly in the Middle East and North Africa and in East Asia and Pacific, and considerably in Latin America and the Caribbean. In Sub-Saharan Africa women's relative participation rates were stable, but in South Asia and in Europe and Central Asia they declined slightly.[13]

In the labor force women and men commonly perform different tasks and work in different sectors. For example, women constitute the vast majority of production workers in the garment sector worldwide. There is persistent occupational segregation by gender in both developed and developing countries, with women underrepresented in better-paying

Figure 1.4   Trends in Female Labor Supply Vary across Regions

Women as a share of total labor force

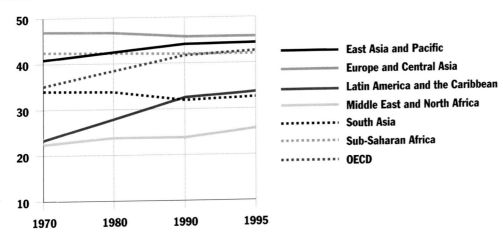

Source: World Bank (1999d).

formal sector jobs and overrepresented in the unpaid and informal sectors. Moreover, female employment is on average less secure than male employment, with women more often involved in subcontracting, temporary, or casual work, or work in the home.

One measure of occupational segregation by gender divides the proportion of all working women employed in a particular occupation by the proportion of all working men employed in that occupation. So, a ratio greater than one indicates that women are overrepresented, a ratio less than one that women are underrepresented. When this measure is applied to data from both developed and developing countries, several dimensions of occupational segregation emerge (figure 1.5). For example, women are overrepresented in service occupations, professional and technical jobs, and clerical and sales jobs—in both developed and developing regions. And men are greatly overrepresented in production jobs as well as in higher-paying administrative and managerial positions.

There appears to have been some decline in employment and occupational segregation by gender over the past several decades. For example, a recent study by Tzannatos (1999) examines a measure of "employment

Figure 1.5   Women and Men Hold Different Occupations

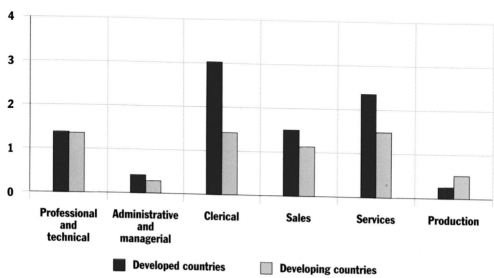

Note: See appendix 1 for included countries and years and glossary for a definition of the occupational representation ratio.
Source: Based on data from Anker (1998).

dissimilarity" called the Duncan index and analyzes changes between the 1950s–60s and 1980s–90s.[14] The study finds slight convergence in female and male employment profiles across industrial sectors, with faster convergence in wage employment than in self-employment or family work. There is also some evidence of convergence in occupational profiles between female and male wage employees, but little evidence of such convergence among self-employed or family workers. In developing countries, even with recent increases in the relative education and work experience of women in the labor force, occupational segregation remains a salient feature of labor markets.

Women also continue to earn less than men. Recent empirical studies from 71 countries indicate that on average in developed countries women earn 77 percent as much as men, and in developing countries, 73 percent as much (table 1.2).[15] These averages, derived from the latest estimates available for these countries, mask wide variation across countries. Among developed countries, for example, the female to male earnings ratio ranges from 43 percent in Japan (1993–94) to 87 percent in Denmark (1995); among developing countries, it ranges from 43 percent in Nicaragua (1991) to 90 percent in Thailand (1989) and 101 percent in Chile (1996). While most studies do not measure the gender earnings ratio for exactly comparable groups of workers over time, evidence from several countries in Asia, Latin America, Sub-Saharan Africa, and the OECD suggests that female earnings tend to be rising relative to male earnings (appendix 3).

But comparing an unadjusted ratio of earnings for women and men can be misleading for three reasons. First, the average earnings (or wage)

Table 1.2 Relative Earnings of Women and Men

	Female to male earnings ratio	Gender gap	Portion of gap unexplained (percent)
Developed countries (n = 19)	0.77	0.23	80.4
Developing countries (n = 42)	0.73	0.27	82.2

Note: The gender gap in earnings is the proportional difference between average female and male wages (1 minus the female to male earnings ratio). The unexplained portion of the gender gap in earnings is the portion not explained by an individual's characteristics, such as educational attainment and work experience, and by job characteristics. See appendix 3 for periods covered.

Source: Various studies; for details, see appendix 3.

data generally used to compute the ratio have not been adjusted for the characteristics of workers, such as education, work experience, and skills training. To the extent that women and men have different levels of education or experience, unadjusted ratios are not comparing earnings across similar types of workers. Second, data on earnings (or wages) reflect differences in occupations, and as previously shown, women and men tend to be concentrated in different types of occupations. And third, earnings figures often reflect differences in hours worked, since a larger proportion of men than women work full-time. If women work fewer hours per month for pay than men, a comparison of the monthly earnings of women and men would indicate lower relative earnings for women than would a comparison of hourly wages. The greater the gender differences in hours worked for pay, the lower the unadjusted gender earnings ratios will be relative to ratios that adjust for differences in hours worked.

Studies in developed and developing countries have analyzed the relative wages of women and men, controlling for such worker characteristics as education and experience. They usually decompose the gender gap in observed wages to separate the effect of discrimination from other factors. In the Republic of Korea women's wages are 51 percent of men's, with half of the gap explained by differences in the characteristics of workers (Horton 1996). In Brazil women earn 70 percent of what men earn, but only 10 percent of this difference is due to differences in measured characteristics (Psacharopoulos and Tzannatos 1992). In Denmark, France, Germany, and the United Kingdom differences in measured human capital characteristics account for 20–30 percent of the earnings gap—and in Portugal and Spain, even less (Rice 1999). In general, workers' characteristics explain about a third or less of the gender earnings gap in developing countries. This suggests that although the way households allocate human capital investments between boys and girls has direct consequences for their children's prospects in the labor market, other important forces are at work.

Few studies of developing countries include measures of job attributes, usually because of lack of data. Those that do indicate that gender differences in job characteristics affect relative wages to some degree (controlling for worker characteristics)—but the impact appears to differ considerably across developed and developing countries. In developed countries adjusting the gender earnings gap for information on job characteristics significantly reduces the proportion of the gap that remains unexplained, confirming that men, on average, hold better-paying jobs

(Rice 1999; Zabalza and Tzannatos 1985). Different patterns of employment explain up to a third of the gender wage gap in some countries (Tzannatos 1998). But occupational segregation appears to account for a relatively small share of the gender wage gap in developing countries. In Latin America employment differences between women and men appear to account for little, if any, of the earnings differences.[16]

In sum, in developed and developing countries differences in observed worker and job characteristics explain only about 20 percent of the gender gap in earnings (see table 1.2). The rest of the gap results from factors that are difficult to measure directly, such as differences in workers' abilities or differences in labor market treatment (discrimination).

Voice

Limited command over productive resources and weaker ability to generate incomes—whether in self-employed activities or in wage employment—constrain women's power to influence resource allocation and investment decisions within the home. Unequal rights and poor socioeconomic status relative to men also limit women's ability to participate in political processes as active agents and to influence decisions in their communities and at the national level. Chapter 4 discusses how command over income, assets, and other resources affect women's voice, autonomy, and power in the household. This section examines disparities in women's and men's voice in society more broadly, as captured by their participation and representation in politics.

Women in the 20th century have gained the right to vote in nearly all countries. The gender gap in voting is declining, especially in countries where a high proportion of the population votes. Even so, substantial disparities still exist in more active forms of participation, such as demonstrations and boycotts. And women remain significantly less likely to discuss politics than men, especially among older cohorts and those with less education (Inglehart 1997).

Moreover, there still are large gender disparities in political participation and representation at all levels of government—from local councils to national assemblies and cabinets. Women continue to be vastly underrepresented in elected office (figure 1.6). In all regions except East Asia and the Pacific and Europe and Central Asia, the average shares of parliamentary seats held by women remained at less than 10 percent between 1975 and 1995. In East Asia women's share has consistently

Figure 1.6   Women Are Vastly Underrepresented in Parliaments

Women's share of parliamentary seats

Percent

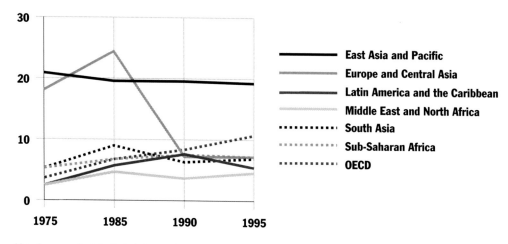

East Asia and Pacific
Europe and Central Asia
Latin America and the Caribbean
Middle East and North Africa
South Asia
Sub-Saharan Africa
OECD

Note: See appendix 1 for included countries.
Sources: Parliamentary data from WISTAT (1998); population weights from World Bank (1999c).

been just less than 20 percent. The most dramatic change has occurred in Europe and Central Asia, where the high levels of female representation (relative to most of the rest of the world) fell dramatically in the late 1980s—from nearly 25 percent to 7 percent—following the start of the economic and political transition.[17] Substantial gender disparities also persist in local and regional assemblies.

Women also remain vastly underrepresented in the executive branch of government. In no developing region did women make up more than 8 percent of cabinet ministers in 1998 (UNDP 2000). In the Middle East and North Africa women held only 2 percent of cabinet positions, while in East Asia and Pacific they held 4 percent, and in South Asia and Sub-Saharan Africa, roughly 6 percent. In Latin America and Eastern Europe and Central Asia women made up between 7 and 8 percent of cabinet ministers. Female representation in subministerial positions tends to be only slightly greater, and in South Asia, it is lower.[18]

Women who do hold cabinet appointments are more likely to be in ministries of women's or social affairs than ministries of finance, economics, or planning, which make mainstream policy and budgetary decisions. Of the 466 female ministers holding portfolios in 151 countries in early 2000, 95 (about 20 percent) were heads of ministries of women's and social affairs, but only 22 (just less than 5 percent) were heads of ministries of finance and of the economy and development (IPU 2000).

Patterns of Gender Inequality within Regions and Countries

HIGHLIGHTING DIFFERENCES AMONG REGIONS CAN MASK diversity within regions and countries. Recognizing this diversity is critical to deeper understanding of the gender dimensions of development and to better informed policymaking. Consider Sub-Saharan Africa and South Asia.

In Sub-Saharan Africa gender gaps in enrollment rates for 6- to 14-year-olds—and in the proportion of 15- to 19-year-olds who have completed grade five—tend to be substantially larger in Central and West Africa than in the rest of the region (Filmer 1999). And while this subregional pattern is strong, there are noteworthy exceptions. Ghana stands out with enrollment rates and grade five completion rates at near parity for girls and boys—a pattern similar to those observed in East and southern Africa. Conversely, while most of the countries in East and southern Africa have high gender equality in basic education, considerable gender gaps persist in Comoros and Mozambique, which (in this respect) resemble West African countries more than they do their neighbors.

The variation in gender inequality is also considerable in South Asia, even within countries. Several studies examining diversity within the region—in particular, the north-south dichotomy in India's kinship systems—have found different patterns in women's autonomy and status (Dyson and Moore 1983; Basu 1992; Malhotra, Vanneman, and Kishor 1995). Perhaps as a result of the differences in kinship systems, gender inequalities in education and health often vary more among states in India and provinces in Pakistan than among countries in the rest of the world. For example:

- A band across India's northwestern states (extending into several provinces in Pakistan) has the largest gender disparities in child mortality rates in the world. The gap is more than a standard deviation higher in the Indian states of Haryana, Punjab, and Uttar Pradesh and the Pakistani provinces of Balochistan and Punjab than in Egypt, the country with the largest gender gap in child mortality of any non–South Asian country (figure 1.7;

Figure 1.7   Variation in Gender Disparity Is Large in South Asia—Even Larger Than among All Countries

Female to male child mortality ratios

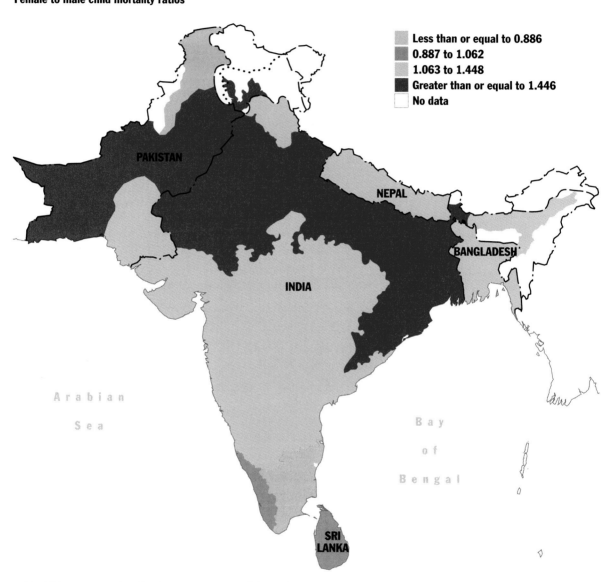

Note: This map was produced by the Map Design Unit of The World Bank. The boundaries, colors, denominations, and any other information shown on this map do not imply, on the part of The World Bank Group, any judgment on the legal status of any territory, or any endorsement or acceptance of such boundaries.

Source: Filmer, King, and Pritchett (1998).

Filmer, King, and Pritchett 1998). In contrast, the Indian states of Tamil Nadu and Kerala have a much smaller gender gap in child mortality than the average for non–South Asian countries.

- For school enrollment rates, the variations in gender disparities within India and Pakistan—and certainly within South Asia—are nearly as large as the differences among the world's countries. Although South Asia has the largest average gender gaps in school enrollments, Sri Lanka has closed the gender gap in basic education. Moreover, India has states with no gender gap (Kerala) and states in which girls are only half as likely as boys to attend school (Rajasthan). In Pakistan the gender gap is twice as large in Balochistan as in the Punjab.

Gender and Poverty

TO WHAT EXTENT ARE GENDER INEQUALITIES ASSOCIATED with poverty? Are gender inequalities more severe among the the poor than the nonpoor? Do persistent inequalities in rights, resources, and participation translate into gender differences in poverty? Are particular groups of women (or men) more likely to be poor?

Gender Inequalities Tend to Be Greater among the Poor

Gender inequalities persist among both the rich and the poor, but they are often greatest among the poor, particularly for household investments in education and health. A recent study by Filmer (1999) analyzes gender differences in school enrollment among 6- to 14-year-olds, using Demographic and Health Survey data from 41 countries in Central, South, and Southeast Asia; Sub-Saharan Africa; Latin America and the Caribbean; and the Middle East and North Africa in the 1990s.[19] It ranks households by wealth according to an index aggregated from asset variables that reflect a household's living standard. Defining the rich as the richest 20 percent of households and the poor as the poorest 40 percent of households within each country, it compares disparities in school enrollments between rich and poor households.

The study finds that gender disparities in school enrollment rates tend to be greater among the poor than among the rich (figure 1.8). In

Figure 1.8 Gender Disparities Tend to Be Greater among the Poor than the Rich

Male to female enrollment ratio among the poor

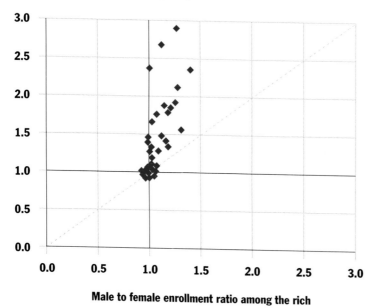

Male to female enrollment ratio among the rich

Note: The enrollment ratio pertains to the proportion of children ages 6–14 enrolled in school, regardless of education level. Poor households are defined as those in the bottom 40 percent of a "wealth" distribution; rich households, those in the top 20 percent. The diagonal line signifies equal gender gaps among the poor and among the rich. See appendix 1 for included countries and years.
Source: Filmer (1999).

21 of the 41 countries gender disparities in enrollment among 6- to 14-year-olds—expressed as a ratio of male enrollment rates to female rates—are greater among the poor than the rich.

In figure 1.8 the diagonal line indicates equal degrees of gender inequality between the richest 20 percent and the poorest 40 percent of households in each country. In countries that lie above the line, gender disparities are larger among the poor than the rich.

Filmer (1999) identifies two subgroups of countries among those in which gender gaps in schooling are greater among the poor than the rich. In one, gender inequality is low or moderate among the rich (a male to female ratio less than 1.5) and moderate among the poor (a ratio between 1.1 and 1.5). In the second, inequality is low or moderate among the rich (a ratio less than 1.5) but high among the poor (a ratio greater than 1.5). The second group includes Benin, Burkina Faso, the Central African Republic, Côte d'Ivoire, India, Mali, Morocco, Niger, Pakistan, and Senegal—many of the countries that have the highest average levels of gender inequality in education.

In no country studied are gender disparities in school enrollment larger among the rich than among the poor. Similar analysis was carried out for 29 developing and transition economies using household survey data from other sources that use consumption rather than wealth as the measure of household welfare, including the Living Standards Measurement Study and Social Dimensions of Adjustment surveys. Very similar patterns of gender disparities in education were found between the rich and the poor for countries that have not achieved universal primary education.[20]

Similar patterns are observed between the rich and poor for mortality of children under five. Analysis of Demographic Health Survey data from 32 developing countries, using a wealth ranking procedure similar to that used by Filmer (1999), indicates that about two-thirds of the countries have patterns of under-five mortality in which female advantage is smaller (or male advantage is larger) among the poor than among the rich. As in schooling, the tendency to favor boys is stronger among the poor than the rich.[21]

The relationship between poverty and gender inequality can differ significantly across countries as well as across dimensions of inequality, and higher incomes do not always imply greater equality in every dimension. In some contexts specific forms of gender disparity confer status on the family. In some societies with rigid gender divisions, for example, the higher a family's socioeconomic status, the greater the investment in female modesty and seclusion—symbols of that status (Chen 1995). Nonetheless, there is a strong association between poverty and gender disparities in basic education and health that are critical to girls' and boys' ability to participate in development and to attain a basic quality of life.

Are Women Poorer Than Men?

Little is known about the relative numbers of women and men in poverty (measured by income or consumption). One widely quoted estimate suggests that 70 percent of the world's poor are now women (UNDP 1995). But a recent study by Marcoux (1998) illustrates that there are no plausible demographic assumptions under which this sexual division of poverty could hold. The 70 percent estimate implies a ratio of 2.3 poor females to every poor male—or a sex imbalance among the world's poor of 900 million women and girls to 400 million men and boys. Population data do not support such conclusions.

Estimating the number of men and women living in poverty is difficult. Why? There is no adequate summary measure of individual welfare that can be compared for males and females. The most commonly used indicator of poverty (or current welfare) is consumption. But most household-based surveys collect consumption data on households, not individuals. While this may partly reflect a traditional view of the household as the basic unit of economic decisionmaking (an issue addressed in detail in chapter 4), it also reflects serious difficulties in measuring individual consumption. For example, many goods consumed by household members, such as housing and consumer durables, are consumed jointly. It is thus difficult, if not impossible, to assign some elements of household consumption to specific household members. This makes direct comparisons of consumption poverty between female and male members of the same household problematic.[22]

The lack of adequate data on individual consumption has led to a tendency to compare poverty between female-headed and male-headed households. The interest in such poverty comparisons has arisen from both substantive and statistical concerns. One substantive concern is that the proportion of female-headed households has been rising in several countries (Baden and Milward 1995; Bruce, Lloyd, and Leonard 1995). Another is that these households may be more vulnerable economically, both because they tend to have poorer access to productive inputs and because they have fewer working-age males who earn income, other factors being equal (Haddad and others 1996).

Analyses of poverty among male-headed and female-headed households across a large number of developing countries have found mixed evidence.[23] A recent review of 61 studies on headship and poverty finds female-headed households to be disproportionately represented among the poor in 38 cases (Buvinič and Gupta 1997). In 15 cases only certain subgroups of female-headed households are disproportionately among the poor; in 8 cases there is no evidence of a higher incidence of poverty among female-headed households.

A separate study analyzes 11 data sets from 10 developing countries using a variety of poverty measures and consistent methodologies across countries (Quisumbing, Haddad, and Pena 2000). In contrast to Buvinič and Gupta (1997), this study finds robust and statistically significant differences in poverty between female- and male-headed households in only two cases. Other recent studies, including a review of 58 World Bank poverty assessments undertaken during the 1990s, find that the evidence varies across countries, studies, and methodologies (Haddad and others 1996; UN ECLAC 1998; Ye 1998; Lampietti and Stalker 2000).

It is difficult to draw hard conclusions about the gender dimension of poverty from standard headship analysis. Male- and female-headed households can be extremely heterogeneous in any society, ranging from young, single, well-educated men and women to two-parent nuclear or extended families to single-parent households and widows. Although households headed by widows or divorced women may be disproportionately represented among the poor, other female-headed households may be better off. For example, single-person households of young, unmarried women working in urban labor markets, or households to which an absent husband regularly sends remittances, may experience relatively low levels of poverty. Moreover, even sophisticated headship studies provide only limited information about poverty among females and males, since they tell little or nothing about the relative welfare of females in male-headed households or males in female-headed households.

A much smaller number of studies have analyzed data on individuals' food intake or nutrition to assess the relative welfare of females and males. This approach avoids the problem of assigning to individuals the household goods that are jointly consumed. These studies have found gender disparities in nutrition in South Asia but little systematic evidence of gender differences in other regions (Appleton and Collier 1995; Alderman 2000). Even in South Asia the evidence is not uniform—in part because the extent of disparities can vary according to the season and because gender biases often manifest themselves in subtle ways. In Southern India there is gender discrimination in calorie intake only in the lean season, not in the surplus (Behrman 1988). And in Bangladesh apparent pro-male biases in calorie intake disappear after gender differences in caloric need or in energy exerted at work are taken into account (Chen, Huq, and D'Souza 1981; Pitt, Rosenzweig, and Hassan 1990).[24] Evidence from Bangladesh also indicates that the most severe gender inequalities often are not in calories consumed, but in the distribution of preferred foods rich in micronutrients (Bouis 1998).

In sum, even while there is extensive evidence on persistent gender inequalities in rights, resources, and voice that affect the relative abilities of women and men to participate in and benefit from development, the evidence on how such disparities translate into poverty (measured by consumption) is still very limited. This argues for efforts to collect new types of data and to develop empirical methods better suited to capturing the gender dimensions of poverty (as traditionally defined). At the same time, the combined evidence makes clear the importance of focusing on a variety of dimensions of female and male well-being to understand the full implications of gender disparity (box 1.2).

Groups at Particular Risk—Widows, Older Women Living Alone

Widows and elderly women heading households or living alone face a particularly high risk of being poor. That is what evidence on income and consumption suggests for both developed and developing countries. In OECD countries, for example, elderly people living alone are more likely than other groups to be in the bottom decile of the income distribution— and most of the elderly living alone are women (World Bank 1994b). In República Bolivariana de Venezuela two-thirds of the elderly in the lowest

---

Box 1.2   Are Women "Time Poor" Relative to Men?

WORLDWIDE, WOMEN PERFORM THE BULK OF child care and household maintenance. Women in most settings combine household work with market or nonmarket work to generate income or raise household consumption—work often not captured in traditional labor force statistics. And women tend to work significantly more hours than men when both market and household work are taken into account (Bevan, Collier, and Gunning 1989; Juster and Stafford 1991; Brown and Haddad 1995; UNDP 1995; Ilahi 2000).

The gender differences in time spent working vary across developing countries. But women commonly work an hour or more a day than men. In rural Kenya women work nearly three hours more a day than men. While few studies compare time use by gender across households at different income levels, evidence suggests that gender disparities in time use tend to be greater among the poor than the rich (Ilahi 2000).

This raises questions about how women's primary responsibility for household work, along with more total hours of work, affects their welfare relative to that of men. To the extent that the gender division of labor in the family means that women undertake household work at the expense of income-generating activities, this limits their bargaining power and decisionmaking capacity in the home. And that has implications for their well-being (see chapter 4). Moreover, gender disparities in hours worked imply that even if there are no gender biases in consumption in a household, women will work more hours than men to achieve the same consumption (Lipton and Ravallion 1995).

income decile are women. And in Australia, Chile, and the United States elderly women are more likely than elderly men to qualify for means-based social assistance (World Bank 1994b; Cox-Edwards 1999).

Consumption data show the same. In India households headed by widows have lower per capita expenditures than those not headed by widows, and specific subgroups of widow-headed households, such as those with unmarried children, experience higher-than-average poverty (Drèze 1990). The relationship between widowhood and poverty in India is particularly strong if one accounts for possible economies of scale in household consumption, since the households in which widows live are typically much smaller than those without widows (Drèze and Srinivasan 1998).[25]

In Eastern Europe older women—especially female pensioners living alone—are also often at high risk of being poor. In Russia female pensioners living alone are much more likely to be poor than are male pensioners. In Hungary both the incidence of poverty and the severity of poverty are greater among single female pensioners than among other groups. And in Poland female heads of household age 70 or above are disproportionately represented among the poor (Lampietti and Stalker 2000).

Why are widows and female pensioners at high risk of being poor? Like many young and working-age women, older women tend to have poorer access to education and other productive assets, weaker property rights, and fewer savings than men. Older women are also less likely than men to have economic support through marriage (worldwide about 79 percent of men age 60 and older are married, compared with 43 percent of women). And they are less likely to be in the labor force or to have pension income. In some societies widows face cultural constraints that limit their ability to ensure a basic standard of living in old age. In much of India, for example, customary restrictions on remarriage, employment, place of residence, and inheritance and ownership of property all limit their abilities to provide for themselves. Yet with the exception of their sons, widows often have little outside economic support (Chen 1998).

In many regions widows already make up an important subgroup. By the mid-1990s more than half of all women over 65 in Asia and Africa were widows, while only 10–20 percent of men were widowers (World Bank 1994b). But the vulnerability of widows to poverty will take on more importance in the 21st century as the world's population ages. Declining mortality and fertility around the world mean that the proportion of the population that is elderly—in both developed and developing countries—will become much larger (World Bank 1999b). The world population age 60 and older is projected to more than triple in the next half century from 593 million to 1,970 million—increasing from 364 to 1,594 million in the less developed regions and from 31 to 181 million in the least developed regions. This will raise the share of older people in the population from 10 to 22 percent (Behrman, Duryea, and Székely 1999).

Such demographic shifts have major implications for gender issues in the 21st century. As women's life expectancy relative to men's improves with development (see figure 1.3), hundreds of millions of women will become widows. At the same time, potential support ratios (of people ages 15–64 relative to those 65 and older) are projected to decline from 9 to 4 between 1999 and 2050—from 5 to 2 in more developed regions, 12 to 4 in less developed regions, and 18 to 8 in the least developed regions. Given the vulnerability of widows to poverty, this will have important implications for the way governments think about social protection and other issues. For example, women's health concerns will shift increasingly from reproductive health to the health issues of aging persons (cancers, cardiovascular problems). The focus of caregiving will shift from children to aging parents. Social services will thus need to shift from infant and maternal health care and child schooling to health, pension, and social protection policies focused on the aging.

———

This chapter has reviewed the state of gender inequality—both across and within developing regions and among the rich and poor within countries. Gender disparities have narrowed in the past several decades. And women have made significant progress in absolute terms and relative to men—strengthening their ability to act as agents of change and positioning themselves for further progress. But important gender disparities remain. While gender gaps have narrowed on average, they have done so unevenly over time and across geographic regions and socioeconomic divides.

The world continues to face a number of old gender challenges—as well as some new ones. Women and girls still experience systematic disadvantages in rights, resources, and voice in almost all parts of the developing world. At the same time, recent changes (and persistent gender stereotypes) have unleashed new risks for males in some places. Whether related to emerging female advantage in schooling in Latin America or to recent declines in male life expectancy in Eastern Europe, these trends underscore the need to think about gender in terms of both women and men. Traditional gender roles and persistent gender disparities affect people's life prospects and well-being regardless of their sex.

Though policymakers often treat gender issues largely as women's issues, a substantial body of evidence now indicates that the costs and consequences of gender inequality are much broader—that gender is a development issue. For example, when low investments in female education translate into poorer health and nutritional practices by mothers, all children feel the effects. This can have significant impacts on the health, well-being, and productivity of an entire generation. And when gender discrimination or social norms that restrict women's activities prevent large segments of the female population from participating fully and productively in society—whether in the economy or in community or national affairs—then a great deal of a country's talent, skill, and energy remains untapped. This, again, can have important consequences for countries' capacities to generate economic growth, to reduce poverty, and to govern effectively. Chapter 2 examines a large and growing body of evidence on the costs to individuals—both male and female—and to societies of allowing gender inequality to persist.

Notes

1. In general, the international community's definitions of gender equality tend to focus on equality of opportunity and equality under the law. For example, in 1985 the Nairobi Forward-Looking Strategies for the Advancement of Women defined equality as "a goal and a means whereby individuals are accorded equal treatment under the law and equal opportunities to enjoy rights to develop their potential talents and skills so that they can participate in…[development]…both as beneficiaries and active agents" (UN 1985, paragraphs 10 and 11). The Beijing Declaration and Platform for Action built upon this with the aim of accelerating the implementation of the Nairobi Forward-Looking Strategies and of removing all the obstacles to women's active participation in all spheres of public and private life (UN 1995). For examples of other definitions of gender equality from multilateral

and bilateral development agencies see DAC (1998), DFID (1998), WHO (1998), CIDA (1999).

Along with *gender equality*, the term *gender equity* is sometimes used in the context of development. While they are often used interchangeably, *equity* tends to be associated more directly with the concept of fairness than the term *equality*. Even though concepts of fairness and justice are integral to any discussion of gender equality, some people are concerned that cultural interpretations of what is "fair" may actually be used to justify discriminatory behavior. But the term *gender equality*, too, has limitations. It could be interpreted to imply that women and men should pursue the same goals and achieve the same outcomes—even though in an environment of equal opportunity women and men may choose to pursue different goals and outcomes. Since both terms have their strengths and limitations, this reports follows the current practice of the international development community and uses *gender equality*.

2. Evidence from a broad range of countries indicates that women and men often have different social values and preferences. For example, women and men often have different views on what they consider justifiable and unjustifiable social behaviors (see table 2.2). Similarly, women and men often have different preferences that translate into different patterns of household expenditures and investments, depending on the extent to which women or men control income or assets (see chapter 4). For instance, resources controlled by women tend to be invested more heavily in children (at the margin) than resources controlled by men. So, women and men may well make different choices and pursue different outcomes in an environment of equal rights, opportunities, and voice.

3. Humana (1986, 1992) uses a scale of 0–3 rather than the scale of 1–4 used in this report.

4. The measure of rights to political and legal equality for women refers to Article 2 of the Universal Declaration of Human Rights, which specifies that everyone is entitled to all the rights and freedoms set forth in the declaration, without distinction of any kind, such as race, color, sex, language, religion, political or other opinion, national or social origin, property, birth, or other status. In assembling the measure, it is recognized that while women may enjoy political and legal equality under the constitution of a given country, this may not prevent inequality in such rights in practice. The measure of rights to social and economic equality for women refers to Article 23(2) of the declaration, which states that everyone, without discrimination, has the right to equal pay for equal work. The measure of "equality of sexes during marriage and for divorce proceedings" refers to Article 16(1) of the declaration, which states that men and women "are entitled to equal rights as to marriage, during marriage and at its dissolution."

5. Average rights indexes for OECD countries are provided for comparative purposes (see figure 1.1). As in developing regions, women in OECD countries do not experience full equality of rights with men. While OECD countries tend to score higher than developing countries on these indexes, only two countries, Finland and Sweden, scored 4 (unqualified respect for gender equality in rights) for political and legal equality. No country, industrial or developing, scored 4 on social and economic equality.

6. The data shows declines between 1985 and 1990 in political and legal rights and social and economic rights in the Middle East and North Africa that are not statistically significant.

7. Adopted in 1979, CEDAW is regarded as the international bill of rights for women. It prohibits any distinction, exclusion, or restriction on the basis of sex that impairs or nullifies women's human rights and fundamental freedoms (see chapter 3).

8. Established in 1889, the Inter-parliamentary union (IPU) is the world organization of parliaments of sovereign states. It has 138 members and 5 associate members. It is a center for dialogue and parliamentary diplomacy among legislators representing political systems and all the main political leanings in the world. The IPU shares objectives with the United Nations and works in close cooperation with it.

9. Gross enrollment rate, the total enrollment in a specific level of education, regardless of students' age, expressed as a percentage of the official school-age population corresponding to the same level of education in a given school year, can exceed 100 because the numerator, unlike the denominator, is not limited to youths of a given age. Early entry into school and grade repetition are among the reasons that the numerator may include youths outside the appropriate age range.

10. For details on the methodology for computing DALYs, see Murray and Lopez (1996).

11. This Disability Adjusted Life Expectancy (DALE) measure reflects the proportion of the population surviving to each age, calculated from birth and death rates, the prevalence of each type of disability at each age, and the weight assigned to each type of disability, which may or may not vary with age. Survival at each age is then adjusted downward by the sum of all the disability effects to obtain a figure for life expectancy at birth that accounts for disability. For further details, see WHO (2000).

12. World Bank staff calculations based on data from a nationally representative household survey in rural Bangladesh in 1991/92 (see Khandker 1998 and Pitt and Khandker 1998 for descriptions of the data).

13. Particularly in less developed countries, labor force statistics tend to understate female participation in economic activities. Some of the measured gender differences in labor force participation arise because much of women's work takes place in the home and is not captured in the labor force data.

14. The Duncan index is a measure of "employment dissimilarity" that can be used to analyze employment differences between any two groups of workers (Duncan and Duncan 1955). The index ranges from 0 to 1, with 0 indicating identical distributions of workers across sectors or occupational categories and 1 representing complete dissimilarity in the distributions of workers across sectors or occupational categories. Between the 1950s–60s and the 1980s–90s the dissimilarity in sectors of employment between all female and male workers, as measured by the Duncan index, declined worldwide from 0.3458 to 0.3058. Dissimilarity in the sectoral distribution of female and male wage employees declined faster than that among all workers: from 0.3948 to 0.3097. Occupational dissimilarity among all female and male workers exhibited essentially no change over the period. The Duncan index for the 1950s–60s was 0.3860, while the index for the 1980s–90s was 0.3804. But female and male wage workers did experience some convergence in occupational profiles, with the Duncan index declining from 0.4421 to 0.4030 over the period (Tzannatos 1999).

15. The survey reviewed evidence from 19 developed countries and 42 developing and transition economies. For a list of the studies and data on female to male earnings ratios, see appendix 3.

16. Adjusting for gender differences in hours worked has an impact on estimates of female to male earnings ratios. For example, Rice (1999) finds that Denmark and Portugal have narrower gender earnings gaps than are suggested by unadjusted wage figures, while Germany has a wider gender gap. However, at least half the countries that report earnings by gender (mostly in the developing world) do not report hourly wages. For more estimates for OECD countries see Blau and Khan (1992).

17. Time series data are lacking for most countries in Eastern Europe, so this pattern is based on data from only five countries: Albania, Bulgaria, Hungary, Poland, and Romania. The steep decline in female representation in parliament is attributed to the abolition of Eastern Europe's 25–33 percent quotas for women (UN 2000). This decline in female representation took place precisely at the time that national parliaments were beginning to play an active role in policymaking and governance in those countries.

18. In South Asia women held less than 1 percent of subministerial positions (UNDP 2000). Compare this with about 4 percent in the Middle East and North Africa, 6 percent in East Asia and the Pacific, approximately 8 percent in Sub-Saharan Africa and Eastern Europe and Central Asia, and 13 percent in Latin America and the Caribbean.

19. The study examines data from 57 Demographic and Health Surveys collected during the 1990s. In several cases multiple surveys were conducted for a given country (see Filmer 1999).

20. The Living Standards Measurement Study and Social Dimensions of Adjustment surveys are household consumption and expenditure surveys conducted in a number of developing and transition economies with the support of the World Bank. Findings are based on World Bank staff's analysis of household survey data from Armenia, Bulgaria, Burkina Faso, Côte d'Ivoire, Djibouti, Ecuador, Egypt, The Gambia, Ghana, Guinea, Guinea-Bissau, Jamaica, Kazakhstan, Kenya, Madagascar, Mauritania, Nepal, Nicaragua, Niger, Pakistan, Panama, Peru, Romania, Russia, Senegal, South Africa, Tanzania, Uganda, and Vietnam during the 1990s.

21. Estimates based on Demographic and Health Survey data on child mortality were provided by Jeffrey Hammer of the World Bank's Development Research Group. For the majority of countries in which the data suggest relatively greater male advantage among the poor than the rich, the female to male mortality ratio is less than one for both the rich and the poor. This indicates lower mortality rates for females than males—although the advantage is smaller among the poor than the rich. In a small subset of countries—including Benin, the Dominican Republic, Madagascar, Niger, and Peru—the female to male mortality ratio is greater than one for the poor and less than one

for the rich. That is, female mortality rates exceed male rates among the poor but not among the rich. In another small group of countries—Bangladesh, Brazil, Burkina Faso, Ghana, and Kenya—female mortality rates exceed male rates among the rich but not among the poor. It should be noted, however, that the mortality rates among the rich are only a tiny fraction of those among the poor, so the absolute levels of mortality are low for both rich females and males in these cases.

22. Consumption data tend to be preferred to income data for measuring poverty, particularly in developing countries. For example, because income can vary from year to year (because of a variety of production shocks), while consumption is more stable, consumption is generally considered a better measure of long-term welfare. Moreover, income tends to be subject to more measurement error than consumption. For assessing the welfare of individuals within households, income and consumption data share some limitations. Particularly in rural areas of developing countries, many elements of household income are jointly produced, such as income from family-run farms or nonfarm enterprises. Therefore, like consumption, income is often difficult to assign to specific individuals within a household. And as with consumption, often little is known about how income is shared among different members of a single household.

23. Important methodological differences across studies make direct comparisons difficult. For summaries of the methodological issues associated with headship analysis, see Rosenhouse (1989) and Lampietti and Stalker (2000).

24. Analysis of a nationally representative household survey from rural Bangladesh in 1991/92 also indicates that an apparent pro-male bias in calorie consumption disappears once gender differences in caloric need are taken into account. See Khandker (1998) and Pitt and Khandker (1998) for descriptions of the data set.

25. A demographic study from India suggests that widows age 45 and above have mortality rates nearly double those of married women of the same age (Mari Bhat 1994, cited in Drèze and Srinivasan 1998).

CHAPTER 2

Gender Inequality Hinders Development

GENDER INEQUALITIES UNDERMINE DEVELOPment—so improving gender equality has to to be part of any sustainable strategy for development. Inequalities in rights, resources, and political voice generally disadvantage women, but they also disadvantage the rest of society and impede development. Even more striking: the costs of gender inequality are particularly large in low-income countries. And within countries they are larger for the poor.

Foremost among the costs of gender inequality is its toll on human lives and on the quality of those lives. It is not easy to identify and measure these costs, but evidence from countries around the world demonstrates that societies with large, persistent gender inequalities pay the price of more poverty, more malnutrition, more illness, and more deprivations of other kinds.

This chapter examines how gender inequalities impose large costs on men, women, and children in developing countries. It begins by showing the negative impacts on people's well-being, such as their health. For example, gender inequalities in schooling and urban jobs accelerate the spread of HIV in Sub-Saharan Africa. And a mother's illiteracy and lack of autonomy directly disadvantage her young children. Traditional gender roles in society, though valuable in many respects, also entail expectations and social pressures that are punishing for men, for women, and for their families. During economic shocks, such as those in the transition economies of Eastern Europe, rapidly worsening unemployment has produced such high anxiety (especially among men) that alcoholism, suicide, domestic violence, and the dissolution of families have risen considerably. These, in turn, have their own impacts on women and children.

Yet many, if not most, of the costs of gender discrimination are hidden, suffered in silence by individuals or latent and invisible until the future. Even those potentially quantifiable are often not measured—for three main reasons. Extensive personal data are expensive and difficult to obtain. Some topics are considered too sensitive for societies or their governments to raise in surveys. And policymakers often do not recognize the value of gender-disaggregated information.

The toll on human lives is a toll on development—since improving the quality of people's lives is development's ultimate goal. In addition, gender inequalities impose an indirect cost by hindering productivity, efficiency, and economic progress. By hampering the accumulation of human capital through prejudice in the home and the labor market—and by systematically excluding women or men from access to resources, public services, and certain productive activities—gender discrimination diminishes an economy's capacity to prosper and provide for its people. This chapter discusses micro-level evidence that shows this. For example, in Kenya giving female farmers the same schooling and access to farm inputs as males could raise farm yields by as much as a fifth. This chapter also reviews the results of a growing macroeconomic literature on the relationship between gender equality and economic growth.

Finally, gender inequality weakens the quality of governance in a country—and thus the effectiveness of development policies. New research on corruption suggests that policies promoting gender equality can help clean up governments and businesses.

Costs to Well-Being

PEOPLE'S WELL-BEING IS NOT SIMPLE TO MEASURE. SEN (1984) concludes that "happiness and desire-fulfillment are serious enough candidates for capturing the idea of personal well-being" (p. 32). This definition implies that well-being is multidimensional, encompassing many facets of people's lives, and highly subjective.

Chapter 1 alludes to a more limited definition of well-being by presenting quantifiable measures, such as availability of rights, average life expectancy, education levels, and political participation, among the indicators of gender inequality. This section presents a few selected markers and traces them to gender roles and discrimination in society. It considers the evidence for the current generation of women and men—and for youths and future generations.

Both Women and Men Bear the Costs

Although women, especially poor women, often bear the brunt of gender disparities, men cannot escape the consequences. Unequal rights to own land or apply for credit deprive women of resources for their livelihood and for security in old age, leaving them more dependent on male relatives. Wide gender disparities in schooling produce correspondingly different abilities for women and men to acquire and process information and to communicate. The gender imbalance in resources and power has consequences for the relative autonomy of women and men and their influence in household decisionmaking. The resulting dependence and stereotyping are a common source of oppressive anxiety and helplessness for both men and women, leading to even worse outcomes. Consider AIDS and gender-related violence.

The AIDS epidemic. Gender inequality accelerates HIV infection rates (figure 2.1). A study of the capital cities of 72 developing countries finds that two measures of gender inequality are associated with higher infection rates among both high-risk and low-risk adults, after controlling for six other socioeconomic variables (Over 1998). First, among high-risk adults (sex workers and patients at clinics treating sexually transmitted diseases), a high ratio of male to female urban residents in the most sexually active age group is a statistically significant predictor of higher infection rates. Male to female ratios as high as 1.2 are probably associated with greater per capita demand for commercial sex, which would speed the spread of HIV both within and outside the small pool of sex workers (who are mostly women). Second, among low-risk adults, such as pregnant women, infection rates are higher in cities where there is a larger gap between the male and female literacy rates. In a pooled regression, both variables are statistically significant.

As chapter 1 discusses, the AIDS epidemic in developing countries will spread rapidly over the next decade until up to one in four women and one in five men become HIV infected, already the case in several Sub-Saharan countries. In the heavily affected countries, women will bear a larger share of the mortality and morbidity burden. Their economic status will also suffer. Because women are the primary caregivers for children and bedridden adults, the epidemic will rob healthy women of wages by pulling them out of the labor market to care for AIDS patients and orphans.

Governments can help women—and other AIDS victims—by adopting prevention and mitigation policies. Most governments have been

Figure 2.1   More Gender Inequality—More AIDS

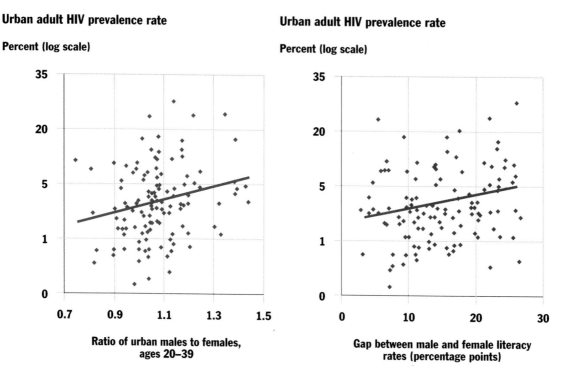

Urban adult HIV prevalence rate

Percent (log scale)

Urban adult HIV prevalence rate

Percent (log scale)

Ratio of urban males to females,
ages 20–39

Gap between male and female literacy
rates (percentage points)

Note: Data are for 72 countries (32 in Sub-Saharan Africa, 20 in Latin America and the Caribbean, 15 in Asia, 4 in the Middle East, and 1 industrial country). Points on each plot represent data for individual countries after removing the effects of other societal variables included in the regression analysis (including religion, GNP per capita, an income inequality index, and the proportion of the population that is foreign born). See appendix 1 for included countries.

Source: Over (1998).

reluctant to confront sexuality and intravenous drug use, but some governments, such as those of Senegal and Thailand, encourage safe behavior among those most likely to contract and spread HIV. The immediate beneficiaries include predominantly male groups (soldiers, sailors, and truck drivers) and predominantly female groups (sex workers and hotel and restaurant workers). For example, an intervention with female sex workers by a medical researcher in Calabar, Nigeria, led to the organization of a sex workers union that insisted on condom use by clients and resisted exploitation by police and landlords (Esu-Williams 1995). To slow the epidemic where it has begun to spread outside the groups at greatest risk, governments must also institute policies that improve the relative status of women—policies that narrow the education and urban employment gaps between the sexes and that open jobs to women in large urban areas (World Bank 1999a).

Violence as a matter of gender. The extent to which violence is related to gender is not easy to ascertain. At one extreme, nearly all violence outside war can be attributed to gender.[1] Male to male violence can be interpreted as men's way of handling conflict, and male to female violence as the expression of men's need to reinforce well-entrenched gender roles, exacerbated by grossly unequal power (physical and otherwise) between men and women.[2] For example, according to a recent study, men in Bangladesh tend to view wife-beating as a right and as a normal way to keep women's "unruly nature" in check (Narayan and others 2000). The *machismo* culture in some Latin American and Caribbean countries is characterized by chronic domestic violence, infidelity, and desertion within a structure of consensual unions, and by aggressive and highly intransigent male to male relations (Sara-Lafosse 1998). Suicide attempts can arise from the interaction between gender roles and the pressures of economic change and social restructuring. In wartime, rape and other abuse against women have been widely used weapons of terrorism and humiliation (Turshen 1998).

This view—that all violence is gender-related—may seem implausible. But there is evidence that gender roles and expectations produce reactions and behaviors that lead to violence. The traditional expectation that men are the dominant breadwinners and decisionmakers in their families may have caused men in transition economies a lot of anxiety. In Russia an epidemiological study links the notable increase in men's mortality rate between 1990 and 1997 to greater stress and depression over job losses (Gavrilova and others 1999). Rates of cardiovascular diseases, suicide, domestic violence, and alcoholism have been significantly higher among men than women. And almost all Eastern European countries have seen larger declines in men's life expectancy than in women's since the beginning of the transition (UNICEF 1999b).

Echoing these statistics are interviews of men and women conducted in the Republic of Georgia as part of the World Bank's *Voices of the Poor* study: for men a "sense of emasculation and failure often leads to a host of physical ailments and sharply increasing mortality, alcoholism, physical abuse of wives and children, divorce and abandonment of families" (Narayan and others 2000, p. 194). Interviews in Latvia and the former Yugoslav Republic of Macedonia portray similar situations.

The paramount cost of the violence is pain and suffering for victims and their families. But violence can also lead to permanent disability, depression, and alcohol and drug abuse, as well as loss of self-esteem (Heise, Ellsberg, and Gottemoeller 1999). It is difficult to quantify these costs because they permeate many aspects of life and because cause and effect are not easy to separate. Also difficult to assess are the negative consequences for children who become orphans, who become separated from their parents, and who witness recurring domestic violence. Their emotional development and survival are also at risk.

Violence leads to other negative outcomes—lower productivity, more absence from the workplace, increased homelessness, greater demand for medical and community support services, and larger expenditures for police and judicial services—but these costs are difficult to estimate as well. Some cost estimates: domestic violence reduced women's earnings by more than 2 percent of GDP in Chile in 1996 and by 1.6 percent in Nicaragua (Morrison and Orlando 1999). The cost of violence against women in Canada is about $1 billion each year, or about 1 percent of Canada's GDP (Day 1995). But another Canadian study estimates the costs to be more than three times larger, in excess of $3.2 billion in 1993 (Greaves, Hankivsky, and Kingston-Riechers 1995, as cited in Buvinič, Morrison, and Shifter 1999), illustrating the challenge of estimating these costs.

Next Generations Are Disadvantaged, Too

Gender bias and inequalities harm future generations as well and perpetuate disparities. Chapter 1 mentions the large imbalance in the sex ratio at birth in several countries in East Asia and South Asia, one of the clearest manifestations of gender discrimination. There are others. The singular role of the mother in a child's early years, difficult to dispute, is a principal pathway for gender discrimination to affect next generations. The influence of a mother on her child begins in the womb and continues through preschool and later childhood. Poor health and nutrition can have devastating effects on her pregnancy and her ability to nurse her infant. In critical ways she determines her child's early intellectual stimulation and physical development. A mother's illiteracy and dependence on others deprive her of knowledge and self-confidence, weakening her ability to nurture and protect. Missed opportunities for stimulating the development of mental, emotional, and motor skills cannot be easily retrieved (Currie 1999; Deutsch 1998). And for children in poverty—with limited access to formal child care and preventive care—mothers constitute the first and only defense.

Poorer nutrition and higher child mortality. While most parents care about their children's welfare, they often do not recognize the results of their own action or inaction. Mothers' education changes this—it improves nutrition directly through the quality of care that mothers provide and through mothers' ability to mitigate adverse shocks, such as price changes, that might reduce food intake (Thomas and Strauss 1992). Across the developing world there is a strong negative association between mothers' average schooling and child mortality. The latest Demographic and Health Surveys in more than 40 developing countries show that the mortality rate of children under five is lower in households where mothers have some primary schooling than in households where they have no schooling, and much lower in those where mothers have some secondary schooling.

Because education levels are positively correlated with economic indicators, this observed correlation between mothers' education and child mortality could be spurious—or weaker than the numbers suggest. This is why multivariate analyses of household survey data that control for other socioeconomic factors better depict the relationship. Reviews of many such analyses published in the 1980s conclude that the more educated mothers are, the lower their children's mortality, even after controlling for household income and other indicators of socioeconomic status (Jejeebhoy 1995; Schultz 1993). A more recent analysis of household survey data from 22 countries casts doubt on the strength of this relationship, however, since the inclusion of program variables in the equations considerably reduces the coefficient of mothers' education (Desai 1998). Even so, it finds that mothers' education has a large effect on program use and health-promoting behavior, such as immunization.

Household studies confirm this finding. In the Philippines mothers' education protects child health in communities without piped water or good sanitation and in communities farther from health facilities—an effect larger than that of household income (Barrera 1990). In Guatemala women with more education are more likely to use child care, particularly formal care, and to have their children immunized completely (Pebley, Goldman, and Rodriguez 1996). In urban Niger and Nigeria mothers' education is also positively related to immunization (Gage, Sommerfelt, and Piani 1997).

The positive relationship between mother's schooling and child immunization rates is observed more broadly across world regions. Figure 2.2 does not control for other factors that might affect immunization rates—thus the focus is not the magnitude but the direction of the effect of mother's education. In all regions, but especially in the lower-income regions of South Asia and Sub-Saharan Africa, the percentage of children immunized is larger when mothers have some secondary education than when mothers have only some primary schooling, and even larger than when mothers have no schooling.

The gender gap in education is not all that matters for children's well-being. The balance of power between women and men in the home also matters. In Brazil additional income in the hands of women has a greater positive impact on child survival and nutrition than does additional income in the hands of men (Thomas 1990, 1997). Increases in household income—regardless of who controls that income—are associated with improvements in child survival probabilities and in child height-for-weight and height-for-age measures. But the marginal impacts are

Figure 2.2   Child Immunization Rates Rise with Mother's Education

Share of children 12–23 months who had been immunized, by mother's educational level

Percent

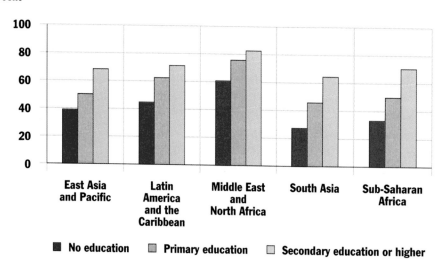

Note: See appendix 1 for general notes and included countries.

Sources: Education and immunization data from latest Demographic and Health Surveys for selected countries; population weights from World Bank (1999d).

substantially greater if the income is in the hands of the mother. For child survival the marginal effect of female income is almost 20 times as large. For weight-for-height measures, about 8 times as large—and for height-for-age, about 4. At the margin additional income in the hands of women enlarges the share of the household budget devoted to education, health, and nutrition-related expenditures.

In Côte d'Ivoire increasing women's share of cash income in the household significantly increases the share of the budget their households allocate to food and reduces the share spent on alcohol and cigarettes—controlling for average per capita expenditure (income), household size, and demographic composition (Hoddinott and Haddad 1995). In Bangladesh borrowing by women from Grameen Bank and other microfinance institutions appears to have a greater impact on child welfare than does borrowing by men. It has a greater positive impact on both girls' and boys' enrollments and a large and statistically significant effect on children's nutritional status (Khandker 1998; Pitt and Khandker 1998).

These findings are based on household data. What about studies that use country-level data? Causality, a methodological issue covered later in the chapter, is more difficult to establish in country analyses because controls are limited. Several studies that account for the effects of per capita income and other factors, though without fully addressing causality, nevertheless conclude that women's schooling lowers child mortality. For example, one study that measures women's schooling by past female primary enrollment rates observes that a 10 percentage point increase in female enrollment appears on average to lower the infant mortality rate by 4.1 deaths per 1,000 live births, controlling for such factors as GDP per capita (Hill and King 1995). A similar rise in the female secondary enrollment rate is associated with another 5.6 fewer deaths per 1,000 live births.

In addition to average level of education, the gender gap in education seems to matter. According to the same study, countries where girls are only half as likely to go to school as boys have on average 21.1 more infant deaths per 1,000 live births than countries with no gender gap, again controlling for other factors (Hill and King 1995). A separate study estimates that if Sub-Saharan Africa had the same female to male ratio of years of schooling as Eastern Europe—that is, at about parity—Africa's under-five mortality rate would have been more than 25 percent lower than it was in 1990 (167 per 1,000), after controlling for income, average levels of schooling, and other regional differences (Klasen 1999a).

A recent cross-country study of 63 countries also concludes that gains in women's education made the single largest contribution to declines in malnutrition in 1970–95, accounting for 43 percent of the total (Smith and Haddad 2000).[3] Changes in women's relative status, measured by the ratio of female to male life expectancies at birth, contributed an additional 12 percent.[4] This smaller impact of women's status reflects the small improvement in women's relative status, not the importance of status in reducing malnutrition. In South Asia, where women's status increased considerably, the gains accounted for 23 percent of the total decline in malnutrition. In Sub-Saharan Africa declines in women's relative status weakened the positive impacts of other determinants on malnutrition.

Autonomy, another measure of women's status, yields similar findings in a recent study (Boone 1996). Women's autonomy is defined as their ability to control their lives, to have a voice in matters concerning themselves and their families, and to make and implement decisions. The study finds that, controlling for the independent effects of per capita income, greater autonomy among women is associated with lower infant mortality.[5] A fall of one point in the autonomy index from 4 (least autonomy) to 3 predicts a 50 percent decrease in infant mortality for countries with per capita incomes of $500 and below.

These results demonstrate the crucial role of mothers in the early years of a child's life and thus the costs of keeping women illiterate, uninformed, and without resources.

Higher fertility. The impact of population growth on development varies across the world. But in the poorest countries—threatened by hunger, housing shortages, and environmental degradation—high fertility can exacerbate the adverse effects of poverty on children. For example, the effects of female literacy on indicators of malnutrition can work through its effects on the total fertility rate. Higher female literacy is negatively associated with stunting and low weight among children under five when there are no additional controls for fertility—but this effect disappears after controlling for the total fertility rate (Klasen 1999b). Higher fertility thus appears to be significantly correlated with higher prevalence of stunting and underweight children.

A large number of empirical household studies offer "unambiguous, although qualified, support for the widely held belief that fertility reduction is one consequence of improvements in female education and consequent changes in women's autonomy" (Jejeebhoy 1995, p. 177).[6]

Better-educated women bear fewer children than less-educated women—for many reasons. They marry later and have fewer years of childbearing. They have better knowledge of ways to control fertility and have more confidence and power to make decisions about reproduction. They have higher aspirations for their children and recognize the tradeoffs between realizing such aspirations and having many children.

Cross-country studies find the same relationship between women's education and fertility, even accounting for differences in per capita income and the average education of men. Using data on 100 countries in 1990, Klasen (1999b) finds that an additional year of female education reduces the total fertility rate by 0.23 births. When a longer period is analyzed, the effect is even larger: an additional year of women's schooling, holding constant the level of men's schooling, decreases the fertility rate by 0.32 births (Gatti 1999). In other words, a three-year increase in the average education level of women is associated with as much as one fewer child per woman.[7]

Women's rights relative to men's also matter. Using data across countries on women's rights (from Humana 1992), Gatti (1999) finds that the higher women's relative status within marriage, controlling for women's education, the lower the fertility rate.

Costs to Productivity and Growth

THE PRECEDING SECTION DISCUSSED THE COSTS OF GENDER inequalities for people's well-being—for today's men and women as well as for future generations. The impacts on adult and child health, knowledge, and freedoms—each important in its own right—also influence people's lives through economic growth. Constraints on access to information or to land and physical capital—and unfair labor practices or limits on the type of work one can engage in—are obstacles to men's and women's abilities to earn a living. And because women's status affects the cognitive development, health, nutrition, and schooling of their children, it also influences a country's long-run prospects for economic growth.

This section discusses the effect of gender differences on child schooling, an indicator of the skills of the future workforce. It also discusses output lost as a result of prejudice in the labor market and unequal distribution of capital between men and women.

Less Schooling—Missed Opportunities

Just as there are strong positive correlations between a mother's schooling and her children's birthweight, health, and nutritional status, a mother's schooling is positively linked to her children's educational attainment. Why? First, education improves the efficiency of human capital production: better-educated mothers are better able to guide their children—through home schooling and the use of more educational inputs, and as role models. Second, the educational achievement of mothers is an indicator of their unobservable or innate abilities, which are positively correlated with those of their children (Rosenzweig and Wolpin 1994).

Higher education levels of mothers enhance children's intellectual achievement. In the United States each additional year of maternal schooling prior to birth adds 1.6 points to a child's mathematics and reading achievement test scores and 2.1 points to a child's picture vocabulary test score, both of which are statistically significant. A mother's enrollment during the first three years of her child's life adds 1.7 points and 3.1 points to these test scores, respectively, per additional year of enrollment (Rosenzweig and Wolpin 1994). In India children of more literate mothers study nearly two hours more a day than children of illiterate mothers in similar households (Behrman and others 1999).[8]

This intergenerational benefit is another compelling reason for improving women's schooling—because higher levels of education and skills allow people to adopt and profit from new technology and reallocate resources better in response to economic cycles and shocks (Foster and Rosenzweig 1995, 1996; Schultz 1961). Restricted schooling for women implies missed opportunities for a better-educated and more productive future generation.

Lost Earnings

Female illiteracy and low female education hurt productivity and earnings—for women and for the economy (see, for example, Schultz 1991, 1993; Psacharopoulos and Tzannatos 1992). The private rate of return to an additional year of schooling for women is generally at least as large as that for men. Marginal returns for women are higher in Bolivia, Brazil, Côte d'Ivoire, Indonesia, and Thailand, but they are about equal for men and women in Colombia and Peru (Schultz 1991). This implies that women can benefit marginally more than men from one additional year of schooling—because women have lower average schooling—but not that women earn more than men from the same level of schooling.

Even in rural economies where wage work is scarcer, reducing the gender gap in schooling or other resources increases productivity. Female farmers are no less efficient than male farmers (Moock 1976; Bindlish and Evenson 1993; Saito, Mekonnen, and Spurling 1994; Udry 1996).[9] Instead, the lower yields by female farmers generally reflect lower levels of inputs or education relative to male farmers. In Kenya increasing the education and input levels of female farmers to those of male farmers could increase yields by as much as 22 percent (Quisumbing 1996).[10] The short-term productivity effects of gender inequality in education are also compounded over time through the effect on technology adoption. Lower education levels make female farmers less likely than male farmers to adopt new agricultural technologies that may raise farm productivity.

And less schooling may mean more limited capacity to upgrade technical skills. Male rice farmers in Vietnam who were given pest-management training acquired better knowledge of pest-management techniques than did female farmers with the same training—and a substantial part of this knowledge gap is explained by the gender differences in schooling before training (Chi and others 1998).

Inefficient Allocation of Labor

One impact of taboos and prejudice against hiring women is that households may not be able to use their labor resources efficiently. Suppose that good weather or a new technology has led to an unexpectedly good harvest, requiring additional hired labor on farms. Depending on relative productivity in the home and the farm, the household may want to hire nonfamily workers to work on the farm or in the house to release family members for farm work (Gertler and Newman 1991; Ilahi 2000). Without a local labor market for female workers, households are limited to hiring male workers. As male workers become more fully employed, increased demand drives up their price, preventing households that are not able to afford the higher wages from applying the efficient amount of labor on their farms. Such labor shortages could lead eventually to labor-saving technological change—but in the short run the prejudice against hiring women will have negative consequences on production.

Losses in output also result from inefficiencies in the allocation of productive resources between men and women within households. In Cameroon, as a result of gender asymmetries in the control of income from different crops, female farmers prefer to work on their sorghum plots, for which they control the proceeds, than on rice, for which they don't (Jones 1986). Reallocating female labor from sorghum to rice could increase household incomes by 6 percent. In Burkina Faso intrahousehold inequalities in fertilizer and labor allocations to plots managed by men and women also produce inefficiencies that reduce household output. Output could be increased by 6–20 percent simply by reallocating inputs more efficiently between men's and women's household plots (Udry and others 1995; Udry 1996). But gender-related customs in land use prevent this.

In the formal wage sector two phenomena reveal gender discrimination in the labor market—around the world women's earnings are on average lower than men's, and women and men are on average occupationally segregated (see chapter 1). These reflect several biases:

- More investment in the human capital of sons than of daughters.
- Employers with discriminatory preferences about whom to hire or pay well.
- Sexual harassment in the workplace that makes working conditions unpleasant and dangerous and reduces worker morale and productivity.
- Women's dominant role in raising children and maintaining the household.
- Social and religious norms that restrict women's ability to choose to work outside the home and to choose among kinds of work.
- Labor laws and legislation intended to protect women against occupational hazard that keep them out of certain jobs instead.

All these biases imply that norms and prejudice rather than efficiency determine the labor supply and labor demand in an economy. The resulting misallocation of labor means that some competent female workers are overlooked because of their sex.

Few studies have estimated the effect of gender discrimination in the labor market on the economy. This is understandable given the data requirements of such a task and the number of simplifying assumptions needed to make the task manageable. Tzannatos (1999) provides a rough approximation of this estimate for selected countries in Latin America and the Caribbean (table 2.1).[11] His method involves first estimating output under prevailing conditions of occupational and wage differences within industries in each country, and then reestimating the output assuming that the occupational differences within industries are eliminated. The difference between the two estimates of output is supposed to be the potential or maximum welfare gain from attaining gender equality in the labor market and the family.

Tzannatos (1999) concludes that substantial increases in women's wages can be had with relatively small loss in male wages, partly because there will be a significant expansion of output. These shifts are supposed to come from a reallocation of labor across occupations—that is, a shift of women to men's jobs and vice versa. The data from Latin America and the Caribbean suggest that if female and male wages had been equal, output would have been 6 percent higher. But wage equalization would require a redistribution of about a fifth of the labor force. The author is quick to point out that a labor reallocation of this magnitude is difficult and politically costly in the short run.

Table 2.1 Women Would Gain, Men Would Lose (a Little) if Occupational Segregation Ended

Country and year data collected	Percentage change in			Percentage of labor force that must change occupation to achieve gender wage equality
	Female wages	Male wages	Output (GDP)	
Argentina 1987	38	−9	4	25
Bolivia 1989	50	−9	6	28
Brazil 1980	96	−8	9	23
Chile 1987	41	−6	3	18
Colombia 1988	46	−8	5	20
Costa Rica 1989	35	−6	3	18
Ecuador 1966	59	−13	9	37
Guatemala 1989	25	−6	2	14
Jamaica 1989	61	−8	8	28
Uruguay 1989	30	−8	3	16
Venezuela, R.B. de 1987	24	−6	2	12

Source: Tzannatos (1999).

Links to Economic Growth: Cross-Country Evidence

What if gender inequality were good for growth? An influential study finds that it might be. Barro and Lee (1994) find that countries with lower starting per capita incomes have higher growth rates ("conditional convergence") and that the partial correlation between female secondary schooling and economic growth is significantly negative while that between male education and growth is positive. The authors suggest a possible explanation—by interpreting the gender gap as a measure of economic backwardness:

> The puzzling finding, which tends to recur, is that the initial level of female secondary education enters negatively in the growth equations; the estimated coefficient is −0.0084 (standard error = 0.0045). One possibility is that a high spread between male and female secondary attainment is a good measure of backwardness; hence, less female attainment signifies more backwardness and seemingly higher growth potential through the convergence mechanism. (p. 18)

This result contradicts the microeconomic evidence on the relationship between productivity and gender inequality discussed earlier. It also contradicts a growing body of cross-country analyses that support the micro-level evidence. Indeed, several recent econometric studies demonstrate that the growth–gender equality relationship is sensitive to the particular specification of the growth equation (box 2.1). In addition to the issue of the nature of this relationship, there is the issue of causality.

Two studies find a negative relationship between gender inequality in education and growth that is statistically significant and substantial. Esteve-Volart (2000) examines the link between growth in per capita GDP and gender inequality in primary schooling in the base year, using data for about 90 countries and controlling for such factors as overall secondary education and regional dummy variables. The study shows that a 1 percent increase in the female to male primary enrollment ratio increases the growth rate by more than 0.012 percentage point.

Knowles, Lorgelly, and Owen (forthcoming) examine the long-run relationship between growth in GDP per worker and the time-averaged stocks of male and female education using data for about 70 countries. They find that the elasticity of GDP per worker with respect to the

Box 2.1   Establishing That Gender Equality Affects Economic Growth

THE DEBATE OVER THE EFFECT OF GENDER equality on growth centers on two key issues: Is the relationship between gender equality and development positive? Does gender equality affect growth, or vice versa, or both—or do common factors determine both simultaneously?

In order to answer the first question, recent studies have attempted to reconcile findings of a positive relationship with the contrasting results of Barro and Lee (1994) by examining alternative econometric specifications of the growth equation. One method has been to identify "outlier" countries that could be influencing the Barro and Lee findings. Stokey (1994) suggests that these apparently puzzling findings might derive from the East Asian "tigers" (China; Hong Kong, China; the Republic of Korea; Singapore; and Taiwan, China), which have had very fast growth but comparatively lower female education. Lorgelly and Owen (1999) use statistical techniques to identify outlier countries. Excluding them from the growth regression is sufficient to weaken the significance of the partial correlation between female education and growth, though it remains negative. Dollar and Gatti (1999) find that, by omitting regional dummy variables from their model, they are able to reproduce the estimates of Barro and Lee. This is because the Latin American economies grew more slowly than predicted by the other variables in the growth equation at the same time that the region had high female secondary attainment. Hence, if the regional dummy variables are excluded from the growth regression, Latin America's poor growth gets attributed to the female education variable, resulting in a negative coefficient on female education.

Moreover, because of the high multicollinearity between male and female education in the Barro-Lee specification, there is very little independent variation to allow a disentangling of their separate effects

on growth. Excluding the male education variable switches the sign of the coefficient on female education from negative and significant to positive and insignificant (Lorgelly and Owen 1999).

Knowles, Lorgelly, and Owen (2000) use a different specification of the growth regression. They average data over the entire estimation period of 1960–90 for the explanatory variables to estimate a long-run relationship. They find that the effect of female education on output per worker is significantly positive. But when they reestimate their model with base-period values of human capital stocks as Barro and Lee did, they reproduce the contrasting Barro-Lee results of a negative significant relationship with respect to female education, and a positive one with respect to male education.

The second issue is concerned with the direction of causality. If the positive relationship between gender equality and growth is due to a two-way relationship or underlying common factor determining both simultaneously, then ordinary least squares regressions of income growth on measures of gender equality would be biased. This is particularly true when different variables pertain to the same period. Recent studies have attempted to unravel the cause and effect relationship between gender equality and economic growth—but have run into problems of measurement and statistical inference.

The most common technique is estimation using instrumental variables. This method is based on identifying exogenous variables that affect gender equality but not growth directly, and using measures of gender equality predicted from these variables as determinants of growth. Dollar and Gatti (1999) use data on religion and civil liberties as variables that affect income only through their effect on gender equality in education. Klasen (1999a) uses education spending as a share of GDP, initial fertility levels, and

(box continues on following page)

Box 2.1 continued

the change in the same variables as instruments for levels of and changes in the female to male ratio of years of education, requiring that these instruments pass overidentification restriction tests. Both studies conclude that gender equality has a significant impact on growth.

Other techniques usually support this result. Dollar and Gatti (1999) use time-series data on gender equality and income levels from more than 100 countries over the past three decades to address some of the endogeneity issues, and show that greater gender equality in secondary education is associated with higher income. Klasen (1999a) estimates panel regressions using regional and decadal dummies after formal tests

indicated that this specification is superior to one with country fixed effects or random effects. The education achievement variables used in the regressions are gender-specific total years of schooling in 1960 and the change in the same between 1960 and 1992. Since the education investments needed to change those achievement variables must have been made approximately between 1930 and 1975, it is unlikely that these investments were caused by income growth after 1960. Thus Klasen concludes that it is more likely that the positive association between the female to male ratio of schooling and income growth indicates that a higher female to male schooling ratio contributed to higher income growth, and not the other way around.

stock of female education ranges between 0.2 and 0.45, while it ranges between –0.3 and 0.1 with respect to the stock of male education.

But these studies do not resolve the causality between gender inequality and growth. Recent studies that specifically address causality suggest that gender inequalities in education impede economic growth (box 2.1). What would have happened if Sub-Saharan Africa, South Asia, and the Middle East and North Africa had had the same initial female to male ratio in years of schooling as East Asia did in 1960 and had closed their gender gaps in schooling at the same rate as East Asia between 1960 and 1992? According to one study, average per capita growth rates in those regions would have been 0.5–0.9 percentage point higher per year, a substantial increase over the actual growth rates of 0.7 percent per year in Sub-Saharan Africa, 1.7 in South Asia, and 2.2 in the Middle East and North Africa (figure 2.3; Klasen 1999a).

Indeed, between 1960 and 1992 average annual growth in per capita income in Botswana exceeded 5.5 percent, while in Ghana it was less than 0.3 percent (Klasen 1999a). Controlling for differences in initial income levels, investment rates, economic "openness," and population and labor force growth over the period—as well as initial levels and growth of male educational attainment—the analysis suggests that as much as

Figure 2.3 Faster Progress in Closing Gender Gaps in Schooling Would Accelerate Economic Growth

Average annual growth in per capita GNP, 1960–92

Percent

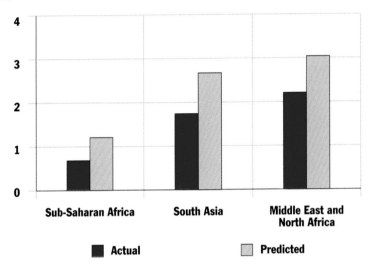

Note: "Predicted" represents the average predicted GNP growth rate for a region if its gender gap in education had started at East Asia's level in 1960 and had narrowed as fast as East Asia's did from 1960 to 1992.

Source: Simulations based on regression results from Klasen (1999a).

1.3–1.6 percentage points of the 5.3 percentage point difference in annual growth between the two countries can be accounted for by differences in gender inequalities in education. Further, for middle- and upper-income countries with relatively high education levels, an increase of 1 percentage point in the share of women with secondary education, holding constant men's secondary education, is associated with an increase in per capita income of 0.3 percentage point (Dollar and Gatti 1999). These results imply that failure to provide girls with the same levels of education as boys impedes economic growth on average.

Gender inequality in other dimensions besides education is associated with lower growth rates. Greater employment opportunities for women may increase national output—at least the part measured in national income accounts. Employment outside the home will lead to a substitution of unrecorded female labor within the home for recorded female labor in the formal economy that is captured in standard national income accounting. This will enhance the visibility of women's labor and increase measured output—even if true output (recorded and unrecorded) is unchanged. To the extent that this substitution involves an increase in productivity, actual economic output and growth will increase as well.

There is limited macroeconomic evidence to show that gender inequality in employment adversely affects economic growth. Controlling for such factors as initial income, population growth, gender inequality in education, and macroeconomic openness, Klasen (1999a) finds that the female share of the working-age population in the formal sector has an economically and statistically significant positive correlation with economic growth. This result should be interpreted with some caution, however, because it may be growth that is drawing women into employment, not the other way around.

Costs to Governance

A COUNTRY'S QUALITY OF GOVERNANCE AND PUBLIC LIFE IS A mark of its level of development—as much as it is a factor of development. The first premise is obvious to most people and requires no evidence; the second, less apparent, has received a boost from recent cross-country studies. A country whose political regime has checks and balances and is able to enforce laws is more stable and has better prospects of development than an autocratic one. Studies find a significantly negative association between corruption and economic growth and development, suggesting that the prevalence of corruption weakens the effectiveness of development policy (Knack and Keefer 1995; Mauro 1995; Olson, Sarna, and Swamy forthcoming). Reducing corruption and promoting a cleaner government thus become challenges for governments and development agencies.

A few other studies explore the possible contributions of greater participation by women in the political arena to decisionmaking about public matters. Do women raise a different set of concerns and represent a different perspective in policy dialogues? Do they bring a different style of governance?

Corruption

Recent studies suggest that gender equality is correlated with corruption. But is this relationship real or spurious? There are two possible hypotheses about why it might be real. First, if egalitarian and participatory societies are more likely to eschew gender discrimination and more likely to institute social checks and balances that make corrupt practices less profitable, then gender equality and corruption would appear to be negatively correlated. Second, there may be intrinsic differences in the behaviors of women and men that lead to cleaner government when more women are in key government positions. The notion that on average women and men respond to social and economic situations in different ways is not radical. Some part of these behavioral differences stems from gender differences in schooling, experience in the workforce, and access to information and technology, among other things. If these differences are accounted for, are the behavioral differences between men and women still statistically significant? While both of these hypotheses warrant further examination, existing studies already offer intriguing findings.

Studies in behavioral and social sciences suggest that men and women differ in behaviors that have to do with corruption, the general conclusion being that women are more community-oriented and selfless than men. Some control experiments find that women are more likely to exhibit generosity and altruism than men—but other experiments contest these results.[12] Other analysis based on data collected by the World Values Surveys from 18 countries in 1981 and from 43 countries in 1991 shows that women are less accepting of dishonest or illegal behaviors than men (Swamy and others forthcoming). And a significantly higher proportion of women than men believe that certain behaviors can never be justified, with differences ranging from 4 to 9 percentage points (table 2.2).

But are the results the same after considering differences in observable characteristics of men and women? When employment status and several individual characteristics (such as age, education, and marital status) are taken into account, men are 3.3 percent more likely to accept a bribe in their job than women (Swamy and others forthcoming). There is some variation across countries, however. In seven of the 43 countries in 1991 men were less likely to accept bribes. But in the rest of the 43 countries in 1991 and in all 18 countries in 1981, the results imply that women were less likely to take bribes—although the estimates are not statistically significant in about a third of these countries. So, while statistically significant gender differences are not found in all countries, gender-differentiated attitudes toward corruption seem to be more or less a worldwide phenomenon.

Enterprise surveys show that women in business are less likely than men to pay bribes to government officials, whether because of risk

Table 2.2   He Says, She Says—What Is Unjustifiable Social Behavior?

Behavior	Percentage who say behavior can "never be justified"	
	Male	Female
Claiming government benefits you are not entitled to	63.7	67.9
Avoiding a fare on public transport	60.3	64.9
Cheating on taxes if you have the chance	54.4	61.5
Buying something you know is stolen	72.9	79.5
Taking and driving a car belonging to someone else	83.1	87.2
Keeping money that you have found	43.9	51.6
Lying in your own interest	45.1	50.9
Accepting a bribe in the course of duty	72.4	77.3
Fighting with the police	52.0	57.1
Failing to report damage you have done to a parked vehicle	61.8	67.6
Throwing away litter in a public place	69.1	74.4
Driving under the influence of alcohol	74.2	83.4

Note: Data are from 18 countries in 1981 and 43 countries in 1991. Sample sizes vary from 52,107 to 83,532. All differences are significant at the .0001 level.

Source: Adapted from Swamy and others (forthcoming).

aversion or higher standards of ethical behavior. In the Republic of Georgia firms owned or managed by men are 10–14 percent more likely (depending on the multivariate econometric method used) to make an unofficial payment to government officials than are those owned or managed by women (Swamy and others forthcoming).[13] These results control for characteristics of the firm (sector and size) and characteristics of the owner or manager (education). Without these controls, firms managed by men are twice as likely to use bribes.

The above findings, based on individual and firm survey information, are echoed by recent analyses of cross-country data. Kaufmann (1998) finds a negative correlation between a corruption index and an index of women's social and economic rights in a sample of more than 80 countries.[14] Since this result does not control for other variables that might be driving the result, such as income, the direction of causality, if any, has not been ascertained. When Kaufmann's results are extended to control for per capita income, the negative relationship between corruption and women's rights is weakened but remains significant—indicating that women's rights have an association with lower corruption independent of income (figure 2.4).[15] To the extent that lower corruption results in higher

Figure 2.4   More Equal Rights for Women—Less Corruption

Corruption index

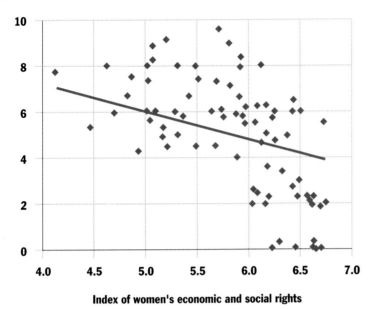

Index of women's economic and social rights

Note: The corruption index uses data from the International Country Risk Guide (ICRG) and transforms it: corruption index = 10 – (ICRG Index – 1) x 2. A vaule of 0 indicates low levels of corruption, a value of 10 indicates high levels. The women's rights variable is the Women's Economic and Social Human Rights (WESHR) Indicator developed by Purdue University's Global Studies program. A score of 7 is interpreted as gender equality in economic and social rights. The figure controls for per capita GDP in each country. See appendix 1 for included countries.
Sources: World Bank staff estimates; see also Kaufmann (1998).

investment and thus growth, gender equality indirectly affects growth through that channel.

Besides rights, broader participation by women also appears to matter. Governments are less corrupt when women are more active in politics or the labor force (Dollar, Fisman, and Gatti forthcoming; Swamy and others forthcoming). For example, corruption falls as the proportion of parliamentary seats held by women rises (based on the International Country Risk Guide's Corruption Index and Transparency International's Corruption Perceptions Index), controlling for national income and other factors shown to affect corruption, including the extent of civil liberties, average years of schooling, trade openness, and ethnic fractionalization. A one standard deviation increase in the proportion of women in lower houses of parliament from the sample average of 10.9 percent is accompanied by no less than a 10 percent decrease in corruption (Swamy and others forthcoming). Although still only suggestive, these findings lend additional support for having more women in politics and in the labor force—since they could be an effective force for good government and business trust.

Exclusion Narrows Perspectives

Chapter 1 shows very low representation of women in parliaments and in ministerial positions across the world's regions, developing or industrial. How large are the development costs of systematically excluding women from government and public decisionmaking? While the studies on this topic generally argue that gender-based exclusion has substantial costs to society, the empirical evidence is still primarily suggestive rather than conclusive. This section cites the results implying that women bring new perspectives to decisionmaking, enhance the legitimacy of governance, and enrich political processes by contributing new skills, styles, and visions.

According to a recent survey by the Inter-Parliamentary Union (2000) of 187 women holding political office in 65 countries, about nine-tenths of respondents believe they hold a different view of politics and society than their male counterparts. And while they feel special responsibility to represent the interests of other women, they are also more likely to act as advocates for other parts of society. They say that they have put new and different issues on the agenda. Some examples: laws on violence against women and initiatives on electoral laws in El Salvador, a land redistribution law to alleviate women's poverty in Ethiopia, and legislation on labor, social security, and children's rights in Russia.

The survey data suggest that women's greater presence has altered the traditionally male approach to social welfare, legal protection, and transparency in government and business. Many respondents believe that if the partnership between men and women were to increase in politics and society, politics would better meet the needs of society. The great majority of respondents claim that their motives for entering politics stem from the desire to make a difference in society, particularly in social justice. Eighty percent believe that women's participation restores trust in politics. They also feel that women advocate a conciliatory approach to politics and can contribute to the mediation of disputes (IPU 2000).

These data represent the views of women in political office. But do women and men in political positions really articulate different priorities?

Do they have different impacts on policy? These questions remain unanswered, especially in developing countries. Even in the United States and Western European countries women legislators do not think they are necessarily more effective than men legislators, even though they are more likely than men to attend party meetings and conferences and work longer hours (Davis 1997).[16] Because they come from outside the traditional networks of legislators, women must work longer hours to compensate for their lack of social and political capital. And women bureaucrats may be limited to only certain areas of policymaking, such as women's affairs and social development.

Because economic class and ethnicity, as well as gender, divide societies, women civil servants and political leaders are not necessarily going to be the allies of all other women—and the same is true for men. But controlling for these factors, if women and men bring different perspectives to decisionmaking within political bureaucracies, then keeping women outside of government at any level will limit the effectiveness of the state and its policies.

More broadly, systematic discrimination against and exclusion of large segments of the population in basic services, political rights, and economic opportunities inspire distrust and resentment, which influences the larger social climate and jeopardizes development prospects. Several recent studies have argued that trust (or social capital, social cohesion)—the willingness of people within a society to cooperate or collaborate across different groups in order to achieve common goals—determines the effectiveness of a society's institutions (Putnam 1993; Fukuyama 1995; Woolcock 2000). Using data from the World Values Survey (1990–93) for a measure of trust, La Porta and others (1997) estimated the effect of trust on government effectiveness and participation in civic organizations. They found that holding GNP per capita constant, a one standard deviation increase in trust raises judicial efficiency by 0.7, bureaucratic quality by 0.3, and tax compliance by 0.3, and decreases corruption by 0.3 of a standard deviation.[17]

Why Gender Disparities Persist: a Framework

THIS CHAPTER HAS REVIEWED A COMPELLING BODY OF evidence on how societies that discriminate on the basis of gender pay a significant price in the well-being of their people, in their economic growth, in their governance, and in their ability to reduce poverty. These costs are widespread and quantitatively significant. Especially in low-income countries, such as those in South Asia and Sub-Saharan Africa, more education and greater autonomy for women would help alleviate some of the worst manifestations of poverty— including HIV/AIDS, child mortality, and severe malnutrition. Yet prejudice and discriminatory practices exclude women from resources, markets, and politics, leaving large segments of each country's talent, skill, and energy untapped.

The evidence leads to several questions. If gender inequalities harm people's well-being and a country's prospects for development, why do they persist in so many societies? Why are gender inequalities in some domains much more difficult to eliminate than in others? For example, improvements have been rapid in health and access to schooling, but much slower or nearly absent in political participation and equal rights to property. What factors stand in the way of transforming gender relations and eliminating pernicious gender disparities?

This section offers a framework for understanding how harmful gender disparities persist. The framework is based on three important factors that influence gender equality:

- Institutions, including social norms, laws, and markets.
- Households and families.
- The economy.

These factors also provide critical entry points for public and civic action to promote gender equality in development. The next three chapters discuss each of the three factors in turn—and the ways they contribute to gender inequalities.

Underlying the gender disparities described in chapter 1 are social and cultural norms that shape the roles of and relationships between men and women. These norms, reflected in legal and regulatory frameworks as well as in economic institutions, shape prevailing gender structures in society and the economy. Social norms are part of a broad institutional environment that also includes customs, rights, laws, and market institutions. These influence what resources women and men have, what activities they undertake, in what forms they can participate in politics and the economy. They embody incentives that tolerate or discourage prejudice. Some of them, such as social norms, can be difficult and slow to change—but are far from static. And public policy can shift incentives in ways that promote or inhibit gender equality (see chapter 3).

Like institutions, households and families shape gender relations from early in a person's life, transmit them from one generation to the next, and determine the opportunities available to people. Households are where many of life's basic decisions are made—having and raising children, engaging in work and leisure, investing in the future. How tasks and productive resources are allocated among sons and daughters, how much autonomy they are given, whether expectations differ among them—all these create, reinforce, or mitigate gender disparities. But families do not make decisions about allocating and investing their resources in isolation. They make them within the context of communities, reflecting the influence of incentives established by the larger institutional and policy environment (see chapter 4).

The economy, too, determines the opportunities people have for improving their standard of living. Rising household incomes can lead to more equal human development (such as health status and schooling) for females and males. Higher incomes mean that households have fewer resource constraints that would force them to choose between investing in sons or daughters. And the factors that yield higher incomes also tend to raise the costs of unfairly excluding people from economic production.

But whether the expansion of economic opportunities reduces gender disparities depends on what type of income-generating activities are available, how they are organized, how effort and skills are rewarded, and whether women and men are equally able to participate. Many factors get in the way. The gender division of labor in the home, social norms and prejudice, and unequal capacities and assets prevent women and men from taking equal advantage of economic opportunities—or from coping with risk or economic shocks. These factors partly explain why women and men often work in different sectors of the economy—and thus are not equally affected by shifts in relative prices or by the growth or decline of particular sectors. Failure to recognize these gender-differentiated constraints when designing policies can compromise their effectiveness—in both equity and efficiency (see chapter 5).

But institutional change and economic growth are not enough to eliminate persistent gender inequalities. These transformations take time, and even development policies that are apparently gender-neutral can have gender-differentiated outcomes—in part because of the ways institutions and household decisions combine to shape gender roles and relations.

Government's Role in Promoting Gender Equality

IMPROVING EQUITY IS COMMONLY VIEWED AS A CENTRAL concern of the state. Most national constitutions promise equal basic rights and freedoms for all citizens—and most explicitly promise to safeguard equality regardless of age, race, or sex. Nearly all governments have signed the Universal Declaration of Human Rights, and most have signed several international conventions protecting women and children—such as the Convention on the Elimination of All Forms of Discrimination against Women, regarded as the international bill of rights for women. But as chapter 3 discusses, these promises and agreements provide no guarantee when the domestic rule of law is weak, when laws and regulations to ensure constitutional rights and international treaties are absent, and when political considerations supersede good intentions.

While improving equity may be reason enough for states to address gender disparities, other reasons are important in formulating government policy and action. For one, greater equality also brings greater stability and cohesion to society. These benefits are public goods, improving the workings of society and the economy. In addition, there are efficiency reasons to consider—to help inform how the state should intervene to promote gender equality.

The Economic Rationale for State Intervention

A compelling argument for state intervention is the spillover effects of greater equality, what economists refer to as "positive externalities." Gender equality benefits those directly affected, such as women who experience discrimination, and society as a whole. Especially at low incomes (as in much of South Asia, Sub-Saharan Africa, and parts of East Asia), more schooling, resources, and autonomy for women can help alleviate some of the worst manifestations of poverty, including child mortality and malnutrition. And there is now growing evidence that gender equality is positively associated with better living conditions and with cleaner governments.

By implication, government action is also justified when it reduces the negative externalities of gender inequalities. That is, individuals or groups, if left on their own, can indulge their prejudices (and fears) at the expense of others. But if individuals or groups internalize this harm they will be more invested in ending or reducing gender inequalities. This is the case when men who have daughters become more aware and concerned about abuses against women. Are there negative externalities when women discriminate against other women and girls? Yes, because the harm a woman directly experiences (or internalizes) is only a portion of the total harm that her action causes.

The presence of externalities, coupled with the high human costs of gender inequality, makes a powerful case for public intervention. And just as the costs and benefits of achieving gender equality go beyond what any individual experiences, what is required to reduce inequalities often falls outside what an individual can reasonably accomplish. Entrenched social norms, customs, and legal institutions that create gender inequalities are extremely difficult, if not impossible, for an individual or small group to change.

Moreover, market failures in the availability of information—which contribute to gender discrimination—are pervasive and costly to overcome. For example, more information in the labor market on worker productivity has large externalities (that is, gains beyond what one employer internalizes)—but accurate information may be too costly for one employer to acquire. So, employers use information markers, such as sex, though they are flawed and unfair. Subsidizing improved availability of information in the labor market is thus something the government can do to promote gender equality.

The state can intervene in many ways. It can tax and subsidize, persuade and regulate, prohibit and punish, or provide services. It can tax to finance (or subsidize) investments to counterbalance gender inequalities in investments by others—such as when it subsidizes more schooling for girls or more job skills training for women. It can directly prohibit prejudicial behavior—such as when it requires enterprises to hire workers on the basis of skills rather than on the basis of sex, and sanctions or fines violators.

Whatever instrument the state chooses, if it intervenes it is making a judgment about fairness, about how much to disallow some people's right to discriminate (at home, in the workplace, in politics), and thus about how large a cost to impose on them in order to protect others. There are certainly win-win scenarios in improving gender equality, as the evidence earlier in this chapter shows. But it would be naive to expect that everybody wins when discrimination is prohibited. For example, redesigning the delivery of public health services to give rural women better access is probably a win-win change. But fortifying laws against sexual harassment in the workplace is not—the government has to make a judgment about who will bear what proportion of the cost of redressing gender-related abuse.

An intrinsic problem of redistributive actions, however, is that it is not always easy to define what is or is not fair and to decide how much to intervene. One of the more difficult areas for state intervention is the household, where inequalities stem partly from biological differences, from traditional norms about gender roles, and from unequal bargaining power between females and males. Should the government intervene in the household? Should it have a say in household decisions about investments, consumption, reproduction, and work to ensure equality between females and males? Although the government may be unwilling to make explicit interpersonal (or intergroup) comparisons of welfare, inaction is also implicitly a judgment in favor of perpetrators. How forcefully to intervene is a question that warrants a different response in different situations.

Even when the costs of gender discrimination can be identified, the state may not be the best party to address the inequalities. And there is still the question of how the state should intervene, if it does. Often government's failure to redress gender inequalities is part of a larger failure to establish and enforce a rule of law based on basic human rights or to design and implement appropriate policies that support vulnerable groups. Governments are not omniscient, selfless "social guardians"—and public policies and interventions are not costless (Krueger 1990). Moreover, governments in many developing countries face innumerable challenges, and they do so with limited fiscal and administrative capacities.

Part of the challenge, then, is for governments to select their roles strategically, partly by focusing on responsibilities that the private sector is unlikely to take on—or to take on well. Prevailing wisdom calls for governments to intervene when and where spillover effects or externalities are especially important—and to choose a role that fits its capability. Such selectivity of intervention and targeting, as opposed to indiscriminate and blanket actions, saves scarce administrative skills and fiscal resources and makes it easier to identify the social costs associated with policy (Bardhan 1990). Under this discipline, governments will be better able to address gender issues constructively and competently.

In most circumstances the first role of the state is to "level the playing field" for women and men. For the regulatory framework, this means safeguarding basic rights for all; mitigating or removing discriminatory elements embodied in civil laws, government functions, and market structures; and enforcing such laws and regulations. But institutional reforms and economic development take time to bear fruit; thus, active policies are often warranted to catalyze change or to redress persistent gender disparities. Policymakers possess a broad range of policy levers—both untargeted and targeted—to affect the relative access to resources and bargaining power of women and men within the household.

As the financier and provider of key public programs, the state must recognize the influence of household economics and power relations to understand how programs are likely to affect females and males differently. Contrary to prevailing wisdom, public policies and programs are not generally gender-neutral in their impacts—or, as many have claimed, even in their intent. Even policies that pay specific attention to gender can have unexpected impacts if the balance of power and resources between women and men is not well understood. Consider changes in family laws designed to benefit women and children. Or labor market legislation intended to protect women. Or agricultural programs intended to increase productivity on female-managed farms. For each, the failure to understand gender relations can lead to unanticipated and often undesirable outcomes, as the next chapters illustrate. Ignoring the gender-differentiated effects has costs not only for equity but also for the efficiency and sustainability of public policies and programs.

Civil Society and the International Community

But what if the state, captured by interests favoring the gender status quo, is unwilling—or unable—to exert its influence for gender equality? Despite the strong case for public action, even well-intentioned policymakers can find it difficult to implement unpopular policies. Moreover, government agencies themselves tend to function under the prevailing views about gender roles and relations. In many cases, then, local civil society and the international community can be an important force for change. Civil society groups have caused social and economic change by initiating public debate, lobbying the state, empowering communities, and undertaking informed advocacy.

In any country civil society comprises a heterogeneous collection of interest groups. Some groups are committed to promoting greater gender equality while others benefit from active discrimination and exclusion. But many groups, local and international, have made difficult and time-consuming efforts to build political support in the face of resistance and have helped get gender issues onto the policy agenda, urging governments to move more quickly and forcefully. Some examples:

- International conventions that have focused on gender issues—such as those in Beijing and Copenhagen in 1995 and in New York in 2000—have stimulated major efforts to analyze the state of gender equality and the impact of public policy and action. They have fostered public discussion and provided critical leverage for local efforts to promote gender equality.
- Civic action has influenced institutional reforms, such as recent land reforms in Latin America, strengthening women's land tenure rights. Civil society groups in South Africa and Uganda helped ensure that the countries' new constitutions contain guarantees of equal rights for women and men.
- In the Indian state of Kerala local women's groups have organized to audit the implementation and impact of local government anti-poverty programs (Goetz 1999).
- Where public institutions have failed to protect women against gender-related violence, nongovernmental organizations (NGOs) have stepped into the breach, providing such services as safe motherhood programs and microfinance schemes. NGOs have raised women's legal literacy, pressed for better enforcement of rights, undertaken dispute resolution in local communities, and provided support to female victims of violence (see, for example, Matin and others 2000).

This chapter has presented a wide range of evidence showing why gender equality is a development issue. Equity considerations are a forceful argument for state intervention, for the costs of gender inequalities to human lives are often large. But there are also compelling efficiency reasons, more often asserted than argued with evidence, that further strengthen the justification for public action. The next three chapters elaborate on the effects of institutions, household dynamics, and economic policy on gender inequalities. The last chapter examines the many opportunities for intervention by the state and civil society.

Notes

1. For recent debates on this view, see Fukuyama (1998), Ehrenreich (1999), and Ferguson (1999).

2. Men do not have a monopoly on violence, however. Historical evidence shows that women are capable of perpetrating or condoning violence against both men and women. For example, in South Africa many women supported apartheid, firmly convinced that racial divisions and violence were necessary to ensure order (Goldblatt and Meintjes 1998).

3. In this study children under five are considered malnourished if their weight for age is more than two standard deviations below the median based on the standards of the National Center for Health Statistics and the World Health Organization. These values reflect the estimated contribution of each determinant as a share of total change in reduction of child malnutrition. These estimates are obtained by multiplying the coefficients on the proxy variables for each determinant by the change in the proxy from 1970 to 1995. The proxies for each determinant are health and environment—access to safe water; women's education—female secondary enrollments; women's status—ratio of female life expectancy to male life expectancy; and food availability—daily per capita dietary energy supplies.

4. Smith and Haddad (2000) measure relative status as the ratio of female life expectancy at birth to male life expectancy at birth. Most measures available in the literature are multiple-indicator indices vulnerable to charges of arbitrariness in composition and aggregation method (Deaton 1997). While there is no agreed-upon measure of "women's relative status," Smith and Haddad (2000) choose the ratio of female life expectancy at birth to male life expectancy at birth because "the extension of human life reflects the intrinsic value of living as well as being a necessary requirement for carrying out a variety of accomplishments (or 'capabilities') that are generally positively valued by society. It is also associated with an enhanced quality of life. Inequalities in this variable favoring males reflect discrimination against females (as infants, children, and adults) and entrenched, long-term gender inequality" (Smith and Haddad 2000, p. 21, referencing Sen 1998 and Mohiuddin 1996).

5. Using Humana's (1992) data on rights, Boone (1996) finds that on a scale of 1–4, with 1 representing the most autonomy and 4 the least, the average index across the world is about 2. The author refers to the degree of women's autonomy (or lack thereof) as the index of gender oppression.

6. But the conclusion is qualified because the impact is not linear. While women's education reduces fertility, there appears to be a threshold of education (between primary and secondary) beyond which a marked reduction in fertility is generated, but below which women's education may have little or even a positive effect on fertility. This threshold tends to be higher in less developed and more gender-stratified countries.

7. This finding reflects the impact on fertility not only of the level of women's education but also the gender gap in education (represented by holding constant men's education in the regression). Hill and King (1995) and Klasen (1999) find that a smaller gender gap is indeed associated with lower fertility.

8. Some studies have found mothers' education to have a larger positive effect on daughters' education than on sons', but overall the findings are mixed. In Malaysia, while both the mother's and the father's education have significant positive effects on their children's schooling, the mother's education has a far greater effect on daughters' than on sons' education, while the father's education has a greater impact on sons' (Lillard and Willis 1994). Cases of maternal education having a larger impact on sons' schooling are not unknown, a hypothesis that requires further study (see chapter 4).

9. See Quisumbing (1996) for a review of recent evidence on gender differences in agricultural productivity.

10. Much of the empirical evidence on differences in the productivity and efficiency of female and male farmers comes from Sub-Saharan Africa. Part of the reason is that men and women commonly manage separate plots, making direct gender comparisons more straightforward empirically.

11. Zabalza and Tzannatos (1985) estimate that Britain's Equal Pay Act of 1970 led to a 15 percent increase in the wage bill across all sectors.

12. For example, Eckel and Grossman (1998) used an "anonymous dictator" game in which each subject in the study was asked to divide $10 with an unknown partner without risk of rejection. On average, women chose to donate $1.60 to their unknown partner, while men donated half this amount. Andreoni and Vesterlund (forthcoming) compared gender behavior in similar games and found that women gave more overall and were more likely to divide game tokens evenly despite different monetary values, while men became less generous as the value of the tokens increased. However, Bolton and Katok (1995) ran a similar experiment using different subjects and found no gender difference in donations. In general, results of laboratory experiments to determine gender differences in ethical behavior and risk aversion are highly sensitive to social context, the sequence of experiments, and the price of displaying integrity or taking risks (Eckel and Grossman 1996; Anderson, Rodgers, and Rodriguez 1998).

13. Swamy and others (forthcoming) estimate the relationship using ordinary least squares (producing a coefficient estimate suggesting that the presence of a male owner or manager increases the incidence of bribe-giving by 10 percentage points); a probit model (13 percentage points); and an ordered probit model (14 percentage points). Interestingly, they find no gender differences in the amounts paid, conditional on a bribe having been paid. The authors suggest that this finding is consistent with other evidence that bribe markets in the Republic of Georgia operate at known prices and that agents have discretion only over whether to pay.

14. See the scatter plot of the corruption index against the women's rights index in Kaufmann (1998).

15. Kaufmann (1998) uses an index of women's rights that differs from the Humana (1986, 1992) index used throughout this report. However, the results underlying figure 2.2 are qualitatively similar even when the Humana index is used.

16. A similar situation is noted in several developing countries by studies included in Staudt (1997).

17. La Porta and others (1997) measure trust by the percentage of people who said "yes" when asked, "Generally speaking, would you say that most people can be trusted or that you can't be too careful in dealing with people?" The higher-trust countries are in Scandinavia, where almost two-thirds of respondents believe that strangers can be trusted; the lower-trust countries are in Latin America. The various measures of government effectiveness were obtained from different databases and are defined in table 1 of the study (La Porta and others 1997, p. 335).

CHAPTER 3

Social Norms, Laws, and Economic Institutions

D EVELOPMENT OCCURS IN AN INSTITUTIONAL environment defined by customs, social norms, and implicit codes of conduct—and such formal structures as laws, regulations, and economic institutions. These structures underlie many of the gender inequalities described in chapter 1. Why boys attend school longer than girls in most countries. Why men but not women inherit land in some societies. Why adolescent girls and women are placed under purdah in some societies. Why girls and women are sometimes maimed or killed for "honor." Why men but not women usually go to war. Why women typically live longer than men. And so on.

This chapter examines the gender structures embedded in social, legal, and economic institutions, how they affect gender relations and gender outcomes, and the scope for policy and action. These institutions establish the incentives, opportunities, and constraints that determine people's choices and actions. They shape power relations within the family, society, and the economy. From early on children are taught in accord with societal expectations, and throughout life, formal and informal structures reinforce the behaviors expected of them as women and men. Institutions are at the heart of the problems of—and the solutions to—gender inequality.

To achieve gender equality development strategies must transform legal and regulatory frameworks, markets, and organizations into institutions based on the principles of equal rights, equal opportunity, and equal voice for women and men. A fundamental step is to establish equal basic rights, especially in family law, protection against gender-related violence, property rights, and political rights. At the start of the 20th century the Nordic countries extended to women rights to vote equal to men's. In China the government-sponsored Marriage Law of 1950 established standards of equal rights for women and men with respect to marriage, divorce, and control of children. In Colombia and Costa Rica in the 1980s land reform measures that explicitly addressed gender inequalities in inheritance traditions expanded women's land ownership considerably. In Egypt in early 2000 a loose coalition of the highest government leaders and civil society groups broadened women's rights in family law.

Another step in transforming a country's institutional framework is to improve economic institutions—so that productivity rather than gender (or race or age) is the primary criterion for employment and compensation in labor markets. And so that information is widely available and not limited to elite networks. The relative wages of men and women, the returns to productive assets, and the prices of goods and services are all determined, in large part, by the structure of markets. Even the presence or absence of certain markets can make a tremendous difference for women and their families. Where markets exist for water or fuel or child care, they reduce the domestic workload and facilitate economic participation outside the household, especially for women and girls. Where labor markets are open to women, they raise the expected rate of return to women's human capital, strengthening incentives for families to invest in the knowledge and skills of girls.

But laws that institute equal basic rights—and markets that are more open and competitive—often are not enough to eliminate persistent gender inequalities embedded in a country's institutional foundation. Targeted laws and regulations, when used selectively and judiciously, can be effective in addressing critical gender inequalities in opportunities and voice.

Indeed, there is tremendous scope for policy to transform institutions so that they support the principle of gender equality. But there are many challenges—and substantial risks. A country's social norms, customs, legal frameworks, markets, and hierarchies—the elements of its institutional framework—often reinforce one another, so it is difficult to effect societal change by changing only one part of the framework. And often there is strong resistance to institutional reform not only from those who might lose directly from the change but even from those who stand to benefit—because they fear the uncertainties that change might bring. But societal institutions are far from static. Institutions reflect past deliberate actions, both by government and civil society. But they also reflect the impact of past political and social upheavals, major economic events, even natural catastrophes—and also of everyday forces for change, such as mass media and migration.

Gender in Norms and Customs

S OCIAL NORMS AND CUSTOMS GO A LONG WAY TOWARD explaining the gender disparities discussed in chapter 1. They determine the roles that women and men have in the family and the community. They shape individual preferences and power relations between the sexes. They dictate the type of work considered appropriate for women and men. Men may be ridiculed for doing what is termed women's work, while women may be regarded as unfeminine or inviting sexual interactions when they work in male-dominated jobs. Social norms thus create powerful incentives that guide people's behavior—as spouses, parents, citizens, and workers—and behavior outside the accepted boundaries can unleash formal and informal systems of social sanction (Narayan and others 2000).

These systems of gender norms and customs vary across regions— and across and within countries—with evident consequences for the autonomy and status of women and men (box 3.1). In the northern part of South Asia kinship systems tend to be highly gender-stratified (Dyson and Moore 1983). The tradition of female seclusion, or purdah, is prevalent, significantly limiting women's freedom of movement and autonomy (Mason, Smith, and Morgan 1998). And following the tradition of exogamous marriage, brides move to their husband's (often distant) village upon marriage, leaving behind their natal kin. This practice leaves many

---

Box 3.1 Gender Norms Differ across Countries—but Women and Men Agree More Often Than They Disagree

THE WORLD VALUE SURVEYS CONDUCTED between 1990 and 1993 asked women and men in 40 countries about the appropriate division of labor in the family (Inglehart, Basañez, and Moreno 1998). A higher proportion of men than women agreed that "when jobs are scarce, men have more right to a job than women." A higher share of women than men agreed that "a woman has to have children in order to be fulfilled" (see figure). But women and men did not disagree much—their responses were highly positively and significantly correlated (with a correlation coefficient of 0.85 for the first question and 0.99 for the second). The more strongly women and men believed a child to be crucial to a woman's self-fulfillment, the more likely they were to think that men should have more right than women to jobs (with a correlation coefficient of 0.60 for both women and men).

(box continues on following page)

Box 3.1 continued

Men's and Women's Views of Gender Roles
(percentage agreeing with statement)

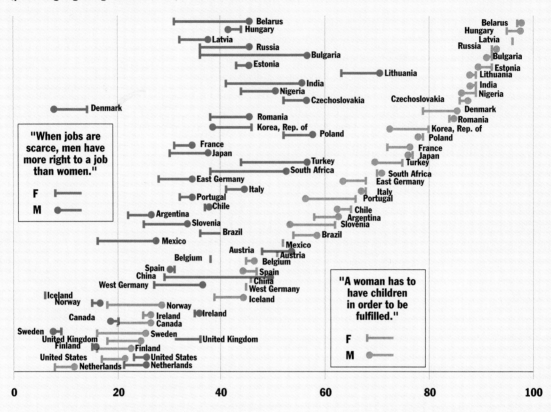

Source: Based on data in Inglehart, Basañez, and Moreno (1998).

The responses can be roughly classified into three groups: a small group of countries where only a small proportion of women and men agreed with both statements, a middle group where 40–60 percent of respondents agreed with both statements, and a third group where there was considerably more agreement on the second statement than the first. The Scandinavian countries, the Netherlands, and North America, including Mexico, generally belong to the first group. This pattern is consistent with the widespread view of Scandi-

navian societies as models of gender equality and suggests that women and men hold similar views about gender roles. A notable exception is Denmark, where there is high agreement that women need children to be fulfilled, but also disagreement that men have more right to jobs, implying that women are expected to have both children and jobs.

Also noteworthy are the responses from Europe and Central Asia, where the largest percentage of women and men agreed that children were necessary

(box continues on following page)

Box 3.1 continued

for women's self-fulfillment. But fewer than half the women and men agreed that men have priority over jobs, except in Lithuania. In the former Soviet states female employment was encouraged by measures that gave women equal rights with men to expand their education and work skills. But women were expected to continue to bear the burden of family responsibilities, with the aid of public day care facilities close to their job (Lapidus 1993).

A similar survey in Japan, the Republic of Korea, and the United States in the early 1990s asked respondents to agree or disagree that "it is better for everyone if men earn the living and women keep house" (Inoue 1998). Eighty-two percent of men agreed in Korea, 63 percent in Japan, and 36 percent in the United States. Among women, the percentages were smaller but still markedly different among the three countries—71 percent in Korea, 54 percent in Japan, and 36 percent in the United States. The responses also indicate that women and men in the United States hold similar views on this question.

---

young brides alone and estranged from their relatives and is said to lead to higher female mortality (Kishor 1993).[1]

These practices also explain why families are often unwilling to send girls to schools for as long as they send boys—because girls marry at very young ages (under 15 and often even younger than 10) and leave their natal families when they marry, and because they are not expected to have to work for pay in the labor market (Jejeebhoy 1995; Alderman and King 1998).[2] And schooling itself may be considered a threat if contact with boys cannot be avoided, if schooling is perceived to be teaching girls aspirations contrary to custom, or even if it simply takes girls away from work and care activities at home.

In contrast, family systems in Southeast Asia and Latin America are generally more egalitarian. Women are rarely secluded, disparities in literacy and economic opportunity are relatively narrow, and son preference is rare (Jejeebhoy 1995). Women in Southeast Asia are often expected to play important economic roles in the family by working outside the home, managing family finances, and providing support for their elderly parents. This higher status results in greater mobility and higher family investments in females. Yet even in these settings social norms and customs embody gender structures that result in occupational segregation, high rates of gender-related violence, and persistent gender gaps in earnings not attributable to worker characteristics. The culture of *machismo* in Latin America and elsewhere, for example, exalts masculine virility and physical strength and aggression as a means of resolving disagreements—including the use of force with women (Sara-Lafosse 1998).

The wide variation in gender roles and inequality across and within regions is associated in part with differences across castes, social classes, and ethnic and religious groups—and with the interaction of these group identities. Countries with homogeneous ethnic, religious, or kinship structures have fairly common gender structures, but even small countries can have multiple systems of gender norms that vary across ethnic groups or geographic communities. In Burkina Faso social norms relating to land rights and to wives' labor differ substantially between its ethnic groups. The Mossi, the country's largest ethnic group, and the Bwa often live in close proximity—but the norms about women's obligations to work on their husband's farms are less stringent among the Bwa than the Mossi. In both groups women receive land rights predominantly through marriage. But because marriage institutions are more stable among the Mossi and land tenure is more secure, agricultural productivity is significantly higher on plots farmed by women in Mossi than in Bwa areas, controlling for other factors (Vishwanath and others 1996).

Like ethnicity, religion influences gender relations and outcomes—but findings from several cross-country studies on the effects of specific religious affiliations are mixed.[3] This is hardly surprising. The practice of religion is influenced by the larger social context—cross-country studies take only limited account of this interaction, which is more the province of micro studies. For example, a study comparing the Muslim populations of several Asian countries found a large variation in the autonomy felt by Muslim women in different contexts (Mason, Smith, and Morgan 1998). On the whole women have less autonomy in South Asia than in Southeast Asia, regardless of religion. Within each country Muslim women's freedom of movement is more constrained than that of non-Muslim women, but their autonomy in participating in decisionmaking about economic matters and family size is not consistently less. This suggests that other factors besides religious affiliation are producing differences in women's autonomy.

Embedded in entrenched kinship and religious systems, social norms and customs related to gender are difficult and slow to change—but they do change. And they change for many reasons. Across the generations the concept of gender equality and gender roles and relations have evolved in response to environmental changes, economic crises and progress, and innovations—as much as to broader political and social transformation.

But deliberate actions by the state and civil society groups, through re-forms of a country's legal framework and economic institutions, also have played an important role in this change in modern times. Governments—with or without support from the majority of civil society—have used laws and regulations, part of a country's institutional environment, to cata-lyze change in these norms and customs. The next sections discuss how they have done so and the scope for further policy and action.

Rights and Laws

A COUNTRY'S LEGAL SYSTEM OFTEN INCLUDES A COMBINATION of national statutory law, customary or traditional law, religious law, and commitments to ratified international conventions. *Statutory law* pertains to all parts of the formal legal system, from legislation issued by different levels of administration to regulations and directives issued by government agencies. Here the term refers also to judicial rulings and laws made by judges. *Traditional* or *customary law* pertains to rules that exist side by side with statutory law but derive their legitimacy from tradition and custom rather than a government act. And where there are diverse religious and ethnic subgroups within a country, customary law is likely to be fractionalized.

The different parts of this legal framework reflect—and codify—social norms and customs about gender roles and relations. For example, in various countries tax allocation and land registration are associated with the head of the household. But since the head of the household is usually identified or presumed to be male in many societies, except when a man is absent, women's claims on income or property may be over-looked. But the legal system does not only codify norms and customs; it can specify how society should operate along the principle of equality. In this it serves as an instrument for societal reform.

Human Rights—de Jure and de Facto

National constitutions around the world affirm the principle of basic human rights. At least in principle, many of them also contain an explicit reference to nondiscrimination between women and men with respect to these rights. But national constitutions are neither automatically nor necessarily effective. Many constitutions now give women and men the right to vote and to be elected to public office—but gender disparities in literacy and access to information still limit women's participation in political forums. Many countries have introduced mandatory education laws recognizing basic schooling as a human right, with no discernible discrimination by gender—but the way education is delivered deters girls more than boys from going to school in many settings. So, failure to consider the impact of gender stratification and inequalities on the practice of basic rights weakens the power of constitutional mandates.

Systemic obstacles also stand in the way of translating into reality what appears to be a national commitment to gender equality. As discussed in the next section, other parts of a country's legal framework (such as customary law or procedural laws) may continue to give unequal rights to women and men, effectively countermanding that commitment. In addition, a country's capacity for effective implementation and enforcement is often limited, again in part because statutes could conflict with more dominant traditional or religious legal structures within the country and in part because administrative agencies may be absent or weak.

An important influence on national law, especially on human rights, is international law. International law has framed gender equality as part of a larger global concern about human rights and basic freedoms—for economic and political rights, for claims to basic health and education services, and for reproductive decisions. Many countries recognize, at least in principle, the international standards set by the general human rights instruments of the United Nations, starting with the Universal Declaration of Human Rights adopted in 1948, and international laws—and the conventions that have developed norms to address gender discrimination.

The Convention on the Elimination of All Forms of Discrimination against Women (CEDAW), established in 1979, is regarded as the international bill of rights for women. It prohibits any distinction, exclusion, or restriction on the basis of gender that impairs or nullifies women's human rights and fundamental freedoms. It establishes women's rights on par with those of men to political participation (Articles 7–8), education (Article 10), work (Article 11), health (Article 12), access to credit facilities (Article 13), and marriage, reproductive choice, and divorce (Article 16). A state is obliged to report on its efforts to meet CEDAW's goals within one year of signing the convention and every four years thereafter.

The Declaration on the Elimination of Violence against Women of 1993 further insists that states should "condemn violence against women and should not invoke any custom, tradition or religious consideration to avoid their obligations with respect to its elimination." The World Summit for Social Development in Copenhagen in 1995 endorsed similar commitments that refer to women's human rights. Most recently, the Beijing Declaration and Platform for Action of 1995 reaffirmed commitments to international human rights standards recognizing "full implementation of the human rights of women and of the girl child as an inalienable, integral and indivisible part of all human rights and fundamental freedoms" (UN 1997).

As of early 2000, 165 United Nations member countries (all but Afghanistan and Islamic Republic of Iran) had ratified the conventions. But again, implementation and enforcement are another matter. Signatory governments are obligated to bring their laws, policies, and practices in line with the provisions of the ratified treaty, but many countries have not followed through (UN 1997). Moreover, many countries have ratified the treaty with reservations, in many cases diluting the standards provided for by the convention.[4]

A Foundation of Equal Rights

Gender equality in rights is an important development goal in its own right. Legal, social, and economic rights provide an enabling environment in which women and men can participate productively in society, attain a basic quality of life, and take advantage of the new opportunities that development affords. Greater equality in rights is also consistently and systematically associated with greater gender equality in education, life expectancy, and political participation—effects independent of income (figure 3.1).

Based on time series data from about 85 countries, figure 3.1 shows the relationship between an index measure of gender rights (Humana 1992) and four indicators of gender inequality. As chapter 1 explains, the gender rights index is an average of three measures pertaining to rights in politics and the law, social and economic matters, and marriage and divorce. Controlling for GDP per capita (in natural logarithm, with a quadratic term, to capture the nonlinearity in the relationship), the multivariate analysis finds a significant positive association between

Figure 3.1   Where Rights Are More Equal, Gender Gaps Are Smaller

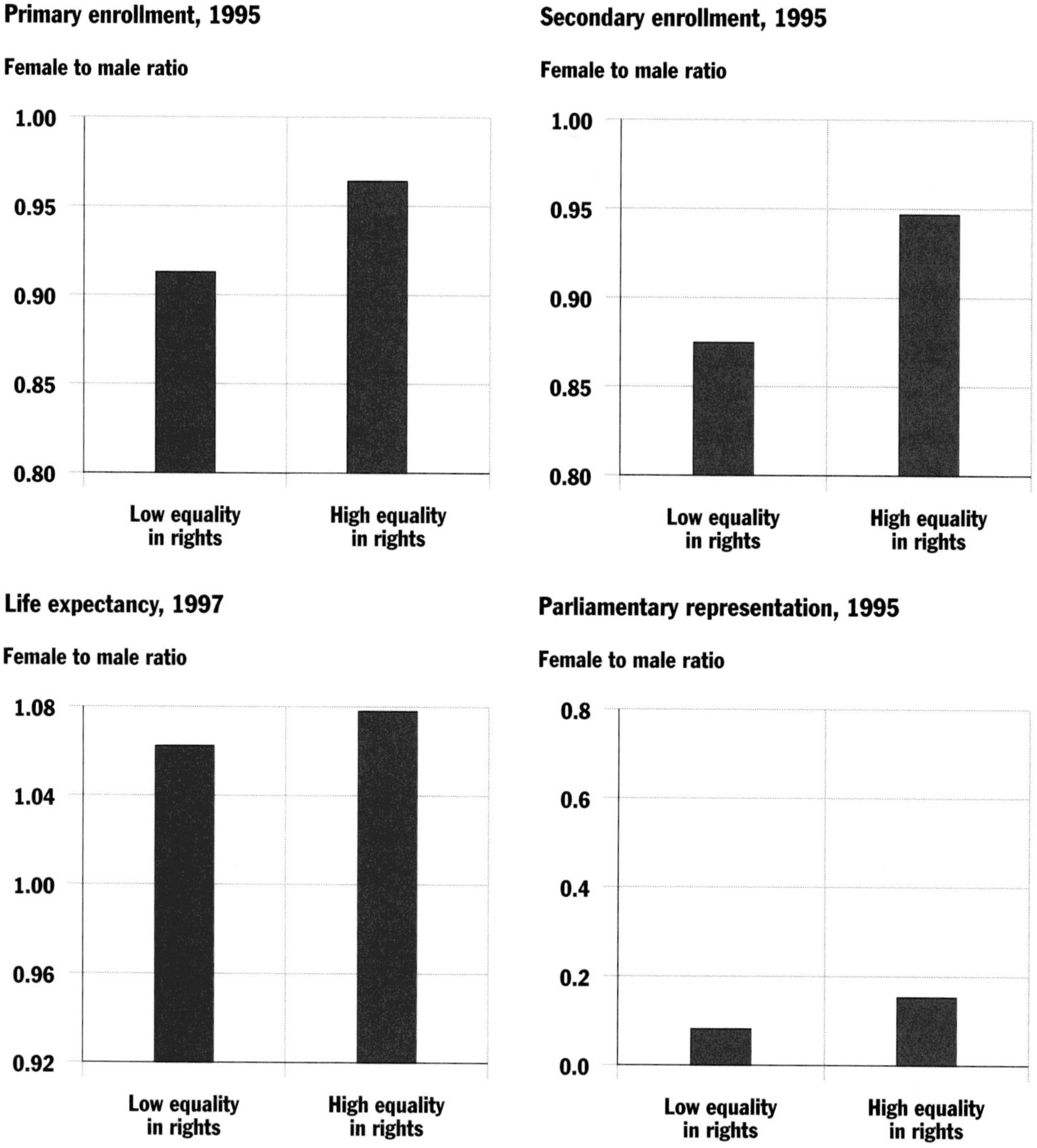

Primary enrollment, 1995

Female to male ratio

Low equality in rights / High equality in rights

Secondary enrollment, 1995

Female to male ratio

Low equality in rights / High equality in rights

Life expectancy, 1997

Female to male ratio

Low equality in rights / High equality in rights

Parliamentary representation, 1995

Female to male ratio

Low equality in rights / High equality in rights

Note: The rights indicator is an average of three indexes of gender equality in rights (equality of political and legal rights for women, equality of social and economic rights for women, and equality of rights for women in marriage and divorce) collected for more than 100 countries by Humana (1992). An average score of 2.33 or less represents low equality in rights, and an average score of 2.67 or greater, high equality. See box 1.1 for description of gender equality in rights indexes, appendix 1 for general notes and included countries, appendix 2 for underlying regression results, and glossary for definitions of ratios.

Sources: Equality in rights data from Humana (1992); parliamentary data from WISTAT (1998); population weights from World Bank (1999d).

gender equality in rights and gender differences in schooling, life expectancy, and political participation.[5]

The countries for which data are available were classified as either "low-equality" or "high-equality" according to the median value of the rights index. The "predicted" value for each country grouping was calculated using the coefficient estimate for rights, while adjusting for the effect of income levels, and taking a population-weighted average. The differences in the gender ratios between the two categories vary across the indicators. For example, for primary education there is a 5 percentage point difference in the gender ratio between low-equality countries and high-equality countries—and a slightly larger difference (7 percentage points) for seats in parliament, representing a near doubling of the ratio.[6]

To improve equality in rights and thus establish the institutional basis for equal protection and opportunity for women and men, significant statutory changes must be taken, especially in family law, protection against gender-related violence, land rights, and political voice. The rest of this section discusses selected legal systems with respect to these areas and the scope for legal reforms. By no means comprehensive, the discussion highlights a few specific points relevant to the role of public policy.

Family law. Family law regulates women's and men's autonomy in and control of family matters—including marriage, divorce, reproductive decisions, child custody, control of conjugal property, and inheritance. It is an area where blatantly unequal rights still prevail (see chapter 1) and where the impact of gender norms and customs is probably most felt. Inequality in family law is particularly contentious because family law pertains to very basic issues of family life—the relationship between husband and wife, the size of a family, and the rights of parents over their children.

Alongside civil statutes, customary laws and religious codes stipulate family rights that may or may not be consistent with the statutory system. The potential effect of statutory reform thus depends on the extent to which it relates to these other legal structures.

For example, Uganda's Divorce Act of 1964 provides for equal rights upon divorce but is silent on division of conjugal property. Customary laws prevail, so women gain access to land through their husband and on widowhood must depend on male relatives for access to land (Gopal and Salim 1998). In Zimbabwe a civil marriage under the Marriage Act is supposed to be a monogamous union, and neither man nor woman can contract a second marriage. But a registered marriage under the

Customary Marriages Act is potentially polygamous—a man may contract other marriages but a woman cannot (Hellum 1998). Like many other countries Uganda and Zimbabwe face contradictions between traditional family forms and norms and the aim of gender equality.

China's Marriage Law of 1950 is an example of how legal reform brought rapid change in traditional norms for the family (Honig 1985; Hooper 1984). With the law the government sought to eliminate arranged marriages, polygyny, bride-price, and child-marriage. Women were given the right to choose their partners, demand a divorce, inherit property, and share control of their children.[7] They were urged to enter the labor force in great numbers—and to make this possible collective dining halls and nurseries were established to relieve women of some household chores. This legal reform is regarded as having played a major part in increasing gender equality in China, but not without cost. Eliciting violent resistance from male peasants and older women, the law is said to have led to several tens of thousands of suicides and murders of women within a few years.[8]

Egypt's New Marriage Contract law enacted in 2000 gives women divorce rights similar to those traditionally given to men. The previous statute gave men the unilateral and unconditional right to divorce their wife, while women faced insurmountable difficulties in obtaining divorce through the court and in enforcing judgments for alimony (Zulficar 1999). The new law came after more than a decade of campaigning by a coalition of government officials, human rights activists, and Muslim scholars who saw no contradiction between the provisions of the new law and Islamic teachings.

Should the state intervene in what many people regard as personal—and thus private—affairs? Changes in family law have direct consequences for the welfare of women and men. Take recent legal reforms in Canada. Before the 1970s women's claims on assets and property upon the dissolution of marriage were limited. Changes in divorce laws in Ontario and British Columbia altered this, improving women's expected settlement upon divorce. A study of annual suicide rates by age group in 1960–94, controlling for unemployment rates, finds a fall in suicide rates for older, married women, coinciding with the reform in the two provinces. It finds no similar declines among men or unmarried women in the two provinces or among older, married women in another province where the divorce laws did not change. The study concludes that the fall in suicide rates was a direct result of the reform in property rights within marriage (Hoddinott and Adam 1998).

Gender-related violence. In many countries laws against gender-related violence contain biases that discriminate against victims or render the laws ineffective. Laws ostensibly intended to address violence against women often define violence very narrowly or entail evidentiary requirements for proving violence that are extremely burdensome (Heise, Pitanguy, and Germain 1994; A. Goldstein 1999). In some Latin American countries the law defines some sexual offenses as crimes only if committed against "honest" women or girls. Laws in Chile and Guatemala exonerate a man who agrees to marry the girl he has raped, as marrying the victim is perceived as restoring her honor (Heise, Pitanguy, and Germain 1994). In Jordan and Pakistan a man who maims or kills his wife to protect his honor receives more lenient punishment, if punished at all, than criminals who commit similar offenses against others. There is thus a need to identify and address the implicit (or explicit) gender biases in existing laws.

In the United States rates of interpersonal violence decrease in response to policies and laws that make violent behavior more costly to the abuser. So, legal reform that strengthens women's rights as victims of violence can make a big difference (Heise, Elsberg, and Gottemoeller 1999). In fact, developed countries have relied heavily on the criminal justice system to achieve this goal—and in response to women's activism, many developing countries have followed suit. Although the legislation varies, most laws include some combination of protective or restraining orders and larger penalties for offenders. Protective orders allow judges to remove an abuser temporarily from the home and to order him to seek counseling, get treatment for substance abuse, and pay maintenance and child support. And if a man violates a protective order, he can be arrested and jailed.

A formidable barrier to protection against gender-related violence is often enforcement. Procedural barriers and the traditional attitudes of law enforcement officials can—and do—undermine the law's ability to deter violence against women (Gopal and Salim 1998; A. Goldstein 1999). Laws are often enforced by male judges, prosecutors, and police officers who may share the abusers' views. Thus, in addition to creating adequate protections under the law, reeducating, and in some cases replacing, the enforcers at different stages of the legal process is critical (A. Goldstein 1999). Legal literacy campaigns and judicial training programs need to do more than focus on abstract human rights guarantees. They need to make clear the extent to which domestic law itself is part of the problem of violence against women. But women too have to be reeducated if the laws are to be effective—about their rights under the law and how to claim those rights (Heise, Elsberg, and Gottemoeller 1999).

Land rights. Land is a very important asset, but women and men do not have equal rights to land in most settings. Evidence from Latin America demonstrates the potential impact of land reform measures, such as land titling and registration, on women's access to land. After Costa Rica's land reform, women represented 45 percent of land titling beneficiaries between 1990 and 1992, compared with 12 percent before the reform. In Colombia, after a ruling on joint titling, land titled jointly to couples made up 60 percent of land adjudications in 1996, compared with 18 percent in 1995. Land titled exclusively to men declined from 63 to 24 percent over the same period (Deere and Leon 1999).

But not all Latin American countries improved gender equality in land rights during their recent reforms.[9] In Bolivia and Ecuador, for example, women's land rights were not raised as major issues in the negotiations that led to new agrarian codes, and there was no movement toward joint titling or the provision of special rights for women. Indeed, a powerful lesson from the experience in Latin American countries is that the intent of statutory reform can be thwarted by failure to consider how social norms and customs interact with the reform. Because past land reform programs stipulated that household heads were to be the direct beneficiaries of the reform and because custom dictated that men are the household heads, there was a real danger that women would lose from such programs (Deere and Leon 1997). But by including provisions for joint titling and for land titles for women when land was distributed to couples in consensual unions, land reform measures in several parts of the region successfully strengthened women's legal rights to land.

Laos offers a similar example of how women could lose their rights to land unless gender-related issues in land titling are addressed. The Forest Law of 1996 and the Land Law of 1997 provide the comprehensive legal framework for land use and ownership rights. Both laws are intended to be gender-neutral in that women are not explicitly excluded from or included in land allocation or titling processes. But in practice, land titling, allocation, and other registration procedures use official forms that ask for the head of household—usually the husband, if he is present. Thus, while custom allows Lao women to inherit land from their parents, as legal documents supplant customary property rights with procedures that exclude women, men are acquiring greater control of land rights at the expense of women (Viravong 1999).

When gender structures of land ownership in customary law prevail, attempts to strengthen land rights solely through statutory law may worsen, rather than improve, women's access to land. In much of

Sub-Saharan Africa conflict between customary and statutory law in land rights is common, exacerbated by interactions with women's social position (Dey Abbas 1997; Kevane and Gray 1996). Women's use rights to land are generally guaranteed through customary channels, but norms against women owning land mean that women are generally denied title to land. Even where local norms give women strong rights to use land, women acquire those rights through men—so these rights are precarious, contingent on a woman's marital status (box 3.2).

In Kenya women have not necessarily gained from the formalization of land rights. Widows can farm, but not own, land registered in their husband's name. The introduction of statutory inheritance laws has endangered widows' entitlement to the use of land. Sons who inherit land legally can sell it without their mother's permission, often leaving widows without a livelihood (Davison 1988).

Land reform programs in Kenya have to navigate overlapping legal systems that reflect differences in the cultural and religious backgrounds of its people—customary law, Islamic law, Hindu law, and statutory and civil law, each with different provisions and restrictions on female property rights. Some customary laws give sons the exclusive right to inherit, while wives and unmarried daughters have the right to be maintained, and married daughters have no claim on their deceased father's property. Islamic law grants widows with children an eighth of property upon their husband's death, while childless widows receive a fourth. Daughters are entitled to half the amount their brothers inherit. Hindu law gives widows the right only to maintenance. But statutory law gives a widow the right to continue living in the matrimonial home and the right to benefit from her husband's assets if her husband named her as a beneficiary to an insurance policy covering the assets (Martin and Hashi 1992).

But in some settings statutory and customary laws may reinforce each other. Among Akan households in Western Ghana the evolution toward individualized land tenure systems has strengthened women's access to land (Quisumbing and others 1999). This has resulted from a practice of men giving gifts of land to their wife in return for planting cocoa trees on the land. With the implementation of the Intestate Succession Law this land can become the legal property of wives, a right traditionally denied them by customary law. Among female-headed households the land gifts account for about 50 percent of land acquired, indicating that the statutory reform can have a large impact on how much land women legally own.

Box 3.2   Land Rights of Women in Africa

THE SOCIAL SYSTEMS OF SUB-SAHARAN AFRICA ARE more heterogeneous than those in much of the rest of the world. African women gain and lose access to land as members of social groups—or through the provision of labor services, through purchases, and through evolutionary changes in statutory and customary law.

Women have had the strongest rights to land in areas where they inherit land under the precepts of Islamic law—in eastern Sudan, among Swahili peasants, and on parts of the Tanzanian coast. Local norms also give strong land rights to women in parts of Western and Central Africa. For example, among the Lemba of Zaire women live in their natal villages after marriage and allow their husbands to use their land.

But in much of Africa women have unequal access to land, gaining rights chiefly through marriage.

- In Sahelian West Africa women are granted rights to use land controlled by their husband's lineage, but lose these rights upon divorce, widowhood, or relocation. Plots may not be alienated without permission from the lineage head.

- In East Africa, under the "house-property" system, a husband allocates land and cattle to each of his wives. While a woman's land rights do not depend on her husband's goodwill, they do depend on having sons and on the goodwill of those sons. If a widow dies without a son her deceased husband's kin inherit her property.

- Land tenure systems in Southern Africa are more complex. While some areas give strong rights to women, men generally control the land. Married women obtain land rights from their husband and keep them as long as the marriage endures. But they are likely to lose these rights when widowed, except in isolated examples of female control and statutory laws favoring women, as in Zimbabwe.

- In isolated parts of Africa matrilineal inheritance prevails. But even though lineage and property are traced through the mother's line, men own and control the property. So, women's rights to land are not necessarily more secure under the matrilineal system. Indeed, a widow can lose her land rights to her deceased husband's family quite easily. Among the Akan of Ghana a widow may lose her land rights to her dead husband's brothers, or to his sister's son.

Sources: Kevane and Gray (1996); Lastarria-Cornhiel (1997).

And in South Africa where custom stresses "universal access to land and to other factors of subsistence [and] priority of use so that families with more land than they can use should transfer it to the land-hungry" (Jacobs 1998, p. 81), the government has chosen an innovative way of dealing with the complexities of rural land tenure and gender inequalities. Recognizing that land titling through market mechanisms could formally leave women with less access to land than under customary law, the government passed the Communal Property Association Act in 1996, which allows individuals to acquire land through membership in a communal property association. It is too early to tell whether this innovation will indeed protect women's access to land, but it is a case worth watching.

Participation and voice. The right to engage in public debate, the right to vote, and the right to run for public office are rights that many people now take for granted. Nearly all countries now give both women and men the right to elect political leaders. But this has not always been the case—even in principle. Even in more developed countries this right has existed for less than a century (except in New Zealand, which gave women the right to vote in 1893, followed closely by Australia in 1901), mirroring the persistent limitations on women's other rights.

In many developing countries equal voting rights came with independence—but in two countries, Kuwait and the United Arab Emirates, the right to vote is still given just to men. In many countries colonial interests and racial and ethnic prejudice prevented both men and women in indigenous and minority groups from voting long after women in the majority group gained the right to vote. This was the case in Australia, Canada, and South Africa, among others. And in several countries educational or property requirements excluded a large majority of women from the polls. In Portugal women were given the right to vote in 1931, but only to women who had completed at least secondary education—whereas men only had to be literate. This differential requirement was revoked nearly 20 years later. Many other countries have imposed literacy requirements on voting rights, as Bolivia, Syrian Arab Republic, and Zimbabwe; and property requirements, as in the Bahamas and Kenya (WISTAT 1998; Sokoloff and Engerman 2000).[10]

Most countries gave women the right to be elected to public office even later than they gave them the right to vote, and this right often was given under various restrictions. For example, Greece allowed women to vote in 1930—but to stand for office in municipal and communal elections only in 1949 and at the national level in 1952 (WISTAT 1998).

As chapter 1 shows, women, on average, make up less than 10 percent of seats in parliament in developing regions (except in East Asia). But some countries have made noteworthy efforts to increase women's representation in government through legal reforms. In India two constitutional amendments in 1992 required that at least a third of the seats in *panchayats* (or local councils) and municipal councils—and the same proportion of chairpersons—be reserved for women. Within the first two years of implementation more than 350,000 women had political positions (Sen 2000). And more women are getting out to vote.

Uganda, too, has taken several steps to increase women's involvement in politics, including reserving official positions for women within the local administrative structures and in district representation in the legislature. The result: many more women in government. Since 1989 women have occupied 18 percent of National Assembly seats, higher than in many industrial countries (Ahikire 1994; Goetz 1998). And in the Philippines a "party list system" was established in the early 1990s with the intention of increasing the number of seats for women (and such interest groups as farmers) in the House of Representatives (NCRFW 1999). This has had a visible impact on such gender-related policies as protection from domestic violence and women's reproductive rights—but whether this provision will continue to result in a net gain in female representation remains to be seen.

Economic Institutions

BESIDES A COUNTRY'S LEGAL FRAMEWORK, ECONOMIC institutions influence the resources to which women and men have access, the activities they can undertake, and the ways in which they can participate in the economy. Economic institutions pertain to markets and hierarchies that have sets of rules governing transactions and influencing decisionmaking about consumption, savings, investment, work, and reproduction. And like legal systems they reflect prevailing social norms and customs, including gender structures that discriminate against women:

- Apparently gender-neutral practices in the labor market, such as hiring only workers who can work full-time during set hours, effectively shut out mothers who need flexible hours. They contribute to perpetuating a sharp division of labor in the home.
- Information networks about job opportunities are typically centered around formal organizations, public or private. This makes information more accessible to people already associated with those organizations, usually leaving out more women than men.
- Undeveloped health insurance markets usually leave women without access to health insurance or only through spouses employed in formal sector jobs. And the absence of a formal old-age security system, coupled with unequal rights to property, forces women to rely primarily on male relatives for support in old age.

• Credit markets that require ownership of land or house to secure loans are out of reach for women who do not or cannot own land independently—or who lack social or business networks. Such women need their husband or other male relatives to co-sign loans, making it more difficult for women to establish or maintain viable business enterprises (Fafchamps 2000).

But gender stratification in markets and hierarchies is often more explicit and deliberate than these examples imply. In the land market property rights laws determine who can possess land and who can buy and sell property. In the labor market employers who believe that all women workers will eventually leave the labor force to get married or have children—or always allow family responsibilities to interrupt their work—often deny women work. The result: even when education and work experience are accounted for, women are relatively restricted to lower-paying, low-skill occupations, while men are freer to find employment in a wider range of occupations.[11]

Prejudice and limited access to information networks also help explain why women workers are overwhelmingly underrepresented in managerial and administrative jobs across the world. Hiring and promotion practices, management hierarchies, and information networks constitute the internal culture within such organizations as private firms and government bureaucracies. Discriminatory attitudes within firms raise invisible barriers, the "glass ceiling," to promotions for women, keeping them from top management positions (box 3.3). This internal culture reflects norms and customs in the broader society. But organizations, particularly large, long-standing ones, may also have developed their own mix of standards and incentives that regulate worker behavior and performance.

Neoclassical economic theory views discrimination as a self-correcting phenomenon, one that embodies the seed of its own demise. The argument: as markets develop and thicken, competitive pressures rise. This change is supposed to make it more costly for individuals and firms to discriminate (Becker 1971). In the long run discriminating employers are driven out, and overall discrimination is expected to fall. In contrast, markets that are protected and overregulated are more likely to breed discriminatory behavior, as those individuals with greater power are better able to impose their personal preferences on the market and to influence policies to their advantage.

Box 3.3   The "Glass Ceiling"

THE INTERNAL CULTURE OF FIRMS AND government bureaucracies generally reflects—and perpetuates—norms and customs that prevail in broader society or in segments of society. Within such organizations invisible barriers to promotion create a "glass ceiling" that bars women from top management positions (see figure).

Gender concerns enter organizations in various ways. One is through hiring policies, including recruitment practices, job assignment, and salary decisions. A second pathway is through bias in promotion policies and practices. The two ways are linked since new hires form the labor pool or "pipeline" for higher-level posts.

Women's career paths often block progress to top positions. If they are hired only in dead-end jobs or in nonstrategic positions—rather than in professional and line management jobs that have well-defined promotion ladders—the top positions are likely to be out of reach. Indeed, "glass walls" are also an issue if women cannot move laterally into such strategic areas as product development and corporate finance and are restricted to personnel management, research, and labor relations (ILO 1997).

A third way for gender concerns to enter organizations is through the firm's informal culture, as reflected by gender norms in its hierarchies, social networks, and information channels. Even women who break through the glass walls and ceilings often encounter glass barriers of traditions, preconceptions, and biases that keep them out of the "old boys' club" of senior managers and away from decisionmaking. Women may also be subjected to sexual innuendoes and other forms of sexual harassment by male co-workers.

While there is evidence to support this discrimination model, it is nevertheless simplistic and incomplete. Many industries, even mature ones, are not highly competitive—not only in developing countries but also in industrial ones. Indeed, monopoly power is pervasive. In many countries a large proportion of skilled jobs are found in government and in monopolistic state-owned enterprises (Birdsall and Sabot 1991). And as long as there are large employers with sufficient resources, stable wage differentials can coexist with greater competition. In addition, in times of economic decline when jobs are fewer, the cost of discrimination declines, allowing employers to hire those they prefer without offering a higher wage (Mueser 1987).

Another model explaining why discrimination persists in the economy stresses information problems. While some employers discriminate out of prejudice, others may discriminate because they lack information about worker productivity, leaving them to rely on stereotypes about gender, race, age, and school credentials when hiring. At the firm level this view implies that as information about a worker becomes more available and more accurate, such as when tenure in a job increases, promotion and pay would be adjusted according to the overall compensation structure in the firm. Economywide this view implies that discrimination in the marketplace will decrease as information markets develop, making the acquisition of information cheaper for any one employer.

But these competition and information models underestimate the influence of social norms and customs on individual and group behaviors. Who works well with whom and under what circumstances matters within enterprises because this determines productivity and thus profitability (Williamson 1975). Further, social networks overlay business relationships, creating durable connections even among apparently competing employers (Granovetter 1985). These connections not only reduce the cost of discriminatory behavior—they sustain it.

But caution is warranted when attributing gender wage and employment gaps to discrimination in the labor market: discrimination by employers or other workers does not explain all of these observed gender gaps. Gender gaps also stem from norms and traditions that encourage families to confine women's work to the home. And traditional views about the appropriate role of women encourage households to invest less in girls' schooling or women's training—thus restricting girls' and women's mobility and preventing them from transacting business independently outside the home. Household decisions and behaviors are discussed in the next chapter.

Regulation in the Labor Market

Countries have used active legal or regulatory measures to address various gender issues in the labor market. Some states have been activists, regulating directly firms' hiring and firing decisions, workers' compensation, and labor relations more generally. Some states have established support for care activities and some are addressing the gender implications of their pension system. This section reviews evidence on the direction of regulatory change in the labor market and whether formal sector interventions have been beneficial in absolute and relative terms for women and men.

Equal pay. Many countries have adopted legislation that ensures equal treatment for women and men in the workplace. Equal pay for equal work legislation, for example, aims to "level the playing field" for women and men in labor markets by requiring employers to provide equal pay for workers performing the same job with equal efficiency, regardless of gender.

The policy has been successful in such countries as Australia, Canada, Greece, and New Zealand, where female pay has been typically prescribed in collective agreements as a percentage of the male wage for a similar task, or when centralized wage-setting mechanisms are in place (Tzannatos 1999). Evidence is mixed in the United Kingdom, according to a comparison of the gender pay gap of two cohorts of workers, since it is difficult to separate the effect of improvements in women's human capital from the effect of the equal pay laws (Makepeace and others 1999). The European Union has endorsed "measures to ensure the application of the principle of equal opportunities and equal treatment of men and women in matters of employment and occupation, including the principle of equal pay for equal work or work of equal value" for its member countries (as cited in Heide 1999, p. 383). This legislation has apparently led to revisions of domestic law in its member states, and individual cases challenging national rules and practice have contributed to clarifying the law and increasing the effectiveness of the supranational instruments.

Equal pay legislation has had less impact in the United States, where wage setting is more decentralized. It would also have less impact in countries where there is gender segregation in employment and where the principle of similar or like work does not apply. In such cases gender wage gaps may be driven by employment segregation, with occupations dominated by women paying less, not by unequal pay for the same kind of work—although this explains only a small proportion of the wage gap, as discussed in chapter 1. Among developing countries published evidence on the effect of equal pay laws is very limited.

More recently the traditional equal pay concept has been replaced by comparable worth policies. These policies are distinct from equal pay for equal work policies because pay comparisons are made not only between jobs with similar titles but also between jobs with similar content, regardless of title, and jobs that are distinct in that one may be largely male-dominated and the other largely female-dominated. The comparisons pertain to the requirements of the job, not performance in it—and usually involve weighting and scoring job requirements such as skill, responsibility, and effort level (England 1999). In the United States studies of the impact of comparative worth policies suggest that they have increased women's relative pay in two states by 6–10 percent (Sorensen 1990 as cited in World Bank 1994c). Critics of these policies argue that requiring employers to raise the wage in female-dominated occupations would decrease hiring in those jobs. This is an area that requires more study, especially in the few developing countries that have adopted similar policies but have not yet assessed impact.

Can developing countries enforce and benefit from equal pay policies? One lesson from the experience in wealthier countries is that the administrative responsibility associated with implementation and enforcement is quite heavy. In Canada, the Netherlands, and the United Kingdom specialized intermediary or enforcement agencies are required to apply these policies. A second consideration is that the potential of applying these policies is largely limited to the formal sector; thus their relevance depends on the relative size of a country's formal and informal sectors.

Another concern is that equal pay laws can displace women from jobs—unless equal opportunity laws also ensure that women have access to new opportunities. But the net effect of these two types of policies on women is uncertain. The Republic of Korea's Gender Equal Employment Act of 1987 created new opportunities for women in higher paying professional and technical jobs (Rodgers 1999). It requires firms to provide equal opportunities for women in such areas as recruitment, hiring, job placement, training, and promotion. But while the law led to employment gains for women, it did not necessarily help women break into administrative and managerial positions. Neither did it improve their earnings relative to men's by as much as their education and experience would warrant, despite equal pay policies.

Special protection and affirmative action. Many countries have addressed gender discrimination in the labor market through special protection measures and affirmative action. Many governments have labor laws that protect women's time with newborns after childbirth and limit women's exposure to strenuous or hazardous activities. While these laws may have benefits, their costs are often borne by the same women they protect. By raising the cost to employers of hiring women, they reduce women's employment or wages.

The traditional approach has been to protect women against unreasonable hours and types of work. Laws have excluded women from such sectors as construction and mining, considered hazardous occupations. Working hour restrictions were popular in Europe and the United States during their industrialization period (Goldin 1988; Nataraj, Rodgers, and Zveglich 1998). Most Asian countries have overtime limits that apply to both men and women. The strictest policies are in South Asia, where women's overtime work is forbidden.

By decreasing women's employment and hours worked, restrictions in Taiwan, China, slowed women's earnings growth (Zveglich and Rodgers 1999). Without the special protection law male earnings would have increased 12 percent while female earnings would have increased 5 percent. With the law male earnings grew close to predicted levels but female earnings grew only 0.6 percent, widening gender pay differences more than would have occurred without a protective measure.

Many protection measures are responses to pressure from interest groups. As with basic human rights, the international community, in collaboration with national interests, has promoted special protection in the labor market.[12] But recently there has been a shift away from protective measures, a change influenced by women's organizations (World Bank 1994c).

Whether a special protection mandate benefits women depends on several things. Foremost is who bears the cost of the mandate. In labor markets the degree to which the cost is borne by employers or can be shifted to the government or to women themselves determines the size of its potentially negative employment effect. If wages can be adjusted downward to reflect the cost of the mandate to employers, the cost of employing the targeted group does not have to increase—and there should be no adverse employment effect. But if the primary intent of the mandate is to promote gender equality by shifting some of the cost of childbirth away from women, the wage adjustment subverts that intent.

Now consider affirmative action policies. Some believe that equal opportunity policies are not enough to redress the effects of past (and present) discrimination and that affirmative action policies—policies designed to reduce specific inequalities across groups through the use of group-specific quantitative targets and measures that help meet these targets—will fill the void. More analysis of the impact of such policies is clearly needed in both developed and developing countries, but measuring their impact is not easy—for several reasons. One is that a central mandate is likely to apply to all workers, offering few controls or comparison groups, and with the exceptions differing systematically in ways that bias the attempts to compare them. Another is that enforcement may be weak (Leonard 1996). In the United States several assessments of the federal antidiscrimination policy known as Title VII yield different conclusions. Some attribute the dramatic narrowing of the gender wage gap between 1980 and 1990 to Title VII (Smith and Welch 1984; Fields and Wolff 1997), but others attribute it to an increase in the average tenure of women on the job during the decade (Smith and Ward 1989; Leonard 1996).

Affirmative action policies cause controversy mainly because of the fear that preferential treatment in hiring for a job or for admission into a school or training post compromises quality and efficiency (Holzer and Neumark 1999). There is controversy even within the groups targeted by these policies: being marked for preference can mean being perceived as poorly qualified—and can breed resentment among those not so preferred.

But affirmative action programs in employment can do more than impose a quota on hires, the element that attracts the most resentment. They can also influence a wide variety of activities by employers— special recruitment efforts, special assistance programs (such as training), changes in screening practices, and changes in hiring, pay, and promotion standards.[13] In the United States survey data from firms in four cities showed that these programs indeed change the hiring and training practices of employers.

Although these programs have been the subject of considerable political debate, they have increased female and minority employment and occupational status (see, for example, Leonard 1985, 1996; Rodgers and Spriggs 1996; and Holzer and Neumark 1998, 1999). Moreover, despite concerns about reverse discrimination and productivity costs of the programs, there is little empirical evidence that affirmative action hires are less productive than other workers. On the contrary, the main costs to employers in the United States appear to be one-time costs associated with upgrading recruits' skills rather than ongoing efficiency costs from the employment of less productive workers. In fact, such programs may well lead to productivity gains for firms and the economy (Holzer and Neumark 1998, 1999).

A primary weakness of affirmative action is its limited scope in societies where most employment continues to be in agriculture or in the informal sector—or where government monitoring and enforcement capabilities are weak. The implication is that the scope for such policies expands with urbanization and the formalization of labor markets.

Family support. Women spend much more time in nonmarket and care activities than men—and these activities impose costs on their leisure, health status, paid employment, and autonomy. Recognizing these costs, many countries now have legislation that supports the reproductive roles of women, although it is sometimes ineffective and sometimes has adverse effects on women. Consider two types of legislation: maternity benefits and support for child care.

Maternity leave. Most developing countries have maternity leave legislation. The benefits often include paid leave at some fraction of previous earnings, protection against dismissal during the leave, paid nursing breaks, and mandatory postnatal leave of a given duration. In Africa nearly all countries provide paid maternity benefits to formal sector workers, typically with compensation rates of 50–100 percent—in principle. Maternity leave varies from 30 days in Tunisia to 15 weeks in the Republic of Congo, with the average at 12–14 weeks. In Latin America and the Caribbean maternity benefits vary from 8 weeks in the Bahamas to 18 weeks in Chile, Cuba, and República Bolivariana de Venezuela. Maternity leave in Asia tends to be at least 12 weeks, often fully compensated and funded by employers (Rodgers 1999).[14]

Besides the health benefit for mothers and their newborns, maternity leave helps women avoid exiting the workforce temporarily and later having to find new employment. Not having to leave employment after childbirth can boost women's wages by increasing their job tenure and overall work experience (Rodgers 1999). But maternity leave also entails costs for women, particularly if employers are expected to bear most or all of the cost of maternity leave. Part (or all of) the costs may be passed to women in lower wages or in decreased hiring of women of childbearing age.

What has been the impact of these policies? In Japan and the United States more women with maternity benefits returned to work after childbirth than women without these benefits (Gruber 1994; Waldfogel, Higuchi, and Abe 1998). But since these women also lost ground in wages in the United States the net gains are not clear.[15] In Western European countries, which have much more generous paid maternity benefits, the effects depend on the duration of the leave. During 1969–93 rights to short periods (three months) of paid parental leave increased the employment ratio by 3 to 4 percent while having little effect on wages. More extended leave entitlements (nine months) increased the employment ratio by about 4 percent but reduced hourly wages by about 3 percent (Ruhm 1998). In Taiwan, China, mandated maternity benefits have expanded women's employment but have had a negative (though not statistically significant) effect on wages (Zveglich and Rodgers 1999). In contrast, following legislation to lengthen maternity leave in Costa

Rica, women's wages fell significantly, but employment did not change (Gindling and Crummet 1997).

Costa Rica also illustrates that how a mandate is funded influences its effectiveness. The government's Social Security Administration covers half the cost of maternity benefits, thus shifting some of the cost away from employers and women—and perhaps explaining why there was no negative effect on employment, though not why wages fell. Another option would be to share costs by expanding insurance coverage to pay for at least a fraction of maternity benefits. While this would likely increase the health insurance premium paid by men and women (since most married couples are likely to share a family plan), it would also lighten the cost incurred solely by women.

Support for child care. A number of developing countries require that firms provide support for child care—or that the state does. Low-cost child care allows mothers to work without breaks in employment. As with maternity leave benefits child care is supposed to reduce work interruptions and the toll they take on accumulated work experience, promotion possibilities, and future earnings. Different countries provide different modes of child care assistance—legislation providing for paid paternity leave, outright public provision of child care, income transfers to families or specifically to mothers to cover the cost of child care services, and wage subsidies to mothers if they remain in the labor force. Depending on specific conditions the different modes each have a benefit-cost calculus.

How do the richer countries support child care? They vary widely in the amount of publicly provided or publicly subsidized child care for working parents. Greece, Ireland, Italy, the Netherlands, Spain, and the United Kingdom have a family-based system with relatively low levels of child care provision. Austria and Germany have a dearth of such services for children under three. But Belgium, Denmark, Finland, France, and Sweden have well-developed child care systems (Plantenga 1999).

Lack of child care services can be a major obstacle to women's labor force participation, as the next chapter discusses. In Russia simulations of the effect of a full subsidy of child care costs show that reducing the out-of-pocket costs to zero increases women's labor force participation by 12 percent and their hours of work by 3 percent (Lokshin 2000). Alternatively, a wage subsidy to all working mothers that would cost the government the same as a child care subsidy would increase labor force participation by less than 6 percent and hours of work by less than 1

133

percent. A full subsidy to child care allows mothers to earn an additional 0.50 ruble per ruble spent by the state, while the wage subsidy increases mothers' earnings by an additional 0.24 ruble.

Old-age support systems. Old-age support systems are not directly related to discrimination in the labor market, but market failures give rise to the problem of social security. Informal community and family arrangements are the mainstay of social security in most developing countries. Most elderly people live in extended family arrangements with their children, and this is more common for women than men (Wong and Parker 1999; Cox-Edwards 2000). Elderly men and women who live apart from their children often depend on interhousehold transfers for support. This is evident from the pronounced life-cycle patterns of private interhousehold transfers. In both developing and industrial countries private transfers are generally targeted to women. In Colombia, for example, being female raises the probability of transfer receipts by almost 33 percentage points (Cox and Jimenez 1998).

Modernization, urbanization, and migration have weakened traditional and informal old-age support systems. And mandatory formal security programs could hasten the process—without providing the safety net needed by those not covered by employment-based systems.[16] Market solutions, such as individual saving and investing for old age, may help fill the gaps left by the breakdown of family support systems, but these are subject to market failures. Individuals could be shortsighted and unwilling to save for their old age when they are young. They may lack information about capital markets and investment. These conditions argue for public action in reforming social security systems—action that explicitly takes account of the different circumstances of women and men and of the family-based, informal mechanisms.

Recognizing the significance of an extensive old-age security system to poverty reduction and overall social welfare, most countries have established formal safety nets for the elderly. But only about 15 percent of the world's 6 billion people have access to a formal system of retirement income support (World Bank 1994b). Social security coverage in developing countries tends to be concentrated in the public sector and in large private sector firms. Pension participation is related to gender, marital status, education, age, occupation, income level, formality of employment, and household composition—and women are less likely than men to participate in pension plans (Bertranou 1998).

There are several reasons for this: women's lower average education, lower labor force participation, more transient employment, and greater likelihood of working in the informal sector or for small employers who cannot afford social security benefits. If women are affiliated with a social security system they are likely to contribute for fewer years. Low-income workers, many of whom are women, often prefer higher take-home pay to future benefits. Any employment-related system thus offers lower annual benefits for women. Under privately managed security systems that usually ignore those with limited experience or high mobility, women are clearly at a disadvantage.

In recent years a number of countries have reformed their pension schemes, moving away from traditional pay-as-you-go defined benefit systems that could not be sustained financially because of the excessively high costs associated with growing elderly populations and associated old-age dependency ratios (World Bank 1994b). Often reforms have replaced these old systems with multipillar systems that include a fully-funded defined contribution pillar (in which retirees get back their accumulated contributions plus interest) and a redistributive public pillar, such as a minimum pension guarantee or a flat (uniform) benefit to all eligible workers.

Depending on the details of the old and new systems, these reforms can increase income inequality between older men and women. Moreover, they greatly alter how different groups of women fare. Why? Because the old systems often gave generous benefits to women and men who contributed only for short periods, including those from middle-income families, whereas the new systems tie benefits more closely to contributions in the defined contribution pillar while redistributing to low earners through the public pillar. And the new systems tend to penalize early retirees while the old systems subsidized them—and women often retire early.[17]

Detailed simulations for Chile, the first country to implement a multipillar system, indicate that on average women's pensions will fall in the new system and will do so relative to men's pensions—because women work for fewer years, earn lower wages, and therefore make smaller contributions. But this drop will be unevenly distributed among women. It is almost nonexistent for primary and secondary school graduates who have full labor force participation and who continue working until the male retirement age of 65. The relative position of women with lower incomes—the chief recipients of the redistributive minimum pension guarantee—will rise. Widows, too, will gain because they are protected by the joint annuity that their husbands must provide, in addition to their own pension. Nonworking women will be protected by the means-tested, noncontributory social assistance program. But those who do not meet the means test—be they nonworking women or women with few working years—will lose under the new system (Cox-Edwards 2000).

Thus, the public pillar is particularly important from a gender perspective because it can be a poverty reduction and redistributive mechanism. In Mexico the government offers a minimum pension guarantee and also contributes a "social quota"—a flat proportion of the minimum wage—to each person's pension account. These provisions protect the welfare of low-income and less-educated groups. For example, women with five years of schooling or less living in semiurban areas can expect an annuity of 80 percent of the minimum wage with the guarantee and the social quota, but only 30 percent of the minimum wage without these protections. The impact of this safety net is much larger for women than for men. The share of the public pillar in the expected annuity is 61 percent for women but only 32 percent for men (Wong and Parker 1999).

Finally, in systems requiring more years at work, relatively few women will receive this benefit. Chile and Mexico require only 20 years of contributions to be eligible for the minimum pension, whereas Argentina requires 30 years to be eligible for the flat (uniform) pension that it pays in its public pillar. In some industrialized countries the public pillar is based on residence and age rather than on employment, and is financed out of general revenues. The Netherlands offers a generous flat benefit, the United Kingdom a much less generous basic benefit, and Australia a broad means-tested benefit that excludes only the richest third of the income distribution. These arrangements reduce pension disparities between men and women—but they are expensive, one reason why they are rarely found in developing countries. More targeted public pillars, as in Chile or Mexico, are very helpful to women with low incomes. But for the majority of women, lower earnings and fewer work years will still translate into lower pensions.

Regulation in the informal sector. In general, labor market laws and regulations can contribute to improving equality in employment, working conditions, and compensation for women and men. But the impact is limited in most developing countries by the large number of workers beyond the reach of formal regulations. Many workers are employed in the informal sector—generally in family enterprises or in small and frequently unregistered firms. The size of the informal sector tends to be larger in less developed countries, exacerbating the problem of ineffective labor laws, and smaller in more developed countries. For example, the informal sector employs about three-quarters of workers in Burkina Faso and only about a quarter in Argentina (World Bank 1995).

It is generally claimed that women are predominantly employed in the informal sector—but data belie this, if available cross-country data are to be believed. Using the official definition of informal sector employment—which includes a continuum of employment, from seasonal, small-scale, home-based self-employment to full-time wage employment in enterprises employing fewer than 5 or 10 employees, depending on the country's official definition—women account for a disproportionately larger share of informal sector employment in only about a half of the countries for which data are presented in figure 3.2. We arrive at this conclusion by comparing women's share of the informal sector labor force with their share of the total labor force. Hence, while women account for 40 percent of the informal sector labor force in Mali and a little more than 40 percent in Brazil, women are not concentrated in the informal sector in Mali but they are in Brazil.

This is similar to the conclusion by Charmes (1998) that women are not systematically overrepresented in the informal sector. But obtaining accurate data about the size of the informal sector is tremendously difficult—the reported numbers are undoubtedly underestimated, especially for women who are more likely to be employed in the more invisible home-based informal sector or for whom work in the informal sector may be a secondary employment.

In most countries the full range of labor laws does not apply to informal sector workers—and even when it does, enforcement is weak and spotty at best. In only a few countries do labor laws provide extensive rights to informal sector workers. Brazil's Federal Constitution of 1988 broadened coverage to domestic, household, and agricultural workers, providing for minimum wage setting, a thirteenth-month paycheck, compensation for a weekly rest period, annual paid vacation, paid maternity leave of 120 days, paid paternity leave, social security benefits, and a month's notice of termination (World Bank 1994c). And the penalties for violating these laws are similar to those for the formal sector. Honduras, too, has special provisions governing domestic workers, piece-rate workers, and home-based workers, although less extensive than in Brazil.

Figure 3.2 Women's Presence in the Informal Labor Market Varies across Countries

Women's share in the informal sector is...

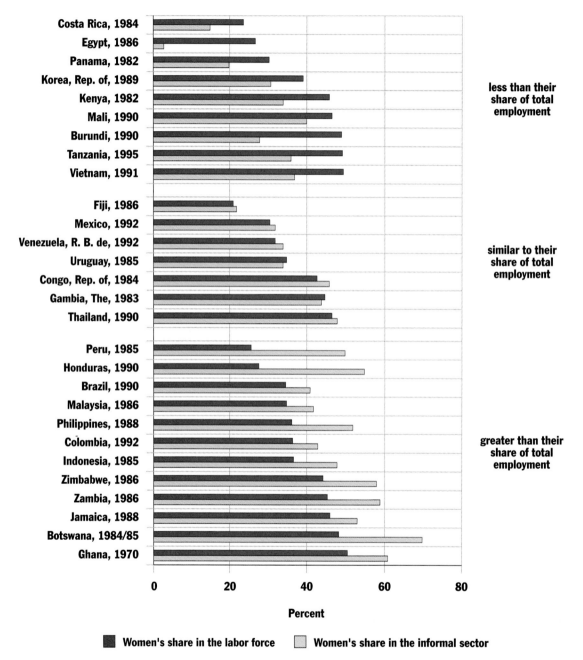

Note: The informal sector consists of small-scale and household-based enterprises producing and distributing goods and services outside the recognized regulatory framework. These enterprises generally lack legal recognition and may not be subject to labor and other standards prescribed by the legal code.

Sources: Informal sector data from Sethuraman (1998); labor force data from World Bank (1999d).

Other laws and regulations affect small-scale self-employment—with their own explicit or implicit gender bias. These include laws that regulate entry into business, access to credit, and tax allocations. Credit institutions that require traditional forms of collateral are likely to exclude women as borrowers since on average women are less likely than men to own property. Also, provisions about minimum loan sizes and restrictions regarding the type of business that qualifies for a loan make it more difficult for women to borrow financial capital (Honig 1998). And complicated application procedures in starting a business, capital requirements, and required political contacts can prevent women from registering enterprises.

In many countries tax deductions, exemptions, and other tax preferences in individual tax filing systems are often assigned to husbands—with deterrent effects on incentives for women to establish a business (Stotsky 1997). In the Netherlands until 1984, a married man was entitled to a larger tax-free allowance than a married woman. In Jordan when a husband and wife file separately, certain deductions are available only to the husband (unless the husband requests differently). In Zimbabwe a married man who is a sole earner is entitled to a special credit—but a married woman who is a sole earner is not.

Is regulation in the informal sector the answer for reducing gender inequalities there? The informal sector in developing countries accounted for roughly half of the total official labor force in 1998—ranging from 54 percent in Sub-Saharan Africa to 49 percent in Latin America and the transition economies in Europe and Central Asia and 46 percent in Asia (Schneider 2000). But this share is not fixed; it depends in part on the level of restrictions imposed on the formal sector. An analysis of cross-country evidence concludes that the size of the informal sector is larger the higher the tax rates and the more numerous the regulations in the formal economy. And perhaps even more important than laws and regulations is the ineffective and discretionary application of tax rates and regulations (Johnson, Kaufmann, and Zoido-Lobaton 1998). Within the informal sector more government restrictions could trigger a shift to even more hidden enterprises, making it harder to monitor gender disparities. Imposing more regulations is thus not necessarily the appropriate means for increasing gender equality. And unless regulations are implemented and enforced effectively—a huge challenge in what is sometimes referred to as the "hidden" or "shadow" economy—regulatory change is not likely to have any impact.

Institutional Change: What Does It Take?

WHAT STANDS IN THE WAY OF INSTITUTIONAL CHANGE TO promote gender equality? Raising this question is necessary if we are to sharpen the focus of policy and action—but it is difficult to answer fully and nearly impossible to address completely with policy. Yes, legal reforms of the types discussed in this chapter have brought about substantial changes in the institutional fabric of many societies—by mandating change that signals commitment to gender equality, by establishing incentives that make equality more appealing, by imposing penalties that make discrimination more costly. And yes, targeted laws and regulations have improved the conditions for workers, men and women, in labor markets, even as these regulatory instruments continue to adjust in response to broad economic changes and ideological shifts in the international environment. But there are also many potential pitfalls for policy. And the burden of reform does not belong only to the state and bureaucracies—it is best shared by more groups in society.

Promise and Pitfalls of Central Mandates

If laws are to be reformed, three aspects of the legal framework have to be kept in mind. First, in many developing countries individual rights are derived not from one legal system but from several—statutory, customary, and religious—that exist side by side. Those systems can mutually reinforce or contradict each other with respect to the rights that women and men can claim, resulting in legal ambiguities, social tension, and noncompliance (Gopal and Salim 1998). Many countries have attempted statutory reforms to improve gender equality, and formal procedures for changing statutes (and for distinguishing and overriding case law) are well established. But reconciling contradictory statutes and customary law continues to perplex and challenge. The earlier example of Kenya illustrates that customary laws often have their own dynamic, at times thwarting the intent of statutory reform.

While there are real benefits from establishing a unified legal framework, there are also real risks in formalizing rules that ignore the norms and customs of different parts of society. And it may be impossible for one set of rules to take into account wide diversity of laws within a population. In such cases customary law may be the effective system of rules governing the behavior of less powerful groups. These considerations imply that statutory reform is not necessarily the best or the only vehicle to ensure gender equality in a country's legal framework.

Second, statutory law does not necessarily reflect social consensus. In fact, its legitimacy may come not from a majority vote but from a powerful minority. It may also be effective mainly in formal transactions or formal relations, and thus practically irrelevant to large sections of the population. The question then is, will statutory reform improve the conditions of the majority or will it simply codify the dominant position of the minority? For while statutory reform can indeed ignite broader social change that benefits the majority, the very same process can also be used to legitimize inequalities.

Third, customary laws are dynamic, flexible, and responsive to environmental factors. As seen in customary land tenure systems, demographic pressure (such as from population growth) as well as economic change can lead to adjustment (Migot-Adholla and others 1991). Recent increases in land values in Burkina Faso, for example, have expanded women's access to nonhousehold land. Landowners, unwilling to lease untilled land to men who might claim greater rights to the land through use, have been more willing to lease their land to women farmers, contrary to traditional practice (Kevane and Gray 1999).

Even if a country were able to pass laws that support gender equality, there are still no guarantees of progress. Laws are ineffective unless they are clear, focused, and unambiguously phrased. And even more important are supportive institutions and personnel to implement and enforce those laws—if equality in principle is to be translated into equality in fact. Without explicit enforcement mechanisms the law has no impact. And in an institutional environment in which support for the law is missing, enforcement of gender equality in rights may be lost amid the deeper and broader problems of governance and participation.

For example, the Labor Standards Law of Taiwan, China, which restricts women's work hours and requires employers to provide maternity benefits, had little impact on hours worked or female employment until three years later, after the government created a cabinet-level enforcement structure (Zveglich and Rodgers 1999). Similarly, changes in Costa Rica's legislation to lengthen maternity leave had little positive impact on employment until the government improved enforcement and imposed stricter penalties on firms that violated the law (Gindling and Crummet 1997).

Inadequate implementation of laws reflects, among other things, gender biases within the implementing institutions and among relevant personnel. Those responsible for interpreting the law may be unwilling or unable to uphold it. For example, conservative judges may interpret the behavior of the victims of rape and other forms of violence according to their traditional notions about gender roles and gender relations, blaming the victim of violence rather than the perpetrator. Moreover, even statutory reform can only achieve so much. The institutional framework that shapes social preferences and constrains behavior resides not only in formal laws, which the state can change, but also in societal norms and customary laws that are more difficult to change by mandate.

So, establishing gender equality in rights and using regulatory policies to address specific areas of gender inequality are critical roles for the state. But government failures are a potential pitfall. Serious gender inequalities may persist not because countries lack an institutional environment that supports gender equality—but because of deeper systemic failures from poor governance and a weak government commitment to basic rights. For more than 100 countries, those with high levels of gender inequality in basic rights generally have highly limited political and ethnic rights as well (Boone 1996). In other words, government commitment to basic rights is highly correlated across several spheres.[18] And where the state's capability and commitment are weak, the private sector and civil society have an important role to play in transforming gender structures, through markets and through political involvement.

Beyond the State and Policy

A basic premise of the discussion thus far is that deliberate public policy is the prime mover for change in gender structures. Indeed, governments possess a range of instruments for catalyzing social transformations, including legal and regulatory policies. But state action also needs the broad support of society in order to effect a deep and lasting change. State effectiveness is greater when civil society groups, especially women's organizations, are able to organize and participate actively in open dialogue. In fact, behind many government actions to promote gender equality have been civil society groups providing support—or pressure—for change. And through treaties, conventions, and donor assistance the international community has supported or pressed national governments to recognize and eliminate gender inequalities (box 3.4).

Box 3.4   Leveraging International Support to Promote Gender Equality

TWO RECENT CIVIC INITIATIVES—ONE IN Botswana, the other in Guatemala—show that court action and strategic use of international support mechanisms can promote gender equality under the law.

Botswana's Nationality Law. Botswana's 1984 Citizenship Act declared a person to be "a citizen of Botswana by birth and descent if, at the time of his birth—(a) his father was a citizen of Botswana; or (b) in the case of a person born out of wedlock, his mother was a citizen of Botswana…" Women's rights groups had long argued that the Act violated the country's constitutional equal protection guarantee. In 1992 a woman named Unity Dow filed a suit before the High Court challenging the constitutionality of the Act (Attorney General v. Unity Dow).

The High Court ruled in favor of Dow, concluding that the Act violated the constitution. The government initially ignored the ruling, refusing to introduce legislation to make the Act comply with the constitution. So women's groups in Botswana organized national and international pressure in support of the High Court's ruling and made the issue a focus of their preparations for the United Nations' Fourth World Conference on Women in Beijing in 1995. Shortly before the Conference the government passed the Citizenship Amendment Act, which complied with the High Court's ruling (in some respects going further than the Court required) and with Botswana's obligations under international law.

Guatemala's Civil Code. Before 1999 the Guatemalan Civil Code had a number of provisions that discriminated against married women. The provisions set a lower minimum age of marriage for females than males, gave wives primary responsibility for child care and care of the home, made husbands the sole legal representative of the conjugal unit, and gave husbands veto power over their wife's decision to work outside the home.

In 1992 María Eugenia Morales Acuña de Sierra, "Deputy State Attorney for Human Rights," filed a case with the Guatemalan Constitutional Court alleging that nine code provisions violated the Guatemalan constitution's guarantee of equality between men and women. In 1994 the Court ruled that none of the challenged provisions was discriminatory, and Morales, with support from the Center for Justice and International Law (a nongovernmental organization), filed a petition with the Inter-American Commission on Human Rights (IACHR), part of the Organization of American States' human rights system.

In response to the petition the executive branch of the Guatemalan government sent a legislative proposal to Congress in 1996 to change the Civil Code "in accordance with the Guatemalan Constitution, the Convention on the Elimination of All Forms of Discrimination against Women, and the American Convention." While the Guatemalan Congress initially appeared unreceptive to the idea of civil code reform, in March, 1998, the IACHR ruled that the petition appeared to provide evidence of a violation of the American Convention. Congress later amended eight of the nine provisions at issue in the petition.

Source: A. Goldstein (1999).

Moreover, profound changes in gender structures often occur as part of wider social and economic transformations not necessarily aimed at altering gender systems. Broad political events—the communist revolutions in China and Russia and the end of apartheid in South Africa—have profoundly affected gender relations and outcomes. The rapid growth in Asia's economic tigers and the return to a market system in the transition economies of Eastern Europe have shifted incentives for work and investment for women and men. These have influenced gender roles and equality between women and men.

Take also the case of colonial America, where women were essentially the property of men, either their father or their husband (Geddes and Lueck 1999). Women could not own property or enter contracts independent of their husband, and they had to relinquish property and wages to him. They had no custodial rights to their children, could not vote or hold political office, and were routinely excluded from social and professional organizations. These restrictions, common in 1776—and more severe than those in developing countries today—no longer exist in the United States. Why? Increases in per capita wealth, women's activism, and women's education all contributed to broadening women's rights (Geddes and Lueck 1999). In the next chapters we discuss these as major factors that help reduce gender inequalities.

———

Social, legal, and economic institutions together underlie observed gender inequalities and are barriers to, as well as instruments for, reducing those disparities. Institutional reform that promotes gender equality must be the first element of a strategy to engender broad-based, sustainable development. In the short run societal institutions are difficult and slow to change. Yet even dramatic transformation is possible—though often in the face of great resistance and at high cost. The state clearly has a role to play in giving a strong mandate through reform of laws and regulations. But the effectiveness of statutory reform depends largely on the state's capacity to implement and enforce—and on the leadership and action of other groups in society. Markets, too, can reduce gender discrimination. When markets function openly they facilitate information exchange and embody a powerful set of incentives for making choices on the basis of productive efficiency rather than gender, ethnicity, or age. Institutional reform can have a profound impact on the decisions and behaviors of individuals and households, ultimately affecting the effectiveness of development strategies.

Notes

1. The rules of marriage exogamy ensure a bride's subservience to her husband's family. When a girl marries and moves to her husband's village, she moves to a place where "she does not know anyone, and custom requires that she remain with her head bowed and not speak…the spiritual rebirth of a girl when she goes to her husband's family is sometimes emphasized by their giving her a new first name…She is at the bottom of the household hierarchy, and the more onerous household tasks are given to her" (Das Gupta 1996, p. 217).

2. In Uttar Pradesh child brides end up having more autonomy in household decisionmaking than women married at older ages, possibly because the transition from marriage to cohabitation gives the bride time to develop a closer bond with her husband and his parents (Desai, Rao, and Joshi 2000).

3. One cross-country multivariate regression study found a significant negative relationship between the proportion of a country's population that is Muslim and school enrollment rates, controlling for other factors, with the effect on girls being greater (Schultz 1987). Similarly, two other studies found a positive association between whether a country is predominantly Muslim and indices of gender inequality (Boone 1996; Forsythe, Korzeniewicz, and Durrant 2000). One of these two studies found that Christianity had a negative but statistically insignificant effect on an index of gender oppression (Boone 1996). A fourth study found that Islam has a negative impact on measures of gender equality but only its effect on equality within marriage is statistically significant. Hinduism is associated with lower female education relative to male, but its effect on other measures of gender inequality is not statistically significant (Dollar and Gatti 1999). This study also tested the joint statistical significance of different religion variables taken together in explaining indicators of gender inequality and concluded that while the effect of individual religions is not clear, on the whole religion is a significant determinant of gender inequality.

4. For example, Bangladesh's reservation to CEDAW does not bind it to certain articles that conflict with the Sharia law that is based on the Qur'an and Sunna.

5. These results are based on ordinary least squares regressions of the gender equality indicator on income and income squared (in natural logarithms) and on average gender rights. The coefficients on rights and on the joint income terms are positive and significant for all indicators. Given the limitation of the data, it is not possible to determine whether this is a causal relationship. See appendix 2.

6. The relative effects of the components that make up the composite rights measure were examined. In all cases the three rights areas are jointly statistically significant in their effect on the development outcomes, again controlling for a country's GDP per capita. But of the three rights indexes, equality of rights in politics and the law and in marriage and divorce matters appears to have a larger effect on gender equality in education, health, and political participation than does equality of rights in social and economic matters.

7. Female cadres attached to the Women's Federation were responsible for implementing these policies in villages and households (Honig 1985; Hooper 1984).

8. Some historians claim that the state successfully eliminated polygyny, reduced the incidence of arranged marriages, and increased the domestic autonomy of young women (Davin 1976 as cited in Das Gupta and others 2000). Others argue that the state backed down from its policy because implementation of the law slackened after the protests, as cadres that failed to implement the campaign were immune from heavy criticism (Honig 1985).

9. For detailed reviews of the gender impacts of two generations of land reforms in Latin America, see Deere and Leon (1997, 1999).

10. In Latin America the right to vote was commonly reserved for adult males until the 20th century. When a number of countries relaxed their restrictions based on landholding or wealth during the 19th century, they almost always chose to rely on a literacy qualification (Sokoloff and Engerman 2000).

11. Chapter 1 shows that women throughout the world earn less than men, on average, with the gap

varying considerably across countries. That gap has narrowed over the past three decades—if unevenly. It has narrowed quite substantially in such countries as Australia, Indonesia, the Republic of Korea, Sweden, the United Kingdom, and the United States, only moderately in Japan and Thailand, and hardly at all in Taiwan, China (Blau 1998; Horton 1996; Zveglich, Rodgers, and Rodgers 1997).

12. Protective legislation for workers has evolved in Europe and the United States since the 1800s and in Asia and Latin America since the 1950s. Some of the changes in the special protection laws in industrialized countries were made in response to conventions sponsored by the International Labor Organization. There were further shifts in attitudes toward these measures in the 1960s, and by the late 1970s the ILO formally recommended that countries review and update their protective legislation.

13. The idea of affirmative action in recruitment has tended to be less politically controversial than affirmative action in hiring.

14. Compared to OECD countries these benefits are modest. In Europe maternity leave ranges from 14 weeks in Germany, Spain, Sweden, and the United Kingdom to 22 weeks in Italy. And compensation during the leave varies from 75 percent in Sweden to 100 percent in France, Germany, the Netherlands, and Spain. The United States is less generous: the Family and Medical Leave Act entitles employees to 12 weeks of unpaid leave for pregnancy and childbirth or other care responsibilities (Rodgers 1999).

15. In the United States, for example, comprehensive maternity benefit provisions adopted by many states during the mid-1970s resulted in a fall in wages and a rise in hours for married women between ages 20 and 40 (Gruber 1994). A substantial part of the costs of maternity benefits was shifted to the wages of women but without much effect on total labor input. In Japan, as in the United States, controlling for factors such as prebirth tenure, women covered by maternity leave benefits were much more likely to return to their prebirth employers

than those who were not. Moreover, nearly half of women workers were covered by the child care leave law and those covered were about twice as likely to return to work after childbirth as those who were not (Waldfogel, Higuchi, and Abe 1998). In contrast, once the length of prebirth tenure is taken into account, women with coverage in the United Kingdom were no more likely to return than were those without.

16. A study suggests that income stability is negatively related to private transfers (Cox and Jimenez 1998). Public transfers crowd out informal, private arrangements for old-age support. Using the Peruvian Living Standards Survey, the authors found that private transfers from young to old would have been nearly 20 percent higher if the elderly did not have access to social security benefits. The crowding-out effect is larger in the Philippines, where the incidence of private transfers is higher. A dollar increase in public pensions would be associated with a decline in private transfers of 37 cents, leaving a net benefit of only 63 cents. Therefore, social security makes elderly pensioners better off, but not as much better off as its expenditures would suggest.

17. For example, the old economic system in the former Soviet Union provided relatively uniform wages and pensions to all; women had a high labor force participation rate and also got pension credit for childbearing years. In contrast, the new economic system has increased inequality in wages and years of employment, and consequently in pensions. When a multipillar system replaced the fiscally unsustainable pension system in Kazakhstan, pensions fell by 44 percent for women but only 21 percent for men, compared with the average wage in the economy (Castel and Fox 1999).

18. For example, the correlation between the extent of restrictions on women's rights and restrictions on political rights within countries is 0.56. The correlations between gender rights and violent forms of political oppression (that is not gender-specific) and between gender rights and oppression of ethnic minorities are higher at 0.62 and 0.63, respectively (Boone 1996).

CHAPTER 4

Power, Incentives, and Resources in the Household

HOUSEHOLDS AND FAMILIES SHAPE GENDER relations, transmit gender norms from one generation to the next, and determine the opportunities available to household members based on their gender. People make many of life's most basic decisions within households—decisions about having and raising children, about work and leisure, about what to consume, and about how to invest in the future. Decisions within families about the allocation of time and other productive resources, including investments in children, can intensify or lessen gender disparities. In fact, the evidence suggests that they do both.[1]

Families do not make decisions about allocating and investing resources in a vacuum. They make them in a broader institutional environment. Decisions to allocate labor in a particular way or to invest in some children rather than others are influenced by social and cultural norms, economic incentives, and individuals' aspirations and power to influence the process. Factors that change the institutional and policy environment inevitably alter the constraints, opportunities, and incentives that women and men face and respond to in their households. Even when these changes are not inherently gender-specific, they commonly affect women and men and girls and boys differently.

As chapter 3 discusses, mortality rates among young girls in India are highest (relative to those of boys) in regions where a bride relocates to her husband's village—and where her parents have to pay substantial dowries at marriage (Kishor 1993). But this excess female mortality is lower where female labor force participation rates and female earnings are relatively high (Rosenzweig and Schultz 1982; Kishor 1993; Murthi,

Guio, and Dreze 1996). Moreover, relative female survival rates are significantly higher in regions where technical changes in agriculture have raised returns to female human capital (Foster and Rosenzweig 1999). Neither technological changes nor policies that affect returns to female labor are generally undertaken with their gender impacts in mind. But such changes commonly have different effects on females' and males' opportunities and well-being.

Such gender-differentiated effects are pervasive across many dimensions of life—including work and leisure choices, investments in children, and access to productive resources. This chapter examines how economic incentives, public investments, and the distribution of power within households affect family resource allocations and investments by gender. In doing so, it highlights policy approaches that can promote greater gender equality in command over resources.

Two main messages emerge from the evidence. First, household resources are allocated in the face of competing preferences and unequal bargaining power among members. This conflicts with the traditional view of economists and policymakers that household members pool their resources and allocate them according to a unified set of preferences. One implication is that the distribution of resources within a household, not just the level of resources, matters. Policies that alter the distribution of resources among household members shift the balance of power among those members, with implications for gender equality and family welfare.

Consider microfinance programs in Bangladesh, which show that access to credit empowers women. Female borrowing is associated not only with increased earning capacity and control of household assets by women, but with more autonomy and decisionmaking power within the home, and greater demand for formal health care for women (Pitt and Khandker 1998; Khandker 1998; Kabeer 1998; Nanda 1999; Zaman 1999). A growing body of evidence indicates that more resources in the hands of women mean greater household allocations to children. These effects can be substantial. In Brazil additional income in the hands of mothers is associated with substantially larger improvements in child survival and nutrition than additional income in the hands of fathers. For child survival the marginal effect of female income is nearly 20 times larger than that of male income. And for child nutrition, the effect is four to eight times larger (Thomas 1990, 1997). Together these factors make a strong case for targeting programs toward women and girls to increase their command over resources.

Second, policymakers can reduce disparities in women's and men's access to resources in the household through a number of means—by using pricing policy, by designing service delivery with gender in mind, and by investing in selected infrastructure.

- *Pricing policy.* Household investments in education, health, and nutrition for females tend to be more sensitive to changes in prices than similar investments for males. Among low-income households in Pakistan a decrease in the price of a doctor's services would increase female use by 58 percent more than male use (Alderman and Gertler 1997). Either targeted or untargeted subsidies for basic services can thus be expected to strengthen demand for female education and health care and to reduce gender disparities in human development. Similarly, subsidizing the costs of out-of-home child care can facilitate women's labor force participation, raise women's (and household) incomes, and increase school attendance among adolescent girls.

- *Better-designed service delivery.* Designing service delivery—whether school systems, health facilities, agricultural extension services, or financial institutions—in ways that account for gender differences and disparities can promote greater gender equality in access to productive resources. In Bangladesh and elsewhere group-based lending has eliminated women's need for traditional forms of collateral (which they often lack), significantly increasing their ability to obtain credit.

- *Investments in infrastructure.* Infrastructure investments generally benefit females and males alike. But selected investments in infrastructure—particularly investments that help women and girls save time on household work—can enhance gender equality in economic participation and access to resources. In poor rural areas investments in basic water and energy infrastructure can significantly reduce the time girls and women spend collecting water and fuel. By doing so, such investments enhance girls' ability to attend school and free women to earn additional income, participate in community affairs, and the like.

By helping to reduce gender disparities in command over resources, these levers strengthen both women's ability to bargain and influence decisions in the home and their capacity to participate productively in society more broadly.

The next two sections explore how households pass gender roles from one generation to the next by the ways they allocate and invest family resources. The chapter then examines evidence on the links between resource control, bargaining power, and intrahousehold allocations and investments—and on policy levers to promote greater gender equality in command over resources. It concludes by summarizing the main policy lessons.

What Is a Household?

ALTHOUGH MOST PEOPLE GROW UP AND LIVE IN HOUSEHOLDS, defining the household is not as straightforward as it might seem. In their most basic form households center on childbearing and rearing, earning income (or otherwise meeting basic consumption needs), and equipping the next generation to function productively in society. To carry out these functions household members—together or individually—decide how to allocate often-scarce resources across activities, including consumption, production, and investment. But the specific form and characteristics of households often depend on context—a combination of social and cultural norms and economic incentives. And how households are constituted changes in response to demographic and economic changes as well as changes in norms.

Economic surveys in developing countries usually define the household as "a group of people who live together, pool their money, and eat at least one meal together per day" (UN 1989, cited in Glewwe 2000, p. 135). In reality, however, none of these conditions necessarily holds. For example, while most households share living quarters, some don't (Hammel and Laslett 1974; McDonald 1992). The members of a household may co-reside for some purposes but not for others, as in parts of Africa where members of the same residential group may split into separate cooking and eating units, and spouses may live in separate residences. In polygynous relationships, particularly common in West Africa, wives frequently maintain separate dwelling units and may even be unaware of the existence of other wives.[2] Moreover, as migration has become increasingly prevalent across developing countries, members not linked to households through proximity may be linked functionally through remittances.

Similarly, while households are generally thought to pool their financial resources for consumption and production, this may not be the case.

In Burkina Faso and Ghana husbands and wives do not commonly pool resources or have common budgets for household expenditures (Kevane forthcoming; BRIDGE 1994). Separate budgets appear to be the norm in West Africa, and spouses often have separate spheres of responsibility for both production and expenditure. In many parts of Sub-Saharan Africa wives bear primary responsibility for household food security, while husbands bear primary responsibility for cash incomes. Among the Ashanti in Ghana, men traditionally have been expected to contribute "chop" (food) money and pay for children's school fees, while women take care of additional expenditures for children, such as clothing (Abu 1983).

Nor are household labor resources necessarily pooled. In parts of Sub-Saharan Africa men have some claim on their wife's labor for household (and sometimes personal) fields (Dey Abbas 1997). These claims can take precedence over women's rights to farm their own fields or earn other income. But women generally have no such claims on their husband's labor.

These asymmetries in rights and decisionmaking power in the household can be reinforced by household structure. In Bangladesh, as in many parts of South Asia, young brides who move from their parents' household to their husband's—as required by the patrilocal system of residence—must adapt to a large, extended family where they are subservient to their mother-in-law and other female relatives (Adnan 1993). This gives young wives little power to influence family resource allocation or investments, even when their views differ considerably from those of other family members.

Households Reproduce Gender Roles

NO MATTER WHERE THEY ARE OR HOW THEY ARE ORGANIZED, households regularly transmit gender roles to the next generations. Households are the first place of gender socialization, passing along knowledge, skills, and social expectations. Children acquire a gender identity that shapes the set of socially acceptable activities for women and men and the relations between them. Children are socialized through explicit instruction, through punishment for inappropriate behavior, and by observing and imitating their parents and other female and male role models in the family (Whiting and Edwards 1988).

Allocating resources is another way households shape gender roles. In extreme cases differences in the allocation of food, health care, and attention to young boys and girls mean greater female malnutrition, limiting girls' ability to learn and women's capacity to participate productively in society. But even in less extreme cases family decisions about investing in boys' or girls' education—or about involving sons in farming but daughters in household maintenance and care activities—all help reproduce and reinforce socially accepted gender roles.

The difference in girls' and boys' gender roles become more pronounced as children get older. In most of the world differences in household expenditure on girls' and boys' education tend to increase when children move from primary to secondary school. When girls reach adolescence they are generally expected to spend more time on such household activities as cooking, cleaning, collecting fuel and water, and caring for children. Meanwhile, boys tend to spend more time on farm or wage work. When young children get sick, teenage girls, not boys, tend to increase their time providing care—often at the expense of their schooling (Pitt and Rosenzweig 1990; Ilahi 1999a). Meanwhile, boys are increasingly engaged in market work, preparing to become the main breadwinner of their own household.

This division of tasks by gender means that by the time girls and boys become adults and form new households, women generally work longer hours than men, have less experience in the labor force, and earn less income. In almost all countries—both developed and developing—there is a strikingly consistent gender division of labor, in which men work more in the market and women more in the home (figure 4.1; UNDP 1995).[3] Moreover, women often undertake multiple activities at once—such as taking care of children while working in the household or in home- or farm-based income-generating activities (Floro 1995).

Even when women work in the labor market they continue to do most of the unpaid work at home. For example, women in the former Soviet Union had a relatively high level of equality with men in labor force participation and occupational attainment, but they still tended to be responsible for most in-home child care (Lapidus 1993).

This division of time and tasks has important implications. For instance, if parents consider it unlikely that their daughters will join the labor force and earn income as adults, they may see less justification for sending their daughters to school. This is true whether or not women become part of their husband's family after marriage (a custom that reduces parents' incentives to invest in girls' schooling relative to boys').

Figure 4.1 Men Work More in the Market, Women More in the Home

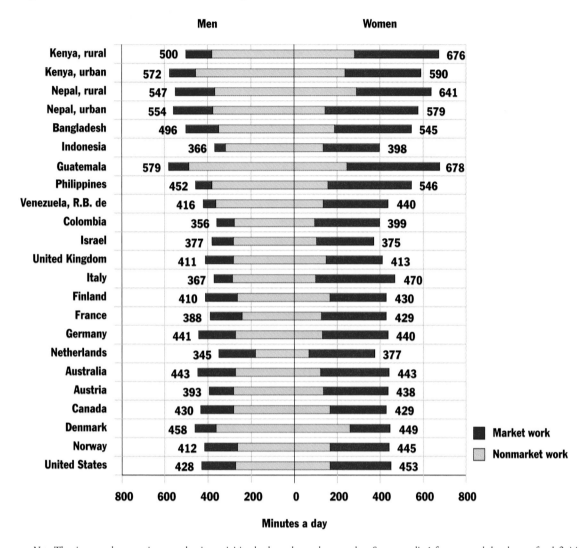

Note: The time use data pertain to productive activities, both market and nonmarket. See appendix 1 for years and the glossary for definitions of market and nonmarket work.
Source: UNDP (1995).

In addition, lower education and labor force participation generally mean lower incomes for women—and thus limited power to influence resource allocation and investments in the home.

Since much of women's work in developing countries is unpaid and done inside the home, it is often "invisible" and not accounted for by policymakers.[4] But failing to recognize gender divisions of time and task

153

allocations within households can result in policies that don't achieve their objectives or that produce unintended outcomes. For example, policies that increase demand for female labor may not elicit the expected supply response if women cannot reduce their time on household maintenance or care activities. Or girls may be taken out of school to cover for mothers who enter the labor force (Grootaert and Patrinos 1999; Ilahi 1999b; Lokshin, Glinskaya, and Garcia 2000). Understanding how households allocate time and other resources by gender can thus provide the basis for more effective policies—and policies that generate fewer unintended and undesirable consequences.

Resource Control and Bargaining Power Affect Household Allocations

TRADITIONALLY, ECONOMISTS AND POLICY ANALYSTS HAVE tended to view the household as a unit that pools income and allocates resources for consumption, production, and investment as if it had a single set of preferences. This view has influenced the way policies and programs have been conceived and designed. For example, within this "unitary" household framework, total income—but not its distribution across household members—is critical in determining how resources are allocated. Wages and other prices are also seen as important. But a broader set of factors that affect individuals' bargaining power in the household—such as their control of resources or laws and norms that shape their options outside the home—are not typically seen as integral to household allocations and investments.[5]

The unitary household model does not imply that households will allocate resources equally by gender. Rather, to the extent that gender disparities arise they are thought to reflect different returns to or costs of investment in male or female household members, in the context of a common set of preferences among household members regarding resource allocation, or the preferences of a "dictator" within the household: someone capable of imposing his or her will on other household members. Nor is the unitary model silent on the roles of income, prices, and wages in reducing gender disparities. In fact, this traditional household model and the empirical evidence it has generated provide policymakers with powerful tools for promoting gender equality.

For example, increases in household income tend to reduce gender disparities in education, health, and nutrition (see chapter 5). When household incomes are low (given prices), families frequently ration spending on children's schooling, health care, and nutrition, often at the expense of girls. But when household incomes rise, families generally increase spending in these areas, with girls benefiting more than boys— although generally from a lower starting point. Similarly, household demand for girls' education and health is often more sensitive to price changes than boys'. As a result, pricing policy can often raise not only the absolute but the relative education and health status of girls.

Even so, resource allocation decisions within households are commonly inconsistent with the unitary household model. Rather, these decisions appear to reflect different preferences among household members, by gender. They also reflect differences among them in control of resources, such as income, assets, and education. And they reflect factors outside the household that affect women's and men's economic "fallback" positions and their options to leave the household under bad circumstances. In other words, it is the distribution of resources, not just their aggregate level, that matters in household allocations and investments. These allocations also appear to reflect the relative bargaining power of different household members (box 4.1).

Box 4.1   Factors Influencing Bargaining Power

DIRECTLY MEASURING ONE'S BARGAINING POWER IN the household is difficult if not impossible. Even so, recent literature on intrahousehold resource allocation has focused on several factors that influence bargaining power and thus how households allocate resources. A body of recent microeconomic analysis has focused on command over economic resources, such as assets, unearned income, and transfer payments or welfare receipts (that is, factors external to labor supply) as a major determinant of bargaining power.[1]

If a person owns or controls assets and is able to take these assets when they leave, they have some power over how household resources are allocated. In Indonesia the assets a man or woman brings to marriage are thought to be a good indicator of bargaining power, since in most of the country spouses can recover what they brought into the marriage if the marriage is dissolved (Thomas, Contreras, and Frankenberg 1997; Quisumbing and Maluccio 1999). But in many developing countries children, the elderly, and women have only limited ability to leave

(box continues on the following page)

Box 4.1 continued

even abusive relationships—both because they are financially dependent on a (male) breadwinner and because gender norms restrict their "exit" options.

The broader institutional environment is thus critical in determining individuals' bargaining power within the household. This includes women's and men's legal rights within marriage (such as their right to transact business independently), rights to own land or other assets, and rights relating to the division of property in a divorce. Not only the existence of laws (or rights) but their enforcement are critically important. For example, if enforcement of alimony and child support payments makes divorce more costly to men, women should have more power within marriage.

Similarly, people's social or economic "fallback" options influence their bargaining power in the household. This includes the extent to which gender norms either allow or proscribe women's or men's economic activities. It also includes the nature of economic opportunities available in the economy and such factors as parents' wealth and social status. One's personal or social networks—such as membership in organizations, access to kin, or access to social capital more broadly—can also influence a person's power to affect household decisions. This is evident in Bangladesh, where women's membership in solidarity groups and nongovernmental organizations has helped break down traditional gender norms and increase women's power in economic decisionmaking (Kabeer 1998).

Individuals' characteristics, such as education, skills, knowledge, and the capacity to acquire information, influence their bargaining power in the household. Physical stature can also be important. Indeed, some people use physical dominance, violence, or the threat of violence to influence household resource allocations or to extract resources from spouses or their families, as with dowry-related violence in India (Rao 1998; Bloch and Rao 2000). Here again, community attitudes toward domestic violence and how the legal and institutional environment punishes or condones perpetrators affect the influence violence has on household allocation decisions.

1. For example, Doss (1996); Thomas, Contreras, and Frankenberg (1997); Quisumbing (1994); and Quisumbing and Maluccio (1999) analyze the role of assets. Schultz (1990) and Thomas (1990) focus on unearned income. Lundberg, Pollak, and Wales (1997) and Rubaclava and Thomas (1997) focus on transfer payments and welfare receipts.

Who Controls Resources Matters

Empirical evidence on the role of resource control and bargaining power in influencing resource allocation and investment within households now exists for a large number of countries and a wide range of household activities, including consumption, labor, production, risk pooling, and investment in human development. Studies have sought to test the unitary model of the household—for example, by examining the impacts of female and male control of labor income, nonlabor income, assets, and public transfers, as well as female and male education levels, on a number of outcomes, including household consumption and expenditure patterns, child survival, nutrition, and education. Under the unitary model, whether females or males control income and assets should not affect household resource allocations. But in general, studies that use different types of data, different measures of bargaining power, and different methodologies find that who controls income or assets does matter to household outcomes (box 4.2; appendix 4).

Box 4.2 Empirical Tests of the "Unitary" Household Model

A NUMBER OF RECENT EMPIRICAL STUDIES HAVE tested the unitary household model. The tests have focused on underlying assumptions of the model, such as income pooling and the efficient allocation of household resources. This growing body of evidence calls into question the unitary model as a description of household behavior for a wide range of household activities, including consumption, labor, production, risk pooling, and investment in human development.

Tests of income pooling. A number of studies have used household survey data to test the basic assumption of the unitary model that households pool their income.[1] Under the assumption of income pooling, the marginal impact of additional resources accruing to the household should be independent of the identity of the person controlling them. To test this assumption studies examine whether female and male control of income, assets, education, credit, or government transfers, have differential effects on household consumption or child welfare. In contrast to what is implied by the unitary model, the studies generally find that who controls resources matters to intrahousehold resource allocation.

A key methodological issue is the possible "endogeneity" of income in these analyses. If the same factors that affect current income also affect the outcomes of interest, then estimates of the effects of income could be biased (Behrman 1997; Hoddinott, Alderman, and Haddad 1997). Efforts have been made to collect better data on "exogenous" measures

of bargaining power in the household—for example, assets brought to marriage as opposed to current income or assets—and to control econometrically for the endogeneity of income. Methodological and data challenges remain. But together these studies, which use different measures of resource control, different methodologies, and data from a diverse range of countries, provide compelling evidence against the assumption of income pooling.

Tests of household labor supply. Studies also reject the unitary model in the context of household labor allocation. In the case of household labor supply, the unitary model implies that the impact of (income-compensated) changes in a husband's wage on his wife's labor supply should be identical to the impact of (income-compensated) changes in the wife's wage on her husband's labor supply (Lundberg 1988). In other words, for the unitary model to hold, the "cross-wage" effects on husbands and wives should be equal. But this symmetry is rejected in a number of studies (Ashenfelter and Heckman 1974; Ashworth and Ulph 1981; Killingsworth 1983; Kooreman and Kapteyn 1986; Alderman and Sahn 1993; and Fortin and Lacroix 1997; see appendix 4 for details on additional relevant studies).

Tests of production efficiency. Another assumption of the unitary household model (and some categories of bargaining models of households) is that intrahousehold allocations are "Pareto efficient." That is, no reallocation of household resources can be made without making at least one member worse off. Pareto

(box continues on following page)

Box 4.2 continued

efficiency implies, among other things, that households allocate their resources to maximize profits (income) from productive activities. A few studies use household- and farm-level data from Sub-Saharan Africa to examine this. And the evidence indicates that intrahousehold allocations to production are not necessarily efficient. In Cameroon, for example, labor is misallocated across plots farmed by women and men within households (Jones 1983, 1986). In Burkina Faso, households allocate too little labor and other inputs on plots farmed by women relative to Pareto-efficient allocations (Udry 1996; Udry and others 1995). In both cases Pareto efficiency is violated; household output and incomes could be increased significantly by reallocating currently used factors of production within the household.

Tests of intrahousehold risk pooling. Building on the empirical literature on consumption-smoothing and risk pooling, recent studies of Ghana and Ethiopia examine whether husbands and wives in the same household pool risk as a unit in the face of economic shocks (M. Goldstein 1999; Dercon and Krishnan 2000). If households pool risk as a unit, husbands' and wives' consumption would be expected to vary together in response to economic shock. In Ghana husbands' and wives' consumption do not move together, suggesting that husbands and wives do not pool risk. In fact, women appear to pool their risk with other women, while men have a wider and less-defined risk pool. In both Ghana and Ethiopia there is evidence that intrahousehold risk-sharing behavior is inefficient, violating the Pareto-efficiency assumption of the unitary household model.

1. See appendix 4 for more on relevant studies.

Household consumption patterns. Studies from a diverse set of countries, including Bangladesh, Brazil, Canada, Côte d'Ivoire, Ethiopia, France, Indonesia, South Africa, Taiwan (China), and the United Kingdom, indicate that women's and men's relative control of resources has significant—and different—impacts on household consumption and expenditure. While the precise effects of female and male resource control differ from place to place, some consistent patterns emerge across countries. The most obvious: increases in the relative resources controlled by women generally translate into a larger share of household resources going to family welfare, and especially to expenditures on children—even after controlling for per capita income and demographic characteristics of the household. Greater resource control by women also leads to expenditure patterns and outcomes that strengthen women's well-being and status in the household.

How do women's contributions to household income affect household expenditure patterns? In Côte d'Ivoire increasing women's share of cash income in the household significantly increases the share of the household budget allocated to food, controlling for average per capita expenditure (income), household size, and demographic characteristics (Hoddinott and Haddad 1995). It also decreases the shares devoted to alcohol and cigarettes. In Brazil it is the same story. At the margin additional income in the hands of women results in a greater share of the household budget devoted to education, health, and nutrition-related expenditures (Thomas 1997).

Because the same factors that affect income control may affect household expenditure choices (see box 4.2), the Brazil and Côte d'Ivoire studies attempt to control econometrically for the possible "endogeneity" of current labor income using two-stage least squares. Moreover, the Brazil study analyzes both labor and nonlabor income. While not completely immune to concerns about endogeneity, nonlabor income may be less influenced by such factors as past or current labor supply choices that affect the outcomes of interest. In Brazil the finding that female and male income control have different effects on household expenditure patterns is robust to the choice of the income measure.

Another study analyzes the impact of assets brought to marriage by women and men and of relative education levels on resource allocation and investment in households in Bangladesh, Ethiopia, Indonesia, and South Africa (Quisumbing and Maluccio 1999). Comparable methodologies are used across countries. The data were collected specifically to analyze intrahousehold allocations and investments and to address concerns about the endogeneity of labor and nonlabor income. In particular, the assets and education men and women bring to marriage are exogenous to decisions made within the marriage.[6]

As in Brazil and Côte d'Ivoire the unitary household model is rejected in all four country cases. While the precise impact of female and male asset control and education differs across countries, the general patterns are consistent with those in the earlier studies. Additional resources and bargaining power in the hands of women have a greater impact on expenditure allocations toward the next generation—such as on education, health, and nutrition—than additional resources in the hands of men.

A policy change in the United Kingdom that transferred income from fathers to mothers led to similar patterns. In the late 1970s the national Family Allowance program transferred control of a substantial child allowance benefit from fathers to mothers. This shift was followed by significant changes in household expenditure patterns that benefited women and children. Relative spending on women's and children's goods (such as clothing) rose, while relative spending on men's goods (clothing and tobacco) fell (Lundberg, Pollak, and Wales 1997; Ward-Batts 1997).[7]

From children's well-being to women's empowerment. Female and male control of income, assets, and education affect more than household consumption patterns. In Brazil additional labor and nonlabor income in the hands of women tends to have a greater positive impact on child survival and nutrition than additional income in the hands of men (Thomas 1990, 1997). Regardless of who controls it, an increase in total household income is associated with improvements in child survival and nutrition (as measured by child height for weight and height for age). But at the margin, improvements are substantially larger if the mother controls the income.

Additional evidence on the gender-differentiated impacts of resource control on household outcomes comes from recent microfinance initiatives in Bangladesh.[8] Two related studies examine the impact of female and male borrowing—from Grameen Bank, the Bangladesh Rural Advancement Committee (BRAC), and government program RD-12—on such outcomes as per capita household expenditure (income) and girls' and boys' schooling and nutritional status (Khandker 1998; Pitt and Khandker 1998). The impacts often differ substantially based on whether the borrower is a woman or a man—and often the marginal impacts of borrowing are greater for women than for men.

For all three microfinance programs the impact of female borrowing on per capita household expenditure (income) is about twice as large as the impact of male borrowing (table 4.1). A 10 percent increase in female borrowing is associated with a roughly 40 percent increase in per capita expenditure—an effect that is strongly significant statistically.[9] Compare this with a roughly 20 percent increase in per capita expenditure associated with the same percentage increase in male borrowing. Female borrowing also has a greater impact than male borrowing on households' ability to "smooth" consumption over time (Khandker 1998; Menon 1999).

As with other forms of resource control, female borrowing also appears to have a greater impact on child welfare than male borrowing does. For example, except for BRAC, female borrowing has a greater positive impact on children's school enrollments than male borrowing does. Moreover, in contrast to male borrowing, female borrowing has a large and statistically significant impact on children's nutritional well-being.

160

Table 4.1 Impacts of Female and Male Borrowing on Selected Household Outcomes
(percentage change for a 10 percent increase in borrowing)

Household outcome	Grameen Bank		BRAC		RD-12	
	Male borrowing	Female borrowing	Male borrowing	Female borrowing	Male borrowing	Female borrowing
Per capita spending	0.18	**0.43**	0.19	**0.39**	0.23	**0.40**
Net worth	**0.15**	**0.14**	**0.20**	**0.09**	**0.22**	0.02
Boys' school enrollment	0.07	**0.61**	−0.08	−0.03	**0.29**	**0.79**
Girls' school enrollment	**0.30**	**0.47**	**0.24**	0.12	0.07	**0.23**
Boys' height for age[a]	**−2.98**	**14.19**	**−2.98**	**14.19**	**−2.98**	**14.19**
Girls' height for age[a]	**−4.92**	**11.63**	**−4.92**	**11.63**	**−4.92**	**11.63**
Contraceptive use	**4.25**	**−0.91**	0.40	−0.74	0.84	−1.16
Recent fertility	−0.74	−0.35	0.54	0.79	−0.74	0.50

Note: Figures in bold are based on coefficient estimates that are statistically significant at the 10 percent level or better.
a. Percentage changes reported for boys' and girls' height for age represent average impacts across all three microfinance programs.
Source: Khandker (1998).

At the same time, male borrowing has a greater impact on household net worth than female borrowing. This suggests that while at the margin women seem to invest relatively more than men in the human capital of their children, men appear to invest more than women in physical capital.

Female and male borrowing also have different impacts on household reproductive behavior, suggesting that women and men do not share the same preferences relating to contraception or fertility. For example, female borrowing decreases contraceptive use and, except for Grameen Bank borrowing, increases fertility, whereas male borrowing increases contraceptive use and, except for BRAC borrowing, decreases fertility. At first glance the findings on the impact of female borrowing on contraceptive use and fertility may seem counterintuitive, since a body of empirical literature suggests that factors increasing the opportunity cost of women's time—such as increased education, wages, or labor market opportunities—tend to reduce fertility.[10] But low-income women in Bangladesh may see additional children as assets capable of assisting them with what are often home-based, self-employment activities.[11]

Increasing women's independent access to credit also empowers them in other dimensions. For example, female borrowing increases female control of nonland assets (Pitt and Khandker 1998; Khandker 1998).

Women who participate in the credit programs report an increased role in household decisionmaking (Kabeer 1998) and greater acceptance by their husband of their participation in market-based economic activities (Agarwal 1997). A study of BRAC's microfinance program finds that female borrowing enhances women's ability to sell assets without asking their husband's permission (Zaman 1999). Specifically, women who have borrowed more than 10,000 taka are 46 percent more likely to be able to sell poultry without their husband's permission than members who have not borrowed. These borrowers are also twice as likely to be able to sell jewelry and 35 percent more likely to have control of their savings. And women who participate in credit programs have significantly higher demand for formal health care than women who do not (Nanda 1999).[12]

Inefficiencies in Production—and Gender-Specific Risk

Households do not necessarily pool resources for production, and the resulting inefficiencies can have important implications for household income and welfare. In Burkina Faso too little labor and fertilizer are used on plots controlled by female farmers, while too much is allocated to plots controlled by men within the same households (Udry 1996; Udry and others 1995). As chapter 2 discusses, these inefficiencies impose high costs on household production and income. Total household production could be increased by as much as 20 percent if some of the production inputs used on men's plots were reallocated to women's plots.

In Cameroon households often allocate labor inefficiently across agricultural plots controlled by wives and husbands (Jones 1983, 1986). Wives allocate more than optimal amounts of labor to sorghum production (they control the income) and less than optimal amounts of labor to rice production (husbands control the income). As in Burkina Faso, total household income could be increased substantially by reallocating inputs to production—in this case by reallocating wives' labor from sorghum to rice. But in Cameroon wives prefer cultivating plots for which they control the income, even though their husbands compensate them for their labor in rice production. Moreover, relative bargaining power appears to play a role in wives' compensation. Senior wives in polygynous households and women whose husbands still owe bride-price receive higher compensation than other women (Jones 1983).

In southern Ghana households do not necessarily act as a unit in pooling risk or responding to shocks, whether related to illness or unexpected agricultural production shortfalls (M. Goldstein 1999). Instead, women seem to pool their risk with other women in the village, while men appear to pool their risk with a wider, less-defined group that includes clan members in and outside their village. In addition to highlighting the gender-specific nature of risks, at least in some contexts, these findings underscore the importance of social networks in providing informal insurance. At least for women in southern Ghana, it is transfers from nonfamily friends—not from the spouse or extended family—that respond to consumption or production shocks. So, government interventions to mitigate the impact of shocks need to consider that the capacity to deal with shocks may differ systematically for women and men, even within the same household.

A Case for Gender-Based Targeting—and Understanding the Context

The evidence on determinants of intrahousehold resource allocation and investments makes a strong case for targeting interventions by gender—to promote gender equality and more effective development. Interventions that aim to increase female access to productive resources and assets can improve women's autonomy and status within the household. They can also enhance household and child welfare more effectively than interventions that aim to improve access to productive resources to the household as an undifferentiated unit. The case for gender-based targeting applies not only to transfer payments or programs to enhance individuals' command over productive resources. Since, at least in some contexts, women and men within a household do not share risk as a unit, interventions designed to mitigate risk may be more effective if they focus on gender-specific rather than household risk and insurance.

The patterns discussed here are empirical regularities based on a growing number of studies in different countries and regions. But understanding the specific nature of gender relations within a given context—and how social institutions affect intrahousehold resource allocations in that context—is critical to designing policies that promote gender equality.

For example, the link between greater maternal resource control and greater investment in children is generally clear, based on evidence from many countries. But the relationship between maternal and paternal resource control and investments in girls rather than boys within households is much more complex and context specific. In Brazil, Ghana, and the United States maternal resources more strongly affect girls; paternal resources more strongly affect boys (Thomas 1994). Evidence from other countries is mixed, however. In Côte d'Ivoire women's share of household income significantly increases boys' height-for-age relative to girls' (Haddad and Hoddinott 1994). In South Africa fathers' education has a significant positive impact on the schooling of adolescent girls, while mothers' education has a positive impact on boys' schooling (Quisumbing and Maluccio 1999).[13]

Why might mothers prefer boys' education to girls'? Social norms and practices may make parents consider children of one sex more or less desirable—say, for family lineage. In Bangladesh a wife's status is linked to whether she has sons (Adnan 1993). And economic considerations may differ for sons and daughters. Where boys are often important sources of old age security and women tend to live longer than men, favoring boys may reflect an investment strategy by mothers to ensure that they are cared for in their old age (Quisumbing and Maluccio 1999). In highly gender-stratified settings women are especially vulnerable to risk, and thus may rely on sons not only for security in old age but for insurance against risk and as a means of legitimizing their position in their marital family (Das Gupta 1987).

So, mechanisms underlying the links between parental income control and investment in boys and girls can be complex. And in countries where gender systems perpetuate boy preference, special efforts may be needed to strengthen incentives for parental investments in girls.

In addition, a detailed understanding of gender systems may prevent interventions from having unintended and adverse consequences. For example, a recent project in The Gambia aimed to increase productivity of rice cultivation (traditionally women's work) and, in so doing, increase women's share of household income. While rice yields increased under the project, the commercialization of rice associated with the project shifted control of cultivation from women to men. With this shift men gained greater claim over female labor, as women were obligated to contribute labor to crops controlled by men. Moreover, women's share of household income declined (von Braun and Webb 1989; Dey-Abbas 1997). An early understanding of the asymmetric rights, obligations, and relative bargaining power of women and men might have enabled policymakers to design the program to achieve both its goals (Alderman and others 1995). More generally, a thorough understanding of local gender systems is often critical to ensuring that programs are designed and implemented in ways that indeed foster greater gender equality.

Policy Incentives and Public Investments Affect Gender Equality

INCREASING WOMEN'S COMMAND OVER RESOURCES CAN IMPROVE women's status and enhance family and child welfare. But what are the appropriate policy levers for achieving this? Policymakers have a number of instruments at their disposal to influence the allocation of household resources and in so doing promote greater gender equality in workloads, in investments in children, and in command over productive resources. This section focuses on three major sets of instruments: prices and physical access to services, the design of service delivery, and investments in (time-saving) infrastructure.

Prices and Physical Access to Services

Pricing policy and other mechanisms that reduce the costs to households of services, such as improving physical access, can be important for promoting gender equality in human development and enabling greater female labor force participation and earning capacity.

Human development. Household demand for female education, nutrition, and health care responds to changes in prices. Moreover, the demand for investment in women and girls tends to be more sensitive to changes in prices (or costs) than demand for investment in men and boys (table 4.2). In Pakistan the price elasticity of demand for doctors is 58 percent higher for females than for males in the lowest-income group, and 14 percent higher in the highest-income group (Alderman and Gertler 1997). In South India the price elasticity of demand for nutrients consumed is much larger for females than for males (Behrman and Deolalikar 1990). A study using data from nearly 90 countries over three decades finds that price elasticities of demand for primary and secondary enrollment as well as total years of schooling are between 12 and 21 percent higher for girls than for boys (Schultz 1987).

The more sensitive demand for investment in girls is due in part to parents' perception that investing in girls yields lower returns to the household than investing in boys. In education, for which the strongest empirical evidence exists, studies on private returns to schooling do not confirm this perception, however. In fact, any systematic differences in returns may favor girls (King and Hill 1993; Schultz 1998).[14] But even

Table 4.2 How Prices Affect Demand for Education, Health, and Nutrition, by Gender

Study	Country	Key findings
Health and nutrition		
Alderman and Gertler 1997	Pakistan	The absolute value of the price elasticity of demand for health care, computed at population means, ranges from 58 percent higher for females than males in the lowest-income group to about 14 percent higher in the highest-income group.
Behrman and Deolalikar 1990	India	Food price elasticities derived from nutrient demand equations are generally larger in absolute value for females. Of 28 estimated food price coefficients, seven are significantly larger in absolute terms for women (and two smaller) than for men. For girls, eight coefficients are significantly larger in absolute terms than for boys.
Education		
Sipahimalani 1999	India	A girl's probability of ever enrolling in school goes down by 1–2 percentage points if distance to primary school increases; the effect on boys is statistically insignificant.
Lavy 1996	Ghana	The coefficients of distance to primary and secondary school show greater responsiveness in schooling for girls (–0.111 and –0.020) than for boys (0.009 and –0.017), though the coefficient of distance to middle school is the same.
Gertler and Glewwe 1992	Peru	Elasticity of demand for education in response to travel time is always higher for girls than for boys—between 5 and 20 percent, depending on average household income and the location of the school.
deTray 1988	Malaysia	The lack of a secondary school in a community lowers girls' attendance more than boys'. It lowers a girl's probability of school participation by 0.171, and a boy's probability by 0.134.
King and Lillard 1987	Philippines	Boys' high school enrollment rates would rise by less than 1 percentage point if the distance to a high school decreased. The effect on girls is larger, about 3 percentage points.
Schultz 1987	Cross-country	Price elasticity for female enrollment rates are –0.76 at the primary level, –1.07 at the secondary level, and –0.86 for total expected years of schooling. For boys the figures are –0.63, –0.91, and –0.77.

Note: The price elasticity of demand is derived from estimates of demand functions. It is the percentage change in demand for a good or service in response to a given change in its price.

166

where the private returns to education do not differ systematically by gender, demand for girls' education could be affected by gender differences in effective returns realized by parents. In societies where women are not expected to be economically independent and thus have limited ability to transfer resources to their parents, parents may regard investments in daughters as less desirable. And as noted earlier, where parents rely on sons for support in old age, they may perceive lower returns to investing in daughters (Alderman and King 1998). The fact that parents' calculations of private returns do not capture the social benefits from investing in girls' education is a market failure that warrants government intervention.

Similarly, the costs of investing in girls' and boys' human capital may differ. Even if tuition is similar for boys and girls, costs for uniforms and travel may be higher for girls. For example, parents may have to pay higher transportation costs if they don't want their daughters to walk long distances, or to walk alone, to school. Similarly, clothing (or uniform) costs may be higher where parents are reluctant to send girls to school without proper attire. In Morocco and Tanzania the direct costs of schooling are considerably higher for girls than for boys (Khandker, Lavy, and Filmer 1994; Mason and Khandker 1996). In Tanzania households spend as much as 14 percent more to send a girl than a boy to school.

The opportunity cost of children's time in school-related activities may also be higher for girls than for boys, especially in poor and rural areas, where girls tend to work longer hours than boys when both market and nonmarket work are considered (Hill and King 1995; Mason and Khandker 1996). This would be so where there are strong gender norms for household tasks and no ready market substitutes. In the absence of information on the opportunity cost of time, several studies have estimated the effect of distance to the nearest school as a way to capture the indirect costs of schooling. The result: distance to school is generally a greater deterrent to girls' schooling than to boys'. In Ghana, India, Malaysia, Pakistan, Peru, and the Philippines household demand for girls' education is more sensitive than boys' to distance to school (see table 4.2).

Some of the strongest evidence on the effect of costs on household demand for girls' education—and perhaps human development more broadly—comes from recent country-level programs that have directly or indirectly subsidized schooling. Program evaluations from a national stipend program for girls' secondary education in Bangladesh, from girls'

167

education projects in rural and urban Balochistan, Pakistan, and from a national school voucher program in Colombia all indicate that interventions that reduce the costs to households of girls' schooling can promote female attendance and improve girls' enrollment and chances of staying in school relative to boys' (box 4.3).

Box 4.3 Subsidizing Girls' Education: Evidence from On-the-Ground Experience

PROGRAM EVALUATIONS FROM RECENT INITIATIVES that subsidize the costs of schooling indicate that demand-side interventions can increase girls' enrollment rates and close gender gaps in education. A school stipend program operating in Bangladesh since 1982 subsidizes various school expenses for girls in secondary school. According to the first program evaluation, over the first five years girls' enrollment rates in the pilot areas rose from 27 to 44 percent, more than twice the national average (Bellew and King 1993). After girls' tuition was eliminated nationwide in 1992 and the stipend program was expanded to all rural areas, girls' enrollment climbed nationally to 48 percent. More girls appeared for exams and enrolled in intermediate colleges (World Bank 1997). Boys' enrollment rates also rose, but not as quickly as girls'.

Two recent programs in Balochistan, Pakistan, illustrate the potential impacts of prices and better physical access. The fellowship program in Quetta, the capital of Balochistan, helped nongovernmental organizations build schools in poor urban neighborhoods, with a subsidy tied to girls' enrollment: the schools could admit boys so long as they made up less than half the enrollment. In rural Balochistan another program helped to increase the number of local, single-sex primary schools for girls by encouraging parent involvement in establishing schools and by subsidizing the recruitment of female teachers from the local community. Girls' enrollment rose 33 percent in Quetta and 22 percent in the rural areas. Interestingly both programs appear to have expanded boys' enrollments also, suggesting that increasing girls' educational opportunities may have spillover

benefits for boys (Kim, Alderman, and Orazem 1999). Before the programs people questioned whether girls' low enrollments were a result of cultural barriers that caused parents to withhold their daughters from school or of an inadequate number of appropriate schools. Program evaluations suggest that better physical access, subsidized costs, and culturally appropriate design can lead to sharp increases in girls' enrollments.

Colombia launched a national education voucher program in 1992 to increase continuation from primary to secondary school. The program tapped into excess private capacity using demand-side financing to ease crowding in public schools. Rather than choosing which private schools to subsidize, the government allowed students and parents to choose among the private schools that agreed to participate in the program (King, Orazem, and Wohlgemuth 1999). Students qualified for the program on the basis of prior attendance in a public primary school, admission to a participating private secondary school, as well as age and socioeconomic status. Vouchers were then assigned to qualified students through a lottery in cities where demand exceeded the supply of vouchers—and neither girls nor boys were more likely to receive them. The vouchers were found to increase secondary schooling among lower-income students. On average, voucher students completed a tenth of a year more schooling, a statistically significant effect that is larger for girls than for boys (Angrist and others 2000). And receipt of a voucher reduced the probability of a student working for pay, an effect larger for boys than for girls.

So, pricing policy and programs that improve physical access to services can increase household investments in women's and girls' human capital in both absolute and relative terms. Since price elasticities of demand for schooling (and health care) are higher for girls than for boys, even untargeted programs that reduce costs will tend to close gender gaps in human development. But targeted approaches are likely to have greater impact at lower budgetary costs.[15] Similarly, that price elasticities tend to be higher for females than for males means that price shocks will likely have more adverse effects on girls and women than boys and men. For example, when countries impose cost recovery for education or health services, use by girls and women is often more vulnerable to price increases than use by boys and men.

Child care. As already discussed, women tend to work longer hours than men, and in virtually all countries women perform a disproportionate share of household maintenance and care activities. These activities often keep women from taking paid work and girls from attending school. When women have limited ability to earn income independently, they have less relative bargaining and decisionmaking power in the household. And when girls cannot attend school, their future capabilities suffer, with implications for their welfare and their children's. The availability of low-cost child care services can reduce the costs to girls and women of care activities, enabling girls to go to school and women to enter the labor force.

In both developed and developing countries the presence of young children significantly reduces the likelihood that mothers will participate in the labor force.[16] In the United States labor force participation among different cohorts of women declines by 10–30 percent with an additional child.[17] In Mexico a newborn decreases its mother's labor force participation by 12 percent, and an additional child between ages one and five reduces it by 9 percent (Cunningham 2000). In urban Brazil an additional child under two reduces female employment by 9–38 percent, depending on the econometric model applied. An additional child between ages two and four decreases female employment by 3–5 percent (Connelly and others 1999). Studies generally do not find that young children decrease men's labor force participation—if anything they have a positive impact on fathers' labor supply.[18]

Labor supply studies also indicate that having "mother substitutes" in the household—usually girls or other women who can provide child care—significantly increases the likelihood that mothers will work outside the home (Wong and Levine 1992; Connelly, DeGraff, and Levinson

1996; Lokshin 2000). But as noted earlier, increases in wages or demand for female labor that draw mothers into the labor force often reduce older girls' school attendance.

The availability of low-cost, out-of-home child care increases the probability that mothers will enter the labor force. In poor neighborhoods of Rio de Janeiro, Brazil, the supply of publicly provided child care facilities is the single most important determinant of mothers working outside the home, either part-time or full-time (Deutsch 1998). In a range of settings—Canada, Kenya, Romania, the Russian Federation, and the United States—reducing the price of out-of-home child care raises demand for such care and enables mothers to enter the labor force (figure 4.2).[19] In Russia subsidizing out-of-home child care can be more cost-effective than such approaches as wage subsidies in bringing mothers into the labor market and raising maternal (and household) incomes.

Low-cost child care can also increase girls' school attendance: in rural and urban Kenya a 10 percent decrease in the price of out-of-home care would be expected to result in a 5.1 percent increase in the enrollment

Figure 4.2 Lower Child Care Costs Put More Mothers in the Labor Market

Percentage increase in mother's labor force participation due to a 10 percent decline in the price of out-of-home child care

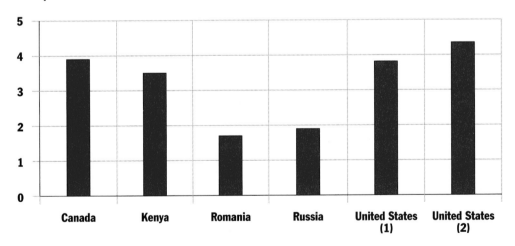

Note: The elasticity of employment with respect to the price of care reported in United States (2) refers to married mothers. Connelly and Kimmel (2000) report an even higher employment elasticity for single mothers.

Sources: For Canada, Cleveland, Gunderson, and Hyatt (1996); for Kenya, Lokshin, Glinskaya, and Garcia (2000); for Romania, Fong and Lokshin (2000); for the Russian Federation, Lokshin (2000); for United States (1), Blau and Robins (1988); for United States (2), Connelly and Kimmel (2000).

rates of 8- to 16-year-old girls (after controlling for other factors)—a statistically and economically significant effect. The results show no significant impact on boys' schooling (Lokshin, Glinskaya, and Garcia 2000).

Design of Service Delivery

Government agencies and donor institutions have tended not to consider gender differences and disparities when designing service delivery, whether school or health care systems, financial institutions, or agricultural extension services. This lack of attention to gender has limited female access to a range of productive resources, if unintentionally. At the same time, institutions designed to account for gender differences and disparities greatly enhance female use of services and thus improve gender equality in command over resources. This section reviews service delivery in three areas: education, financial services, and agricultural extension.

Education. The design of school systems can improve girls' education outcomes. In Balochistan, Pakistan, recruiting local female teachers has been key to breaking down cultural barriers to sending girls to primary school (Kim, Alderman, and Orazem 1998). The presence of female teachers has also been an important determinant of girls' enrollments in Bangladesh (Khandker 1996). In some settings parents are more willing to send their daughters to a single-sex school. And in Bangladesh's coed schools separate toilet facilities are an important determinant of girls' school enrollment and attainment.

Recent project experience highlights an important link between community involvement and participation in the design of culturally appropriate service institutions. In Balochistan, Pakistan, for example, parental involvement in teacher recruitment and other elements of school design has been critical in attracting female students (Kim, Alderman, and Orazem 1998).

Parents' demand for girls' education appears to be more sensitive than their demand for boys' education to the quality of schooling, the extent of learning, and teacher attitudes. In the Northwest Frontier Province in Pakistan girls promoted to the next grade based on academic achievement are 70–90 percent more likely to continue in school than those held back or promoted without learning. Merit-based promotions appear to matter less for boys—those who are promoted for achievement are only 50 percent more likely to continue than those held back or promoted for other reasons (King, Orazem, and Paterno 1999). Similarly, studies based on household survey data from Bangladesh and Kenya suggest that the quality of teachers affects the demand for girls' schooling more than demand for boys' (Khandker 1996; Lloyd, Mensch, and Clark 1998).

A recent study of Kenya found that the experience of primary school can be harsh for both boys and girls—but girls appear to be particularly affected by negative attitudes and discrimination (Mensch and Lloyd 1998). And the quality of the learning environment is directly related to the likelihood that girls will drop out of school. For example, whether teachers think math is important for girls and whether boys and girls receive (and perceive) equal treatment in the classroom significantly affect girls' (but not boys') propensity to stay in school (Lloyd, Mensch, and Clark 1998). Also in Kenya girls seem to underperform in school when teachers think they are naturally less able, controlling for other factors. At the same time, boys' school performance does not seem to be affected significantly by how teachers view them (Appleton 1995).

Parents' attitudes toward their children's schooling have a similar effect. In households where parents think schooling is more important for boys than for girls, sons attain higher exam scores than those in households with no such attitude, other factors held constant. In households where parents think girls are naturally less able than boys, daughters perform significantly worse on exams than those in households without that view (Appleton 1995). Changing attitudes among parents, teachers, and principals will require long-term efforts. To this end, training staff and reviewing and revising school curricula can all play important roles in ensuring that gender stereotypes are not perpetuated in the classroom.

Financial services. Several features in the design of traditional banks or other lending agencies make it more difficult for women than men to borrow or save (Buvinic and Berger 1990; Holt and Ribe 1991). For example, financial intermediaries often require traditional forms of collateral (land, other assets) that women lack access to. Similarly, complicated application procedures and documentation may prevent women with low education and few skills from applying. Minimum loan sizes—and sometimes sectoral priorities for bank lending (such as manufacturing) outside sectors in which female entrepreneurs are concentrated (services and commerce)—also mean that women have poorer access to credit and other financial services. And if the nearest savings institution is far away, limited mobility may prevent women from establishing financial savings accounts.

Financial institutions can facilitate women's saving and borrowing by designing rules, procedures, and operations to account for the constraints that women often face—for example, by allowing substitutes for traditional forms of collateral, by simplifying banking procedures, or by reducing the need for women to travel long distances to save and borrow. Take Ghana's *susu* collectors, who mobilize savings of both women and men by visiting them at home and work (Muntemba 1999). By bringing financial services to clients (rather than the other way around), *susu* collectors have mobilized savings among Ghanaian women and provided small working capital loans for female-run enterprises (box 4.4).

Box 4.4 *Susu* Collectors—West Africa's Mobile Bankers

IN GHANA THEY ARE *SUSU* COLLECTORS OR *OLU*. IN Nigeria they are *esusu* or *ajo*. And in francophone countries they are *tontiniers*. Also known as "mobile bankers," they are informal sector savings collectors who mobilize savings in Ghana and other parts of West Africa by collecting daily deposits. They differ from community banks and group-based organizations, such as Grameen Bank, in a few respects. They visit savers at shops, workplaces, market stalls, and homes to collect a specified amount daily or at regular intervals. Moreover, they are generally individual entrepreneurs who perform a financial service without capital of their own.

Amounts saved with *susu* collectors tend to be small, typically ranging from $0.25 to $2.50 in 1994. In Ghana the amount averaged $0.73 a day per client (Steel and Aryeetey 1994). At the end of each month the savings are returned to the depositors, with the collectors keeping one day's deposit, or 3.3 percent of the monthly savings, as commission. *Susu* collectors sometimes extend an "advance" to clients who save regularly and consistently, and they occasionally lend to nonclients (Aryeetey and others 1994, 1997). Savings collectors screen and monitor borrowers through daily observations while collecting deposits. Evidence suggests that recent growth in petty trading activities in Ghana has enabled *susu* collectors to expand lending in recent years, as their deposit base has increased. But weak links to the formal financial sector still constrain expansion of lending activities.

Why are people willing to pay to save with *susu* collectors?

- The *susu* system functions as a financial management service. Depositors commonly use the accumulated funds as working capital to restock the supplies that enable them to maintain or expand their businesses.
- By pledging to set aside savings for their *susu* collector, people in small businesses—particularly women—can protect their savings from competing claims by family and friends.
- In settings where commercial banks are ill equipped to accept small deposits by often-illiterate savers, depositors willingly pay for the convenience of banking daily at their home or workplace.

How do *susu* collectors facilitate female access to financial services?

- There are no minimum deposit requirements, so women can save small amounts.
- Women do not have to travel long distances.
- The system does not have complicated procedures requiring literacy or high levels of education.
- The *susu* system does not involve formal banking regulations that sometimes act as barriers to women's access—such as co-signatory requirements.

For credit delivery, one of the most important design innovations comes from recent microfinance initiatives, such as Grameen Bank and BRAC in Bangladesh, in the form of group-based lending. Group-based lending replaces traditional collateral requirements—based on ownership of land, buildings, or other physical assets—with a group-based lending contract, which uses social capital and peer pressure as means to promote loan repayment. While this innovation has the potential to enable borrowing among both women and men who lack traditional forms of collateral, in practice group-based lending appears to have been particularly significant in facilitating female borrowing. Between 1985 and 1994 the number of women borrowing from Grameen Bank grew rapidly, from about 100,000 to more than 1.7 million (Khandker, Khalily, and Khan 1995). By 1996 BRAC had grown to about 1.5 million female borrowers (Chen 2000). Women now make up the vast majority of borrowers from these programs. Moreover, smaller microfinance programs in Bangladesh now provide financial services to millions of Bangladeshi women.

In addition to substituting group-based collateral for traditional collateral, microfinance programs often provide training and other activities that help borrowers become better entrepreneurs. Some programs train group members in areas not directly related to microenterprise development, areas intended to help members improve their living standards and quality of life more broadly. For example, Grameen Bank members are often taught about the benefits of education and physical exercise (Khandker, Khalily, and Khan 1995).

Many microfinance programs also help to mobilize savings by encouraging or requiring members to save part of their newly earned income in bank accounts. Intended to stimulate saving habits, this also helps poor women and men build financial assets, providing insurance to them and their families in the event of economic shocks. Some microfinance programs also include contributory funds that serve as insurance.

Agricultural extension. Female farmers tend to have poorer access to resources needed for agricultural production— and production information, training, and technologies gained through national agricultural extension tend to be no exception. In Kenya, Malawi, Nigeria, Tanzania, and Zambia extension agents are more likely to visit male-headed than female-headed farm households (Quisumbing 1994). Similarly, in Vietnam female rice farmers are less likely than male farmers to receive integrated pest management training or consultations from extension service workers or technicians (Chi and others 1998). This has had significant effects on female farmers' functional knowledge of pest management relative to male farmers', even after controlling for education, age, and other relevant personal and farm characteristics.

Staffed predominantly by male agents, extension services have traditionally focused on male farmers because it was assumed that men were the main agricultural decisionmakers and would share relevant extension information with their wives. Neither assumption tends to be accurate. Women are farm managers in many countries. This has long been the case in Sub-Saharan Africa, but is increasingly so in other regions as men leave farming for nonfarm employment. And as with other resources, extension information often is not pooled within households. Although 40 percent of female farmers in Trinidad indicated that they received agricultural advice from their husband, female farmers in Burkina Faso, India, Malawi, Nigeria, Syria, and Thailand reported that they more commonly get information about modern production technologies from friends, neighbors, and relatives (Saito and Spurling 1992; Das 1995). In Burkina Faso only 1 percent of female farmers surveyed indicated that they had heard about production technologies from their husband.

The ability of female farmers to benefit from agricultural extension can improve substantially if services account for gender differences in cropping choices, gender disparities in resource constraints, and cultural restrictions limiting female-male interactions individually or in groups. As with other service delivery systems, the benefits of accounting for gender issues are likely to be greatest when beginning "upstream" in the process—accounting for female farmers as a separate constituency in agricultural extension policies and operational guidelines, recruiting female extension workers (especially where female-male interactions are restricted), and training both female and male extension agents about the different production constraints faced by female and male farmers (Saito and Spurling 1992; Das 1995). In such regions as Sub-Saharan Africa, where female farmers cultivate different crops than male farmers do, this would also include agronomic research on female-cultivated crops.

Investments in (Time-Saving) Infrastructure

Selected investments in basic infrastructure, particularly infrastructure that helps women and girls save time, can increase progress toward gender equality in access to resources and in economic participation. As discussed earlier, investments that reduce distance to school can help raise female enrollment rates (in absolute terms and relative to male rates), in part by reducing the opportunity cost of schooling for girls. Similarly, increasing access to local health care facilities reduces the time women and girls need to spend on in-home care for sick family members (Gutierrez 1998). This can mean fewer interruptions to women's paid work and girls' schooling.

Equally important are investments in basic water and energy infrastructure. In rural areas of developing countries, where water and energy infrastructure is poor or nonexistent, household members spend lots of time going to community water sources (wells) or open access areas (rivers or forests).[20] What would happen if all households in Sub-Saharan Africa were no more than 400 meters (about a six-minute walk) from a potable water source—the national target set by the government of Tanzania? A recent study of five rural areas in Burkina Faso, Uganda, and Zambia found that potential time savings would range from 125 to 664 hours per household per year, on average, in villages where that target had not been met (figure 4.3). In the "worst-case" villages (those where households were farthest from water and fuel supply), potential time

Figure 4.3   Closer Water and Fuel Supply Can Significantly Reduce Time on Collection Activities

Average potential time savings per household per year

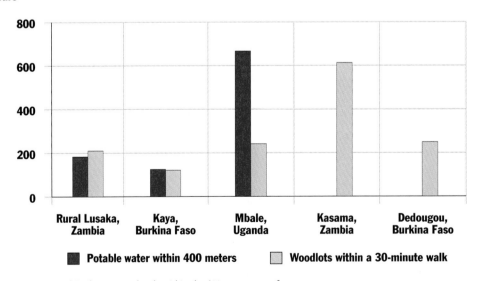

Note: Kasama and Dedougou are already within the 400-meter target for water.
Source: Barwell (1996).

savings would be as high as 942 hours per year per household. Similarly, if woodlots or other sources of household energy were no farther than a 30-minute walk, potential time savings on firewood collection would range from 119 to 610 hours per household per year, on average. Again, in the worst-case village potential savings would be as high as 984 hours a year for households, equivalent to half a year's work for a person working eight hours a day, five days a week (Barwell 1996).

In most settings collecting water and fuelwood is largely the responsibility of women and girls. In Ghana, Tanzania, and Zambia women account for no less than two-thirds of household time devoted to water and fuel collection, while children—mostly girls—account for between 5 and 28 percent of household time spent on these activities (Malmberg Calvo 1994). In rural Nepal and Pakistan poor access to firewood means women spend more hours collecting firewood and fewer hours generating income (Kumar and Hotchckiss 1988; Cooke 1998; Ilahi and Jafarey 1999). The same is true for water in rural Pakistan, where women work longer hours and have less free time than men (Ilahi and Grimard forthcoming). Without adequate water, fuel, or transport infrastructure, these time-consuming activities often come at the expense of girls' schooling or women's time for paid work or leisure.

Investments in time-saving infrastructure—as well as markets for energy, water, and transportation—can reduce the time women spend on household maintenance activities, freeing them for income-earning activities. Greater earning capacity, in turn, can promote a more equitable balance of power between women and men within households. And while better water and energy infrastructure can benefit all household members, it benefits girls in particular. For example, in rural Morocco having wells or piped water increases the probability that both girls and boys will enroll in school. But the impact is considerably larger for girls, who are responsible for collecting water (Khandker, Lavy, and Filmer 1994).

———

This chapter has shown that households distribute resources in the face of competing preferences and unequal bargaining power among members. Putting more resources in the hands of women tends to empower them; it also tends to increase household allocations and investment toward children. The evidence makes a strong case for targeting interventions on the basis of gender. It also highlights several key policy levers—pricing policies, service delivery designed with gender in mind, and investments in specific types of infrastructure—to reduce gender disparities in command over resources.

The broad institutional context (discussed in chapter 3) and household allocation decisions interact to shape gender roles and relations and to determine the extent of women's and men's rights, resources, and voice in society. Neither the institutional environment nor household decisionmaking processes are static, however. As countries grow and develop—or experience shocks and economic decline—societal institutions change, as do the incentives and constraints that individuals and households face. These changes affect investments and opportunities by gender. The next chapter examines how income growth and economic development affect gender inequality in its various dimensions. It also explores how several prominent development strategies have affected progress toward gender equality.

Notes

1. Evidence of excess female mortality in China, Korea, and India (and to a lesser extent in the Middle East and North Africa) and high relative levels of female malnutrition in South Asia (see chapter 1) highlight particularly severe pro-male bias in the allocation of household resources. But some studies find that the household resource allocation can promote greater equity among household members on the basis of gender. For example, Behrman (1988) finds that during the surplus season households in South India transfer more resources to women and girls than would be justified by pure efficiency considerations. Pitt, Rosenzweig, and Hassan (1990) find evidence of compensatory transfers to women in households in Bangladesh. And recent evidence from the Philippines also suggests that the common household strategy of bequeathing land to sons while investing more heavily in daughters' education is an attempt by parents to bestow productive endowments equitably upon children of both sexes (Estudillo, Quisumbing, and Otsuka 1999).

2. Although the prevalence of polygynous households has declined in the past two decades in The Gambia, Guinea, Niger, and Senegal, more than a fifth of household heads are still polygynous, according to survey data collected in the early to mid-1990s (World Bank staff calculations based on household survey data from 15 countries in Sub-Saharan Africa).

3. See also Brown and Haddad (1995) and Ilahi (1999b) for additional evidence on selected developing countries and Lapidus (1993) for evidence from the former Soviet Union.

4. By virtue of being outside the monetized economy, women's economic contribution tends to be undervalued (Elson 1992; Folbre 1998). For example, a much smaller proportion of female work than male work is captured in national income accounting systems. And the asymmetries, by gender, appear to be considerable. In industrial countries about two-thirds of men's total work time is spent in activities that are captured and valued in national accounts; this compares to about a third of women's total work time (UNDP 1995). In developing countries the gap is larger. More than three-quarters of men's total work time is spent in activities captured in national accounts, compared to about a third of women's total work time.

5. See, for example, Samuelson (1956), Becker (1974, 1981), and Singh, Squire, and Strauss (1986). For a critique of the neoclassical view of the household from a gender perspective, see Folbre (1986).

6. This is the case even if assets and education are endogenous due to marriage market selection. For further discussion on assets brought to marriage in the context of analyzing household bargaining behavior see Quisumbing and Maluccio (1999).

7. Before April 1977 the United Kingdom's Universal Child Benefit consisted primarily of a reduction in the amount withheld for taxes from the father's paycheck. There were two separate programs: a taxable Family Allowance payment made to the mother, and a Child Tax Allowance (based on the child's age) available to the household as an income deduction for tax purposes. The Child Tax Allowance generally resulted in an increase in the father's take-home pay, with benefits of about £500 a year for a family with two children—about 8 percent of male earnings on average. Between 1977 and 1979 the government eliminated these programs and instituted a single Child Benefit program that made a nontaxable weekly payment to the mother. The change thus implied a substantial redistribution of income within the family, as the mother became the sole direct recipient of the payment (Lundberg, Pollak, and Wales 1997; Ward-Batts 1997).

8. Quantifying the impact of such programs as microfinance is often problematic. Researchers are rarely able to collect "experimental" data, which would allow them to make inferences that are not confounded by the effects of nonrandom program placement and self-selection of participants into the program. Nonetheless, several recent studies of microfinance programs in Bangladesh use data based on a "quasi-experimental" survey design that enable their authors to correct for these problems (Khandker 1998; Pitt and Khandker 1998; Menon 1999).

9. For all three programs the effect of female borrowing on household per capita expenditure is significant at the 1 percent level.

10. See, for example, Fairlamb and Nieuwoudt (1991), Gertler and Molyneaux (1994), Singh (1994), Diamond, Newby, and Varle (1999), Mencarini (1999),

and Handa (2000). For a summary of this perspective, see World Bank (1999b).

11. Several studies, including Schuler and Hashemi (1994) and Schuler, Hashemi, and Riley (1997), find that female borrowing is associated with greater contraceptive use by women. But analysis by Pitt and others (1999) points out that these studies did not control for individuals' self-selection into the microfinance programs, nonrandom program placement, or other forms of heterogeneity bias. Neither Schuler and Hashemi (1994) nor Schuler, Hashemi, and Riley (1997) examine the impact of male borrowing on contraceptive use.

12. There is a concern raised in the literature on microfinance in Bangladesh that female borrowing has led to increased violence against women in the home (Goetz and Sen Gupta 1996). Violence can erupt when men try to take control of their wife's credit resources or refuse to contribute to loan payments after they have used their wife's loans. Evidence on whether domestic violence has increased is mixed, however, with several studies suggesting that female membership in credit programs tends to be associated with less violence (Hashemi, Schuler, and Riley 1996; Schuler and others 1996; Kabeer 1998).

13. Even within South Africa the impact of mothers' assets and education differs across the African and Indian populations. Indian women who bring relatively more assets to marriage have a positive influence on their daughters' education (Quisumbing and Maluccio 1999).

14. The assessment of relative returns to girls' and boys' schooling is based on review of numerous studies of private returns to education from developed and developing countries. These studies estimate rates of return to female and male education econometrically using "Mincerian" earnings functions (for an overview, see Schultz 1998).

15. See chapter 6 and appendix 5 for analysis of the likely government budget impacts of using targeted and untargeted pricing policies to promote gender equality in primary education.

16. This finding holds even after studies have applied econometric methods to correct for possible endogeneity of the explanatory variables. See Connelly and others

(1999) for a review of the econometric issues related to assessing the impact of young children on mothers' labor force behavior.

17. These estimates are from Rosenzweig and Wolpin (1980), Bronars and Grogger (1994), Angrist and Evans (1998), and Jacobsen, Pearce, and Rosenbloom (1999) which have used the "natural experiment" of twin births in order to address the potential endogeneity bias.

18. In an analysis of intrahousehold time allocation in rural India, Skoufias (1993) finds that the presence of young children in the household reduces women's time in market activities, statistically significant at the 10 percent level. The impact of young children on men's labor supply to market activities is not statistically significant.

19. See Blau and Robbins (1988), Connelly and Kimmel (2000), Cleveland, Morley, and Hyatt (1996), Lokshin (2000), Fong and Lokshin (2000), and Lokshin, Glinskaya, and Garcia (2000). In Lokshin, Glinskaya, and Garcia's study of rural and urban Kenya, entry into the labor force is defined as movement into wage employment.

20. In more than 50 percent of the 68 countries for which data exist, more than half the rural population lacks access to safe water (World Bank 2000).

CHAPTER 5

Is Economic Development Good for Gender Equality?

G ENDER DISPARITIES HARM A COUNTRY'S prospects for economic development in many ways, imposing high costs on people's standard of living. But the relationship between gender equality and economic development goes both ways—that is, income growth and economic development can be good for gender equality, or bad. This side of the two-way relationship is the topic of this chapter.

Evidence from many countries shows that while economic growth has not eliminated poverty, the share of people who are poor has decreased where average incomes have grown (World Bank 2000b):

> Today close to a fifth of the people in the world survive on less than $1 a day. The incidence of this deprivation varies greatly across countries. Not surprising, the richer the country, the higher the average consumption of the poorest fifth of its population—and the smaller on average the fraction living on less than $1 a day. On average, every additional percentage point of growth in average household consumption reduces that share by about 2 percent... [T]he relationship highlights the importance of economic growth for improving the incomes of poor people and for moving people out of poverty. (pp. 46–47)

But these findings do not imply that economic growth necessarily improves gender equality. Yet, to the extent that economic development betters the lives of the poor—by increasing incomes and income-earning opportunities or expanding the availability of such public services as schools, transportation, and health clinics—avenues for improving the well-being of girls and women and increasing gender equality also open.

Economic change affects women and men differently. Chapter 1 shows that women and men possess unequal rights and resources and so are not equally able to take advantage of the opportunities that economic change presents. Since women and men work in different economic sectors and on different tasks, changes in relative prices of goods and services or technological changes are likely to affect them differently.

A more vibrant economy can increase gender equality through several pathways, which this chapter reviews:

- Economic development expands job opportunities and raises worker productivity in labor markets—and leads to the emergence of labor markets where none has existed. These improvements can eliminate some economic inefficiencies, make it more costly for those not employed to remain unemployed, and send signals to households and individuals about the benefits of greater economic participation by both men and women.
- Economic growth is typically accompanied by more investments in infrastructure—for safe water, roads, transportation, and fuel sources. These investments and the development of markets for substitute labor can lighten women's nonmarket work and allow them more opportunities for paid work and leisure, helping to break down rigid gender divisions of labor. Reducing the burden of housework also has potential benefits for women's health, for household income, and for girls' schooling.
- Higher household incomes relax tight budget constraints to investments in human capital. When household incomes rise, gender disparities in education, health, and nutrition tend to fall. Low-income families that have been forced to ration spending on education, health care, and nutrition are likely to increase such spending. And when this happens, gender disparities in human capital tend to decrease.
- When economic development increases the availability and quality of public services, such as health clinics, schools, and roads, it lowers the cost of investments in human capital for the household. If costs decline more for females than males—or if, as evidence from a range of countries suggests, investments in females are more sensitive to price changes than investments in males—females benefit more.

This chapter reviews household and country studies of how economic development has affected gender equality through these pathways. It also examines the development experience of world regions—and how broad development strategies have had different impacts on males and females. A large empirical literature suggests that gender equality, measured in various ways, improves with economic development. But the findings also indicate that some gender inequalities persist despite economic development.

In the East Asian countries that grew rapidly over the past three decades (barring the financial crisis of the 1990s), gender gaps in education and real wages narrowed as women's work opportunities expanded. Yet gender inequality in political representation remains greater than might be expected, given the region's average income per capita. In Eastern Europe and the former Soviet Union the output collapse following the restructuring of the productive sectors and the downsizing of the public sector illustrates the risks that can accompany major economic reforms and the disparities in their effects on women and men. Gender inequalities are resurfacing there as a result of lower incomes, lost jobs, and reduced government support for child care and health care services.

Breaking Down Rigid Gender Divisions of Labor

TECHNOLOGY, THE EXTENT TO WHICH LABOR MARKETS EXIST and function, and prevailing gender norms about divisions of labor together determine the allocation of work and leisure within society. As earlier chapters discuss, women in most societies shoulder the burden of domestic responsibilities—cooking, fetching water, collecting fuel, and caring for children, the sick, and the elderly. On average, women work far longer hours than men—especially when women also work for pay. On the other hand, men are expected to be the primary breadwinners and protectors for their families, and men's self-esteem and status in society are intertwined with their ability to fulfill these expectations. And the more prescriptive and stratified a society's gender roles, the more rigid its gender division of labor.

Economic development introduces incentives and opportunities that can break down entrenched gender roles in the economy—allowing females to participate as males do in the market economy (and not just during economic recession) and males to share in care activities. Economic growth can lighten women's work burden at home, giving them more leisure time and the choice of engaging in market work. And it can allow men to lighten their own market work and induce them to engage in more nonmarket activities.

Lighter Household Work

As household income or wealth rises, studies show, women's work hours decline, holding other factors constant—and this drop tends to exceed the corresponding decrease in men's work hours. In Peru total hours worked by females are highest among the poorest 20 percent of households while total hours worked by males are stable over the income distribution. So, the gender gaps in work and leisure are narrower among higher-income households (Ilahi 2000). Similarly, in Bangladesh and India greater wealth—measured by various forms of nonwage income—is associated with fewer total hours worked (and more leisure) for women relative to men (Khandker 1988; Skoufias 1993).

But not all studies find this pattern. In Pakistan an increase in nonwage income had no appreciable impact on women's work or leisure (Ilahi and Grimard forthcoming; Ilahi and Jafarey 1999). And in the hilly regions of Nepal, both men and women spend longer hours in farm work at higher levels of income, with men's total working hours increasing more than women's (Kumar and Hotchkiss 1988).

Then there is the cross-country evidence. Two measures of gender equality in time use—average hours worked in all activities and average hours worked in nonmarket activities only—are positively related to per capita GDP (figure 5.1). A scatter plot of 23 countries with comparable measures of work hours shows the following patterns: in nearly all the countries women work more hours than men. But this gender gap is smallest (essentially zero) among the highest-income countries where on average both men and women work fewer hours. The difference in the gender gap between countries with per capita GDP greater than $5,000 (1995 dollars, adjusted for purchasing power parity) and those with less is about 100 minutes a day. An important source of this gender gap in total work is the gender gap in time spent in nonmarket activities. This gender gap is also smaller in higher-income countries than in lower-income countries, but the implied effect of economic development is less than that for total work hours, indicating that even with more work options and greater flexibility, the traditional division of labor between women and men persists.[1]

Figure 5.1   Women Work More, Especially in Nonmarket Activities

Total work

Minutes a day

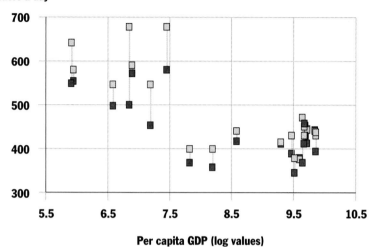

Per capita GDP (log values)

Nonmarket work

Minutes a day

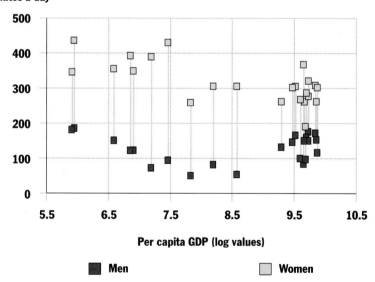

Per capita GDP (log values)

■ **Men**   ▢ **Women**

Note: See appendix 1 for included countries and years, see the glossary for definitions of market and nonmarket work.
Sources: Work data from UNDP (1995); per capita income data from World Bank (1999d).

185

By providing an impetus for increasing the level and quality of infrastructure, economic growth provides opportunities for lightening the burden of household work on women and girls. The improvements in infrastructure, so vital to sustainable economic development, directly affect the efficiency of home production, reducing time spent in household work and releasing time for other activities. There is tremendous potential for this in poorer countries. Consider that the electric power generating capacity (in kilowatts per million people) of high-income countries is about five times that of middle-income countries, and the generating capacity of middle-income countries seven times that of low-income countries (World Bank 1994d). Access to safe drinking water is nearly universal in high-income countries, whereas a fifth of the population in middle-income countries and almost a third in low-income countries do not have access (UN 2000). These numbers suggest the large potential improvements that economic development could achieve.

And where available, hired labor can substitute for family labor on farms or in care activities, thus easing the workload of household members. Low-cost care facilities (for young children, the sick, or the elderly) can substitute for women's labor and increase women's participation in paid work. Or they can subsitute for older girls' time, raising girls' school attendance—as chapter 4 discusses. A market for farm workers enables households to cope with peak season labor demand without pulling older children out of school or adding excessive hours to women's work. But where labor markets are absent or do not function well, substituting hired workers for family labor is not possible, even where it makes economic sense to do so. This results in inefficiencies for households.

More Labor Market Opportunities for Women

Economic development brings dramatic shifts in the structure of employment and in worker productivity. Often it increases urban work opportunities, inducing more people to leave agriculture and move to the cities. When economic change gives rise to a new sector and erodes the dominance of another, it produces winners and losers, especially in the short run as new jobs compete with existing ones and better-equipped workers move to the rising sector.

In the parts of the economy that wane in importance, whether women or men are disproportionately harmed and by how much depend on how quickly they are able to cope with displacement, invest in new skills, and find new employment. Labor market shifts will likely affect women and men differently because they possess unequal work skills, experience, assets, information, and social connections, and so do not benefit from new work opportunities in the same way. Often men move to take advantage of the higher wages in the new sector and women take the lower-paying jobs in the traditional sectors. Agricultural revolutions around the world have led to these types of labor market changes, with accompanying broad social and economic transformations (Boserup 1970). Men migrate to the cities and leave women behind to manage the farm. Or men take over small-scale crop production, traditionally the domain of women, after the crop becomes a major cash crop (Kevane forthcoming).

But women can also gain. Two cases that illustrate this:

- In Bangladesh, with the rise of the export-oriented garment industry and the resulting increase in wage opportunities for young women, families have overcome social resistance to women's work outside the home and are sending women to garment factories. This growth in the ready-made garment industry has already created 1.3 million formal sector jobs, about 90 percent of them filled by women (Bhattacharya and Rahman 1998). The higher employment of women in the country has changed the view of women's economic sphere and has, it is said, increased women's social prestige, their control of income, and their decisionmaking power in the family (Kabeer 2000; Paul-Majumder and Begum 2000).

- In South India women are taking over jobs traditionally held by men in the gem-cutting industry (Kapadia 1999). Married women of the Soliya Vellalar caste of Tamil Nadu typically worked alongside their husbands in gem-cutting workshops, as so-called helpers. With the lowering of tariffs on imported machinery and greater economic liberalization, the synthetic gem industry expanded rapidly, as did the economy overall. Between 1992 and 1997 many men left gem-cutting to take higher-paid, casual, nonagricultural work outside their villages. Women could not benefit as much from these new work opportunities because social and cultural taboos deny them the same mobility. Instead, women were trained to operate the semiautomatic machines in the gem-cutting industry and gradually replaced skilled male workers. While the jobs women took generally paid less than the new jobs taken by men, these jobs tended to pay more than women's alternative employment.

187

Today, two other important trends in labor markets are affecting women's paid work. First, a subset of the informal sector—that of industrial home-based work—is transforming the structure of employment, even in more industrial countries, with significant implications for women's participation. The industrial revolutions of more than a century ago reorganized work around the factory, creating spatial separation between women's work and men's. But there has been a shift back to home-based work as a low-cost, flexible way for formal sector enterprises to meet fluctuating demand and a strategy for lowering labor costs (Anderson and Dimon 1999; Prügl 1999). For married women with children the jobs can be attractive, as the spatial arrangement may allow them to combine paid work with traditional duties. But this benefit could detract from wages (and benefits), as these enterprises can operate outside labor laws and often below legislated minimum wages.

The second trend is the increase in skill-intensive industries, particularly the more intensive use of computers by workers. Consider the United States: in the early 1990s nearly half of workers used computers in their jobs, and women are now much more likely than men to use computers (box 5.1; Weinberg 2000). In developing countries, too, computer use has increased dramatically over the past decade. The number of computers per 1,000 people grew from less than 2 to about 9 in China, 15 in the Philippines, and 30 in Brazil from 1988 to 1998. At the same time the number of computers used nationally has grown between 22 and 36 percent a year in these countries (World Bank 1999d). The new technology is creating new opportunities in all economies—but there is also danger that those without the appropriate skills or the means to access the technology will be left behind. There will be notable gender disparities as gaps are compounded by differences between the poor and the nonpoor and between urban and rural residents.

Lower Labor Market Participation by Men

As women's labor force participation rates have risen in many parts of the world in the past decades, older men's labor force participation has been falling noticeably. Across world regions participation rates have been declining since 1960 for men ages 55–64 and 65 and above, bringing them closer to women's participation rates (figure 5.2). The drop has been notably steeper in Europe and North America than in other regions for

Box 5.1 Computer Use and Women's Employment

THE PAST TWO DECADES SAW UNPRECEDENTED growth in the use of computers at work. In the United States the fraction of workers directly using a computer rose from roughly a quarter in 1984 to more than a third in 1989 and further to half by 1993 (Weinberg 2000). Controlling for a variety of individual characteristics, including education, experience, race, and gender, workers who use computers earn 10–15 percent more than workers who do not (Krueger 1993). In fact, computer use accounted for about 40 percent of the increase in returns to education between 1984 and 1989.

In the United States more women than men use computers at work. For example, in 1993 in the United States women were 33 percent more likely to use computers than men (Weinberg 2000). Breaking down the sources of growth in women's employment using cross-industry regressions, the increased use of computers can account for more than 50 percent of the growth in women's employment between 1984 and 1993.

In developing countries women are still underrepresented among computer users. While 50 percent of Internet users in the United States are women, the proportion is 35–37 percent in Brazil and China, and only about 6 percent in the Middle East (Nua Internet Surveys 2000). And even though the proportion of information technology users who are women is increasing, women are not necessarily moving toward equal labor market participation with men. In Brazil large numbers of women attend computer training, but they are enrolled mainly in word processing courses for support and secretarial positions, rather than in networking or programming courses that might equip them for higher-paying and career-path jobs (Taggart and O'Gara 2000). In India and Malaysia, though information technology has increased women's employment, a large fraction of the new workers occupy low-skill clerical positions (Meng 1993). As more people use computer technology, the differences in the use of the technology, rather than use rates, are likely to determine whether women or men will benefit from the technology revolution.

men ages 55–64, but all regions show a similar rate of decrease for men ages 65 and older. While a third of men in many European countries generally worked past age 65 in the 1960s, the average retirement age for men is now well below 60. The participation rates for men ages 60–64 declined from more than 60 percent in the early 1960s to only 15–40 percent in the 1990s for Belgium, France, Germany, Italy, and Spain (Gruber and Wise 1998). In the United States the particpation rate of men over 60 has been falling continuously since 1930, with more dramatic declines since 1950 (Wise 1997). The fraction of men ages 55 and older in the labor force dropped from 61.4 percent in 1940 to 52.7 percent in 1970 and to 39.4 percent in 1990.

In general, labor force participation rates for these two age groups of men are much higher in Africa, Asia, and Latin America than in Europe and North America. This is the case although the legal retirement age in

Figure 5.2   Labor Force Participation Rates of Older Men and Women are Converging

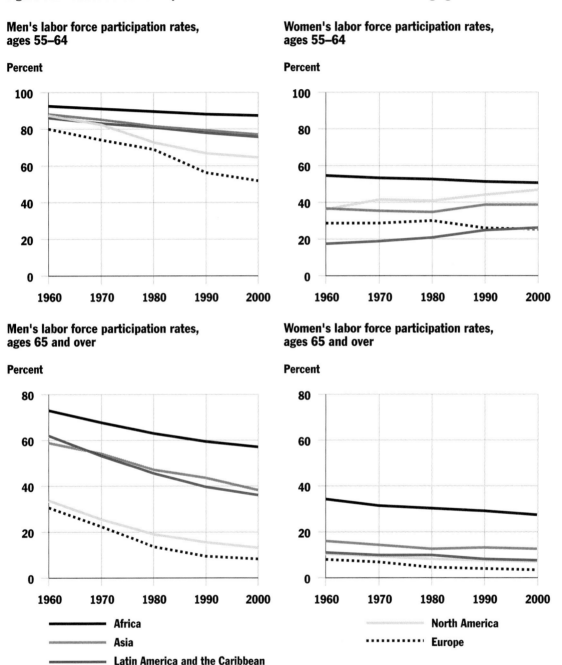

Men's labor force participation rates, ages 55–64

Percent

Women's labor force participation rates, ages 55–64

Percent

Men's labor force participation rates, ages 65 and over

Percent

Women's labor force participation rates, ages 65 and over

Percent

————— Africa

~~~~~~~ Asia

————— Latin America and the Caribbean

~~~~~~~ North America

··········· Europe

Note: Participation rates show the number of economically active individuals as a percentage of the total population in the relevant age and gender category. Data for 2000 are based on projections by the International Labour Organization.

Source: ILO (2000).

poor countries tends to be lower than in richer countries—for example, an average of 57 years in Sub-Saharan Africa compared with 64 years in OECD countries (World Bank 1994b). But even in developing regions the participation rate of men ages 55–64 is decreasing, and the decline accelerates for those ages 65 and older. In contrast, the participation rate has risen for women ages 55–64 or has stayed constant for those ages 65 and older, except in Africa.

There are several possible explanations for the pattern for older men, but consider those relating to economic development. First, increased incomes and the resulting higher demand for leisure—the chance to enjoy one's life earnings—are enticing workers to retire earlier. But perhaps more important, financial incentives for early retirement in the form of public social security or occupational pension schemes have become more available during the past decades (Blöndal and Scarpetta 1997; Wise 1997). In fact, pension schemes are making it costly for men to continue working beyond a certain age because of forgone pension and continued contributions. One study of 15 OECD countries estimates that a 10 percentage point increase in this implicit tax on work between ages 55 and 65 decreases participation rates among older men by 2 percentage points on average (Blöndal and Scarpetta 1997).[2]

This increased availability of formal old-age security programs, a benefit of economic development, has changed the labor market behavior of older men with possible consequences for their old-age security, health, and gender roles. Indeed, the trend raises several questions that pertain to gender equality: as labor supply patterns of men and women converge, will patterns in nonmarket activities also converge so that care responsibilities are more equally shared? To the extent that the decline in participation is voluntary and predictable, will less market work improve men's life expectancy? How will women benefit from this trend in male labor force participation? As men begin to dissave at a younger age and live longer, what are the implications for their wives? Note that women do not benefit from the old-age security programs to the same extent as men because they accumulate fewer work years on average and often may not have access to such programs.

Research on these questions is increasing in industrial countries where the decline in older men's participation rate is more pronounced. One focus of the research is the appropriate design of pension programs. As chapter 3 discusses, the design of pension programs can have different impacts on men and women; the next chapter discusses this issue further.

Strengthening Incentives for Equal Investments in Human Capital

HOUSEHOLDS DECIDE ABOUT WORK, CONSUMPTION, AND investments partly in response to prices and other market signals that determine the costs and benefits of these decisions. Shifts in these signals lead households to reallocate resources among activities and among individuals. Evidence from a range of countries suggests that investments in females are more sensitive to price changes than investments in males, so policies that lower the costs or raise the returns to these investments are likely to benefit females more and thus close the gender gaps in human capital.

Lower Cost of Investments

The discussion of resource allocation in the household in chapter 4 indicates that households make decisions in response to price shifts, among other factors. Those price shifts result from several factors, not least of which are market forces and public policy. When, for example, a stronger economy makes it more affordable for the state to provide health clinics and schools (because, say, tax revenues are higher), the cost of health care and schooling likely declines for low-income households. Moreover, the supply expansion need not originate from the public sector. A stronger economy also gives rise to increased private service delivery, especially if there is a perceived growing demand for human capital. In addition, a stronger economy will enable some poorer households to afford these services even without a price decline—but a decline enables more low-income households to afford the services.

How does this affect gender equality? Although expanded service delivery may not be specifically targeted to girls or women, they can benefit disproportionately. The fall in the effective cost of investments may be larger for them than for males. Building more schools to reduce the average distance to school is likely to raise enrollment for both boys and girls, but it may be particularly beneficial for girls previously not attending school because of distance. As chapter 4 discusses, distance to school is typically a deterrent to girls' education—especially in settings where parents fear for their daughters' safety and reputation. Another example: mothers and older daughters are the primary caregivers for young children. Improving the availability of rural health services for young children and of low-cost child care reduces the cost of caring for mothers and their daughters, raising their welfare. It also allows older daughters to devote more time to schooling (Lokshin, Glinskaya, and Garcia 2000).

Higher Perceived Returns to Investments

The perception that the benefits of human capital investments are lower for women than men tend to dampen investments in females significantly. So, factors that increase returns to these investments and improve the perception of those returns are important incentives for more equal investments.

Inaccurate perceptions stem from information failures, which are pervasive in less-developed economies. For example, gender differences in wages do not accurately reflect gender differences in the effects of schooling on productivity (particularly when there is prejudice in the labor market) and so do not encourage optimal investments in human capital. Estimating the impact of schooling on wages in Indonesia and taking household decisions about schooling explicitly into account, Behrman and Deolalikar (1995) conclude that while women receive lower wages, on average they receive wage increments that are higher than those that men receive for every additional year of primary schooling. At the secondary level the impact on women's wages is 50 percent larger than that on men's. Though there are dissenting studies (for example, Kingdon 1998), a number of studies of other countries support the findings for Indonesia (Schultz 1993, 1998).

Information failures—both in workers receiving information about how the market operates and rewards particular skills and in workers sending signals about their productivity and attachment to the labor market—are likely to be larger for women than for men for several reasons. One is that women's work is still predominantly outside the market. While women have some information networks to rely on, other networks will be unavailable to them. For example, limits on the scope of paid employment for women restrict their ability to realize market returns from their human capital, reducing the signals about the desirability of girls' schooling (Alderman and King 1998).

The creation of markets and the expansion of work opportunities for women in those markets reduces information failures relating to the returns to women's human capital. A few studies in industrial countries estimate the impact on schooling decisions of market signals about the returns to human capital. They find that enrollment choices respond not only to the price of schooling, as discussed in chapter 4, but also to market signals about returns, though the studies do not indicate whether the signals have different effects for females and males (see, for example, Altonji 1991).

Finally, markets produce real incentives. Sustained increased demand for labor in the economy can permanently improve gender equality in human capital investments—by raising market returns to women's human capital they help break down rigid divisions of labor.

Higher Household Incomes

Economic development can improve gender equality in investments through both supply and demand—by increasing service provision, raising the expected rates of return to human capital, and expanding household resources. Recall the evidence in chapter 1 that gender disparities are more pronounced in poorer households than in nonpoor ones. Undeveloped capital markets prevent people from borrowing against expected future income, so the poor are likely to be even more constrained where such markets are thin. For this reason, increases in household incomes can stimulate larger investments in human capital, especially among the poor. And where economic development raises incomes for the poor, there are large potential gains for gender equality. These income gains are likely to have unequal effects for daughters and sons, for when budgets are tight households tend to invest more in sons than in daughters, and when incomes rise the demand for daughters' human capital is more responsive (Alderman and Gertler 1997).[3]

The magnitudes of the income effect vary across settings, but they are often economically important (table 5.1). In Rajasthan, India, a 1 percent increase in per capita household income raises boys' probability of enrollment in middle school by an insignificant 1 percentage point, and girls' by 4 percentage points (Basu 1997).[4] In Malaysia a 1 percent rise in household income increases the probability of girls' school attendance by 18–20 percentage points, but that of boys' attendance by 5–6 percentage points (de Tray 1988).

Similar patterns are found in household demand for nutrition and health care. In Ghana gender discrimination in nutrition among siblings is apparent mainly among low-income households (Garg and Morduch

Table 5.1 How Income Affects Demand for Education, Health, and Nutrition, by Gender

Study	Country	Key findings
Health and nutrition		
Rose 1999	India	Unexpectedly heavy rainfall, a proxy for income, increases girls' survival probabilities during the first two years more than boys' survival probabilities.
Hoddinott and Kinsey 2000	Zimbabwe	Women's mean body mass index fell 3 percent during drought; there was virtually no variation for men.
Alderman and Gertler 1997	Pakistan	Income elasticities of demand for health care are 36–48 percent higher in absolute value for females than for males; there is variation by income group and type of provider.
Garg and Morduch 1996	Ghana	The effect of per capita household expenditure on the probability of being underweight is 50 percent larger for girls than for boys; the effects on the probability of being stunted or wasted are not significantly different.
Behrman 1988	India	During the lean season parents give more weight to a given health-related outcome for boys almost 5 percent more than an identical outcome for girls.
Education		
Ilahi 1999a	Peru	The coefficient of (log) per capita wealth on grade for age is 1.97 for girls and 1.02 for boys, and on the probability of attending school full time, 1.01 and –0.08. Coefficients for boys are statistically insignificant.
Sipahimalani 1999	India	A 1 percent increase in income increases girls' probability of ever being enrolled by 9–13 percentage points, and boys' by 7 percentage points.
Behrman and Knowles 1999	Vietnam	The income elasticity is 6 percent lower for boys than for girls for grades passed per year of school, 22 percent smaller for their exam score in the last completed grade, and 40 percent larger for their age when starting school.
Tansel 1998	Turkey	The coefficient of per adult expenditure on school attainment is higher for girls than boys at the primary (1.10 and 0.36), secondary (1.00 and 0.86), and high school (1.13 and 0.69) levels.
Mason and Khandker 1996	Tanzania	The coefficient of per capita expenditure in girls' secondary enrollment equation is 10 percent higher than the coefficient in boys'.
Basu 1997	India	The coefficient of (log) per capita household income on enrollment is 1.05 percentage points higher for girls than boys. The differential is 3.92 percentage points for the poorer half of households, but 0.89 percentage point and insignificant for the richer half.
de Tray 1988	Malaysia	A 1 percent increase in income increases boys' enrollment probability by 0.05–0.06, and girl's probability by 0.18–0.20.
Schultz 1985	Cross-country	Income elasticities for enrollment are 0.43 for girls and 0.24 for boys at the primary level, 0.65 and 0.30 at the secondary level, and 0.50 and 0.28 for total expected years of schooling.

Note: The income elasticity of demand is derived from estimates of demand functions. It is the percentage change in demand for a good or service in response to a given percentage change in a measure of income.

1996, 1998). In those households a marginal increase in per capita household expenditure reduces the probability of being underweight by 50 percent more for girls than for boys. In Pakistan, at the average household income, a 1 percent increase in per capita income raises the demand for doctor's care by 15–20 percent for girls and by 8–11 percent for boys (Alderman and Gertler 1997).

The flip side of the finding that rising household incomes have a larger positive effect on females—thus improving gender equality in schooling, health, and nutrition—is that economic shocks that erode incomes are also likely to have more devastating effects on females than males. The drought in Zimbabwe in the mid-1990s reduced women's body mass index, a measure of nutrition, by 3 percent, but did not affect men's (Hoddinott and Kinsey 2000). In rural India there are no significant differences in nutrient allocations between sons and daughters when food is abundant, but sons get more food during the lean season (Behrman 1988). These findings suggest that social protection and safety net programs can be critical for women and girls during economic downturns.

Reducing Discrimination through Competitive Markets

COMPETITIVE MARKETS MAY NOT BE THE BEST WAY TO eliminate gender discrimination, so government has a role to play in regulating markets and in providing critical economic infrastructure. But as the world becomes smaller—with national boundaries disappearing with air travel, the new information technology, and regional trade communities—sustained development depends not only on national but also on global conditions. The forces that widen access to basic knowledge in science, medicine, and engineering and engender freer cultural exchanges also tend to expand and open markets. This brings with it potential for economic gains as well as risks.

How do competitive forces, strengthened by open and freer markets, affect gender disparities? A number of empirical studies examine the relationship between the level of trade openness and competition in the economy and gender differences in wages. One study analyzes the effect of greater competition in the manufacturing sector in the United States from the 1960s to the 1980s. It finds that the gender wage gap narrowed beyond what can be explained by relative improvements in women's education and work experience (Black and Brainerd 1999). A 10 percentage point increase in an industry's import share leads to a 6.6 percentage point decline in the gender wage gap.[5] A similar study concludes that deregulation of the banking industry in the United States, a reform that relaxed entry of firms into the industry, is associated with a significant improvement in the relative wages of women, controlling for other factors (Black and Strahan 1999). In addition, women's share of managerial positions increased by 10 percent of the mean, again controlling for measured worker characteristics. A third study finds that enterprises that have weak market power tend to pay women and men more nearly equal wages, while firms that are large relative to the market tend to discriminate (Hellerstein, Neumark, and Troske 1997).

A few similar analyses on developing countries provide supporting evidence:

- One study examines Mexico's experience during a recent period of trade liberalization and finds results that are weakly consistent with the U.S. evidence. Of the change in the gender wage gap between 1987 and 1993, the portion not explained by either female education or experience is smaller in more competitive industries and declines faster in less competitive industries that became exposed to greater competition through liberalization (Artecona and Cunningham 2000).
- Two studies on China, one of rural and another of urban China, conclude that more competitive hiring practices reduce the scope for gender wage discrimination (Meng 1993; Maurer-Fazio and Hughes 1999). Comparing the gender wage gap between employees whose jobs were assigned through administrative mechanisms and those who found their jobs through a competitive job search, the studies find that the proportion of the gap attributable to discrimination is higher among workers in assigned jobs than among those in jobs obtained competitively. The studies control for education and job experience.[6]
- An analysis of industry-level data from 16 middle- and high-income countries finds support for the country-specific findings: gender wage gaps favoring men narrow when domestic markets are open to more and freer international trade (Behrman and King

2000).[7] For middle- and high-income countries, improving the openness of product markets reduces gender wage gaps.

While the results from these different studies are suggestive, little is still known about the magnitude or economic significance of the effects in other developing countries. As concerns about the impact of globalization are being expressed increasingly in public forums, more studies are needed to evaluate the quantitative impact of shifts in competitive pressure on gender inequality in these countries.

Growth with Gender Equality: What Macro Studies Find

THE MICROECONOMIC EVIDENCE ON THE EFFECT OF household income on human capital investments leads one to expect a similar link between economic growth and gender equality at the national level. Several macroeconomic studies have tried to establish a causal link from economic growth to gender equality. These studies have attracted some attention in the development community, and their findings are reviewed here. But consider first the patterns from plots of cross-country data and simple multivariate regressions.

Scatter plots of cross-country data suggest that countries with higher per capita income have higher school enrollment rates for both girls and boys—and longer life expectancy for males and females—than do countries with lower per capita income (figure 5.3).[8] The graphs also show fitted regression lines that summarize the statistically significant relationships between each of the education and life expectancy measures and GDP per capita (in logarithmic values), controlling for equality of rights in each country (see chapter 3). The leveling of the line for primary education has to do with countries in the middle-income ranges already reaching universal enrollment. The same pattern is not yet visible for secondary education.

Are females better off relative to males in countries that have higher incomes? The graphs showing gender ratios for countries at various income levels suggest that they are. Gender equality (at least in terms of the three indicators shown) is higher in countries that have higher income than in countries with lower income. The education gender ratios

Figure 5.3   Gender Equality Is Higher in Countries with Higher Incomes

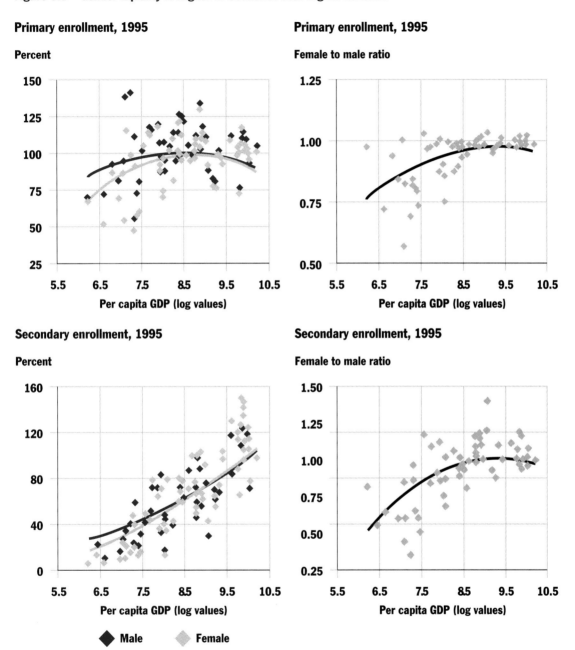

Primary enrollment, 1995

Percent

Per capita GDP (log values)

Primary enrollment, 1995

Female to male ratio

Per capita GDP (log values)

Secondary enrollment, 1995

Percent

Per capita GDP (log values)

Secondary enrollment, 1995

Female to male ratio

Per capita GDP (log values)

◆ Male   ◆ Female

(figure continues on following page)

199

Figure 5.3 continued

Life expectancy, 1997 — Years — Male / Female

Life expectancy, 1997 — Female to male ratio

Note: See appendix 1 for included countries and appendix 2 for regression results.
Source: Authors' calculations based on data from World Bank (1999d).

are generally around 1 for countries with GDP per capita of about $5,000 (1995 dollars, adjusted for purchasing power parity) and above. The life expectancy ratio, also increasing but with a flatter slope, is higher than 1, for reasons discussed in chapter 1.

The cross-sectional association between gender equality and income is evident also in women's political participation. Female representation in parliament, minuscule in most countries, is highest in some, but not all, high-income countries. With few exceptions, the ratio of females to males in parliament lies in a band between zero and 0.2—but in countries with per capita income of around $15,000 (1995 dollars, adjusted for purchasing power parity) and above, it reaches 0.65. Even at the higher income, however, the female to male ratio falls below 0.2 in most countries (figure 5.4).

Figures 5.3 and 5.4 show a positive relationship between income and gender equality in several dimensions—but the relationships are not necessarily causal. The regression lines in figure 5.3 are estimated from

Figure 5.4   Few Women in Parliament—Even in Countries with Higher Income

Female to male ratio

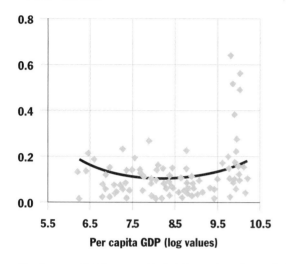

Per capita GDP (log values)

Note: See appendix 1 for year and included countries and appendix 2 for regression results.
Source: World Bank staff calculations based on parliamentary data from WISTAT (1998) and per capita income data from World Bank (1999d).

cross-country data spanning 20–25 years, adjusted for a year variable and an index of gender equality in rights. The values for the most recent year of data are shown in the scatterplot. Because the regression coefficients are based on multiple years of data, the slope of the regression lines represents an average progression for a country as income increases; the intercept of the line reflects year-specific effects. However, causality cannot be determined without a longer time series on the data for gender equality in rights, a central feature of the model. These results simply serve as a baseline for comparison with the results of similar empirical studies that establish causality.

Unless causality from economic growth to gender equality is proved, we cannot conclude that lower-income countries will reach the level of gender equality that higher-income countries enjoy. Today's lower-income countries differ from today's higher-income countries in many important respects besides average income. Some of the higher-income countries may have started off with greater gender equality than today's average low-income country because they had a more egalitarian tradition to begin with. Conversely, some of today's low-income countries may not develop as egalitarian a tradition as today's average high-income country. A key to establishing causality is to separate the effect on gender equality of economic growth (as measured by income growth) from the effects of all other variables, measured or not. Box 2.1 discusses the methodological issues associated with ascertaining causality.

Recent cross-country analyses have examined the effect of income on various measures using a different and richer set of variables—and have reached varying conclusions.[9] However, most of these studies do not deal fully with the statistical issues of establishing a causal relationship, especially issues of unobserved or unmeasured variables that may link income and gender equality. Dollar and Gatti (1999) use two variables—the black market premium and a rule of law index—that are expected to affect growth but not gender inequality directly, as instrumental variables. Analyzing data from up to 127 countries over four time periods, they examine whether income growth leads to greater gender equality in secondary school attainment, life expectancy, and women's political representation.[10] For all three indicators they find sufficiently robust evidence to conclude that increases in income lead to greater gender equality.

Moreover, they find that the relationship is nonlinear. For example, the proportion of women in parliament shows little improvement at low per capita incomes—but increases rapidly once countries reach lower-middle- to upper-middle-income status, controlling for other factors. They also find this convex relationship between income and gender equality in secondary school attainment.[11] This suggests that for many low-income countries, the salutary impacts of income growth alone may take a long time to be realized—at least for some dimensions of gender inequality.

That the relationship may be nonlinear was recognized three decades ago when Boserup (1970) argued that development has to reach a certain threshold before gender gaps close with further economic growth. In her book, *Woman's Role in Economic Development*, Boserup suggests that in the initial stages of development greater urbanization and industrialization tend to intensify the gender division of labor in the home and the workplace. Further expansion of markets begins to erode these traditional gender structures. Tighter labor markets put pressure on employers to relax the exclusion of women from wage activities, and eventually households take advantage of greater labor and consumption opportunities and encourage women to work outside the home.

The overall evidence from different types of data and empirical analyses supports the conclusion that economic development provides an enabling environment for gender equality—though its effects are not immediate or without costs, at least in the short run. The evidence pertains to average effects (though taking into account other factors that might also affect gender equality), meaning that economic development may not benefit all women and men. Knowing who is likely to fall in this group is key to finding a remedy for those who do not benefit or those who are harmed by economic development.

The following sections examine another set of evidence on the links between economic development and gender equality, reviewing the economic strategies that developing regions have followed in recent decades.

Do Development Paths Lead to Gender Equality? Regional Views

THERE IS NO SINGLE PATH TO DEVELOPMENT. BUT THE development strategy a country pursues will affect gender inequalities, even when the strategy does not aim to do so explicitly. Even small changes can make a difference for the working lives of women and men—affecting where people work, the kinds of tools and machinery they use, the value of work experience relative to that of education, and the relative returns to male and female labor. They also affect the amount of time people spend on tasks, how they work in a team, and how males and females relate at home and in the workplace. In Southeast Asia the introduction of high-yield rice varieties led to changes in harvest tools (in Indonesia from a small finger knife to a sickle) and to different labor arrangements, with accompanying changes in the tasks of women and men in harvest teams (Collier and others 1974; Kikuchi and Hayami 1983).

The industrial revolutions of Europe and North America also demonstrate how new modes of production transform gender relations and outcomes (Boserup 1970; Landes 1980; Goldin 1990). Industrialization in Europe and the United States created new jobs in factories for numerous women (and children) and for men moving out of agriculture. And although work conditions were often oppressive, the expansion of factory jobs eventually led to urbanization, new goods and services, and later to higher schooling levels. The subsequent expansion of the service sector, where education could substitute for work experience, further increased women's economic options. More schooling also had the effect of keeping children in school during the day, allowing more mothers to work. Today, not only are many more married women joining the labor market, but they are also working more weeks a year, more hours a week, and are staying active for longer regardless of the presence of young children in the household (Lombard 1999).

The Nordic countries have successfully combined private ownership and market competition with deliberate policies for achieving an egalitarian income distribution and consensus in political and economic life. One feature of this development strategy that pertains to gender is generous family support, which reduces the costs of nonmarket and care activities for women (box 5.2)

Today growing manufacturing and service sectors in many developing countries are increasing demand for female labor—and slowly but surely changing gender roles and relations in the process. But economic changes are not without risks. Some think that the structural adjustment period, particularly in Sub-Saharan African countries, was too harsh, effectively starving social programs that have not fully recovered. Or that the transition period in Eastern Europe proceeded too quickly, leaving firms and households little time to adjust and cope with dramatic changes in the way the economy or the state functioned. These and similar broad changes in other regions have generated a new set of concerns for women, men, and their families. For example, more families, now with two working parents, must balance the exigencies of child rearing with the demands of paid work. Working women face greater risk of violence, sexual harassment in the workplace, and occupation-related health risks and stress. Indeed, traditional gender relations in the home and in society are being challenged by broad social transformations that have accompanied economic development.

Box 5.2   A Nordic Model

THE NORDIC COUNTRIES ARE OFTEN REGARDED AS pioneers in promoting gender equality. Denmark, Finland, Iceland, Norway, and Sweden granted equal rights of inheritance between 1850 and 1880, and gave women the rights to vote and be elected between 1905 and 1920 (Osterberg and Hedman 1997). The Nordic countries all recognize equal rights, duties, and opportunities for men and women in obtaining

(box continues on following page)

Box 5.2 continued

gainful employment, taking care of the home, and participating in political and social activities. This commitment to equality between the sexes is reflected in most quantitative indicators of gender equality, with the United Nation's Gender-Related Development Index and the Gender Empowerment Measure both ranking these five countries within the top 15 of 174 countries (UNDP 2000).

Despite national differences, the pattern of development in gender equality has been similar among these countries, which differ from other industrial economies in that they have given government a larger role in household and family matters. Although the state is not involved in public production of most material goods and maintains free markets in consumer and producer goods, the household sector has been "monetized" by a substitution of public for privately produced household services on a large scale. This has helped increase women's labor force participation.

For example, employment growth in Sweden since the 1960s can be attributed to the increase in women's entry into the labor force (Rosen 1995). The female share of the adult labor force rose from 29 percent in 1960 to 48 percent in 1998 (World Bank 1999d). How did this happen?

- Boys and girls enjoy the same formal education opportunities, with compulsory nine-year primary schooling paving the way for higher education. The result: universal adult literacy.
- Sweden changed its income tax accounting system from families to individuals in the mid-1960s, with no deductions for dependents. This encouraged secondary wage earners—usually women—who had often been discriminated against under joint income taxation.
- The Equal Opportunities Act (1992) strengthened rules that promoted equal rights at work.

This act prohibited direct and indirect salary discrimination and obliged employers to address sexual harassment, survey salary differences by gender, and make it easier for men and women to combine working life with parenthood.

- Expanding publicly provided child care has decreased the personal costs of labor force participation for Swedish women(Gustafsson and Stafford 1992). Since 1948 the government has paid fixed monthly nontaxable child allowances to families with children under 16. By the mid-1990s 57 percent of preschool children were in publicly provided day care centers, in kindergartens, or with "day mothers" employed by the local government. Publicly provided child care is responsive to the needs of working parents, even covering evening work hours. Since 1975 families have paid only 10 percent of child care costs on average, while the public sector has paid the rest (Rosen 1995).
- The state encourages men to take responsibility for the household and children. Between 1994 and 1996 government agencies gave training to recent fathers and fathers-to-be aimed at increasing their understanding of an active father's role and how to combine professional and family life, and encouraged fathers to take more parental leave to care for sick children.
- Roughly one in five people are elderly and receive a pension (Swedish Institute 1999). The care of the elderly has been a public responsibility for a long time—social welfare legislation in 1956 regulated this care, effectively abolishing children's obligation to care for their parents and relieving the pressure on women. Since the 1970s both help in the home and institutional care have rapidly expanded, with special grants from the central government to expand the availability of home help services.

205

This section reviews evidence on three major economic regimes—rapid growth in East Asia in the 1970s and 1980s, structural adjustment in Africa and Latin America in the 1980s, and the economic transition in Eastern Europe and East Asia from the late 1980s. These regimes have been associated with specific policy approaches for restructuring and stimulating the economy. The cases illustrate how diversely economic change can affect gender equality. It is difficult to weigh the success of one regime against that of another in improving gender equality, but cross-country data and case evidence provide interesting and vital lessons (box 5.3).

Box 5.3   Measuring Policy Impact

DETERMINING EMPIRICALLY HOW BROAD development policies have affected women and men and, specifically, how they have affected gender equality is not a simple and straightforward task. It is important to acknowledge the initial situation and to distinguish it from the impact of a particular policy regime. For example, the adverse effects of an economic crisis that leads to the need for reforms should not be mistaken for the impact of the reforms.

It is necessary to establish how the state would have evolved without the policies and compare this counterfactual state with the post-policy state to assess the effect of the development strategy. But this counterfactual state is extremely difficult to establish empirically, and most assessments are at best rough guesses of whether a particular policy regime has improved what the situation could have been otherwise. And when a policy reform is fairly recent it may not be possible to observe its impact, especially if all the policy's elements have not been implemented.

It is important to focus on the gender impacts of a development strategy, not just its effects on either men or women. Focusing on how particular development strategies affect absolute levels of well-being of either men or women does not reveal their

effect on gender inequality. Evidence on how a particular set of policies has affected females and males differently—for better or for worse—is limited.

The welfare impacts of a development policy are likely to be multidimensional. So, measures that pertain only to selected aspects give us only a partial picture—and it can be easy to draw misleading conclusions. Consider two studies on Ecuador that arrive at opposite conclusions about the overall impact of structural adjustment. One study, of a low-income neighborhood in urban Guayaquil, Ecuador, concludes that cuts in government expenditures on public services forced mothers to increase their time on household and community care activities at the expense of leisure (Moser 1989). Daughters were similarly compelled to reallocate time, taking away from their schooling. The conclusion is that adjustment harmed women and girls. The second study, of the cut-flower industry in rural Ecuador, credits an adjustment-induced boom with expanding the demand for female labor, raising women's incomes relative to men's, and increasing women's leisure time (Newman 2000). Men in cut-flower producing areas increased their time in home maintenance and care activities compared with men in other areas. The study concludes that adjustment has benefited women.

Growth and Crisis in East Asia

Nearly a decade ago developing countries were seeking lessons to catapult themselves onto an economic trajectory similar to East Asia's. From 1965 to 1990 the 23 economies of East Asia grew faster than all others. Most of this spectacular growth was attributable to Japan, the four "tigers"—Hong Kong, the Republic of Korea, Singapore, and Taiwan, China—and the newly industrializing economies of Indonesia, Malaysia, and Thailand (World Bank 1993). From 1960 to the pre-crisis period of the late 1990s, these economies grew more than two times as fast as the rest of East Asia, almost three times as fast as Latin America and South Asia, and five times as fast as Sub-Saharan Africa. Moreover, other development outcomes, not just income growth, improved considerably. Life expectancy and education levels rose faster than in any other region, as chapter 1 shows.[12]

How did the East Asian countries do it? They let their product and factor markets operate freely within an environment of appropriate macroeconomic policies. Governments intervened but generally with caution, pragmatism, and flexibility. A striking feature of these economies has been their superior export performance. As a group they increased their share in world exports from 8 percent in 1965 to 13 percent in 1980 to 18 percent in 1990, with manufactured products fueling most of this growth. The region's rapid economic growth was accompanied by declining income disparities and lower poverty rates than in other developing countries (World Bank 1993; Deininger and Squire 1996). While 6 in 10 people lived in absolute poverty in 1975 (based on a $1-a-day poverty line in 1975), only 2 in 10 did in 1995. Further, this rate of decline accelerated in the 1980s and 1990s, a pace of poverty reduction faster than in any other region of the developing world (Ahuja and others 1997).

Narrower gender gaps in schooling and employment. But did gender inequality fall while growth accelerated? Did sound macroeconomic policy and getting prices "right" help achieve gender equality? There is little doubt that several features of the East Asian experience have had a large impact on gender outcomes. First, the region eliminated gender gaps in schooling—though this success came mostly from a general push for universal education rather than from policies specifically targeting girls. Basic education for all—a policy for decades and the goal of public spending in which about half of total education expenditures was allocated to the primary level—paid off not only in universal primary education but also in notable gains at higher levels of education. Also remarkable has been the willingness of households to supplement public resources for these higher levels.

Second, a sustained increase in demand for labor during the period of rapid growth drew large numbers of women into the labor force. Such key export industries as textiles and electronics relied heavily on relatively unskilled, but generally literate, women. In 1970 women made up 39 percent of the labor force in Japan and 26–31 percent in Singapore, Indonesia, and Malaysia (table 5.2). By 1995 women's share of the labor force had risen in these countries—to 41 percent in Japan and 37–40 percent in the other three. In the Republic of Korea the share of working women in regular paid work increased from 65 percent in 1965 to 81 percent in 1992, and in mining and manufacturing the female to male employment ratio rose from 0.37 to 0.68 (Fuess and Lee 1994).

The expansion of female labor force participation came partly from restructuring production and employment away from traditional sectors. In Indonesia, the Republic of Korea, Malaysia, and Thailand the share of working women in agriculture decreased, but the shares in industry and services increased (table 5.3). In Hong Kong, where agriculture was not important, the shift was from industry to services. In Taiwan, China, domestic industry became more skill-intensive as firms that relied heavily on low-skill workers moved abroad, largely to mainland China and to Southeast Asia (Ranis 1993).

Table 5.2 Female Share of the Labor Force in East Asia
(percentage of total)

Economy	1970	1980	1995
Hong Kong, China	35	34	37
Indonesia	30	35	40
Japan	39	38	41
Korea, Rep. of	32	39	40
Malaysia	31	34	37
Philippines	33	35	37
Singapore	26	35	39
Thailand	48	47	46

Source: World Bank (1999d).

Table 5.3 Sectoral Allocation of Female Labor Force in East Asia
(percentage of economically active women)

Economy	Year	Agriculture	Industry	Services
Hong Kong, China	1970	4.7	61.2	34.2
	1980	1.2	56.1	42.8
	1990	0.7	33.0	66.3
	1997	0.2	16.4	83.4
Indonesia	1970	65.3	10.0	24.8
	1980	55.8	12.4	31.8
	1990	56.4	12.5	31.1
	1997	39.6	15.4	39.4
Japan	1980	13.0	27.9	57.0
	1990	8.3	26.8	62.2
	1997	5.8	23.3	67.0
Korea, Rep. of	1980	37.5	23.1	35.9
	1990	20.0	29.5	48.7
Malaysia	1970	66.4	9.9	23.7
	1980	49.3	17.7	33.0
	1990	25.6	22.7	51.8
	1997	14.2	29.8	56.0
Thailand	1990	62.8	11.9	22.0
	1997	50.8	16.6	31.2

Note: Rows may not add up to 100 percent due to rounding or omission of the mining sector.
Source: World Bank (1999d).

The faster growing demand for women's labor supply increased women's earnings relative to men's, but at a slower rate than would have been expected given the relative gains in women's education and experience levels. In Japan women's average earnings as a proportion of men's increased from 48 percent in 1968 to 59 percent in 1988 (Horton 1996). In Korea during 1984–88 the gender earnings ratio increased from 42 percent to 51 percent.[13] In fact, the proportion of the gap explained by these measured characteristics declined over the period, suggesting that other factors, including wage discrimination against women, were contributing more to gender earnings differences.[14]

Gender gaps are visible not only in earnings but also in working conditions in manufacturing. As new entrants into the labor force women generally have little formal sector experience and limited knowledge of their rights as workers, and thus are less able to demand fair treatment. One important change in East Asia was the adoption of legislation protecting female workers in accord with international standards—although enforcement has been a problem. For example, a survey of female workers in nonunionized factories in Indonesia found ample documented cases of women being fired because of marriage, pregnancy, or birth (Agrawal 1996). Only 47 percent of those who applied for maternity leave received it, and only 12 percent of those who did were paid for that leave. Women workers are often ill informed about—or ill equipped to claim—their rights from employers, including overtime pay, paid leaves, and compensation (World Bank 1995; Pangestu and Hendytio 1997).

Shifts in other measures of well-being. The two decades of rapid economic growth in East Asia, economic restructuring, increased urbanization, and higher labor force participation rates transformed the lives of women and men also beyond work. Life expectancy increased in the region: between 1970 and 1997 women gained 10 years and men 9 years. Because of more schooling, the resulting delay in marriage, and the greater availability and adoption of contraceptive methods, fertility rates dropped. Japan's fertility rate, already only 2.1 in 1970, did not show a large decline. But Korea's fertility rate dropped from 4.3 to 1.7 during the period, Indonesia's from 5.4 to 2.8, and Thailand's from 5.4 to 1.7.

Because of more schooling and higher labor force participation, the transition period between schooling and marriage and parenthood lengthened, enabling more young women to earn income and enjoy some autonomy. In Hong Kong young women saw paid employment before marriage as a temporary reprieve from their responsibilities at home and from future responsibilities to their own families (Salaff 1981). A study of female workers in Indonesia's textile, garment, and footwear factories in the export sector found that these women won the greater personal independence associated with higher earnings and became aware of new possibilities for contesting gender norms (Agarwal 1997).

But this was not true in all cases. Against the background of traditional intergenerational contracts in Taiwan, China, newly found work opportunities did not necessarily give young women greater personal autonomy. Many parents tightened their control of daughters and expected remittances as repayment for the investments in them (Greenhalgh 1985). In the home the traditional division of labor remains sharp. According to a 1990 survey in Korea, married women spent an average of more than five hours a day on household chores and child care, while men spent an average of 37 minutes. A 1986 survey in Japan found that on average married working women spent two hours and 26 minutes a day on household chores, married men seven minutes (Westley and Mason 1998).

Effects of the economic crisis of the 1990s. The impressive growth in the region was interrupted in the late 1990s. The currency and financial crisis that first emerged in Thailand in 1997 spread quickly throughout the region, bringing bankruptcies, devaluations, painful adjustments in the labor market and in the home, increased poverty where there had been plenty, and a shaken confidence in the region's so-called economic miracle (World Bank 1998b). The crisis reversed some of the gains from the period of sustained growth. Though it is too early to predict the full and long-term impacts of the crisis, it is apparent that the impacts tend to vary by gender, but not always to the disadvantage of one gender or the other.

The immediate impact of the crisis was felt in employment. For example:

- In Thailand male employment was hit harder than female employment because the construction sector, dominated by men, lost the most workers. For wages the effects were similar for women and men, with men faring a little worse (the increases for men and women from 1995 to 1998 were about equal—at 18 percent and 18.2 percent—as were the declines between 1998 and 1999, 8.9 percent and 7.9 percent). The same gender division of labor that limited women's employment during the construction boom before the crisis protected them somewhat during the sector's downturn (Behrman and Tinakorn 1999). But aggregate unemployment rates were higher for women than for men both before and after the crisis, despite the rise in male unemployment.

- In Indonesia the fall in real wages appears to have compelled younger men and women who were part of an unpaid labor force to enter the paid sector, even as older men were exiting. Compared with 1997, slightly higher fractions of men and considerably higher fractions of women were working in 1998 (Frankenberg, Thomas, and Beegle 1999). According to another study, the proportion of women working more than 45 hours a week rose from 20 percent in 1994 to 24.9 percent in 1998, whereas it fell for men (Horton and Mazumdar 1999). At the same time the decline in average hours worked per week was greater for women, especially in the formal sector (Beegle and others 1999). The loss in real wages was larger in urban than in rural areas, and somewhat larger for women than for men.

- In Korea the crisis decreased the employment of men and women in regular jobs but increased women's employment as daily workers by 16 percent by the end of 1998 (Moon, Lee, and Yoo 1999). And although the final word is not in on whether men or women suffered more unemployment, official data indicate that women's share of unemployment declined between 1997 and 1998 primarily because men's unemployment rate rose sharply.

For household expenditures and welfare the impact of the crisis appears to be differentiated between females and males, but not always in the same direction. In Indonesia the percentage of youths enrolled in school fell more for girls than for boys ages 7–12, and more for boys than for girls ages 13–19 (Frankenberg, Thomas, and Beegle 1999). In Thailand overall enrollment and dropout rates were not as seriously affected by the crisis—but there were differences between boys and girls across schooling levels. Girls' enrollment declined at the pre-primary level but increased significantly at the upper secondary level, while boys' enrollment declined in upper secondary education (Pyne 1999).

Also, studies of the impact of the crisis on health and nutritional outcomes reveal gender differences (Pyne 1999). In Indonesia the average body mass index declined, especially among women in poorer households. Access to higher-quality childbirth services declined as well, with more women resorting to less costly traditional birth attendants and midwives. In Thailand anemia increased among pregnant women.

Although the East Asian economies have not fully recovered from the economic crisis, signs of financial stability and business confidence have reemerged (World Bank 1998b, 2000a). The long-term effect of the crisis on people's lives is not yet known. If households and communities cope by, say, pulling relatively more girls or boys out of school or redistributing nutrient intake by gender, the crisis could have significant long-term impacts on gender equality. This is an area that requires further study.

Structural Adjustment

Structural adjustment typically refers to a set of economic policy reforms undertaken by countries beginning in the late 1970s and early 1980s to reverse economic decline or respond to external economic shocks. Such programs aim to stabilize the economy in the short run and put it on a steady growth path for the long run (Jayarajah, Branson, and Sen 1996). Stabilization measures focus on bringing aggregate national demand in line with national product plus external financing. In most cases this means reducing the fiscal deficit by removing subsidies, introducing user fees for public services, and downsizing the public sector. It also means devaluing the currency to restore internal and external balance. Structural reforms have tended to focus on creating more appropriate incentives for sustained economic growth—deregulating trade and domestic goods markets, privatizing government enterprises, and removing regulatory constraints to saving and investment.

One of the most vigorous debates in the gender and development literature has focused on whether structural adjustment programs have harmed or benefited women and girls, especially in Latin America and Sub-Saharan Africa. A large literature argues that women bear the brunt of the costs of structural adjustment programs and are unable to reap many of the benefits from improved economic performance in the long run (see, for example, the reviews by Beneria 1995 and Summerfield and Aslanbeigui 1998). Another set of evidence, however, indicates that these broad reforms have improved living conditions for both women and men.

How adjustment harms gender equality. One side of the debate stresses the negative consequences of declines in public spending, shifts in relative prices of commodities, employment shocks, and the inability of women to benefit from any positive effects of the reform. Short-run stabilization measures have included cutbacks in public spending—reducing the availability of public services or raising the prices of those services through user fees—with greater impact on females' access to services and on their care activities (Sen and Grown 1987). Household investments in women's and girls' education, health, and nutrition appear to be more sensitive to policy-induced income shocks and price changes than similar investments in men and boys.

Macroeconomic policy measures that change the relative prices of commodities can affect women and men differently as well. In Sub-Saharan Africa—because women's work is concentrated in the nontradable sectors (such as food crop production) and men's work in tradable sectors (such as cash crops)—reforms that raise the price of tradables relative to nontradables would increase men's income relative to women's (Collier, Edwards, and Bardhan 1994). In Chile, following substantial trade liberalization, firms laid off female workers first when business declined—although they hired proportionately more female workers when business recovered (Fan, Melitz, and Sever 1996; Levinsohn 1999). Job reallocation rates were also more than twice as high for women as for men.[15]

Similarly, public sector downsizing may hurt women more than men since the majority of workers in many countries' public sector are women (Appleton, Hoddinott, and Krishnan 1999). Indeed, studies of public sector retrenchment programs in Benin, China, Ecuador, Ghana, and Vietnam show that women have often been disproportionately affected.[16] These employment impacts affect the relative incomes of men and women—in turn influencing their bargaining power in the household and the intrahousehold allocation of resources by gender.

Gender inequalities in economic rights and in access to and control of productive resources—and in economic mobility associated with household responsibilities and gender roles—impede women's ability to participate fully in longer-term economic opportunities associated with adjustment (Collier 1988). This in turn has generated concerns about the ability of adjustment programs to achieve their goals, particularly in Africa where women play a central economic role in agriculture (Saito, Mekonnen, and Spurling 1994). Where women do not command sufficient resources or cannot reallocate their resources toward expanding sectors, they are more likely to be "innocent victims" and "spectators" in adjustment rather than "players" (Haddad and others 1995).

How adjustment benefits gender equality. The other side of the debate argues that adjustment can promote gender equality. Adjustment can promote patterns of growth that raise women's relative economic status—by creating new opportunities that break down established economic interests that traditionally discriminate on the basis of gender. Where adjustment has resulted in growth in export manufacturing, this has often led to substantial job growth for literate, often single women, frequently at wages above previously prevailing market levels (Agrawal 1996; Paul-Majumder and Begum 2000; Haddad and others 1995; Lin 1985).

Even in rural areas outside the wage sector women may have had greater economic mobility in response to adjustment than generally thought. In Ghana rural women—both married women and female heads of household—moved into the nonfarm sector faster than men (Newman and Canagarajah 1999). Movement into nonfarm employment helped reduce the incidence of poverty among female-headed households faster than among male-headed households and resulted in relative income gains for women within and outside female-headed households. The difference between male and female real income in Ghana declined from 19 percent in 1987 to 8.6 percent in 1991.

In Uganda the movement of women into nonfarm employment was not as widespread as in Ghana—since more women remained in agriculture in accord with their traditional roles. But women in female-headed households who moved into nonfarm employment in 1992–96 had similar income gains, with poverty among female-headed households in nonfarm activities dropping faster than among male-headed households (Newman and Canagarajah 1999).

While there is evidence to support both sides of the debate about the impact of structural adjustment, on balance the evidence suggests that females' absolute status and gender equality improved, not deteriorated, over the adjustment period. First, in Sub-Saharan Africa and Latin America and the Caribbean gender equality of rights either improved or stayed the same between 1985 and 1990, girls' schooling generally rose relative to boys', and female life expectancy continued to rise (see figures 1.1–1.3). The most obvious exception to these trends is the relative life expectancy of females and males in Sub-Saharan Africa. Women's relative advantage in the region declined between 1980 and the early 1990s—though the decline appears, at least in part, to reflect a longer-term trend that began before the adjustment period.

Second, a number of studies that have estimated the ratio of women's wages to men's wages over time lead to the conclusion that the (unadjusted) gender gap in wages has decreased in countries in Latin America and Sub-Saharan Africa during the adjustment period (see appendix 3). While the studies are not strictly comparable because they use different databases and may refer to different sectors of the economy, they represent the more careful studies of relative earnings of women and men.

A closer look at adjusting and nonadjusting countries. With Sub-Saharan Africa separated into "adjusting" and "nonadjusting" countries—defined by whether a country ever took a structural adjustment loan in the 1980s from the World Bank—the trends in gender equality have been largely similar across categories of countries.

- While primary enrollment rates have been generally static since 1980, both absolute levels of female enrollments and the gender ratio of enrollments remain higher in these so-called adjusting countries than in nonadjusting ones (figure 5.5).
- At the secondary level growth in female and male enrollment rates has been similar between adjusting and nonadjusting

215

Figure 5.5   Trends in Gender Equality Are Similar across Adjusting and Nonadjusting Countries in Sub-Saharan Africa

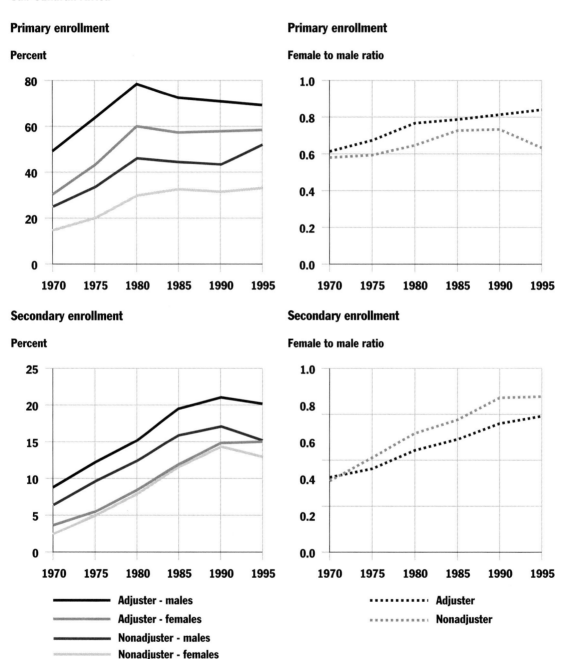

(figure continues on following page)

Figure 5.5 continued

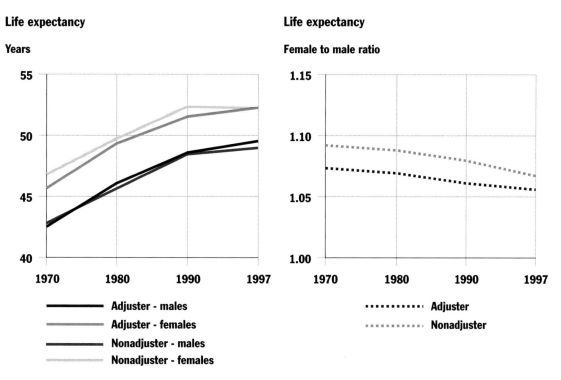

Life expectancy

Years

Life expectancy

Female to male ratio

Legend:
- Adjuster - males
- Adjuster - females
- Nonadjuster - males
- Nonadjuster - females

- Adjuster
- Nonadjuster

Note: See appendix 1 for general notes and included countries.
Source: World Bank (1999d).

countries, but enrollment rates, especially for boys, started at higher levels in adjusting countries. So, while gender equality increased in both adjusting and nonadjusting countries, the ratio of female to male enrollment rates has grown slightly faster among nonadjusting countries.[17]

- Female life expectancy was higher in 1970 in nonadjusting countries than in adjusting countries, with convergence in 1997, while male life expectancy was about equal in both country groups. Thus, the initial gender ratio was higher in nonadjusting than in adjusting countries. Life expectancy then rose with a slight advantage for males over the adjustment period, and with adjusting countries catching up to nonadjusting countries.

In Latin America time series data are relatively scarce for nonadjusting countries, mostly in the smaller countries of Central America, so it is

217

possible to compare only the trends for life expectancy. Initial levels of life expectancy were slightly higher in adjusting than in nonadjusting countries. Even so, women in adjusting countries increased their advantage in longevity slightly, relative to women in nonadjusting countries.

The receipt of an adjustment loan, used to distinguish adjusting from nonadjusting countries in the preceding analysis, does not say anything about the policies implemented or their effect on a country's macroeconomic situation. One study finds that countries that adopted the reforms grew 2 percentage points faster in the 1980s, in contrast to the countries in which the policies worsened and where per capita GDP growth fell more than 2 percentage points (World Bank 1994a). So, if adjusting countries are ranked according to whether or not their macroeconomic policy environment actually improved following the receipt of an adjustment loan, a rather different picture of adjustment emerges.[18]

Female life expectancy increased most in countries that had the largest improvement in their macroeconomic environment (figure 5.6).

Figure 5.6   Better Macroeconomic Environment—Higher Female Life Expectancy in Sub-Saharan Africa

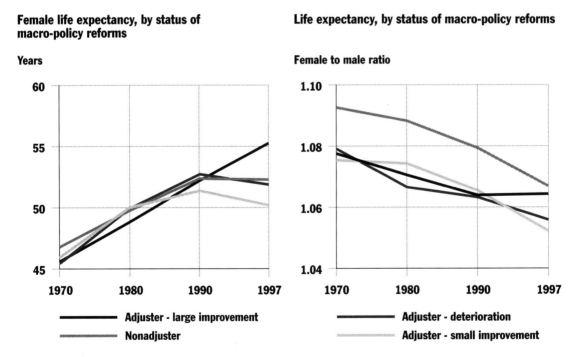

Female life expectancy, by status of macro-policy reforms

Years

Life expectancy, by status of macro-policy reforms

Female to male ratio

———— Adjuster - large improvement

▬▬▬▬ Nonadjuster

———— Adjuster - deterioration

▬▬▬▬ Adjuster - small improvement

Note: Classification of adjusting countries is based on scores for changes in fiscal policy, monetary policy, and exchange rate policy from 1981–86 to 1987–91. See World Bank (1994a) for details. See appendix 1 for general notes and included countries.

Source: World Bank (1999d).

Moreover, these countries were the only group in Sub-Saharan Africa to stem the decline in female life expectancy relative to male life expectancy. In contrast, nonadjusters and countries that did not greatly improve their macroeconomic environment experienced continued declines in female to male ratios over the period (and an absolute deterioration in female life expectancy since 1980). Econometric evidence, based on cross-country data across and within regions, supports the descriptive data. Structural adjustment programs and associated economic policies do not appear to have had significant impacts on gender equality—either positive or negative—independent of their effect on income growth more generally.

In an analysis of the relationship between income growth and gender equality, Dollar and Gatti (1999) find that macroeconomic policy variables, such as the exchange rate policy and the rule of law, do not have a direct impact on gender equality. Instead, the variables affect gender outcomes indirectly through their contribution to growth. Similarly, Forsythe, Korzeniewicz, and Durrant (2000) find no independent impact of structural adjustment on measures of women's status and gender equality, controlling for income growth and social institutions that affect gender norms. Neither the existence nor the size of adjustment loans has independent impacts on gender inequality in education or life expectancy, controlling for initial conditions and subsequent income growth.[19]

While the evidence on the impact of structural adjustment on gender equality appears mixed, when countries that implemented the reforms successfully are distinguished from those that did not, a more positive assessment emerges, on balance. Even so, the experience with the reforms demonstrates that important gender-specific risks as well as context-specific barriers to female economic mobility must be taken into account in policymaking. Policy analysis that accounts for gender differences in the short- and long-term impacts of adjustments can reveal potential hazards that must be addressed. The big areas for attention: country-specific gender norms, the legal framework, the asymmetries in access to productive resources, such as credit, and the nature of intrahousehold allocations.

Transition to a Market Economy

At the end of the 1980s a massive political and economic transformation began in Central and Eastern Europe and spread soon thereafter to the republics of the Soviet Union, as well as to China and Vietnam. Societal change of this scope and depth will certainly have long-lasting repercussions on all aspects of life, including gender roles and relations.

Transition, but little growth, in Eastern Europe and Central Asia. The collapse of communist rule in Europe led to the emergence of 27 countries from the eight that once made up the continent's communist area. The revival of market economies in these countries is expected to bring fundamental changes—away from centralized planning and control of production and labor use toward privatized production, decentralized wage setting, flexible labor markets, and freer trade. But contrary to early predictions, the first five years of transition in Eastern Europe and the former Soviet Union brought a severe drop in GDP, with accompanying sharp drops in the demand for labor and in real wages (Allison and Ringold 1996). The Eastern European countries have emerged from the transition crisis and their economies are beginning to grow again. But the break-up of the Soviet Union left the newly independent states with generally unfavorable economic conditions. The massive political and economic upheaval in these countries has not led to immediate gains. Output has steadily recovered since the mid-1990s, but GDP in several countries is still lower than at the onset of the transition.

Whether women benefited or lost relative to men during this massive political and economic restructuring is contested—and evidence is mixed. Short-run impacts have been different from longer-run impacts. For example, some recent assessments of the impact of the transition on job losses and real wages for men and women contradict earlier findings. There is also disagreement about whether women were really as well off during the previous regime—an attempt perhaps to explain why gender-based conflicts, such as higher rates of gender-related violence, have resurfaced in societies that can still boast of greater gender equality in most measures of welfare.[20]

Before the transition the central mandate of redirecting the family's energies and loyalties from the private to the public domain helped women achieve a level of parity with men. Women's rights were high on the social agenda and created the basis for women's empowerment. Education levels were high and equal for women and men. Women were expected to work full-time, and the state supported them with lengthy paid maternity leave and child care services. On average women accounted for over 40 percent of employment in Eastern Europe and the Soviet Union (table 5.4). Even as early as 1970 in several of these coutries, women made up nearly half of the labor force.

Table 5.4   Female Share of the Labor Force in Eastern Europe and Central Asia
(percentage of total)

Economy	1970	1980	1995
Albania	34	36	41
Bosnia and Herzegovina	31	25	35
Bulgaria	46	47	48
Central Asia[a]	33	39	37
Croatia	34	37	40
Czech Republic	46	48	51
Hungary	41	40	40
Macedonia, FYR	24	31	38
Poland	47	46	45
Romania	46	44	41
Russian Federation	47	50	47
Slovak Republic	36	44	49
Slovenia	33	45	45
Soviet Union (except Central Asia)[b]	45	48	46
Yugoslavia, Fed. Rep. (Serbia/Montenegro)	32	35	40

a. The Central Asian republics were part of the former Soviet Union in 1970 and 1980.

b. This pertains to the republics of the former Soviet Union, excepting the Central Asian republics. In 1970 and 1980 they were part of the Soviet Union.

Source: World Bank (1999d).

Whether women or men have lost more in employment and earnings during the transition varies across countries and depends on the gender composition of the industrial sectors hit hardest by restructuring—and on the occupational structure of job losses. Early studies of Eastern Europe concluded that administrative jobs, dominated by women, suffered more than production line jobs, usually filled by men (Boeri and Keese 1992). But later studies on other countries concluded that heavy industry, agriculture, and mining, the cornerstones of the socialist economy, have lost the most workers. Because the transition resulted in a contraction mainly of heavy industries in the Russian Federation, men were laid off in much larger numbers than women, although women's wages have declined relative to men's (Brainerd 1998). In Estonia and Slovenia the changes in the composition of demand for goods and services also favored women, with the shocks disproportionately affecting the predominantly male sectors (such as manufacturing, agriculture, transportation, and construction), while predominantly female sectors declined very little or expanded (Orazem and Vodopivec 1999).

221

The economic and social shock of the transition—and the instability and vulnerabilities it exposed—has also affected the health and longevity of women and men. On average life expectancy in the transition economies declined by a year for both men and women between 1990 and 1997. Higher rates of cardiovascular diseases, emotional stress and depression, suicide and domestic violence, and alcohol consumption have been recorded (Gavrilova and others 1999). In the Russian Federation age-adjusted mortality rose by almost a third between 1990 and 1994, an increase well beyond the peacetime experience of industrial countries (Notzon and others 1996). The increase has been significantly larger for men than women, 36 percent compared with 23 percent, reducing life expectancy by nearly seven years for men and three years for women. More than three-quarters of this drop can be attributed to increased mortality rates for people ages 25–64.

Gender impacts have also been felt in the home. A dramatic reduction in the provision of child care services affected not only women's employment but also their overall work burden. Preschool services for children in nearly all the republics of the former Soviet Union have declined since about 1990. While attendance and the number of kindergartens rose between 1980 and 1989, after 1990 supply was only 40–80 percent of the 1980 levels, depending on the country (figure 5.7). In the Russian Federation the resulting increase in child care costs has had a stronger effect on women's work hours than have wage shifts (Lokshin 2000). The long-term impact of the change in the provision of child care on women, their children, and gender roles has yet to be examined.

The share of women in parliament has been another casualty of the transition. As chapter 1 shows, Europe and Central Asia had the highest proportion of women in parliament in 1985, 25 percent—but representation fell to 7 percent in 1990. Whether and how women can regain their share in parliament is worth watching.

Transition with growth in East Asia. The transition to a market economy has followed a different path in China and Vietnam. The Chinese economy has been growing at an impressive 8–9 percent a year for well over a decade, transforming employment patterns, consumption habits, and personal lives. The sustained economic expansion has opened new nonfarm employment opportunities for young men and women, mostly in electronics, textiles, and apparel. More than half of China's exports are low-technology products. The greater demand for labor has

Figure 5.7   Number of Kindergartens Has Declined in the Former Soviet Union

Index of kindergarten supply (1980 = 100)

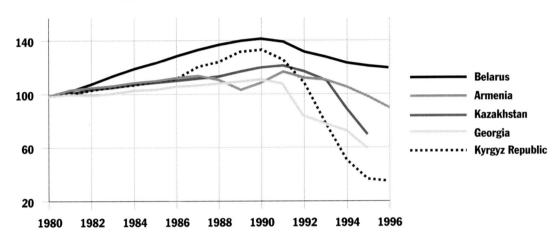

Index of kindergarten supply (1980 = 100)

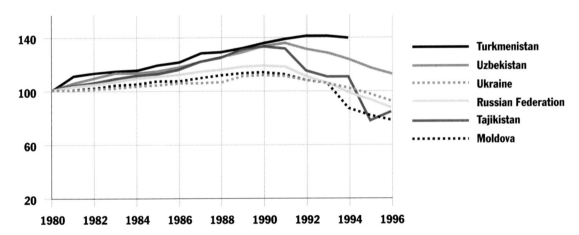

Source: State Committee of the CIS (1999).

been met by a drop in the share of farm employment and a rise in migration from rural areas and in the number of rural residents who commute to urban factories.

Have women and men benefited to the same degree from China's transition to a market-oriented economy? The evidence is mixed. Some women may have lost ground: urban women appear to have been disproportionately laid off from jobs in the state-owned sector (U.S. Department of State 1997). Average gender wage gaps have increased as employment has shifted away from the state to the collective and private sectors (Maurer-Fazio and Hughes 1999). And at least in the early years of reform, women were left to work on farms while men gained access to newly created off-farm jobs (Parish, Zhe, and Li 1995).

But recent growth in the rural nonfarm sector has led to rapid growth of female nonfarm employment in rural areas (Hare 1999; Rozelle and others 2000). Absolute female wages are higher in the private sector than in the state-owned sector (Maurer-Fazio and Hughes 1999). The gender wage gap, at least in the rural economy, has not increased (Rozelle and others 2000). And remittances to parents have increased daughters' status in the family, giving them a greater sense of control of their lives (Hare 1999).[21]

Like China, Vietnam experienced a remarkable economic transformation starting in the mid-1980s. By 1995 GDP was growing at about 10 percent a year, exports had increased tenfold, and there were signs of higher living standards in most of the country (Dollar, Glewwe, and Litvack 1998). There was a move out of agriculture into industry and services for both men and women, but the shift in sectoral allocation of employment was small, with no appreciable gender dimensions. Vietnam continues to be a primarily agricultural economy, with 73 percent of economically active women and 70 percent of men employed in agriculture in 1990.

The move to the market by the Chinese and Vietnamese economies has been accompanied by significant changes in the lives of men and women beyond work. Gender gaps in education closed further over the period. In China gross primary enrollment rates for both boys and girls reached 120 percent in 1996, and girls' secondary enrollment rate rose more rapidly (from 37 to 66 percent) than boys' (54 to 73 percent) in 1980–96. In Vietnam gross enrollment rates in 1985 were already about equal for girls and boys—at least 100 percent at the primary level and more than 40 percent at the secondary level—but gender equality has improved further during the transition.

In a qualitative survey of two communes in Vietnam, respondents from about 80 households describe dramatic improvements in their lives after the program of economic reforms know as *Doi Moi*—in basic infrastructure (water and sanitation), ownership of durable goods, housing, mobility, diets, and access to new information through television (Long and others 2000). Further, women and men alike talked explicitly about changing gender roles, with men agreeing with women that relations within households have become more equal. Despite this change a focus group study reveals that men's authority within the household remains dominant (World Bank 1999c). While women are still responsible for care and household maintenance activities, men are responsible for the family's social affairs.

In sum, while the transition economies share the legacy of centrally mandated gender equality and still possess some of the highest indicators of gender equality in the world, market-oriented policies and the differences in their economic performance have produced different tensions related to gender. In the face of output collapse, a shortage of jobs, and severe cuts in state support for child care, gender inequalities are growing in Eastern Europe and the former Soviet Union. In contrast, in the face of rapid economic growth in China and Vietnam, women and men must adjust to new economic roles and the specific gender-based conflicts these present—but have the luxury of doing so with a higher standard of living.

Best of Times, Worst of Times: Lessons from Regional Experience

Economic growth and policy affect everyone's standard of living as well as women's and men's relative welfare. Indeed, development strategies usually affect men and women differently. Macroeconomic policy reforms and economic development influence gender relations and outcomes, for better or worse, whether or not they target gender issues. And these effects may vary in the short and long terms. When those reforms change fiscal resources and constraints, they alter the availability of public programs on which the poor may be particularly dependent. These reforms also affect the incomes of farmers who sell their produce and workers who sell their labor as well as the prices at which they must purchase food, basic services, and other necessities. And because women and men tend to have different roles—and power—in the home, in the workplace, and in politics and the economy at large, they are usually affected by these broad changes in different ways.

The impact of economic development on gender equality is often neither automatic nor immediate. Nor is it sufficient. It depends largely on the state of rights of women and men, their access to and control of productive resources (such as land and credit), and their political voice. In East Asia's high-growth, low-inequality countries, women's welfare

225

improved and gender disparities decreased in several dimensions—but unevenly and imperfectly, with some gender inequalities persisting. In Latin America, where human capital is generally high and relatively equal for women and men, measures of gender equality may have worsened temporarily during the structural reforms as a result of gender differences in layoffs and wages. But as inflation rates have fallen and growth rates have become positive, there is recent evidence of improvement. An important remaining challenge is how to improve the conditions of women and men in poor rural areas.

In the republics of the former Soviet Union—where levels of human capital are high and generally equal for men and women, but where economies are contracting (if only temporarily)—structural reforms have produced winners and losers. Some people have benefited from the new market opportunities—but some are worse off. Labor has borne a disproportionate share of the cost of change in downsized sectors, although neither women nor men have a monopoly on the losses.

In contrast, in the transition countries in Asia—where the economy is expanding rather than contracting—there is room for more winners and women are benefiting, mostly by taking new jobs in a modernizing economy. Their experience illustrates the positive side of economic development. Although the opening and deepening of markets in these countries and the downsizing of the public sector have produced both winners and losers, the sustained expansion of output, against a background of greater gender equality in rights and in human capital, has tangibly improved gender equality and life in general.

In Sub-Saharan Africa the macroeconomic reforms to address structural problems may have been too harsh or too swift for those that had few resources (human capital or physical), severely destabilizing their lives at home and at work. Partly this is because infrastructure and social and political institutions have not responded to the reforms as readily as have macroeconomic imbalances (Collier and Gunning 1999). Women, who own and control fewer productive resources, have been especially vulnerable in countries where macroeconomic policies did not improve during adjustment.

These observations indicate that policies that enable the economy to grow and prosper, that improve social and physical infrastructure, that generate new jobs, and that raise real wage rates provide a setting more conducive for both females and males to reach higher standards of living and greater equality. But often they are not sufficient. Social policies that combat labor market discrimination or support child care can supplement what economic development or broad institutional reform alone cannot achieve in reducing gender inequalities. In addition, social protection policies that recognize gender differences in market-based and household work and in risks are also important to protecting women (and men) from economic shocks or prolonged economic downturns (box 5.4). Another important challenge for policymakers is minimizing the adverse effects of rapid and wholesale economic change so that households and individuals can benefit from the change.

Box 5.4 Cushioning the Effects of Reform on the Vulnerable

ECONOMIC CHANGE UNLEASHES FORCES THAT CAN undermine traditional protection mechanisms for the poor, the unemployed, and the elderly—and this may occur so rapidly that new social institutions do not have time to evolve. Subsidies for countering the cuts in social services and safety nets (such as skills retraining and public employment programs) for displaced workers would have eased the effects of adjustment policies. But few adjusting countries acted soon enough. These policies should be sensitive to gender-specific risks, to differences in women's and men's command over resources, and to the types of activities societies deem appropriate for women and men. When social protection policies are blind to gender they fail to reach women. Analyses of several recent safety net programs illustrate this point.

A cash-for-work program introduced in Zambia in 1995 as an alternative to food aid was targeted toward women's participation. The program organized different activities for men than women and paid them the same wages based on work targets (Devereux 1998). Preliminary results based on a 1997 survey indicate that women who wanted to participate freed up time by delegating household work primarily to daughters. Domestic constraints, as well as the program's heavy workload, led many women to hire oxcarts to help them with their work on the road. But men owned 80 percent of the

oxcarts, so men benefited not only directly by participating in the program, but also by hiring out their resources to women. In many cases women turned over their cash earnings to males in the household. An analysis of the distribution of benefits from participation shows that only 16 percent of women kept their earnings for personal expenditures, compared with 42 percent of men.

Social protection programs not targeted to women were much less successful in engaging women's participation. Bolivia's Emergency Social Fund, established in 1986, was one of the World Bank's first attempts to address the social costs of adjustment through a compensatory program. The fund financed small, labor-intensive projects that would increase employment among the poor while providing services to the community that would aid development. A 1988 survey shows that 99 percent of workers in the projects were males (Newman, Jorgensen, and Pradhan 1991).

For the first six months of the Trabajar 2 workfare program, which began in Argentina in May 1997, only 15 percent of the participants were women (Jalan and Ravallion 1999). But the net wage gains that accrued to the few who participated were nearly identical to those for men, suggesting that women's low participation may be a matter of choice rather than gender bias in recruitment.

227

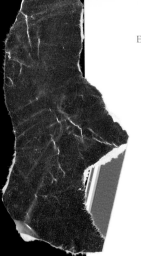

Economic development can improve gender equality in a variety of ways. It does so by creating, deepening, or opening markets, by enabling new investments, by expanding opportunities to increase income, and by redefining the state's role in the economy. If supportive institutional and policy environments exist, economic development could help break down traditional gender divisions of labor within the household and the economy, provide incentives for more equal investments in human capital, and reduce discrimination in the labor market. But these effects may be reinforced by active social policies that promote greater equality in different spheres of society and that protect the vulnerable. What these policies should entail is discussed in the next chapter.

Notes

1.   These findings are consistent with findings from an earlier study on male and female time use for a smaller number of industrial and preindustrial countries by Juster and Stafford (1991).

2.   Regressions control for the unemployment rate, labor market activity rates for the population, the standard age of entitlement to pension, serial correlation of residuals, and heteroskedasticity.

3.   Additional household income can lead to increased demand for human capital in the family, but the effect on gender disparities is determined by a variety of social and institutional factors, as discussed in chapter 3. There is no automatic process whereby increased household resources reduce gender disparities.

4.   Mean age-specific enrollment rates in middle school are 81 percent for boys and 31 percent for girls.

5.   Using the U.S. 1977 Census of Manufacturers, Black and Brainerd (1999) define import share as the ratio of value of the industry's total imports to the value of its domestic shipments.

6.   There is an ongoing debate among Chinese researchers about changes in women's relative status in the labor market since the onset of economic reform. Some researchers suggest that the reduction of government involvement

in the labor market means greater scope for the reemergence of traditional values that would encourage greater gender discrimination in the labor market. Other researchers suggest that increasing competitive labor markets should enhance women's economic standing by "penalizing discriminating firms and rewarding nondiscriminators" (Maurer-Fazio and Hughes 1999). While there is general agreement that increasingly competitive markets are working to limit the scope for gender discrimination, empirical evidence is still mixed on which of the two forces—traditional values and increased competition—are having a greater overall impact on labor market outcomes. See below for further discussion.

7.   The data demands for this study are considerable and did not permit including low-income countries.

8.   All the cross-country relations discussed in this section adjust for gender rights. Coefficients are obtained from the estimates described in appendix 2.

9.   Easterly (1999) finds a significant positive relationship between income growth and gender equality in secondary enrollment rates using a pooled cross-section, time series model, with controls for country fixed effects. However, for primary education, a 10 percent rise in per capita income is associated with a lower female to male enrollment ratio of 1.1 percent. Similarly, using cross-country data from semi-industrialized countries from 1975 to 1995,

Seguino (2000) finds that gender wage inequality is positively related to income growth. Filmer, King, and Pritchett (1998) estimate that while income is positively associated with absolute levels of girls' health and education across subregions of South Asia (also using a cross-country, time series model with fixed effects), it has little or no significant effect on gender disparities. On the other hand, Forsythe, Korzeniewiez, and Durrant (2000) show that higher incomes are associated with higher levels of gender equality as measured by the Gender Development Index developed by the United Nations (1994).

10. To address this issue of causality between income and gender equality, Dollar and Gatti (1999) use two-stage least squares and fixed effects estimation techniques.

11. The "shape" of this relationship seems to be sensitive to the precise measure of inequality used. Dollar and Gatti use the absolute level of female attainment, holding the level of male attainment constant. But focusing on the proportional difference between male and female attainment levels reveals a more linear—or even a concave relationship, as in figure 5.3—depending on the econometric specification.

12. For example, in Indonesia infant mortality declined by as much as 30 percent between 1982 and 1987 and between 1992 and 1997, according to data from the Demographic and Health Surveys (Beegle and others 1999). In Malaysia the proportion of the labor force who had not attended school dropped by two-thirds, while the proportion with secondary education and higher tripled between the 1960s and the early 1980s (Mazumdar 1994).

13. A longer series on the gender earnings ratio in the Korean manufacturing sector is provided by Seguino 1997 using International Labour Organization data: in 1975 it was 47 percent; in 1980, 45 percent; in 1985, 47 percent; and in 1990, 51 percent.

14. In Taiwan, China, too, despite the improvement in women's work experience and education levels relative to men's, the average ratio of women's earnings to men's remained at 65 percent between 1978 and 1992 (Zveglich, Rodgers, and Rodgers 1997). Underlying this, however, are different patterns for less educated and more educated women: women with a middle

school education or less experienced dramatic losses in earnings relative to men, while women with more education made modest gains relative to men. Gender earnings differentials are largely explained by differences in measured characteristics, but at a declining share over the period as women experienced extremely large losses due to unmeasured gender-specific factors.

15. Related evidence from Chile and Colombia indicates that firms' demand for female blue-collar workers is more elastic than for male blue-collar workers over recent periods of trade liberalization (Fajnzylber 2000).

16. See Rama and MacIssac (1999) on Ecuador, Alderman and others (1996) on Ghana, and Rodgers (1999) on Vietnam. While the evidence of gender asymmetries in government retrenchment is not universal, it suggests that women's employment has been disproportionately affected by retrenchment in most cases.

17. Even before the adjustment era in Africa gender equality in secondary education was improving more slowly in adjusting countries than in nonadjusting ones.

18. In Sub-Saharan Africa between 1981–86 and 1987–91 implementation of adjustment policies was often incomplete, inconsistent, or did not occur at all (World Bank 1994a). The World Bank's *Adjustment in Africa* (1994) classified African countries into four categories between 1981–86 and 1987–91: nonadjusters, adjusters whose macroeconomic policy environment deteriorated, adjusters whose macroeconomic policy environment improved slightly, and adjusters whose macroeconomic policy environment improved greatly. These categories are based on an index of change in macroeconomic policies that measures changes in fiscal, monetary, and exchange rate policies between 1981–86 and 1987–91. For fiscal policy a score was assigned based on the change in budget deficit (excluding grants), with adjustments for changes in revenue as a share of GDP. For monetary policy a score was assigned based on the average of change in seignorage and inflation. For exchange rate policy a score was assigned based on the change in the real effective exchange rate for fixed exchange rate countries and a simple average of the change in the real effective exchange rate and the change in the parallel market exchange rate premium for flexible exchange rate countries.

19. To capture the effects of structural adjustment on gender equality, Forsythe, Korzeniewicz, and Durrant (2000) construct an index of four indicators pertaining to 1975–90: the number of bilateral debt restructurings, the number of multilateral debt restructurings over the same period, the number of times a country received extended funds from the International Monetary Fund (IMF), and the total IMF loans received as a percentage of its allotted quota over the period. In a similar exercise World Bank staff examined the impacts of structural adjustment on gender equality in education and life expectancy using measures of Bank adjustment lending in specific countries. See also Bradshaw and Wahl (1991).

20. While indicators of gender equality give high marks to the communist period for reducing inequalities in education, health status, and labor market participation quite rapidly, at least one recent study has questioned this (UNICEF 1999b). The study argues that the previous regime left gender equality issues unresolved, especially with respect to women's position in the home. The study argues that there was substantial occupational segregation by gender, little official support for family life outside the context of work, and a blanket of silence over violence against women. The lifting of centralized state control revealed these gender inequalities.

21. Evidence on changes in wage discrimination, as measured by the portion of the wage gap that is unexplained after controlling for education and work experience, is mixed. Some evidence shows that the largest unexplained wage gaps are in the private sector, while the smallest are in the state sector (Maurer-Fazio and Hughes 1999), suggesting that gender wage gaps are likely to increase as private sector employment becomes increasingly important. Other evidence suggests, however, that the relative share of discrimination in the overall gender wage differential declines substantially from the state to the private sector (Liu, Meng, and Zhang forthcoming).

CHAPTER 6

A Three-Part Strategy to Promote Gender Equality

T HAT GENDER INEQUALITIES EXACT HIGH HUMAN
costs and constrain countries' development prospects provides a compelling case for public
and private action to promote gender equality. The
evidence makes clear that the state has a critical role
in improving the well-being of both women and
men, and by so doing, in capturing the substantial social benefits
associated with improving the absolute and relative status of women
and girls. Public action is particularly important, since many social
and legal institutions that perpetuate gender inequalities are extremely
difficult, if not impossible, for individuals alone to change. Market
failures, too, such as insufficient information about women's
productivity in various jobs (because women spend a greater part of
their work hours in nonmarket activities or because labor markets are
absent or undeveloped), are clear obstacles.

The evidence in this report argues for a three-part strategy to promote gender equality:

- Reform institutions to establish equal rights and opportunities for women and men.
- Foster economic development to strengthen incentives for more equal resources and participation.
- Take active measures to redress persistent disparities in command over resources and political voice.

As chapter 5 indicates, economic development and income growth
tend to promote gender equality. But the positive effects of economic
development can take a long time to play out. And they are not sufficient to eliminate gender disparities. Nor are they automatic. For these

reasons governments and development organizations need to take a more integrated approach to promoting gender equality. The state has a critical role in establishing an institutional environment based on equal rights and opportunities for women and men—and in ensuring equal access to resources and public services.

Recent debates on gender and development have tended to pit growth-oriented approaches against rights-based or institutional approaches (see, for example, UNDP 1995; Cagatay, Elson, and Grown 1995). But the evidence suggests that both gender equality in basic rights and economic development are core elements of a long-term strategy to promote gender equality. Indeed, societies that provide the same basic rights for women and men and that promote economic development are likely to be more effective in reducing gender disparities than societies that focus on growth—or rights—alone.

The relationships among rights, income growth, and gender equality can be seen by examining cross-country data. Greater gender equality in rights and higher per capita GDP are associated with higher female to male ratios in primary and secondary enrollment rates, life expectancies, and participation in parliament (figure 6.1). These differences are particularly large in parliamentary representation and secondary school enrollment.

Figure 6.1 suggests that where per capita GDP and gender equality in rights are low, countries can raise relative outcomes for women both by improving gender equality in rights and by increasing per capita income. Moreover, in low-income countries with high gender equality in rights, increases in income would be expected to result in further improvements in the relative status of women; likewise, in higher-income countries with low gender equality in rights, raising women's relative rights status would be expected to result in additional improvements in relative outcomes for women.[1]

While improving the effectiveness of societal institutions and achieving economic growth and development are widely accepted as key elements of any long-term development strategy, successful implementation of this strategy does not guarantee gender equality. Policies for institutional change and economic development need to account for prevailing gender inequalities in rights, resources, and voice and how these disparities affect women's and men's ability to participate in, contribute to, and benefit from development.

But even an approach that combines improvements in rights and other institutional reforms with economic development may be

Figure 6.1   As Equality of Rights and Income Improve, So Do Other Gender Indicators
Effects of rights and income on education, life expectancy, and parliamentary representation

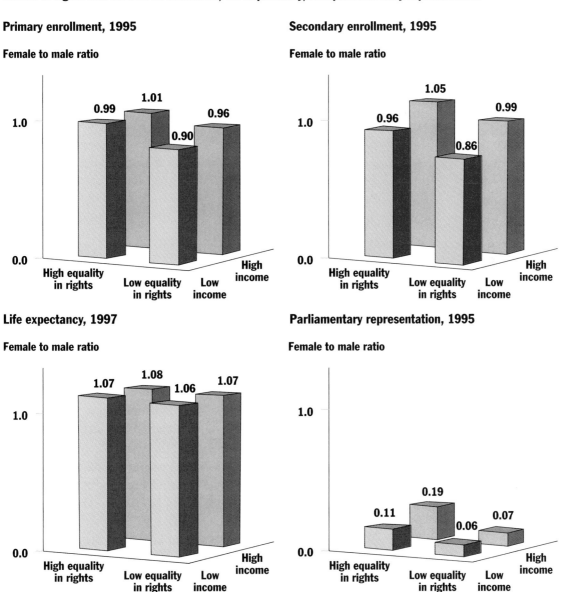

Primary enrollment, 1995

Female to male ratio

Secondary enrollment, 1995

Female to male ratio

Life expectancy, 1997

Female to male ratio

Parliamentary representation, 1995

Female to male ratio

Note: Data are obtained using country-level predictions from regressions of each indicator on per capita GDP, per capita GDP squared (both expressed in logs), and an aggregate index of gender equality in rights, based on data collected by Humana (1986, 1992). Countries are classified by the median value of gender equality in rights (the average of three indexes that capture the relative rights status of women and men in the economy, law and politics, and marriage and divorce) and by per capita GDP (1995 dollars, adjusted for purchasing power parity), with $4,000 being the cutoff between low income and high income. For primary and secondary education relative outcomes are represented by the ratio of female gross enrollment rates to male gross enrollment rates. See appendix 1 for general notes and included countries, appendix 2 for underlying regression results, and the glossary for definitions.

Sources: Rights data from Humana (1992); parliamentary data from WISTAT (1998); all other data from World Bank (1999d).

unable to produce major gains in the short run. As with the effects of growth, institutional reforms and related efforts to strengthen basic rights may take time to have an impact. While institutional reforms can help lay the groundwork for progress toward gender equality, long-standing social practices, discriminatory customs, weak law enforcement, and political opposition all pose potential obstacles to what can be achieved quickly.

In this context, there is a critical role for active policies and programs that:

- Promote gender equality in access to productive resources and earnings capacity.
- Reduce the personal costs to women of their household roles.
- Provide gender-appropriate social protection—through programs that account for differences between women and men in risk and vulnerability.
- Strengthen women's political voice and participation.

Such measures often help promote efficiency as well as gender equality objectives. Moreover, active policies can accelerate progress toward gender equality.

In fact, governments have a range of policy levers to promote gender equality—pricing policy, legal and regulatory reform, better-designed service delivery, selected investments in infrastructure. Chapter 1 shows that there is considerable diversity in the nature and extent of gender disparities, both across and within regions. Thus, which interventions will be most appropriate—and most effective—will likely differ considerably from place to place. For example, gender inequality in access to basic education remains an important priority in South Asia, Sub-Saharan Africa, and the Middle East and North Africa but is less so in other developing regions.

So, while the overall approach laid out here is broadly applicable, the details of its implementation—particularly with respect to active measures—can be expected to vary across countries and regions. Diversity of circumstances across countries and regions underscores the importance of understanding the nature of gender systems and gender disparities in specific locations. It also calls for integrating gender issues into national public policy analyses and debates. And because public resources are limited, it is important to assess the full costs and benefits of pursuing different policy and programmatic approaches for promoting gender equality.

This chapter discusses each part of the strategy in turn, focusing first on institutional reforms, then on economic development and growth, and then on active policy measures. Where data permit, the sections provide indicative estimates of how specific elements of the strategy can be expected to affect equality between women and men in different dimensions. Since governments tend to operate with scarce fiscal and personnel resources, the discussion of active measures begins by outlining several basic principles for choosing among a multitude of options. This builds on the discussion of the role of the state in chapter 2 and on a well-established literature on public economics. The discussion of specific active measures highlights the extent to which particular interventions are likely to benefit development broadly and promote gender equality. While evidence on the relative costs and benefits of active measures tends to be limited, available findings are highlighted, as is evidence on the effectiveness of public versus private provision of services. The report ends with a brief discussion of future challenges for promoting gender equality, including priorities for future policy research.

Reforming Institutions to Establish Equal Rights and Opportunities for Women and Men

ENSURING THAT WOMEN AND MEN HAVE EQUAL RIGHTS IS AN important development goal on its own. But it is important for other reasons, too. Establishing equal rights between women and men creates an environment of equal opportunities and power, critical elements to achieving gender equality in other dimensions, such as education, health, and political participation. While promoting equal rights is important for all countries in all regions, it is a particular priority in South Asia, Sub-Saharan Africa, and the Middle East and North Africa, where inequalities in basic rights are greatest (see chapter 1).

Simulating the effects of increasing gender equality in rights on female to male ratios in primary and secondary education, life expectancy, and parliamentary representation helps to illustrate how improving equality of rights between women and men could affect other gender outcomes (figure 6.2). These simulations are based on the same cross-country regression model discussed in chapters 3 and 5. The regressions control for an index of gender equality in rights, per capita GDP, and per

Figure 6.2   As Equality in Rights Improves, So Do Other Gender Indicators
Simulated effects of greater gender equality in rights on education, life expectancy, and parliamentary representation, by region

Primary enrollment, 1995

Female to male ratio

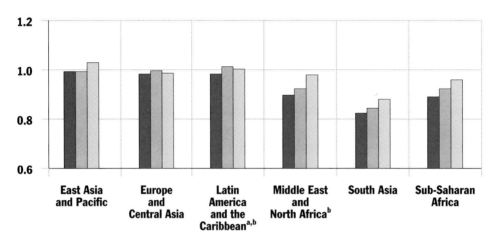

Secondary enrollment, 1995

Female to male ratio

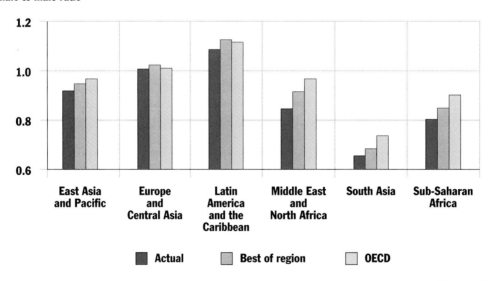

(figure continues on following page)

Figure 6.2 continued

Life expectancy, 1997

Female to male ratio

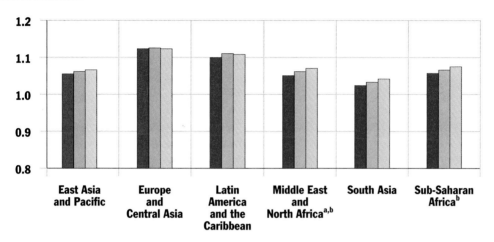

Parliamentary representation ratio, 1995

Female to male ratio

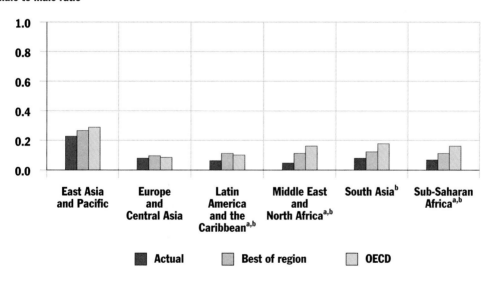

Note: The figures summarize simulation results for the effect of different gender equality of rights scenarios on gender outcomes in developing countries, controlling for income. See appendix 1 for included countries, appendix 2 for underlying regression results, and the glossary for definitions. The differences in the regional means between actual levels and simulations are statistically significant at the 10 percent level or better when indicated as follows:

a. Between actual and best-of-region scenario;
b. Between actual and OECD scenario.
Sources: Rights data from Humana (1992); parliamentary data from WISTAT (1998); World Bank (1999d).

capita GDP squared (with the GDP variables expressed in logs; see appendix 2 for regression details).

The parameter estimates are used to predict gender outcomes for each country under two alternative scenarios:

- If each country in the region were to achieve equality in rights at a level similar to the country with the best record in that region.
- If each country in the region were to achieve gender equality in rights equivalent to the average in OECD countries.

The population-weighted average of the predicted values from individual countries is then calculated for each region. The starting points for the simulations are data for the latest year available, usually from the mid-1990s. One important caveat when interpreting the results: because the number of countries in each region is small and data may be available only for part of this small group (for example, for only 2–5 countries in South Asia, depending on the measure of gender equality), the standard deviation around each regional average tends to be large, thus lowering the statistical significance levels of the differences between the scenarios. In spite of this statistical issue, the simulations suggest that improvements in rights and incomes can bring countries closer to gender equality. Figure 6.2 makes clear which differences in means are significant, given the number of countries with data.

The simulated impact of improvements in rights is a function of both the estimated parameters and the distance between each country's current rights status and the status under the best-in-the-region or OECD average scenarios. (In regions where the OECD average scenario appears to be too optimistic, the best-in-the-region scenario may be more plausible in the short run.) Note that in Europe and Central Asia and in Latin America and the Caribbean the best-in-the-region rights records are actually better than the average OECD record.

Under both the best-in-the-region and OECD average scenarios, enrollment ratios for primary and secondary education become more equal, relative female representation in parliament increases, and the overall advantage for women in life expectancy becomes slightly more pronounced. But the predicted changes are generally largest in South Asia, Sub-Saharan Africa, and the Middle East and North Africa. Using the best-in-the-region record on rights, for example, the female to male parliamentary representation ratio more than doubles in the Middle East and North Africa and increases by more than 60 percent in the other two regions. The female to male secondary enrollment ratio increases by 8 percent in the Middle East and North Africa, 6 percent in Sub-Saharan Africa, and 5 percent in South Asia. Ratios for primary enrollment and life expectancy experience more modest changes.

In the OECD average rights scenario, all four gender equality indicators tend to increase further—in some cases markedly. The exceptions are Europe and Central Asia and Latin America and the Caribbean, where the best-in-the-region equality in rights is higher than the OECD average. The simulations suggest that in most regions substantial improvements in gender equality in rights would go a long way toward achieving parity between girls and boys in primary and secondary school enrollment ratios. Only in South Asia would sizable gender gaps persist.

Establishing Equal Rights and Protections under the Law

Legal reform is a necessary step in improving gender equality in rights—and in establishing a supportive institutional environment more broadly. As chapter 3 discusses, many aspects of the law in developing countries continue to confer unequal rights and status on people based on gender, with important consequences for women's autonomy, security, opportunities, and well-being. Legal reform is important to promote gender equality in many areas, but five stand out:

Family law. Family law, whether based on statutory, customary, or religious law, establishes the level of autonomy and control women and men have in family matters, including marriage, divorce, child custody, control of conjugal property, and inheritance of property. Inequalities in family law directly affect women's welfare, and by weakening their bargaining power in the household can have important second-round effects on family welfare. Reforms that eliminate disparities in legal status between women and men in the family help lay the groundwork for broader progress toward gender equality.

Protection against violence. In many countries laws that ostensibly protect women from gender-related violence contain biases that discriminate against the victims or that render the laws ineffective. Moreover, laws addressing violence against women often define violence in very narrow terms or impose burdensome evidentiary requirements. The first goal of legal reform in this context is to identify and correct gender biases in existing laws. Also required are provisions that make violent behavior more costly to the abuser—an approach that has had some success in developed countries.

Land rights. Equal access to and control of land resources is important for several reasons. Insecure land rights can reduce female farmers' productivity (as in Sub-Saharan Africa) and inhibit women's access to credit, since land is an important form of collateral. Land reforms that provide for joint titling of husband and spouse or that enable women to hold independent land titles can increase women's control of land where statutory law predominates. Where customary and statutory laws operate side by side, their interactions must be taken into account if efforts to strengthen female access to land are to succeed.

Labor law. Labor laws that restrict the types of work women can do or limit the hours they can work, even when couched as "special protection," restrict women's access to the labor market. Such legal restrictions should be eliminated. At the same time, equal employment and equal pay legislation can help form the basis for equal rights and equal protection in the labor market. But such legislation may have limited impact in the short run—both because large numbers of female workers remain in informal sector jobs and because adequate enforcement may be lacking.

Political rights. Equal political rights provide the foundation on which women and men can enjoy equal voice in society. Most countries' statutory codes give women the right to vote and to hold political office; providing these rights in the few places where they are absent is critical. Similarly, restrictions that limit women's ability to exercise these rights should be removed.

While establishing a legal framework that affords equal rights and protections to women and men is critical to leveling the institutional "playing field," statutory reform alone is not sufficient. In many developing countries the capacity and commitment to implement legal reforms remain weak, often undermining progress toward achieving equality under the law. Efforts to strengthen the enforcement capabilities of a country's judicial and administrative agencies are thus integral to realizing greater gender equality in basic rights. Political leadership is almost always decisive.

The law is one part of a broader institutional environment that includes social and cultural norms, economic institutions (such as markets), and service institutions, whether school and health care systems or financial institutions. Policy approaches that work to align legal and economic incentives, as well as the structures of service institutions, are likely to be more effective in reducing gender disparities than approaches that focus solely on the law.

Establishing Incentives That Discourage Discrimination by Gender

The nature and structure of economic institutions can promote or impede gender equality in important ways. The structure of markets, for example, determines in large part the relative wages of men and women, returns to productive assets, and the prices of goods and services. This creates a powerful set of incentives that influence people's decisions and behaviors in work, saving, investment, and consumption—often with different effects on women and men. While not intrinsically "gendered," factor, product, and information markets are effectively so. Why? Because the social context affects who may enter into contracts in these markets and the way contracts are formed. In nearly all countries individuals and organizations in these markets discriminate and exclude participants on the basis of gender.

This discriminatory behavior—like other rent-seeking behavior, such as corruption—is easier where markets are relatively closed or undeveloped. In fact, as chapter 5 discusses, firms operating in more competitive markets appear to engage in less gender discrimination in hiring and pay practices than do firms with significant market power operating in less competitive markets. More generally, policies and investments that deepen markets, redress gender inequalities in access to information—combined with sanctions on those who discriminate—all help strengthen incentives for gender equality in the labor market.

Designing Service Delivery to Facilitate Equal Access

Similarly, service institutions, such as school systems, health care centers, financial institutions, and agricultural extension systems, can promote greater gender equality in access to productive resources if they are designed to account for gender differences and disparities. Gender-appropriate design of service delivery is often an important element of the active measures discussed later in the chapter, but the principle applies broadly to a wide range of services and other program interventions:

- School systems that take account of cultural concerns for girls' privacy, parents' desire for girls to be taught by female teachers, or demand for single-sex facilities have successfully increased girls' enrollment and retention in schools, even in highly gender-stratified societies.

- Health care facilities that include female service providers have increased women's use of formal health care services in many settings.
- Group-based lending programs that substitute social capital for traditional collateral, such as land or physical capital (which women often lack), have increased women's ability to obtain credit.
- Agricultural research and extension services that account for gender differences in cropping choices, gender disparities in resource constraints, and cultural restriction that limit female-male interactions substantially improve female farmers' ability to benefit from training and dissemination of new technologies.

Fostering Economic Development to Strengthen Incentives for More Equal Resources and Participation

ECONOMIC DEVELOPMENT TENDS TO INCREASE PRODUCTIVITY and create new work opportunities that benefit both women and men through more jobs, higher incomes, and better living standards. And in most contexts economic development also reduces gender disparities. By raising worker productivity, economic development increases the (private) returns to women's education—strengthening family incentives to invest in girls' human development and to have women participate in the labor force. Similarly, investments in infrastructure for water, transportation, and fuel that typically accompany development—as well as the deepening of markets—are important for reducing female workloads and facilitating girls' education.

Moreover, when economic development raises income and reduces poverty, gender gaps in education, health, and nutrition tend to narrow. When low-income families are forced to ration spending on education, health care, and nutrition, women and girls tend to bear much of the costs. But as household incomes rise, spending on these items also rises, and women and girls often benefit disproportionately—albeit from a lower starting point.

But just how great an impact are income growth and economic development likely to have on gender disparities in different dimensions? And in which regions? Simulation analysis reveals three main patterns (figure 6.3).

Figure 6.3 As Incomes Rise, Gender Equality Tends to Increase

Simulated effects of higher income on education, life expectancy, and parliamentary representation, by region

Primary enrollment, 1995

Female to male ratio

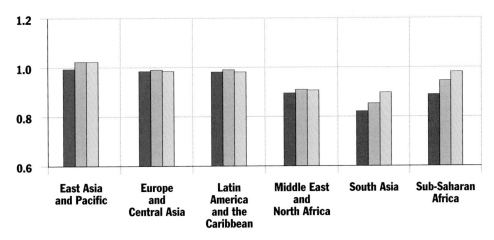

Secondary enrollment, 1995

Female to male ratio

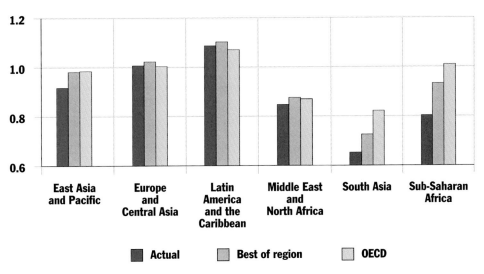

(figure continues on following page)

243

Figure 6.3 continued

Life expectancy, 1997

Female to male ratio

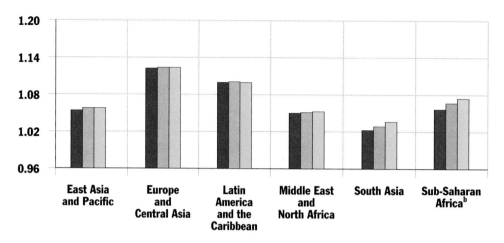

Parliamentary representation, 1995

Female to male ratio

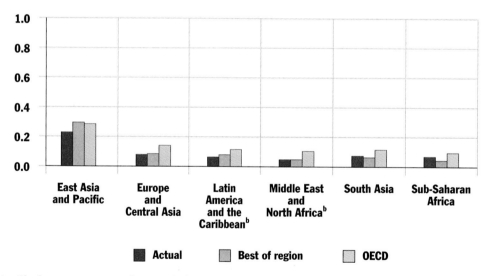

■ Actual   ▨ Best of region   ▢ OECD

Note: The figures summarize simulation results for the effect of different income growth scenarios on gender outcomes in developing countries, controlling for the extent of gender equality in rights. The best-of-region scenario is based on per capita income, the OECD scenario on OECD average income. See appendix 1 for included countries, appendix 2 for underlying regression results, and the glossary for definitions. The differences in the regional means between actual levels and simulations are statistically significant at the 10 percent level or better when indicated as follows:

a. Between actual and best-of-region scenario;

b. Between actual and OECD scenario.

Sources: Rights data from Humana (1992); parliamentary data from WISTAT (1998); all other data from World Bank (1999d).

- For primary and secondary education and relative life expectancies, the largest effects of income growth are likely to come in the poorest regions: South Asia and Sub-Saharan Africa. The effects of growth in average incomes on gender equality in education and life expectancy tend to be minimal in East Asia and Pacific, Eastern Europe and Central Asia, Latin America and the Caribbean, and the Middle East and North Africa. This is consistent with the underlying regression model (see appendix 2), which finds that the marginal effects of income growth are relatively large at low levels of per capita income, but that this effect declines as national income rises.[2]

- The effects of rising incomes tend to be stronger for primary and secondary education than for relative life expectancy. Of the three measures, income growth appears to have the largest marginal impact on gender equality at the secondary school level. Under the best-in-the-region scenario for income, the female to male secondary enrollment ratios increase by 11 percent in South Asia and by more than 16 percent in Sub-Saharan Africa. Under the OECD average income scenario the ratio would increase by 26 percent in both regions.

- Noticeable increases in gender equality in parliamentary representation are likely to come only with very large increases in income. For South Asia and Sub-Saharan Africa the simulations suggest that small increases in income might even be associated with slight declines in the ratio of women to men in parliament. This reflects the fact that some low-income countries, such as Bangladesh, China, Nicaragua, and Uganda, have relatively high levels of female representation in parliament. Since the simulation model controls for gender equality in rights, this finding should not reflect possible trade-offs between income growth and rights. Rather, it may reflect some other factor for which there are no data—such as civil participation.[3]

So, while income growth and economic development help promote gender equality, the positive effect of growth is not, by itself, likely to eliminate gender inequalities, even when national incomes are substantially higher than they are now. Moreover, sizable growth-related benefits in poor regions may be realized only in the long run. Together, the simulations presented in this chapter suggest that societies that give equal rights to women and men and promote economic development are likely to be more effective in reducing gender disparities than those that focus on rights or growth alone.

Care should be taken in directly comparing the effects of increasing gender equality in rights and of raising national incomes because the types of actions and levels of effort needed to improve rights and raise incomes differ. Even so, examining the simulation results for rights improvements and income growth together yield interesting information about the relative role of rights and income in improving different gender outcomes. For example:

- Income growth appears to have a larger potential impact than rights improvements on gender equality in primary and secondary school enrollments in South Asia and Sub-Saharan Africa (figure 6.4). The same seems to be true for gender equality in secondary enrollments in East Asia and Pacific. In contrast, improved rights appear to have greater scope for promoting gender equality in education in Eastern Europe and Central Asia, Latin America and the Caribbean, and the Middle East and North Africa. The role of improved rights appears to be particularly important in the Middle East and North Africa.[4]
- For relative life expectancies the potential effects of improved rights tend to be stronger than those of income growth in most regions, especially in the Middle East and North Africa. The potential effects of income growth are largest in South Asia and Sub-Saharan Africa. In fact, in Sub-Saharan Africa the potential income effects appear to be as large or larger than the potential rights effects.
- As with life expectancy the potential impact of rights improvements on relative representation in parliament is greater than that of income growth in most regions. Because of relatively low levels of gender equality in rights in South Asia, Sub-Saharan Africa, and the Middle East and North Africa, the potential effect of rights improvements appears particularly large.

In sum, even a combination of greater gender equality in rights and higher levels of income may not guarantee the elimination of gender disparities—at least not in the short run. In South Asia combined improvements in rights and increases in income to best-of-region levels do not appear sufficient to achieve gender equality in primary or secondary education (see figure 6.4). And while there appears to be some scope for

Figure 6.4   Rising Income or Greater Gender Equality of Rights: Which Has a Larger Impact?
Simulated effects of improved rights and income on education, life expectancy, and parliamentary representation, by region

Primary enrollment, 1995

Female to male ratio

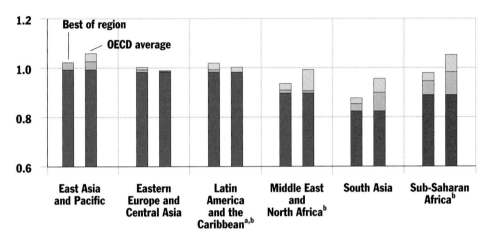

Secondary enrollment, 1995

Female to male ratio

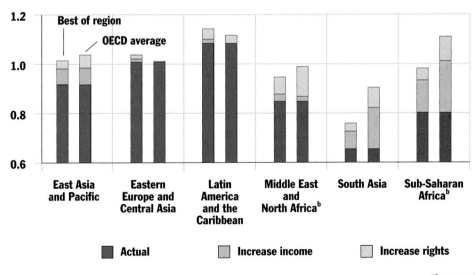

(figure continues on following page)

247

Figure 6.4 continued

Life expectancy, 1997

Female to male ratio

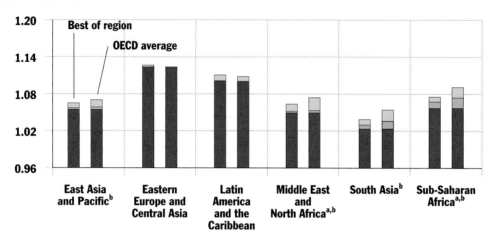

Parliamentary representation, 1995

Female to male ratio

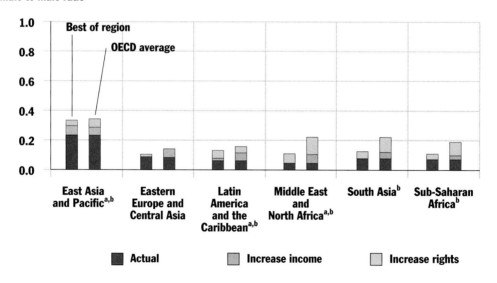

Note: See appendix 1 for general notes and included countries, appendix 2 for underlying regression results, and the glossary for definitions. The differences in the regional means between actual levels and simulations are statistically significant at the 10 percent level or better when indicated as follows:

a. Between actual and best-of-region scenario;

b. Between actual and OECD scenario.

Sources: Rights data from Humana (1992); parliamentary data from WISTAT (1998); all other data from World Bank (1999d).

increasing gender equality in parliamentary representation through rights improvements and (to a lesser extent) through income growth, gender parity in representation is not predicted even after substantial changes in rights and incomes. Factors outside the direct scope of legal and institutional reform or economic development—social norms and practices, gender asymmetries in power in the home—may continue to impede the social and economic transformations necessary to eliminate disparities between women and men.

Taking Active Measures to Redress Persistent Disparities in Command over Resources and Political Voice

BECAUSE THE COMBINED IMPACTS OF INSTITUTIONAL REFORMS and economic development may be limited—and may take time to become apparent—active policy measures to promote gender equality are often warranted.

Active measures are concrete, often targeted steps to redress specific forms of gender discrimination and exclusion in the home, community, or workplace. Like some of the institutional reforms discussed earlier, active policy measures aim at ensuring that women and men have equal access to and command over productive resources, that they can participate fully in productive employment and community affairs, and that they are adequately protected against risks associated with economic shocks or policy reforms. Unlike the legal and institutional issues discussed earlier, however, active measures go beyond simply leveling the playing field. In most cases, they focus on correcting persistent inequalities.

There are two important benefits of active policy measures. First, they can accelerate progress toward gender equality over what would be in their absence. Second, active measures can be used to target specific groups, such as the poor, among whom gender inequalities are often particularly acute.

While there are many types of active measures, the focus here is on four categories of interventions that address consistent patterns of gender disparities and differences highlighted in the report, whether generated by societal institutions, by households, or in the economy. Specifically, this section discusses interventions that:

- Promote gender equality in access to productive resources and earnings capacity.
- Reduce the personal costs to women of their household roles.
- Provide gender-appropriate social protection.
- Strengthen women's political participation and voice.

These four areas are at the heart of public action to promote gender equality in development. Access to productive resources—including education—and earnings capacity are critical to women's and men's ability to participate in and contribute fully to development. They are also central to transforming power relations between women and men. Reducing the costs to women of their household roles enables them to participate more fully in society, whether in the labor force or the community. And gender-appropriate social protection is important to ensuring that both females and males are adequately protected against gender-specific risks—whether from personal and family crises, economic shocks, or specific policy changes. Along with other measures that increase women's autonomy (such as education or access to other productive resources), enacting specific measures to strengthen women's voice in politics and policymaking can enhance women's ability to act as agents of change—to influence and contribute to development.

Table 6.1 presents an extensive (but not exhaustive) list of policy options in each of the four key policy areas. It covers a range of interventions that give policymakers leverage in reducing gender disparities. Given such a wide range of options, how can policymakers decide which active measures deserve priority in the face of limited budgetary and administrative resources? The following section outlines some guiding principles, drawing on an extensive literature on public economics.

Choosing Active Measures

Because implementing active measures has costs, a critical challenge is to choose interventions strategically to attain the greatest social benefit for the resources committed. And because the most effective interventions are likely to differ from place to place, choices about implementing active measures need to be based on a clear understanding of local and national gender differences and disparities, as well as of the bottlenecks to progress.

Table 6.1 Selected Active Measures to Promote Gender Equality

Policy area	Policy options
Promoting gender equality in access to productive resources and earnings capacity	
Education	"Retrofitting" school facilities and teaching staff to address cultural concerns about sending girls to school.
	Providing targeted subsidies, including:
	• Grants, stipends, fellowships, vouchers for tuition and other costs (as in Bangladesh).
	• Capitation grants, subsidizing girls' schools or girls' places in schools (as in Pakistan).
Financial resources (savings and credit)	Reforming financial institutions to give women access to savings and credit (such as allowing substitutes for traditional collateral requirements, simplifying procedures, reducing travel distances, as in Bangladesh and Ghana).
	Providing direct and indirect state (or donor) support for nongovernmental organization or private sector efforts to promote female access to financial intermediation (as in Bangladesh).
Employment and labor market policy	Initiating affirmative action programs in recruitment and job screening for public sector employees and for private firms with government contracts (as in the United States).
Reducing the personal costs to women of their household roles	
Reproductive rights and services	Increasing women's bargaining power and choice in reproductive decisions by increasing female control of resources and earnings (as above).
	Ensuring access to a basic package of reproductive health services, including family planning inputs.
	Initiating information, education, and communication campaigns on reproductive rights and family planning targeted to both men and women.
Out-of-home child care	Providing subsidies for out-of-home care, including vouchers and capitation grants to early childhood development and other child care facilities.
Labor market policy	Legislating maternity benefits for women, including paid postnatal leave (with compensation equal to some fraction of previous earnings), protection against dismissal during the leave, and paid nursing breaks.
	Offering paid paternity leave to fathers (as in Norway).
	Providing public support for paid maternity leave financed through general tax revenues or social security administrations (as in Costa Rica).
	Using insurance and other mechanisms to spread the costs of maternity leave more equitably across female and male workers and firms (as in the United States).
Time-saving infrastructure	Investing in water, power, and transportation infrastructure, particularly in rural areas.
	Increasing provision of and physical access to health and other service facilities.

(table continues on following page)

251

Table 6.1 continued

Policy area	Policy options
Providing gender-appropriate social protection	
Public works and workfare programs	Designing public employment schemes and other safety nets that account for gender differences in types of work considered appropriate for men and women.
Safety nets to protect human development investments	Providing short-term support—scholarships or other grants—to mitigate losses of children's, especially girls', education and health care in the face of economic shocks (as in Indonesia).
Old-age security	Designing or retrofitting pension systems to account for gender differences in employment histories and life expectancies, including: • Eligibility requirements that account for women's briefer employment histories. • Joint annuities and survivor's benefits. • Minimum pension guarantees or other redistributive mechanisms. • Appropriate price indexation. • Statutory retirement age. Providing (means-tested) social assistance to widows and elderly women who are not eligible for pension benefits (as in Chile).
Other social assistance or social insurance	Offering job retraining programs that account for gender differences in education, skills, and placement in the labor force. Training judges and other law enforcement personnel to better protect women's legal rights, including protection against gender-related violence. Training in legal literacy for women. Initiating information campaigns and treatment programs for perpetrators of domestic violence (as in Argentina, Canada, Mexico, Sweden, and the United States). Initiating public health campaigns that address gender-specific risks associated with rising mortality levels.
Strengthening women's political voice and participation	
Political reservation	Reserving positions for women in political parties or in local and national assemblies (as in Argentina, Ecuador, India, the Philippines, Uganda).
"Gender budget" initiatives	Reviewing gender impacts of government allocations on women's access to resources and public services (as in Australia, Barbados, Fiji, Mozambique, South Africa, Sri Lanka, Uganda). Supporting partnerships between government and civil society that promote gender awareness in public spending and strengthen women's voice in policymaking (as in South Africa and Uganda).
Women's participation in program design and implementation	Increasing female participation and consultation with women's organizations in the design of government interventions (as in India). Supporting local "audits" of government program implementation (as NGOs are pushing for in India).

For example, measures to increase females' access to basic education may yield high returns in countries with large gender disparities in schooling (as in South Asia, Sub-Saharan Africa, and the Middle East and North Africa). But they are not likely to provide as large benefits in countries where parity (or near-parity) in school enrollments has largely been attained (as in Eastern Europe and Central Asia or Latin America and the Caribbean). In these countries measures that enable fair and equal access to formal sector jobs or that promote greater female participation in politics may have higher social benefits.

Policy analysis that explicitly incorporates gender concerns is thus central to developing a strategy for implementing active measures—both for identifying policy priorities and for anticipating how specific interventions will affect women and men. Similarly, a process of public deliberation and debate that includes both women and men can help policymakers ensure that interventions are responding to perceived needs and constraints.

A few basic principles can help guide policymakers' analysis and choice of active measures:

- Are there persistent market failures or externalities that call for government intervention? Active measures to promote gender equality will have the biggest impact where private markets fail to supply (or supply enough of) the relevant goods and services—as opposed to areas where government interventions will substitute for (or crowd out) goods and services that the private sector already supplies or could supply. When active policy measures focus on correcting market failures—whether associated with underinvestment in girls' education or with poor access to formal sector jobs—they increase overall welfare in society as well as advance gender equality objectives (see chapter 2).

- How large is the market failure or externality and how much can specific government intervention reduce the failure or capture external benefits? The social costs and benefits of different measures need to be analyzed to identify interventions with the greatest impact on gender equality and on development. When assessing the full benefits and costs of different interventions, policymakers should take into account cross-sectoral links that may make interventions more effective. For example, long hours spent collecting water and fuel, as well as child care responsibilities, often constrain girls' schooling. Selected investments in time-saving infrastructure or public support for out-of-home child care can ease these constraints and, in turn, can make direct efforts to increase girls' schooling more effective.[5] Some measure of the social costs and benefits of alternative interventions should be analyzed—even when policymakers pursue purely distributional (as opposed to efficiency) objectives—to ensure that the chosen interventions will achieve the greatest possible impact.

- Once a case for active intervention is made, what is the most effective entry point for policy? It is important to consider the relative efficacy of different types of interventions—including efforts to address information failures, regulation and enforcement, direct public provision of goods or services, or public subsidies for private provision. In some circumstances providing information—to employers or to the public—may be sufficient to correct the market failure. In other instances regulatory approaches may be cost-effective. And when provision of a service or good is warranted, there may be a case for public financing of private provision rather than direct public provision. For instance, microfinance programs run by nongovernmental organizations (NGOs) have generally been more successful and cost-effective in providing financial services to women than have government-sponsored programs (Morduch 1999a). It is important also to consider the relative efficacy and cost-effectiveness of targeted versus untargeted measures.

Even though there is now a considerable body of empirical evidence on how various factors affect gender equality, further analysis of the gender impacts of specific policies and programs is needed. Moreover, there remains relatively little analysis of the relative costs and benefits of specific interventions. This reflects both the difficulty of measuring the (sometimes wide-ranging) benefits associated with gender equality and a lack of adequate data to support gender analysis. There is thus a critical need to collect and analyze gender-disaggregated data that would allow policymakers to make more informed choices about the most effective measures in specific contexts.[6]

The next section elaborates a number of the policy options listed in table 6.1. While evidence on net social benefits of interventions or on the merits of public or private provision is available only for a small subset of the measures discussed, this is not a justification for inaction. The costs of inactivity are high. But better understanding of impacts and cost-effectiveness of interventions in specific settings remains an important challenge if policymakers are to improve their capacity to promote gender equality with limited budget and administrative resources.

Promoting Gender Equality in Access to Productive Resources and Earnings Capacity

Reducing gender disparities in access to productive resources—whether education, credit, or land—and in earnings capacity can help to enhance both equity and efficiency. It is thus often a key element of an active policy approach to promote gender equality. Land was discussed in the section on basic rights, so the focus here is on approaches to promoting greater equality of access to education, financial services, and employment opportunities in the formal sector.

Education. Both targeted and untargeted measures can raise enrollment rates and achievement levels for girls (or boys) in countries where many are not in school. Since demand for girls' education is often more sensitive to costs, distance to school, and school quality than demand for boys' education, across-the-board improvements in these dimensions all tend to raise girls' school enrollments more than boys' (see chapter 4). For example, Indonesia's drive for universal primary education in the 1980s, which included a massive school-building program, boosted enrollment rates for both boys and girls. And girls' enrollment rates grew faster, since they started lower than boys'.

Reallocating public expenditures from higher to basic education—even without explicit gender targeting—also tends to promote gender equality in education because fewer girls in poor and rural communities continue beyond basic education. Universal primary enrollment rates and high continuation rates for both girls and boys in East Asia's newly industrialized countries have been attributed, in part, to policies allocating at least half of the education budget to primary education (World Bank 1993).[7]

Gender-targeted approaches, too, have improved females' access to education in several countries. As chapter 4 discusses, a national program that provides secondary school scholarships to girls in Bangladesh and a project that subsidized the establishment of private schools with capitation grants pegged to numbers of girls enrolled in Balochistan, Pakistan, have successfully increased the numbers of girls enrolled (World Bank 1997; Kim, Alderman, and Orazem 1998, 1999).

There is now evidence on an array of social benefits associated with female education, as chapter 2 discusses. And estimates using data from Egypt, India, and Pakistan demonstrate that in countries with low levels of female education, promoting girls' education is among the highest return investments a society can make (Summers 1992, 1994). In many settings the budgetary impacts of these investments are likely to be modest as well. Simulation analysis for South Asia and the Middle East and North Africa suggests, for example, that a policy of universal primary education would likely require only small percentage increases in the government primary education budgets of these countries (box 6.1). While the simulations suggest considerably larger budgetary costs in Sub-Saharan Africa, they also indicate scope for budgetary savings through gender targeting of interventions.

Financial resources. Financial institutions can facilitate saving and borrowing by women if they design their services in ways that account for gender differences in demand for savings and credit and for differences in the constraints that women and men face in accessing financial services.

Box 6.1   Budgetary Costs of Promoting Gender Equality in Primary Education in South Asia, Sub-Saharan Africa, and the Middle East and North Africa

GOVERNMENTS CAN RAISE DEMAND FOR PRIMARY schooling and close gender gaps by reducing the cost of education to households—say, by subsidizing school fees and associated costs. But what kind of budget impacts should governments expect from such efforts? Simulation analysis, based on published estimates of price elasticities of demand for boys' and girls' schooling (Schultz 1987) and of the share of private (household) spending in total (public and private) expenditures on primary education in developing countries (World Bank 1993), suggest that in many settings the budgetary costs would be modest.

In South Asia and the Middle East and North Africa achieving gender equality in primary education by promoting universal primary education would require increases in public spending on primary education of just more than 3 percent, on average. The budget costs of achieving universal primary education in Sub-Saharan Africa would likely be considerably higher, however—requiring increases in public spending on primary education of about a third. Why? Household spending on primary education makes up

a much larger proportion of total expenditure on primary education, and primary enrollment rates (for both girls and boys) tend to be lower than in the other regions.

The simulations also indicate that there are potentially significant budget savings associated with adopting targeted, as opposed to untargeted, approaches. For example, in South Asia and the Middle East and North Africa targeting cost reductions to attain universal primary enrollments for girls (only) would reduce the necessary increases in primary education budgets from 3 to about 2 percent, on average. In Sub-Saharan Africa gender-targeting of this type would reduce the required increases in public spending on primary education to about 20 percent.

If policies to reduce households' costs of education were targeted by household poverty status as well as by gender, the required increases in public budgets could be reduced a bit further. In Sub-Saharan Africa, for example, combined poverty and gender targeting could reduce the required budgetary increases to about 15 percent.

Source: World Bank staff estimates. See appendix 5 for details.

Among the relevant design features: allowing substitutes for traditional forms of collateral (such as social capital, to which women have access), simplifying banking procedures, and making savings and credit physically more accessible where women have limited mobility or time to travel.

One of the most important design innovations in financial intermediation for women is group-based microfinance. In group-based lending programs, such as those of Grameen Bank and the Bangladesh Rural Advancement Committee (BRAC), group support and pressure replace traditional collateral based on ownership of land, buildings, or other physical assets. Microfinance programs often use the group setting for a variety of training activities to help female (and male) borrowers become more effective entrepreneurs. Some microfinance programs (those of Grameen Bank, for example) also help members mobilize savings and, through voluntary contributory funds, offer program members and their families various types of insurance.

Recently some policy researchers have questioned the financial sustainability of microfinance programs. One study suggests that even microfinance institutions committed to financial sustainability tend to cover only about 70 percent of their costs (Morduch 1999b). But microfinance programs can be very effective in strengthening women's access to financial resources (Kabeer 1998; Khandker 1998; Zaman 1999). And a recent study of several microfinance programs in Bangladesh suggests that they can also be a cost-effective way to increase household consumption among the poor (box 6.2). In fact, relatively small subsidies to

---

Box 6.2 Cost-Benefit Analysis of Selected Microfinance and Antipoverty Programs in Bangladesh

A RECENT STUDY OF THE SEVERAL MICROFINANCE programs in Bangladesh indicates that microfinance programs can be cost-effective investments in reducing poverty and enhancing women's access to financial resources (Khandker 1998). The study, based on careful analysis of quasi-experimental survey data collected in rural Bangladesh, analyzes the costs and benefits of several antipoverty programs, including two NGO-sponsored microfinance programs, Grameen Bank and the Bangladesh Rural Advancement Committee (BRAC); two credit programs by state-owned agricultural development banks, Bangladesh Krishi Bank (BKB) and Rajshashi Krishi Unnayan Bank (RAKUB); two food-for-work programs, World Food Programme and CARE; and a government-run employment generation scheme, the Vulnerable Group development program.

(box continues on following page)

Box 6.2 continued

The analysis indicates that Grameen Bank lending is more cost effective than other programs aimed at increasing consumption among the poor (box table). For example, the costs of Grameen Bank lending associated with a one taka increase in household per capita consumption—even accounting for explicit and implicit subsidies—is lower than the costs of similar improvements in household consumption arising from the Vulnerable Group Development program and two food-for-work programs in rural Bangladesh. Both Grameen Bank and BRAC programs appear more cost-effective than the government-sponsored BKB and RAKUB programs.

Analysis of the costs and benefits of Grameen Bank and BRAC also suggests that the net benefits of lending to women, measured by increased household consumption, are greater than the net benefits of lending to men. While the cost-benefit estimates in the table are based on the assumption of similar costs of lending to women and men, evidence on relative benefits suggests that the costs of lending to women would have to be from 38 to 63 percent higher than the costs of lending to men before the cost-benefit ratios would shift in favor of men. But analysis of detailed data on the cost components of Grameen Bank lending (available in Khandker, Khalily, and Khan 1995) suggests that such large cost differentials are unlikely. If, for example, all training costs were incurred as a result of lending to women, this would raise the costs of lending to women by only a few percentage points.

Cost-Effectiveness of Programs to Increase Consumption among the Poor

Credit program	Unit	Economic cost per taka of loan outstanding	Benefits		Cost-benefit ratio	
			Women	Men	Women	Men
Grameen Bank	Taka	0.172	0.189	0.116	0.91	1.48
Bangladesh Rural Advancement Committee (BRAC)	Taka	0.444	0.172	0.125	2.58	3.55
Bangladesh Krishi Bank (BKB)	Taka	0.146	0.030		4.87	
Rajshashi Krishi Unnayan Bank (RAKUB)	Taka	0.098	0.030		3.27	

Other programs	Unit	Dollars per ton of grain				
Vulnerable Group Development	Dollars per ton	252	164[a], 153[b]		1.54[a], 1.65[b]	
Food-for-work (World Food Programme)	Dollars per ton	258	151[a], 128[c]		1.71[a], 2.02[c]	
Food-for-work (CARE)	Dollars per ton	299	114		2.62	

(box continues on following page)

Box 6.2 continued

Note: The Vulnerable Group Development program is an employment-generation scheme that uses food (mostly wheat) as currency to promote productive self-employment among poor people not covered by a food-for-work program. Food-for-work programs are employment-generation programs that provide employment, with food as payment, to poor people who have difficulty finding alternative employment during the lean season. The cost-benefit ratios should not be interpreted in the context of full social cost-benefit analysis. The costs are measured as the social costs—including subsidies—incurred for each unit of financial services provided to clients. But the benefits are measured as the effects on private household per capita consumption, which do not necessarily reflect the full social benefits of the relevant programs. The cost-benefit ratios are best interpreted as the social costs associated with increasing household per capita consumption by one unit. For a detailed explanation of the cost-effectiveness calculations see appendix C in Khandker (1998).

a. Data are from the World Food Programme.

b. Data are from the International Food Policy Research Institute.

c. Data are from a joint study of the Bangladesh Institute of Development Studies and the International Food Policy Research Institute.

Source: Adapted from Khandker (1998).

Grameen Bank in Bangladesh, (compared with subsidies to other, less cost effective, programs) have had a substantial impact on women's access to credit and other financial services (Khandker 1998).[8]

While microfinance programs promoting women's access to credit have received much attention recently, it is important to recognize the role of institutions that foster financial savings among women—whether or not they are associated with credit programs. As with the poor more generally, giving women convenient, safe, and reliable means to save can make an important and cost-effective contribution to raising women's incomes and reducing their vulnerability and gender-specific risk. Enabling financial savings among women may be particularly important in such places as Ghana or Ethiopia, where husbands and wives do not pool risk (M. Goldstein 1999; Dercon and Krishnan 2000). Moreover, promoting savings among women can enhance their security in old age or widowhood.

Labor market policy. In countries with fairly well-developed labor markets and reasonable law enforcement, affirmative action employment programs can promote greater gender equality in formal sector employment opportunities (see, for example, Leonard 1985, 1990; Rodgers and Spriggs 1996; Holzer and Neumark 1998, 1999). And despite concerns about reverse discrimination and productivity costs, recent studies from the United States find little empirical evidence that affirmative action hires are less productive than are other workers (Holzer and Neumark 1998, 1999). In fact, where there is serious discrimination in hiring and promotions, affirmative action programs may bring productivity gains to firms and the economy.

Yet affirmative action employment programs tend to be controversial. Among those who benefit from discriminatory practices, there are concerns that affirmative action programs could threaten privilege and cause "reverse discrimination." And among those who stand to gain from affirmative action, there are often concerns about being stigmatized as less qualified and about attracting resentment from nonpreferred groups in the workplace.

But affirmative action employment programs are not limited to hiring quotas—the form of preference that appears to generate the most political heat. Programs can include a variety of activities by employers—special recruitment efforts, broader screening practices, special assistance programs, such as training, and changes in hiring, pay, or promotion standards. Survey evidence from the United States suggests that most people, even those who oppose hiring quotas, tend not to oppose affirmative action policies that broaden recruitment and screening practices (Holzer and Neumark 1998).

Reducing the Personal Costs to Women of Their Household Roles

Women in developing countries generally work longer hours than men—in part because they bear a disproportionate share of the responsibility and time for household maintenance and care activities. Many hours devoted to these responsibilities often mean that women have less opportunity than men to participate in market-based work or earn income independently—which affects their bargaining and decisionmaking power within the household—and less time for rest and personal care. For adolescent girls, who commonly share responsibility for household tasks, these activities often come at the expense of schooling.

Policies and infrastructure investments that reduce the costs to women and girls of their household roles can free women to participate in other activities, whether income generation or community affairs. They can also facilitate increased education for girls, with salutary effects on such broad development objectives as raising living standards and improving well-being—as well as helping to promote gender equality.

Reproductive rights and services. In many developing countries women still have little say in decisions on family size or contraceptive use. Moreover, access to adequate reproductive health services, including family planning, remains limited in many places. Although it is difficult to distinguish between the effects of demand and supply, between 120 and 150 million women who wish to space births or limit further childbearing are not using contraception (UNFPA 1997). This affects the nature and costs to women of their household roles.

There are two main pathways to giving women more say in reproduction. First, interventions that increase women's bargaining power in the household by improving their control of resources and earnings enhance women's role in making reproductive decisions. Higher levels of female autonomy, education, wages, and labor market participation all tend to increase contraceptive use and reduce fertility (see, for example, Fairlamb and Nieuwoudt 1991; Gertler and Molyneaux 1994; Singh 1994; Diamond, Newby, and Varle 1999; Mencarini 1999; and Handa 2000). But strengthening women's bargaining power and reproductive choice may not always lead them to choose smaller families. While access to microfinance empowers women, evidence from Bangladesh suggests that it can lead them to desire more children under some circumstances—say, when they are chiefly engaged in home-based, self-employment activities (as opposed to labor market work) and perceive additional children as compatible with—or even assets to—their enterprises (Khandker 1998).

Second, increased power for women to negotiate reproduction may not translate into greater reproductive choice if women lack access to family planning inputs. It is thus important to ensure that health systems provide a basic package of reproductive health services, including family planning. And since women and men may have different preferences for family size and contraceptive use, it is important to ensure that family planning services, including basic information and education and communication campaigns, are targeted to men and women.

Child care. The availability of low-cost, out-of-home child care options significantly increases the likelihood that mothers will participate in the labor force. A recent study that simulates the impact of subsidies for child care on mothers' labor force decisions in the Russian Federation (Lokshin 2000) finds, moreover, that subsidizing out-of-home care can be more cost-effective than other approaches, such as wage subsidies, in drawing mothers into the labor market and raising maternal (and household) incomes. Low-cost child care also increases girls' ability to enroll and stay in school. As chapter 4 notes, in Kenya reducing the price of out-of-home care has a substantial impact on enrollment rates of 8- to 16-year-old girls, after controlling for other factors (Lokshin, Glinskaya, and Garcia 2000).

Reducing the cost of child care can have efficiency as well as equity benefits for society. For example, if combining nonfamily with family care in the early years gives children a better start than family care alone, subsidizing child care for preschoolers can have positive externalities. Evidence on early childhood development programs in developing countries indicates that investing in such programs when children are very young can improve their academic achievement and cognitive development, nutrition and health status, and earnings potential in the future (Young 1996).[9] Similarly, since out-of-home care results in higher household investments in girls' schooling, this, too, can help support national development efforts and increase gender equality.

If governments support child care and early childhood development programs, should they focus on direct public provision or on financial incentives (say, through vouchers or capitation grants) to private or NGO–run early childhood development facilities? Evidence is limited—and mixed—on the relative benefits and costs of different types of child care providers. For example, a recent study of the quality of child care facilities in four U.S. states found no difference between for-profit and not-for-profit day care centers—except in one state with particularly lax licensing standards (Cost, Quality & Child Outcomes Study Team 1995). In that state the quality of care was considerably lower in the for-profit sector, suggesting that the regulatory environment is important for the quality of care in the United States.

In contrast, a study of child care use among low-income households in the *favelas* of Rio de Janeiro suggests that private providers tend to be of higher quality and offer more flexible hours than public providers (Deutsch 1998). This study also found that the costs of running government facilities are high relative to the subsidies that would be required to expand private provision. So, at least for low-income neighborhoods in Rio de Janeiro, subsidies for private care (say, vouchers) would be more cost-effective in raising female labor force participation and incomes than direct support for public facilities.[10]

Labor market policy. As chapter 3 discusses, many developing country governments already have formal labor market policies intended to help women combine employment and motherhood, including maternity leave legislation that provides for paid leave (with compensation equal to some fraction of previous earnings), protection against dismissal during the leave, paid nursing breaks, and mandatory postnatal leave. Some developed countries have gone further, establishing policies to encourage fathers to take paid family leave time (as in Japan and the United States). Indeed, some have created strong incentives for fathers to share in care activities. Norway's family leave policy, for example, grants fathers paternity leave that is not transferable to mothers, so fathers either use it or lose it.

But these types of labor market policies are often double-edged swords, generating costs as well as benefits for women. For example, when firms bear all the costs of maternity leave, they may bias hiring decisions against women. When women bear all the costs, the incentives to continue work weaken (see chapter 3). Nevertheless, appropriately designed labor market policy can reduce the personal costs to women of providing care and enable them to participate in market work.

For instance, the way programs are financed can affect who benefits and who pays. Measures that spread the costs of maternity (or other family) provisions across employers, workers, and even the state can raise the benefits relative to the costs for women and their families. In some countries the state covers a part of maternity leave benefits through general tax revenue or social security system payments (as in Costa Rica). By sharing some of the costs with firms and with women, this approach can mitigate the negative impacts on female employment and earnings. Alternatively, maternity leave funding can be part of more general firm-level insurance schemes related to health, disability, or worker compensation. Since women and men have different health and disability risk profiles, the costs of childbearing and child rearing are spread more equitably across female and male workers—again reducing the impacts on female employment.

Selected infrastructure investments. While economic development can be expected to increase the overall availability of infrastructure, selected investments in basic infrastructure—especially time-saving infrastructure—can accelerate progress toward gender equality in access to resources and economic opportunity. Infrastructure investments generally benefit people regardless of their gender, but they often benefit women and men differently. An example: investments that reduce distances to schools (and thus the costs of education) tend to raise female enrollment—both in absolute terms and relative to males. Another example: especially in poor, rural areas the absence of basic water and energy infrastructure often means long hours for girls and women collecting water and fuel. In these settings selected investments in water, energy, and transportation infrastructure can substantially reduce the time women and girls devote to household maintenance, freeing girls to attend school and women to participate in more productive activities.

These types of infrastructure investments need not be targeted by gender, but accounting for the benefits to women and girls in benefit-cost calculations would raise the estimated returns (of what are often already high return investments), perhaps raising their priority among competing public investments. Taking account of gender differences in demand for different types of infrastructure would also likely affect the placement and design of such investments.

Providing Gender-Appropriate Social Protection

Women and men often face different risks during economic shocks or policy reforms. Women command fewer resources with which to cushion shocks—while men, as the traditional breadwinners, are particularly vulnerable to stress associated with large changes or uncertain employment. Taking gender differences in risk and vulnerability into account in designing social protection is particularly important because women and men in the same household may not pool risk (box 6.3).

Social safety nets. Social safety nets and other types of social protection programs whose design neglects gender differences and disparities can have important—often unintended—gender impacts. For instance, workfare programs designed without attention to the types of work women and men consider appropriate have excluded women as participants and beneficiaries. At the same time social protection programs that account for gender differences in risk and in demand for services can better protect both men and women. Specific examples include designing scholarship programs or waivers of fees for services during times of economic shock that systematically incorporate gender differences in income and price elasticities of demand for education and health care, or designing short-term job retraining programs for the unemployed that account for differences between women and men in education, skills, placement in the labor force, and employment preferences.

Old age security. In light of current demographic trends female vulnerability in old age will take on increasing importance in the 21st century. Women tend to live longer than men, and in most regions women are more likely to spend time as widows. Widows and other elderly women living alone tend to be much more vulnerable to poverty in old age than men (see chapter 1).[11]

Box 6.3   Gender-Appropriate Social Protection Means Attention to both Women and Men

THERE ARE MANY GOOD REASONS TO FOCUS ON measures that address female-specific vulnerability and risk when considering gender-appropriate social protection. As this report shows, negative price and income shocks often have more harmful impacts on access to and use of basic services for women than for men. Both public and private enterprises often let go female employees earlier and in greater numbers than male employees during economic downturns. And women, because they tend to live longer than men and have poorer command over resources, tend to be particularly vulnerable to poverty in old age.

At the same time several emerging trends argue for greater attention to male-specific issues in designing social protection. Take the relative decline in male life expectancy in the transition economies of Eastern Europe. The trend points to gender-specific risks—related to rising unemployment and growing alcoholism and depression among men—for which gender-targeted social programs may be warranted. Like the many manifestations of gender roles and relations discussed in this report, these problems affect the well-being of men, women, and children: from higher risks of male suicide to higher risks of poverty among affected men and their families to higher risks of domestic violence.

A policy approach that focuses explicitly on both men and women is also warranted in gender-related-violence prevention efforts. Such an approach is necessary to address the underlying socioeconomic causes of male violence against women and should complement efforts to protect and support women as victims of such violence. Several countries already have treatment programs for perpetrators of domestic violence, including Argentina, Australia, Canada, Mexico, Sweden, and the United States (Heise, Ellsberg, and Gottemoeller 1999).

In some countries special attention to gender issues is warranted in raising male as well as female school enrollment and retention. In parts of Latin America and the Caribbean, for example, young men leaving school early is becoming an increasing concern. In Colombia this reflects, in part, the evolution of male roles and expectations in the context of civil conflict and a growing skepticism among young men about the value of education in improving their life prospects. In fact, female advantage in school enrollment is becoming increasingly common in Latin America and the Caribbean. Education interventions or other social policies that target males rather than females may be warranted in these countries.

Measures that strengthen women's command over productive resources in general and over assets and savings in particular reduce women's vulnerability in old age. But other mechanisms are also necessary. Inasmuch as informal (and household-based) insurance mechanisms break down with development (see chapter 3), establishing other, more formal mechanisms for ensuring old age security for women as well as men becomes increasingly important. As more countries reform their social security programs, they can better protect elderly women by taking account of gender differences in earnings, labor force experience, and longevity in the design of their old-age security systems.

Since women tend to spend fewer years in the labor market than men, programs that include a redistributive component that does not require as many years of contributions better protect women in old age. Such components may be based on residence (as the flat benefit in the Netherlands) or may be pro-rated by years of employment—both superior to an all-or-nothing benefit that requires a lifetime of formal market employment.

In many countries the statutory retirement age is lower for women than men. This means that women will retire earlier and receive smaller annuities (other factors equal), since they have fewer years of contributions and more years of expected longevity that the annuity must cover. And if pensions are not indexed properly to inflation, females' living standards fall disproportionately with age because women live longer than men. Even if pensions are indexed to prices, older women's living standards will fall relative to those of younger workers if pensions do not rise as wages grow. Since women's earnings tend to be lower than men's, minimum pension guarantees, survivor benefits, and joint annuities can ensure that women receive a minimum threshold level of benefits (box 6.4). Finally, given that many women work outside the formal sector or do not participate in the labor force, designing old-age security systems (defined more broadly than simply employment-based pension schemes) to provide more general social assistance to low-income groups can help elderly women.[12]

Box 6.4   Gender and the Design of Old-Age Security in Chile

SPECIFIC DESIGN FEATURES OF A FORMAL PENSION system—such as the statutory retirement age, whether there are survivor benefits, and what the eligibility requirements are for a minimum pension guarantee and for noncontributory social assistance—matter to the relative income flows of older women and men. Chile has a multipillar pension system in which the largest component is a defined contribution pillar. Workers contribute to their retirement savings accounts while working, turning this accumulation into an annuity (pension) or gradual withdrawal after retirement.

An average woman with incomplete primary education who retires at 60—the statutory retirement age for women—has accumulated a retirement savings fund that is only 36 percent that of an average man with the same level of education who retires at 65—the statutory retirement age for men (Cox-Edwards 2000). This disparity results from gender differences in both earnings and years of labor market experience. Since the woman is expected to live longer, and gender-specific mortality tables are allowed, this accumulation yields a monthly annuity that is only 29 percent of that of her male counterpart (box figure).

(box continues on following page)

Box 6.4 continued

Pension Design Affects the Relative Benefits to Elderly Women and Men

**Monthly pension income for workers with incomplete primary education
(female to male ratio in parentheses)**

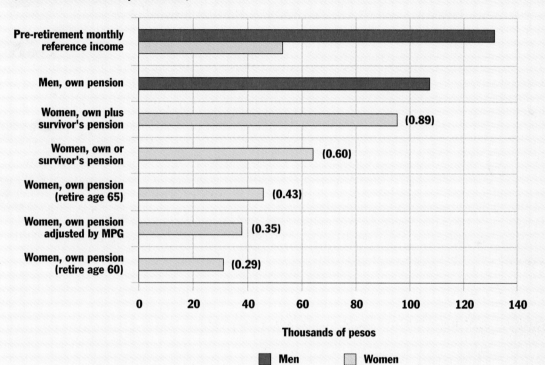

Note: These estimates assume that men retire at 65, women at 60—the statutory retirement ages for men and women, unless otherwise noted. *MPG* stands for the government-supported minimum pension guarantee. The figures are calculated as monthly annuities to urban contributors, assuming 5 percent rate of return with 2 percent secular wage growth. Males are assumed to survive for 15 years after retirement (at 65) and to make provisions for a survivor's pension for 6 years at 60 percent of their own annuity. If females retire at 60, they are assumed to survive for 23 years, and if they retire at 65, they are assumed to survive for 19 years. Pre-retirement reference income represents the average monthly earnings for the last 10 years of contributory wages, weighted by average time worked. Because women, in general, work much more than men, the gender gap shown here is larger than the gender gap in current monthly or hourly earnings. Under the scenario of "women, own plus survivor's pension" a widow is assumed to get survivor benefits as well as her own pension. But when a woman has already exhausted her pension contributions prior to widowhood, she would receive survivor's benefits only.

Source: Adapted from Cox-Edwards (2000).

(box continues on following page)

Box 6.4 continued

What can be done to reduce or eliminate this disparity? Chile has instituted a minimum pension guarantee that is received mainly by low-income women and which raises the relative annuity per month from 29 to 35 percent. If the retirement age were raised to 65 and if women worked from ages 60 to 65 at the same rate that they worked for the preceding five years, this would raise their monthly annuity to 43 percent of male levels.

Husbands are required to purchase a joint annuity when they retire or to withdraw their savings over their own expected lifetime plus that of their wife. The annuity must be indexed to prices to retain its real purchasing power over time. So, in the event of widowhood, the same woman would receive a survivor's pension which, by itself, provides an annuity that is 60 percent of the annuity received by her husband. If she were to receive her own pension in addition to a survivor's benefit, the relative value of the combined annuity would rise to 89 percent.

Patterns are similar for women and men with higher education levels—although the absolute sizes of their pensions are larger due to higher contributions over their years of employment. And because of higher contributions the minimum pension guarantee does not affect the relative annuities for women and men in this group.

In addition to the employment-based pension scheme, Chile finances a means-tested social assistance pension called PASIS, targeted to poor women and men over 65 who are not covered by their own contributory pension, and to disabled people over 18 (Cox-Edwards 1999). PASIS beneficiaries represent between 12 and 13 percent of all old-age beneficiaries. Since elderly women are generally poorer than elderly men, and the very elderly (who are the poorest) are largely women, PASIS benefits are received disproportionately by women and account for a higher share of their retirement income, particularly in rural areas.

Strengthening Women's Political Voice and Participation

Measures that increase women's voice in politics and policymaking can have far-reaching implications for gender equality—because they enhance women's ability to act on their own behalf. And by fostering greater participation, transparency, and availability of information, increasing women's voice in politics and public life can improve the impact of policies and programs, reduce corruption, and strengthen governance (see chapter 2). In all countries—developed and developing—there is considerable scope for increasing female participation and voice in politics and policymaking locally and nationally.

Political reservation. Because economic development and other factors that strengthen women's economic status are likely to contribute to greater political influence only in the long term, more active measures are needed to enhance women's ability to participate in politics and policymaking in the short and medium terms. As chapter 3 discusses, one approach that has increased female representation in local and national governments is political "reservation"—reserving political positions for women in political parties or in local and national assemblies.

More than 30 countries have some form of political reservation, with the form varying by country (UNIFEM 1998). In some countries a prescribed number or proportion of seats is reserved for women. A third of local assembly (*Panchayat Raj*) seats in India are reserved for women (Sen 2000). In other countries political parties mandate that women make up some minimum proportion of their candidates for the elected assembly. In Argentina the minority gender must account for at least a third of candidates on national election lists (Jones 1996).

As with other forms of affirmative action, political reservation is controversial—even among some women's organizations (Sen 2000). While many women's groups support reservation, at least as an interim measure, others worry about the stigma associated with being elected to a reserved position. Other critics argue that reservation may limit women's advancement. They say that by mandating minimum levels of representation, quotas create a psychological ceiling, making it difficult for women to reach the majority status in government that they make up in most electorates. But even these critics acknowledge that reservation has substantially increased female representation in electoral bodies over the past decade.

Partnerships in policy and program design. Strengthening women's participation in the public arena goes well beyond formal representation in local or national government bodies, and several recent initiatives highlight promising examples of efforts to increase female voice in policymaking and governance. Australia, Barbados, Canada, Fiji, Mozambique, South Africa, Sri Lanka, Sweden, Tanzania, and Uganda have recently begun "women's budget" (or "gender budget") initiatives to review the gender impacts of government budgets and promote greater attention to gender equality in budget allocations. In contrast to what the name might suggest, women's budget initiatives are not focused on establishing separate budgets for women and men. Rather, they aim to increase understanding of gender issues in budget processes and allocations so as to improve women's access to resources and government services.

Many of these initiatives are largely government efforts. But others involve innovative partnerships between government and civil society groups. In South Africa, for example, nongovernmental research organizations, women's NGOs, and the new parliament's Joint Standing Committee on Finance are collaborating to evaluate the gender impacts of government taxation and expenditure policies, deliberating on spending priorities, and disseminating information to the public on budget processes and outcomes (box 6.5).

Beyond efforts to promote greater female voice in policymaking in central government, participatory development planning is being promoted as part of government decentralization efforts in India and the Philippines, as well as in municipalities in Brazil, Bolivia, and Uruguay. In Kerala, India, efforts are being made to give poor women control of the selection of beneficiaries for antipoverty program benefits and to increase their participation in drawing up local government annual investment plans (Goetz 1998).

Increasing female participation in the design of government interventions is good for gender equality—and for development effectiveness

---

Box 6.5 Toward Stronger Female Voice in Policymaking: Women's Budget Initiatives in Africa

THE SOUTH AFRICAN WOMEN'S BUDGET INITIATIVE began as an innovative joint venture between several nongovernmental organizations (NGOs) and new parliamentarians in the post-apartheid government. The parliamentarians were members of the Joint Standing Committee on Finance's Gender and Economic Policy Group. And many of the NGO representatives were involved in budget-related and more general policy research.

The initiative highlights the gender dimensions of the government's budget—including taxation, expenditure, and the budget process itself—and ensures that the budget process and subsequent allocations serve gender equity. The first three rounds of analysis focused on the national parliament's budget process. The fourth looked at local government and disseminated the findings and messages to a broader constituency of South Africans—to equip citizens to engage in policy discussions.

The South African initiative inspired a three-year gender budget initiative in Uganda in 1997, led by the Parliamentary Women's Caucus and the Forum for Women in Democracy, an NGO. Like South

Africa's initiative it coordinates the efforts of parliamentarians and researchers from NGOs. The Women's Caucus, already a powerful political force in Uganda, has pushed through several legislative changes, including the clause in local government law stating that at least a third of executive committee members in parishes and villages should be women. The gender budget initiative has focused on better understanding the gender impacts of macroeconomic policy—with a focus on the impacts of structural adjustment on poor women.

A coalition of NGOs is spearheading another three-year gender budget initiative, also started in 1997. Led by the Tanzania Gender Networking Programme, the focus is on understanding the budget processes of the National Planning Commission and the Ministry of Finance, how those processes affect government spending on basic services, and how government spending decisions affect women's and men's access to health and education services. The coalition is disseminating its key findings in "simple language" to make them accessible to a broad range of women and men across Tanzanian society.

Source: Blackden and Bhanu (1999); Budlender (1999); TGNP (1999).

---

more broadly. Studies find that participation by civil society contributes to more effective development projects (Isham, Narayan, and Pritchett 1995) and can be instrumental in improving project impacts on women and girls (Kim, Alderman, and Orazem 1998, 1999). But civil society participation does not always guarantee female participation, because women may not be able to voice their views forcefully in meetings that include both men and women (Narayan 1995; Graham 1996). For that reason, specific measures—such as sex-segregated focus group meetings— are often needed to ensure female participation.

This section has shown that policymakers can choose from a wide range of active policies to promote gender equality. In many cases these interventions will bring high social returns and can therefore be justified on efficiency as well as gender equality grounds. Because the nature and extent of gender inequality differ considerably from place to place, decisions about whether and how to intervene need to be based on a clear understanding of local realities. And because policies and programs to reduce gender disparities have real resource costs, policymakers need to be selective, focusing strategically on the areas where government intervention is likely to have the largest pay-offs—for gender equality and for development. While government intervention is not costless, with appropriate attention to gender when designing programs—whether for public service delivery or for social protection—relatively modest investments at the margin can often yield noteworthy progress toward gender equality.

Challenges for the Future—the Way Forward

THE EVIDENCE PRESENTED IN THIS REPORT MAKES A compelling case for the state to intervene to promote gender equality. Indeed, the state, civil society, and the international community all have critical roles to play in fighting gender discrimination and enabling societies to reap the benefits of greater equality between women and men. Even so, policymakers face several important challenges as they move forward.

Sharpening Policy through Gender Analysis

How to deepen understanding of the links between gender equality and development and how to reflect these links in policy decisions

271

constitute a major challenge. This report brings together extensive evidence on these links, but much remains to be discovered and understood, implying the need for more and better data and for analyses disaggregated by gender. Among the key areas for more analysis:

- What are the gender impacts of specific macroeconomic and sectoral policies? And how do public expenditure choices promote or inhibit gender equality and economic efficiency? Policymakers face numerous competing demands for public resources and attention—and tight fiscal and administrative budgets. Under these constraints information and analysis help governments achieve the maximum social gains from the gender-related interventions they choose. Because gender disparities—and the institutional environment in which they persist—differ among societies, effective policy needs to be grounded in analysis that integrates local and national gender concerns.
- What policies empower women? Increasingly it will be important to look beyond the way policies and programs affect our usual development markers (such as education, health, or labor force indicators) to the way specific interventions improve female autonomy, leadership, and voice, both in the household and in society more broadly. Understanding which interventions are most effective requires more gender analysis.

Addressing Emerging Issues

A related challenge for policymakers is to be forward-looking in the face of rapidly changing circumstances around the world. Indeed, a number of emerging issues require greater attention from a gender perspective by policymakers and policy researchers. For example:

- *The graying of the world's population.* With birth rates declining and people living longer, the world's population is aging and the number of elderly—especially widows—worldwide will increase substantially during the 21st century. The labor force choices of elderly men and women are also becoming more similar. What do these changes imply for social protection, health, and other areas of public policy?
- *The spread of HIV/AIDS.* The incidence of adult deaths due to HIV/AIDS is expected to rise dramatically in developing countries over

the next few decades. Gender disparities help fuel the AIDS crisis, and women will disproportionately bear the costs. In what ways can policy, by taking gender differences and disparities explicitly into account, more effectively stem the spread of AIDS and reduce its human costs?

- *Globalization, technology, and information.* Globalization and new information technologies are transforming the way production is organized and information shared across the world. Will these changes accelerate progress toward gender equality or widen gender gaps in economic opportunity? And how can these forces be harnessed to promote gender equality?

- *Decentralization and localization.* Alongside globalization is a trend toward decentralization of government authority and decisionmaking in many countries. This trend will affect the delivery of public services and the roles of the state and the private sector—often with important implications for relative access to resources, opportunities, and political voice for women and men. Under what conditions does decentralization promote or inhibit progress toward gender equality?

Broadening Partnerships

A third major challenge is for policymakers—in their efforts to promote gender equality—to broaden their partnerships with civil society groups, donors, and others in the international community. While policymakers have an important leadership role, efforts to combat gender inequalities can be enhanced by more active collaboration with civic and international organizations. The donor community can contribute by supporting the collection and analysis of gender-disaggregated data, by incorporating gender analysis into its dialogue with national policymakers, and by sharing good practice based on international experience. Similarly, civic groups and local researchers can contribute critical information and analysis based on local knowledge that will broaden and deepen the policy dialogue.

Fostering broader participation and transparency in policymaking has the potential for tremendous payoffs, both for gender equality and for national development. Opening public deliberations and policymaking to greater participation by women's groups can directly empower women—and can enhance the impact of policies and programs. The research findings on the links between greater female participation in

273

public life and lower levels of corruption are intriguing and deserve further investigation. They suggest that facilitating broader exchanges of ideas and greater transparency in policymaking—and greater female participation in the public domain—can strengthen a country's governance and the effectiveness of its development policy.

Notes

1. Comparing the heights of the "low equality–high income" and the "high equality–low income" bars, it is not possible to generalize that one is always taller than the other. The relative magnitudes differ by indicators. Simulation analyses suggest that the relative impacts of rights and income differ by the measure of gender inequality considered, as well as by region (see below).

2. While the simulations suggest that growth in average incomes would have only a small impact on average indicators of gender equality in education and life expectancy in these regions, evidence presented elsewhere in this report (see chapters 1and 5) suggests that rising incomes among the poor would still play an important role in closing gender gaps in education and health in low-income households, even in these regions.

3. It may also reflect the limitations of analyzing data in cross-section. Specifically, while analyzing data at a single point in time allows identication of patterns across countries at different income levels, it does not permit identification of the effects of changes in income levels within countries over time. There are thus potentially large gains to collecting time series data on rights and analyzing the effects of gender rights and income within a panel data framework.

4. World Bank staff also estimated an alternative model, with per capita income, average gender rights, and their interaction term as right-hand variables. Results were mixed. For the school enrollment variables, gender equality in rights and income had a significantly positive impact on gender equality, whereas the interaction term was negative and significant. This indicates that where gender equality in rights (or income) are lower, increases in income (or gender rights) could still improve gender equality in enrollment. In other words, in countries where equality in rights (or income) are

high, income (or rights) can have only a marginal impact on gender equality in schooling. Improved gender equality in rights (or income) were found to have positive impacts on gender equality in enrollment only for per capita incomes less than $16,000 in 1995 dollars, adjusted for purchasing power parity (or for a gender rights index below 3.6). For the ratio of females to males in parliament, the opposite was true, with gender equality in rights and income being negative and significant and the interaction being positive and significant in the estimated relationship. This indicates that where gender equality in rights (or income) are very low, increased income (or rights) do not promote gender equality in parliamentary representation. Increased equality in rights (or income) had positive impacts on gender equality in parliamentary representation only for per capita incomes exceeding $600 in 1995 dollars, adjusted for purchasing power parity (or for a gender rights index exceeding 2.8). These results indicate that gender equality in rights and income are complementary and reinforce each other. For life expectancy the interaction term was statistically insignificant.

5. Similarly, supply side interventions that increase women's reproductive choices, such as family planning services, are more effective when combined with demand side interventions that enhance women's bargaining power and decisionmaking ability in the household.

6. Several methodologies are available for evaluating the costs and benefits of specific interventions, including rate-of-return and cost-effectiveness analysis (see, for example, Squire 1989 and various studies included in van de Walle and Nead 1995). It is important to recognize, however, that certain types of social benefits are not easily measured by standard forms of cost-benefit or rate-of-return analysis. It may be difficult to quantify the social benefits of increasing women's ability to participate in politics or increasing their voice in policymaking. But even

when the benefits of an intervention are difficult to measure precisely, it is often possible to measure the costs. And in the absence of good information on benefits, understanding the magnitude of these costs can help policymakers rule out some policy options and identify feasible policy priorities (Pradhan 1996).

7. There is some evidence that primary enrollments are also linked to spending at the secondary school level. A study of household demand for schooling using data from Ghana, for example, indicates that increasing expenditure on secondary education raises enrollment rates and improves continuation in primary school (Lavy 1996).

8. To illustrate: in 1994 Grameen Bank received $6.3 million from the government and donors (Khandker, Khalily, and Khan 1995). This support, in forms ranging from explicit grants to interest rate subsidies, helped facilitate lending to about 1.9 million people that year, nearly 1.8 million of them women. In the same year the government of Bangladesh and donors together provided about $80.6 million in grain to food-for-work programs—programs that were not as cost effective (Government of Bangladesh 1999; box 6.2). While Grameen Bank and food-for-work programs are not perfect substitutes (they have somewhat different objectives and often serve different clients), the cost-effectiveness estimates suggest that there is potential for the government of Bangladesh and donors to improve the impact of their same resources by reallocating a portion of their current subsidies away from food-for-work programs toward the Grameen Bank.

9. Evidence from the Philippines, for example, suggests that $1 invested in an early childhood nutrition could potentially return gains in academic achievement valued at $5 in the market (Glewwe, Jacoby, and King forthcoming). Estimates from two separate studies on an early childhood development program in Bolivia suggest that the ratio of quantifiable benefits to costs ranges from 1.7 to 3.1 (van der Gaag and Tan 1998; Todd, Behrman, and Cheng 2000).

10. The fact that the relative costs and benefits of public and private provision differ in different places with different regulatory environments underscores the importance of context-specific policy analysis.

11. Not only do women tend to live longer, but most marry older men and are less likely than men to remarry after divorce or the death of a spouse. Therefore, a much higher proportion of women end up living alone. Moreover, divorce, separation, or death of spouse has a more negative effect on the living standards of women than on those of men because women are more dependent on spousal support (James 1999). A recent study of the United States also found that men generally enjoy economic gains after divorce (Duncan and Hoffman 1985). Five years after a divorce the average divorced woman's household income has fallen to 71 percent of its predivorce level, while the average divorced man's household income has risen by 14 percent.

12. There are a number of critical issues in the design of financially sustainable systems of old-age security in developing countries that are not based on employment and contribution (World Bank 1994b). Nonetheless, from a gender perspective a potentially important benefit of such generalized old-age assistance is that it helps undermine an important rationale for persistent pro-male bias in developing countries by reducing parents' economic dependence on sons in the parents' old age.

Notes and Country Coverage for Text Figures

General

ALL VALUES ARE POPULATION-WEIGHTED AVERAGES. WHERE revevant, the figures are scaled so that a ratio of 1.0 represents equality between women and men. See glossary for definitions of terms; see box 1.1 for a description of the gender equality in rights indexes.

Country Coverage

This section lists the countries covered in various figures.

Summary

Figure 1

East Asia and Pacific—Cambodia, China, Hong Kong, Indonesia, Democratic People's Republic of Korea, Republic of Korea, Malaysia, Myanmar, Papua New Guinea, Philippines, Singapore, Thailand, and Vietnam; *Eastern Europe and Central Asia*—Bulgaria, Czechoslovakia, Hungary, Poland, Romania, USSR (at August 1991), and Yugoslavia (at mid-1991); *Latin American and the Caribbean*—Argentina, Bolivia, Brazil, Chile, Colombia, Costa Rica, Cuba, Dominican Republic, Ecuador, El Salvador, Guatemala, Honduras, Jamaica, Mexico, Nicaragua, Panama, Paraguay, Peru, Trinidad, Uruguay, and Republica Bolivariana de Venezuela; *Middle East and North Africa*—Algeria, Arab Republic of Egypt, Islamic Republic of Iran, Iraq (at August 1991), Israel, Jordan, Kuwait,

Libya, Morocco, Oman, Saudi Arabia, Syrian Arab Republic, Tunisia, and Yemen; *South Asia*—Afghanistan, Bangladesh, India, Nepal, Pakistan, and Sri Lanka; *Sub-Saharan Africa*—Angola, Benin, Botswana, Cameroon, Ghana, Ivory Coast, Kenya, Malawi, Mozambique, Nigeria, Rwanda, Senegal, Sierra Leone, South Africa, Sudan, Tanzania, Togo, Uganda, Zaire, Zambia, and Zimbabwe; *OECD*—Australia, Austria, Belgium, Canada, Denmark, Finland, France, Germany, Greece, Irish Republic, Italy, Japan, Netherlands, New Zealand, Norway, Portugal, Spain, Sweden, Switzerland, Turkey, United Kingdom, and United States.

Figure 2

Bangladesh, Benin, Bolivia, Brazil, Burkina Faso, Central African Republic, Cameroon, Chad, Colombia, Comoros, Côte d'Ivoire, Dominican Republic, Arab Republic of Egypt, Ghana, Guatemala, Haiti, India, Indonesia, Kazakhstan, Kenya, Madagascar, Malawi, Mali, Morocco, Mozambique, Namibia, Nepal, Nicaragua, Niger, Nigeria, Pakistan, Peru, Philippines, Rwanda, Senegal, Tanzania, Togo, Turkey, Uganda, Uzbekistan, Zambia, and Zimbabwe.

Figure 3

Primary enrollment: Low income—Afghanistan, Benin, Burkina Faso, Burundi, Côte d'Ivoire, Ethiopia, The Gambia, Guinea, India, Kenya, Lesotho, Madagascar, Mali, Mauritania, Nicaragua, Niger, Senegal, Sudan, Tanzania, Togo, and Uganda; *Middle income*—Albania, Algeria, Bahrain, Botswana, Bulgaria, Chile, Costa Rica, Cuba, Arab Republic of Egypt, El Salvador, Guyana, Hungary, Iraq, Jamaica, Republic of Korea, Malaysia, Mauritius, Mexico, Morocco, Oman, Papua New Guinea, Paraguay, Poland, Romania, Saudi Arabia, Sri Lanka, Swaziland, Syrian Arab Republic, Trinidad and Tobago, Tunisia, Uruguay, and Republica Bolivariana de Venezuela; *High income*—Australia, Austria, Canada, Denmark, Finland, France, Greece, Hong Kong, China, Irish Republic, Italy, Japan, Kuwait, Malta, Netherlands, New Zealand, Norway, Qatar, Spain, Sweden, and United Kingdom.

Secondary enrollment: Low income—Afghanistan, Benin, Comoros, Côte d'Ivoire, Ethiopia, The Gambia, Guinea, India, Kenya, Lesotho, Mali,

Mauritania, Nicaragua, Niger, Senegal, Sudan, Tanzania, Togo, Uganda, and Zimbabwe; *Middle income*—Albania, Algeria, Bahrain, Botswana, Chile, Colombia, Costa Rica, Cuba, Arab Republic of Egypt, El Salvador, Guyana, Hungary, Islamic Republic of Iran, Iraq, Korea, Malaysia, Mauritius, Mexico, Morocco, Papua New Guinea, Poland, Romania, Saudi Arabia, Sri Lanka, Swaziland, Syrian Arab Republic, Thailand, Tunisia, and Republica Bolivariana de Venezuela; *High income*—Australia, Austria, Canada, Denmark, Finland, France, Greece, Hong Kong, China, Iceland, Irish Republic, Israel, Italy, Japan, Kuwait, Malta, Netherlands, New Zealand, Norway, Qatar, Spain, Sweden, and United Kingdom.

Life expectancy: *Low income*—Afghanistan, Angola, Armenia, Azerbaijan, Bangladesh, Benin, Burkina Faso, Burundi, Cambodia, Cameroon, Central African Republic, Chad, China, Comoros, Democratic Republic of Congo, Republic of Congo, Côte d'Ivoire, Eritrea, Ethiopia, The Gambia, Ghana, Guinea, Guinea-Bissau, Haiti, Honduras, India, Indonesia, Kenya, Democratic People's Republic of Korea, Lao People's Democratic Republic, Lesotho, Liberia, Madagascar, Malawi, Mali, Mauritania, Mongolia, Mozambique, Myanmar, Nepal, Nicaragua, Niger, Nigeria, Pakistan, Rwanda, Senegal, Sierra Leone, Somalia, Sudan, Tajikistan, Tanzania, Togo, Turkmenistan, Uganda, Vietnam, Republic of Yemen, Zambia, and Zimbabwe; *Middle income*—Albania, Algeria, Argentina, Bahrain, Barbados, Belarus, Bolivia, Botswana, Brazil, Bulgaria, Cape Verde, Chile, Colombia, Costa Rica, Cuba, Djibouti, Dominican Republic, Ecuador, Arab Republic of Egypt, El Salvador, Equatorial Guinea, Estonia, Fiji, Gabon, Guadeloupe, Guatemala, Guyana, Hungary, Islamic Republic of Iran, Iraq, Jamaica, Republic of Korea , Latvia, Lebanon, Libya, Lithuania, Malaysia, Maldives, Mauritius, Mexico, Morocco, Namibia, Oman, Panama, Papua New Guinea, Paraguay, Peru, Philippines, Poland, Puerto Rico, Romania, Saudi Arabia, South Africa, Sri Lanka, Suriname, Swaziland, Syrian Arab Republic, Thailand, Trinidad and Tobago, Tunisia, Turkey, Ukraine, Uruguay, Republica Bolivariana de Venezuela, and Federal Republic of Yugoslavia (Serbia/Montenegro); *High income*—Australia, Austria, The Bahamas, Belgium, Brunei, Canada, Cyprus, Denmark, Finland, France, Germany, Greece, Hong Kong, China, Iceland, Irish Republic, Israel, Italy, Japan, Kuwait, Luxembourg, Macao, Malta, Martinique, Netherlands, Netherlands Antilles, New Caledonia, New Zealand, Norway, Portugal, Qatar, Reunion, Singapore, Slovenia, Spain, Sweden, Switzerland, United Arab Emirates, United Kingdom, and United States.

Parliamentary representation: Low income—Angola, Benin, Bangladesh, Bhutan, China, Côte d'Ivoire, Cameroon, India, Kenya, Madagascar, Mongolia, Nicaragua, Pakistan, Democratic People's Republic of Korea, Senegal, Solomon Islands, Sao Tome and Principe, Togo, and Zambia; *Middle income*—Albania, Argentina, Barbados, Bolivia, Botswana, Brazil, Bulgaria, Cape Verde, Costa Rica, Dominica, Ecuador, Arab Republic of Egypt, Hungary, Islamic Republic of Iran, Iraq, Jamaica, Kiribati, Republic of Korea , Malaysia, Mexico, Panama, Paraguay, Peru, Poland, Romania, Sri Lanka, Syrian Arab Republic, Thailand, Tonga, Tunisia, Uruguay, Vanuatu, and Republica Bolivariana de Venezuela; *High income*—Australia, Austria, Belgium, Canada, Cyprus, Denmark, Finland, France, Greece, Iceland, Irish Republic, Israel, Japan, Luxembourg, Netherlands, New Zealand, Norway, Singapore, Spain, Sweden, Switzerland, United Arab Emirates, United Kingdom, and United States.

Figure 4

East Asia and Pacific—Indonesia, Philippines, and Vietnam; *Latin America and the Caribbean*—Bolivia, Brazil, Colombia, Dominican Republic, Guatemala, Haiti, Nicaragua, Paraguay, and Peru; *Middle East and North Africa*—Arab Republic of Egypt, Jordan, Morocco, and Republic of Yemen; *South Asia*—Bangladesh, India, Nepal, and Pakistan; *Sub-Saharan Africa*—Benin, Burkina Faso, Cameroon, Central African Republic, Chad, Comoros, Côte d'Ivoire, Eritrea, Ghana, Guinea, Kenya, Madagascar, Malawi, Mali, Mozambique, Namibia, Niger, Nigeria, Tanzania, Togo, Uganda, Zambia, and Zimbabwe.

Figure 5

Algeria, Argentina, Bangladesh, Barbados, Benin, Botswana, Brazil, Cameroon, Central African Republic, Chad, Chile, China, Colombia, Republic of Congo, Costa Rica, Côte d'Ivoire, Dominican Republic, Ecuador, Arab Republic of Egypt, El Salvador, Fiji, Gabon, The Gambia, Ghana, Guatemala, Guinea, Guinea-Bissau, Guyana, Haiti, Honduras, India, Indonesia, Jamaica, Kenya, Lao People's Democratic Republic, Lesotho, Madagascar, Nepal, Nicaragua, Niger, Nigeria, Pakistan, Paraguay, Philippines, Rwanda, Republic of Korea, Senegal, Sierra Leone,

Singapore, South Africa, Spain, Sri Lanka, Sudan, Tanzania, Thailand, Togo, Trinidad and Tobago, Uganda, Uruguay, Venezuela, Vietnam, Zambia, and Zimbabwe.

Figure 7

Algeria, Angola, Argentina, Australia, Austria, Bahrain, Bangladesh, Belgium, Bolivia, Botswana, Burkina Faso, Cameroon, Canada, Chile, China, Colombia, Republic of Congo, Costa Rica, Côte d'Ivoire, Czech Republic, Denmark, Dominican Republic, Ecuador, Arab Republic of Egypt, Finland, France, Gabon, Germany, Ghana, Greece, Guatemala, Guinea, Guinea-Bissau, Haiti, Honduras, Hungary, India, Indonesia, Islamic Republic of Iran, Iraq, Irish Republic, Israel, Italy, Japan, Jordan, Kenya, Republic of Korea, Kuwait, Libya, Malaysia, Mali, Mexico, Morocco, Myanmar, Netherlands, New Zealand, Niger, Nigeria, Norway, Pakistan, Panama, Paraguay, Philippines, Poland, Portugal, Russian Federation, Saudi Arabia, Senegal, Sierra Leone, Spain, Sri Lanka, Sudan, Sweden, Switzerland, Syrian Arab Republic, Tanzania, Thailand, Togo, Tunisia, United Arab Emirates, United Kingdom, United States, Uruguay, Republica Bolivariana de Venezuela, Yemen, Yugoslavia, Zambia, and Zimbabwe.

Figure 8

Secondary enrollment: Low equality—Afghanistan, Algeria, Bangladesh, Botswana, Côte d'Ivoire, Arab Republic of Egypt, El Salvador, India, Indonesia, Islamic Republic of Iran, Kenya, Kuwait, Malaysia, Morocco, Mozambique, Nepal, Nigeria, Oman, Pakistan, Papua New Guinea, Rwanda, Saudi Arabia, Senegal, Sierra Leone, South Africa, Sudan, Syrian Arab Republic, Tanzania, Thailand, Togo, Tunisia, Turkey, Uganda, and Zimbabwe; *High equality*—Australia, Austria, Belgium, Benin, Bolivia, Bulgaria, Cambodia, Cameroon, Canada, Chile, China, Colombia, Costa Rica, Cuba, Denmark, Finland, France, Germany, Ghana, Greece, Hong Kong, China, Hungary, Iraq, Irish Republic, Israel, Italy, Jamaica, Japan, Republic of Korea , Malawi, Mexico, Myanmar, Netherlands, New Zealand, Nicaragua, Norway, Panama, Paraguay, Philippines, Poland, Portugal, Romania, Singapore, Spain, Sri Lanka, Sweden,

Trinidad and Tobago, United Kingdom, United States, Republica Bolivariana de Venezuela, Vietnam, and Federal Republic of Yugoslavia (Serbia/Montenegro).

Parliamentary representation: Low equality—Afghanistan, Angola, Bangladesh, Botswana, Côte d'Ivoire, Arab Republic of Egypt, El Salvador, Honduras, India, Islamic Republic of Iran, Jordan, Kenya, Malaysia, Nepal, Pakistan, Peru, Rwanda, Senegal, South Africa, Syrian Arab Republic, Tanzania, Thailand, Togo, Tunisia, Uganda, Zambia, and Zimbabwe; *High equality*—Argentina, Australia, Austria, Belgium, Benin, Bolivia, Brazil, Bulgaria, Cameroon, Canada, Chile, China, Costa Rica, Denmark, Ecuador, Finland, France, Germany, Greece, Hungary, Iraq, Irish Republic, Israel, Jamaica, Japan, People's Democratic Republic of Korea, Republic of Korea , Mexico, Netherlands, New Zealand, Nicaragua, Norway, Panama, Paraguay, Poland, Romania, Singapore, Spain, Sri Lanka, Sweden, Switzerland, United Kingdom, United States, Uruguay, and Republica Bolivariana de Venezuela.

Figure 9

Secondary enrollment: Algeria, Australia, Austria, Benin, Botswana, Bulgaria, Cambodia, Canada, Chile, China, Colombia, Costa Rica, Côte d'Ivoire, Denmark, Arab Republic of Egypt, El Salvador, Finland, France, Germany, Greece, Hong Kong, China, Hungary, India, Islamic Republic of Iran, Irish Republic, Israel, Italy, Japan, Kenya, Republic of Korea, Kuwait, Malawi, Malaysia, Mexico, Morocco, Mozambique, Netherlands, New Zealand, Nicaragua, Norway, Oman, Papua New Guinea, Paraguay, Peru, Philippines, Poland, Romania, Saudi Arabia, Senegal, South Africa, Spain, Sri Lanka, Sudan, Sweden, Syrian Arab Republic, Tanzania, Thailand, Togo, Trinidad and Tobago, Tunisia, Uganda, United Kingdom, United States, Uruguay, Republica Bolivariana de Venezuela, Vietnam, and Zimbabwe.

Figure 11

Secondary enrollment: High equality and high income—Australia, Austria, Canada, Chile, Colombia, Costa Rica, Denmark, Finland, France, Germany, Greece, Hungary, Italy, Mexico, Netherlands, New Zealand,

Norway, Spain, Sweden, United Kingdom, United States, Uruguay, and Republica Bolivariana de Venezuela; *High equality and low income*—Bulgaria, Philippines, Poland, Romania, Trinidad and Tobago, and Vietnam; *Low equality and high income*—Botswana, Hong Kong, China, Irish Republic, Israel, Japan, Republic of Korea, Kuwait, Malaysia, Oman, Saudi Arabia, and South Africa; *Low equality and low income*—Algeria, Benin, Cambodia, China, Côte d'Ivoire, Arab Republic of Egypt, El Salvador, India, Islamic Republic of Iran, Kenya, Malawi, Morocco, Mozambique, Nicaragua, Papua New Guinea, Paraguay, Peru, Senegal, Sri Lanka, Sudan, Syrian Arab Republic, Tanzania, Thailand, Togo, Tunisia, Uganda, and Zimbabwe.

Parliamentary representation: High equality and high income—Argentina, Australia, Austria, Belgium, Bulgaria, Canada, Chile, Colombia, Costa Rica, Denmark, Finland, France, Germany, Greece, Hungary, Italy, Mexico, Netherlands, New Zealand, Norway, Poland, Portugal, Singapore, Spain, Sweden, Switzerland, Trinidad and Tobago, United Kingdom, United States, Uruguay, and Republica Bolivariana de Venezuela; *High equality and low income*—Jamaica, Philippines, Romania, and Vietnam; *Low equality and high income*—Botswana, Brazil, Ecuador, Islamic Republic of Iran, Irish Republic, Israel, Japan, Republic of Korea, Kuwait, Malaysia, Panama, South Africa, Thailand, Tunisia, and Turkey; *Low equality and low income*—Algeria, Angola, Bangladesh, Benin, Bolivia, Cambodia, Cameroon, China, Democratic Republic of Congo, Côte d'Ivoire, Dominican Republic, Arab Republic of Egypt, El Salvador, Ghana, Guatemala, Honduras, India, Indonesia, Jordan, Kenya, Malawi, Morocco, Mozambique, Nepal, Nicaragua, Nigeria, Pakistan, Papua New Guinea, Paraguay, Peru, Rwanda, Senegal, Sierra Leone, Sri Lanka, Sudan, Syrian Arab Republic, Tanzania, Togo, Uganda, Zambia, and Zimbabwe.

Chapter 1

Figure 1.1

East Asia and Pacific—China, Hong Kong, Indonesia, Malaysia, Papua New Guinea, Philippines, Democratic People's Republic of Korea, Republic of Korea, Singapore, Thailand, and Vietnam; *Eastern Europe and Central Asia*—Bulgaria, Hungary, Poland, Romania, Turkey, and Yugoslavia; *Latin America and the Caribbean*—Argentina, Bolivia, Brazil, Chile,

Colombia, Costa Rica, Cuba, Dominican Republic, Ecuador, Jamaica, Mexico, Panama, Paraguay, Peru, Trinidad and Tobago, and Republica Bolivariana de Venezuela; *Middle East and North Africa*—Algeria, Arab Republic of Egypt, Iraq, Israel, Kuwait, Libya, Morocco, Saudi Arabia, Syrian Arab Republic, and Tunisia; *South Asia*—Bangladesh, India, Pakistan, and Sri Lanka; *Sub-Saharan Africa*—Benin, Botswana, Cameroon, Democratic Republic of Congo, Ghana, Kenya, Mozambique, Nigeria, Senegal, Sierra Leone, South Africa, Tanzania, Zambia, and Zimbabwe; *OECD*—Australia, Austria, Belgium, Canada, Denmark, Finland, France, Germany, Greece, Irish Republic, Italy, Japan, Netherlands, New Zealand, Norway, Portugal, Spain, Sweden, Switzerland, United Kingdom, and United States.

Figure 1.2

Primary enrollment: East Asia and Pacific—Hong Kong, Indonesia, Republic of Korea, Lao People's Democratic Republic, Malaysia, Papua New Guinea, and Singapore; *Eastern Europe and Central Asia*—Albania, Bulgaria, Hungary, Poland, Romania, and Turkey; *Latin America and the Caribbean*—Chile, Colombia, Costa Rica, Cuba, El Salvador, Guyana, Jamaica, Mexico, Nicaragua, Paraguay, Trinidad and Tobago, Uruguay, and Republica Bolivariana de Venezuela; *Middle East and North Africa*—Algeria, Bahrain, Arab Republic of Egypt, Iraq, Jordan, Kuwait, Malta, Morocco, Oman, Qatar, Saudi Arabia, Syrian Arab Republic, Tunisia, and United Arab Emirates; *South Asia*—Afghanistan, India, Nepal, and Sri Lanka; *Sub-Saharan Africa*—Benin, Botswana, Burkina Faso, Burundi, Republic of Congo, Côte d'Ivoire, Ethiopia, The Gambia, Guinea, Kenya, Lesotho, Madagascar, Malawi, Mali, Mauritania, Mauritius, Niger, Senegal, Sudan, Swaziland, Tanzania, Togo, and Uganda; *OECD*—Australia, Austria, Belgium, Canada, Denmark, Finland, France, Greece, Irish Republic, Italy, Japan, Netherlands, New Zealand, Norway, Portugal, Spain, Sweden, Switzerland, and United Kingdom.

Secondary enrollment: East Asia and Pacific—China, Hong Kong, Indonesia, Republic of Korea, Lao People's Democratic Republic, Malaysia, Mongolia, Papua New Guinea, and Philippines; *Eastern Europe and Central Asia*—Albania, Bulgaria, Hungary, Poland, Romania, and Turkey; *Latin America and the Caribbean*—Chile, Colombia, Costa Rica, Cuba, El Salvador, Guyana, Mexico, Nicaragua, and Republica

Bolivariana de Venezuela; *Middle East and North Africa*—Algeria, Bahrain, Djibouti, Arab Republic of Egypt, Islamic Republic of Iran, Iraq, Israel, Jordan, Kuwait, Malta, Morocco, Qatar, Saudi Arabia, Syrian Arab Republic, Tunisia, and United Arab Emirates; *South Asia*—India, Nepal, and Sri Lanka; *Sub-Saharan Africa*—Benin, Botswana, Republic of Congo, Côte d'Ivoire, Ethiopia, The Gambia, Guinea, Kenya, Lesotho, Malawi, Mali, Mauritania, Mauritius, Mozambique, Niger, Senegal, Sudan, Swaziland, Tanzania, Togo, Uganda, and Zimbabwe; *OECD*—Australia, Austria, Belgium, Canada, Denmark, Finland, France, Greece, Iceland, Irish Republic, Italy, Japan, Netherlands, New Zealand, Norway, Portugal, Spain, Sweden, Switzerland, and United Kingdom.

Figure 1.5

Developed countries—Australia 1990, Austria 1990, Canada 1990, Cyprus 1989, Germany 1989, Finland 1990, Italy 1981, Luxembourg 1991, Netherlands 1990, Norway 1990, Spain 1990, Sweden 1991, and United States 1991. *Developing countries*—Bahrain 1991, Arab Republic of Egypt 1986, Islamic Republic of Iran 1986, Jordan 1979, Kuwait 1985, Tunisia 1989, China 1982, Fiji 1986, Hong Kong 1991, India 1981, Japan 1990, Republic of Korea 1983, Malaysia 1980, Angola 1992, Costa Rica 1991, Ghana 1984, Haiti 1996, Mauritius 1990, Netherlands Antilles 1981 and Senegal 1988.

Figure 1.6

East Asia and Pacific—China, Democratic People's Republic of Korea, Kiribati, Malaysia, Mongolia, Republic of Korea, Singapore, Solomon Islands, Thailand, Tonga, and Vanuatu; *Eastern Europe and Central Asia*—Albania, Bulgaria, Cyprus, Hungary, Poland, and Romania; *Latin America and the Caribbean*—Argentina, Barbados, Bolivia, Brazil, Costa Rica, Dominica, Ecuador, Jamaica, Mexico, Nicaragua, Panama, Paraguay, Peru, Uruguay, and Republica Bolivariana de Venezuela; *Middle East and North Africa*—Arab Republic of Egypt, Iraq, Islamic Republic of Iran, Israel, Syrian Arab Republic, Tunisia, and United Arab Emirates; *South Asia*—Bangladesh, Bhutan, India, Pakistan, and Sri Lanka; *Sub-Saharan Africa*—Angola, Benin, Botswana, Cameroon, Cape Verde, Côte d'Ivoire, Kenya, Madagascar, Sao Tome and Principe, Senegal, Togo, Zambia, and Zimbabwe; *OECD*—Australia, Austria, Belgium, Canada, Denmark, Finland, France, Greece, Iceland, Irish Republic, Japan, Luxembourg, Netherlands, New Zealand, Norway, Spain, Sweden, Switzerland, United Kingdom, and United States.

Figure 1.8

Bangladesh, Benin, Bolivia, Brazil, Burkina Faso, Central African Republic, Cameroon, Chad, Colombia, Comoros, Côte d'Ivoire, Dominican Republic, Arab Republic of Egypt, Ghana, Guatemala, Haiti, India, Indonesia, Kazakhstan, Kenya, Madagascar, Malawi, Mali, Morocco, Mozambique, Namibia, Nepal, Nicaragua, Niger, Nigeria, Pakistan, Peru, Philippines, Rwanda, Senegal, Tanzania, Togo, Turkey, Uganda, Uzbekistan, Zambia, and Zimbabwe.

Chapter 2

Figure 2.1

Algeria, Argentina, Bangladesh, Barbados, Benin, Botswana, Brazil, Cameroon, Central African Republic, Chad, Chile, China, Colombia, Republic of Congo, Costa Rica, Côte d'Ivoire, Dominican Republic, Ecuador, Arab Republic of Egypt, El Salvador, Fiji, Gabon, The Gambia, Ghana, Guatemala, Guinea, Guinea-Bissau, Guyana, Haiti, Honduras, India, Indonesia, Jamaica, Kenya, Lao People's Democratic Republic, Lesotho, Madagascar, Nepal, Nicaragua, Niger, Nigeria, Pakistan, Paraguay, Philippines, Rwanda, Republic of Korea, Senegal, Sierra Leone, Singapore, South Africa, Spain, Sri Lanka, Sudan, Tanzania, Thailand, Togo, Trinidad and Tobago, Uganda, Uruguay, Venezuela, Vietnam, Zambia, and Zimbabwe.

Figure 2.2

East Asia and Pacific—Indonesia, Philippines, and Vietnam; *Latin America and the Caribbean*—Bolivia, Brazil, Colombia, Dominican

Republic, Guatemala, Haiti, Nicaragua, Paraguay, and Peru; *Middle East and North Africa*—Arab Republic of Egypt, Jordan, Morocco, and Republic of Yemen; *South Asia*—Bangladesh, India, Nepal, and Pakistan; *Sub-Saharan Africa*—Benin, Burkina Faso, Cameroon, Central African Republic, Chad, Comoros, Côte d'Ivoire, Eritrea, Ghana, Guinea, Kenya, Madagascar, Malawi, Mali, Mozambique, Namibia, Niger, Nigeria, Tanzania, Togo, Uganda, Zambia, and Zimbabwe.

Figure 2.4

Algeria, Angola, Argentina, Australia, Austria, Bahrain, Bangladesh, Belgium, Bolivia, Botswana, Burkina Faso, Cameroon, Canada, Chile, China, Colombia, Republic of Congo, Costa Rica, Côte d'Ivoire, Czech Republic, Denmark, Dominican Republic, Ecuador, Arab Republic of Egypt, Finland, France, Gabon, Germany, Ghana, Greece, Guatemala, Guinea, Guinea-Bissau, Haiti, Honduras, Hungary, India, Indonesia, Islamic Republic of Iran, Iraq, Irish Republic, Israel, Italy, Japan, Jordan, Kenya, Republic of Korea, Kuwait, Libya, Malaysia, Mali, Mexico, Morocco, Myanmar, Netherlands, New Zealand, Niger, Nigeria, Norway, Pakistan, Panama, Paraguay, Philippines, Poland, Portugal, Russian Federation, Saudi Arabia, Senegal, Sierra Leone, Spain, Sri Lanka, Sudan, Sweden, Switzerland, Syrian Arab Republic, Tanzania, Thailand, Togo, Tunisia, United Arab Emirates, United Kingdom, United States, Uruguay, Republica Bolivariana de Venezuela, Yemen, Yugoslavia, Zambia, and Zimbabwe.

Chapter 3

Figure 3.1

Primary enrollment: Low equality—Afghanistan, Algeria, Angola, Bangladesh, Botswana, Democratic Republic of Congo, Côte d'Ivoire, Arab Republic of Egypt, El Salvador, India, Indonesia, Islamic Republic of Iran, Kenya, Kuwait, Libya, Malaysia, Morocco, Mozambique, Nepal, Nigeria, Oman, Pakistan, Papua New Guinea, Rwanda, Saudi Arabia, Senegal, Sierra Leone, South Africa, Sudan, Syrian Arab Republic, Tanzania, Thailand, Togo, Tunisia, Turkey, Uganda, and Zimbabwe; *High equality*—Australia, Austria, Belgium, Benin, Bolivia, Bulgaria, Cameroon, Canada, Chile, China, Costa Rica, Cuba, Denmark, Finland, France, Ghana, Greece, Hong Kong, China, Hungary, Iraq, Irish Republic, Israel, Italy, Jamaica, Japan, Republic of Korea, Malawi, Mexico, Myanmar, Netherlands, New Zealand, Nicaragua, Norway, Panama, Paraguay, Poland, Portugal, Romania, Singapore, Spain, Sri Lanka, Sweden, Trinidad and Tobago, United Kingdom, United States, Uruguay, Republica Bolivariana de Venezuela, and Federal Republic of Yugoslavia (Serbia/Montenegro).

Secondary enrollment: *Low equality*—Afghanistan, Algeria, Bangladesh, Botswana, Côte d'Ivoire, Arab Republic of Egypt, El Salvador, India, Indonesia, Islamic Republic of Iran, Kenya, Kuwait, Malaysia, Morocco, Mozambique, Nepal, Nigeria, Oman, Pakistan, Papua New Guinea, Rwanda, Saudi Arabia, Senegal, Sierra Leone, South Africa, Sudan, Syrian Arab Republic, Tanzania, Thailand, Togo, Tunisia, Turkey, Uganda, and Zimbabwe; *High equality*—Australia, Austria, Belgium, Benin, Bolivia, Bulgaria, Cambodia, Cameroon, Canada, Chile, China, Colombia, Costa Rica, Cuba, Denmark, Finland, France, Germany, Ghana, Greece, Hong Kong, China, Hungary, Iraq, Irish Republic, Israel, Italy, Jamaica, Japan, Republic of Korea, Malawi, Mexico, Myanmar, Netherlands, New Zealand, Nicaragua, Norway, Panama, Paraguay, Philippines, Poland, Portugal, Romania, Singapore, Spain, Sri Lanka, Sweden, Trinidad and Tobago, United Kingdom, United States, Republica Bolivariana de Venezuela, Vietnam, and Federal Republic of Yugoslavia (Serbia/Montenegro).

Life expectancy: *Low equality*—Afghanistan, Algeria, Angola, Bangladesh, Botswana, Democratic Republic of Congo, Côte d'Ivoire, Arab Republic of Egypt, El Salvador, Honduras, India, Indonesia, Islamic Republic of Iran, Jordan, Kenya, Kuwait, Libya, Malaysia, Morocco, Mozambique, Nepal, Nigeria, Oman, Pakistan, Papua New Guinea, Peru, Rwanda, Saudi Arabia, Senegal, Sierra Leone, South Africa, Sudan, Syrian Arab Republic, Tanzania, Thailand, Togo, Tunisia, Turkey, Uganda, Yemen Republic, Zambia, and Zimbabwe; *High equality*—Argentina, Australia, Austria, Belgium, Benin, Bolivia, Brazil, Bulgaria, Cambodia, Cameroon, Canada, Chile, China, Colombia, Costa Rica, Cuba, Denmark, Dominican Republic, Ecuador, Finland, France, Germany, Ghana, Greece, Guatemala, Hong Kong, China, Hungary, Iraq, Irish Republic, Israel, Italy, Jamaica, Japan, People's Democratic Republic of Korea, Republic of Korea, Malawi, Mexico, Myanmar, Netherlands, New Zealand, Nicaragua, Norway, Panama, Paraguay,

Philippines, Poland, Portugal, Romania, Singapore, Spain, Sri Lanka, Sweden, Switzerland, Trinidad and Tobago, United Kingdom, United States, Uruguay, Republica Bolivariana de Venezuela, Vietnam, and Federal Republic of Yugoslavia (Serbia/Montenegro).

Parliamentary representation: Low equality—Afghanistan, Angola, Bangladesh, Botswana, Côte d'Ivoire, Arab Republic of Egypt, El Salvador, Honduras, India, Islamic Republic of Iran, Jordan, Kenya, Malaysia, Nepal, Pakistan, Peru, Rwanda, Senegal, South Africa, Syrian Arab Republic, Tanzania, Thailand, Togo, Tunisia, Uganda, Zambia, and Zimbabwe; *High equality*—Argentina, Australia, Austria, Belgium, Benin, Bolivia, Brazil, Bulgaria, Cameroon, Canada, Chile, China, Costa Rica, Denmark, Ecuador, Finland, France, Germany, Greece, Hungary, Iraq, Irish Republic, Israel, Jamaica, Japan, Democratic Republic of Korea, Republic of Korea, Mexico, Netherlands, New Zealand, Nicaragua, Norway, Panama, Paraguay, Poland, Romania, Singapore, Spain, Sri Lanka, Sweden, Switzerland, United Kingdom, United States, Uruguay, and Republica Bolivariana de Venezuela.

Chapter 4

Figure 4.1

Bangladesh 1990, Colombia 1983, Guatemala 1977, Indonesia 1992, Kenya rural 1988, Kenya urban 1986, Nepal rural 1978, Nepal urban 1978, Philippines 1975–77, Venezuela 1983, Australia 1992, Austria 1992, Canada 1992, Denmark 1987, Finland 1987/88, France 1985–86, Germany 1991–92, Israel 1991–92, Italy 1988–89, Netherlands 1987, Norway 1990–91, United Kingdom 1985, and United States 1985.

Chapter 5

Figure 5.1

Bangladesh 1990, Colombia 1983, Guatemala 1977, Indonesia 1992, Kenya rural 1988, Kenya urban 1986, Nepal rural 1978, Nepal urban 1978, Philippines 1975–77, Venezuela 1983, Australia 1992, Austria 1992, Canada 1992, Denmark 1987, Finland 1987–88, France

1985–86, Germany 1991–92, Israel 1991–92, Italy 1988–89, Netherlands 1987, Norway 1990–91, United Kingdom 1985, and United States 1985.

Figure 5.3

Primary enrollment: Algeria, Australia, Austria, Benin, Botswana, Bulgaria, Cambodia, Canada, Chile, China, Colombia, Costa Rica, Côte d'Ivoire, Denmark, Ecuador, Arab Republic of Egypt, El Salvador, Finland, France, Germany, Greece, Guatemala, Hong Kong, China, Hungary, India, Islamic Republic of Iran, Irish Republic, Italy, Jamaica, Japan, Kenya, Republic of Korea, Kuwait, Malaysia, Mexico, Morocco, Mozambique, Netherlands, New Zealand, Nicaragua, Norway, Oman, Papua New Guinea, Paraguay, Peru, Poland, Romania, Saudi Arabia, Senegal, South Africa, Spain, Sri Lanka, Sudan, Sweden, Syrian Arab Republic, Tanzania, Togo, Trinidad and Tobago, Tunisia, Uganda, United Kingdom, United States, Uruguay, Republica Bolivariana de Venezuela, Zambia, and Zimbabwe.

Secondary enrollment: Algeria, Australia, Austria, Benin, Botswana, Bulgaria, Cambodia, Canada, Chile, China, Colombia, Costa Rica, Côte d'Ivoire, Denmark, Arab Republic of Egypt, El Salvador, Finland, France, Germany, Greece, Hong Kong, China, Hungary, India, Islamic Republic of Iran, Irish Republic, Israel, Italy, Japan, Kenya, Republic of Korea, Kuwait, Malawi, Malaysia, Mexico, Morocco, Mozambique, Netherlands, New Zealand, Nicaragua, Norway, Oman, Papua New Guinea, Paraguay, Peru, Philippines, Poland, Romania, Saudi Arabia, Senegal, South Africa, Spain, Sri Lanka, Sudan, Sweden, Syrian Arab Republic, Tanzania, Thailand, Togo, Trinidad and Tobago, Tunisia, Uganda, United Kingdom, United States, Uruguay, Republica Bolivariana de Venezuela, Vietnam, and Zimbabwe.

Life expectancy: Algeria, Angola, Argentina, Australia, Austria, Bangladesh, Belgium, Benin, Bolivia, Botswana, Brazil, Bulgaria, Cambodia, Cameroon, Canada, Chile, China, Colombia, Democratic Republic of Congo, Costa Rica, Côte d'Ivoire, Denmark, Dominican Republic, Ecuador, Arab Republic of Egypt, El Salvador, Finland, France, Germany, Ghana, Greece, Guatemala, Honduras, Hong Kong, China, Hungary, India, Indonesia, Irish Republic, Israel, Italy, Jamaica, Japan, Jordan, Kenya, Republic of Korea, Malawi, Malaysia, Mexico, Morocco, Mozambique, Nepal, Netherlands, New Zealand, Nicaragua, Nigeria, Norway, Pakistan, Panama, Papua New Guinea, Paraguay, Peru, Philippines, Poland, Portugal, Romania, Rwanda,

Saudi Arabia, Senegal, Sierra Leone, Singapore, South Africa, Spain, Sri Lanka, Sudan, Sweden, Switzerland, Syrian Arab Republic, Tanzania, Thailand, Togo, Trinidad and Tobago, Tunisia, Turkey, Uganda, United Kingdom, United States, Uruguay, Republica Bolivariana de Venezuela, Vietnam, Zambia, and Zimbabwe.

Figure 5.4

Data are for 1995. Countries include Algeria, Angola, Argentina, Australia, Austria, Bangladesh, Belgium, Benin, Bolivia, Botswana, Brazil, Bulgaria, Cambodia, Cameroon, Canada, Chile, China, Colombia, Democratic Republic of Congo, Costa Rica, Côte d'Ivoire, Denmark, Dominican Republic, Ecuador, Arab Republic of Egypt, El Salvador, Finland, France, Germany, Ghana, Greece, Guatemala, Honduras, Hungary, India, Indonesia, Islamic Republic of Iran, Irish Republic, Israel, Italy, Jamaica, Japan, Jordan, Kenya, Republic of Korea, Kuwait, Malawi, Malaysia, Mexico, Morocco, Mozambique, Nepal, Netherlands, New Zealand, Nicaragua, Nigeria, Norway, Pakistan, Panama, Papua New Guinea, Paraguay, Peru, Philippines, Poland, Portugal, Romania, Rwanda, Senegal, Sierra Leone, Singapore, South Africa, Spain, Sri Lanka, Sudan, Sweden, Switzerland, Syrian Arab Republic, Tanzania, Thailand, Togo, Trinidad and Tobago, Tunisia, Turkey, Uganda, United Kingdom, United States, Uruguay, Republica Bolivariana de Venezuela, Vietnam, Zambia, and Zimbabwe.

Figure 5.5

Nonadjuster: Botswana, Lesotho, South Africa, and Swaziland.
Adjuster: Benin, Burkina Faso, Burundi, Cameroon, Central African Republic, Democratic Republic of Congo, Côte d'Ivoire, Gabon, The Gambia, Ghana, Kenya, Madagascar, Malawi, Mali, Mauritania, Niger, Nigeria, Rwanda, Senegal, Sierra Leone, Togo, Zambia, and Zimbabwe.

Figure 5.6

Adjuster—deteriorate: Benin, Cameroon, Central African Republic, Republic of Congo, Côte d'Ivoire, Gabon, Rwanda, Sierra Leone, Togo, and Zambia.

Adjuster—large improvement in macroeconomic policies: Burkina Faso, Ghana, The Gambia, Nigeria, and Zimbabwe.

Adjuster—small improvement in macroeconomic policies: Burundi, Kenya, Madagascar, Malawi, Mali, Mauritania, Niger, and Senegal.

Nonadjuster: Botswana, Lesotho, South Africa, and Swaziland.

Chapter 6

Figure 6.1

Primary enrollment: High equality and high income—Australia, Austria, Canada, Chile, Colombia, Costa Rica, Denmark, Finland, France, Germany, Greece, Hungary, Italy, Mexico, Netherlands, New Zealand, Norway, Spain, Sweden, United Kingdom, United States, Uruguay, and Republica Bolivariana de Venezuela; *High equality and low income*—Bulgaria, Jamaica, Poland, Romania, and Trinidad and Tobago; *Low equality and high income*—Botswana, Hong Kong, China, Irish Republic, Japan, Republic of Korea, Kuwait, Malaysia, Oman, Saudi Arabia, and South Africa; *Low equality and low income*—Algeria, Benin, Cambodia, China, Côte d'Ivoire, Ecuador, Arab Republic of Egypt, El Salvador, Guatemala, India, Islamic Republic of Iran, Kenya, Morocco, Mozambique, Nicaragua, Papua New Guinea, Paraguay, Peru, Senegal, Sri Lanka, Sudan, Syrian Arab Republic, Tanzania, Togo, Tunisia, Uganda, Zambia, and Zimbabwe.

Secondary enrollment: High equality and high income—Australia, Austria, Canada, Chile, Colombia, Costa Rica, Denmark, Finland, France, Germany, Greece, Hungary, Italy, Mexico, Netherlands, New Zealand, Norway, Spain, Sweden, United Kingdom, United States, Uruguay, and Republica Bolivariana de Venezuela; *High equality and low income*—Bulgaria, Philippines, Poland, Romania, Trinidad and Tobago, and Vietnam; *Low equality and high income*—Botswana, Hong Kong, China, Irish Republic, Israel, Japan, Republic of Korea, Kuwait, Malaysia, Oman, Saudi Arabia, and South Africa; *Low Equality and low income*—Algeria, Benin, Cambodia, China, Côte d'Ivoire, Arab Republic of Egypt, El Salvador, India, Islamic Republic of Iran, Kenya, Malawi, Morocco, Mozambique, Nicaragua, Papua New Guinea, Paraguay, Peru, Senegal, Sri Lanka, Sudan, Syrian Arab Republic, Tanzania, Thailand, Togo, Tunisia, Uganda, and Zimbabwe.

Life expectancy: High equality and high income—Argentina, Australia, Austria, Belgium, Canada, Chile, Colombia, Costa Rica, Denmark,

Finland, France, Germany, Greece, Hungary, Italy, Mexico, Netherlands, New Zealand, Norway, Poland, Portugal, Singapore, Spain, Sweden, Switzerland, Trinidad and Tobago, United Kingdom, United States, Uruguay, and Republica Bolivariana de Venezuela; *High equality and low income*—Bulgaria, Jamaica, Philippines, Romania, and Vietnam; *Low equality and high income*—Botswana, Brazil, Ecuador, Hong Kong, China, Irish Republic, Israel, Japan, Republic of Korea, Malaysia, Panama, Saudi Arabia, South Africa, Thailand, Tunisia, and Turkey; *Low equality and low income*—Algeria, Angola, Bangladesh, Benin, Bolivia, Cambodia, Cameroon, China, Democratic Republic of Congo, Côte d'Ivoire, Dominican Republic, Arab Republic of Egypt, El Salvador, Ghana, Guatemala, Honduras, India, Indonesia, Jordan, Kenya, Malawi, Morocco, Mozambique, Nepal, Nicaragua, Nigeria, Pakistan, Papua New Guinea, Paraguay, Peru, Rwanda, Senegal, Sierra Leone, Sri Lanka, Sudan, Syrian Arab Republic, Tanzania, Togo, Uganda, Zambia, and Zimbabwe.

Parliamentary representation: High equality and high income—Argentina, Australia, Austria, Belgium, Bulgaria, Canada, Chile, Colombia, Costa Rica, Denmark, Finland, France, Germany, Greece, Hungary, Italy, Mexico, Netherlands, New Zealand, Norway, Poland, Portugal, Singapore, Spain, Sweden, Switzerland, Trinidad and Tobago, United Kingdom, United States, Uruguay, and Republica Bolivariana de Venezuela; *High equality and low income*—Jamaica, Philippines, Romania, and Vietnam; *Low equality and high income*—Botswana, Brazil, Ecuador, Islamic Republic of Iran, Irish Republic, Israel, Japan, Republic of Korea, Kuwait, Malaysia, Panama, South Africa, Thailand, Tunisia, and Turkey; *Low equality and low income*—Algeria, Angola, Bangladesh, Benin, Bolivia, Cambodia, Cameroon, China, Democratic Republic of Congo, Côte d'Ivoire, Dominican Republic, Arab Republic of Egypt, El Salvador, Ghana, Guatemala, Honduras, India, Indonesia, Jordan, Kenya, Malawi, Morocco, Mozambique, Nepal, Nicaragua, Nigeria, Pakistan, Papua New Guinea, Paraguay, Peru, Rwanda, Senegal, Sierra Leone, Sri Lanka, Sudan, Syrian Arab Republic, Tanzania, Togo, Uganda, Zambia, and Zimbabwe.

Figure 6.2

Primary education: East Asia and Pacific—Cambodia, China, Hong Kong, Republic of Korea, Malaysia, and Papua New Guinea; *Eastern Europe and Central Asia*—Bulgaria, Hungary, Poland, and Romania; *Latin*

America and the Caribbean—Chile, Colombia, Costa Rica, Ecuador, El Salvador, Guatemala, Jamaica, Mexico, Nicaragua, Paraguay, Peru, Trinidad and Tobago, Uruguay, and Republica Bolivariana de Venezuela; *Middle East and North Africa*—Algeria, Arab Republic of Egypt, Islamic Republic of Iran, Kuwait, Morocco, Oman, Saudi Arabia, Syrian Arab Republic, and Tunisia, *South Asia*—India, Sri Lanka; *Sub-Saharan Africa*—Benin, Botswana, Côte d'Ivoire, Kenya, Mozambique, Senegal, South Africa, Sudan, Tanzania, Togo, Uganda, Zambia, and Zimbabwe; *OECD*—Australia, Austria, Canada, Denmark, Finland, France, Germany, Greece, Irish Republic, Italy, Japan, Netherlands, New Zealand, Norway, Spain, Sweden, United Kingdom, and United States.

Secondary education: *East Asia and Pacific*—Cambodia, China, Hong Kong, Republic of Korea, Malaysia, Papua New Guinea, Philippines, Thailand, and Vietnam; *Eastern Europe and Central Asia*—Bulgaria, Hungary, Poland, and Romania; *Latin America and the Caribbean*—Chile, Colombia, Costa Rica, El Salvador, Mexico, Nicaragua, Paraguay, Peru, Trinidad and Tobago, Uruguay, and Republica Bolivariana de Venezuela; *Middle East and North Africa*—Algeria, Arab Republic of Egypt, Islamic Republic of Iran, Israel, Kuwait, Morocco, Oman, Saudi Arabia, Syrian Arab Republic, and Tunisia; *South Asia*—India, and Sri Lanka; *Sub-Saharan Africa*—Benin, Botswana, Côte d'Ivoire, Kenya, Malawi, Mozambique, Senegal, South Africa, Sudan, Tanzania, Togo, Uganda, and Zimbabwe; *OECD*—Australia, Austria, Canada, Denmark, Finland, France, Germany, Greece, Irish Republic, Italy, Japan, Netherlands, New Zealand, Norway, Spain, Sweden, United Kingdom, and United States.

Life expectancy: *East Asia and Pacific*—Cambodia, China, Hong Kong, Indonesia, Republic of Korea, Malaysia, Papua New Guinea, Philippines, Singapore, Thailand, and Vietnam; *Eastern Europe and Central Asia*—Bulgaria, Hungary, Poland, and Romania; *Latin America and the Caribbean*—Argentina, Bolivia, Brazil, Chile, Colombia, Costa Rica, Dominican Republic, Ecuador, El Salvador, Guatemala, Honduras, Jamaica, Mexico, Nicaragua, Panama, Paraguay, Peru, Trinidad and Tobago, Uruguay, and Republica Bolivariana de Venezuela; *Middle East and North Africa*—Algeria, Arab Republic of Egypt, Israel, Jordan, Morocco, Saudi Arabia, Syrian Arab Republic, and Tunisia; *South Asia*—Bangladesh, India, Nepal, Pakistan, and Sri Lanka; *Sub-Saharan Africa*—Angola, Benin, Botswana, Cameroon, Democratic Republic of Congo, Côte d'Ivoire, Ghana, Kenya, Malawi, Mozambique, Nigeria, Rwanda, Senegal, Sierra Leone, South Africa, Sudan, Tanzania, Togo, Uganda, Zambia, and Zimbabwe; *OECD*—Australia, Austria, Belgium, Canada, Denmark, Finland, France, Germany, Greece, Irish Republic, Italy, Japan, Netherlands, New Zealand, Norway, Portugal, Spain, Sweden, Switzerland, United Kingdom, and United States.

Parliamentary representation: East Asia and Pacific—Cambodia, China, Indonesia, Republic of Korea, Malaysia, Philippines, Singapore, Thailand, and Vietnam; *Eastern Europe and Central Asia*—Bulgaria, Hungary, Poland, and Romania; *Latin America and the Caribbean*—Argentina, Bolivia, Brazil, Chile, Colombia, Costa Rica, Dominican Republic, Ecuador, El Salvador, Guatemala, Honduras, Jamaica, Mexico, Nicaragua, Panama, Paraguay, Peru, Trinidad and Tobago, Uruguay, and Republica Bolivariana de Venezuela; *Middle East and North Africa*—Algeria, Arab Republic of Egypt, Islamic Republic of Iran, Israel, Jordan, Morocco, Syrian Arab Republic, and Tunisia; *South Asia*—Bangladesh, India, Nepal, Pakistan, and Sri Lanka; *Sub-Saharan Africa*—Angola, Benin, Botswana, Cameroon, Democratic Republic of Congo, Côte d'Ivoire, Ghana, Kenya, Malawi, Mozambique, Nigeria, Rwanda, Senegal, Sierra Leone, South Africa, Sudan, Tanzania, Togo, Uganda, Zambia, and Zimbabwe; *OECD*—Australia, Austria, Belgium, Canada, Denmark, Finland, France, Germany, Greece, Irish Republic, Italy, Japan, Netherlands, New Zealand, Norway, Portugal, Spain, Sweden, Switzerland, United Kingdom, and United States.

Figure 6.3

See figure 6.2.

Figure 6.4

See figure 6.2.

Basic Cross-Country Regression Model and Coefficient Estimates

T HIS REPORT USES A MULTIVARIATE REGRESSION model as the basis for the cross-country figures in chapters 3, 5, and 6 and for the simulations discussed in chapter 6. The model was estimated using cross-country data from a number of years, generally starting with 1970 and ending with the latest year for which data are available, usually around 1995. Comparable development indicators from a large number of developing countries differentiated by gender are generally limited. They are usually available for some education and health information through the databases maintained by the World Bank's Development Data Group and through the Women's Indicators and Statistics Database. Humana (1986, 1992) also provides data on measures of rights across countries, but these are available for two years at the most—limiting the ability to do time series analysis. To not lose information on the rest of the variables, we assume that the two data points for rights apply to the years closest to them.

The model estimated is:

$$g_{it} = \alpha + \beta y_{it} + \chi y^2 + \delta R_{it} + \theta T_t + \varepsilon_{it}$$

where:

g_{it} is the indicator of gender equality—female to male ratios of primary and secondary enrollment rates, female to male ratio of life expectancy, and female to male share of seats in parliament.

y_{it} is per capita GDP (natural logarithms) in 1995 dollars, adjusted for purchasing power parity. To fit the data better, we also introduce a quadratic term for this variable.

R_{it} is the average of gender rights, as defined by Humana (1986, 1992). This is the simple average of three rights indexes—equality of social and economic rights, equality of political and legal rights, and equality of rights in marriage and divorce proceedings. The three individual rights are not continuous variables, and are defined on a scale of 1–4 (4 being the highest degree of equality). The averages, however, are closer to a continuous variable.

T_t is a year dummy.

ε_{it} is an error term.

i denotes country i.

t denotes year t.

Coefficient Estimates from Regressions on Gender Ratios

The key coefficients from the regressions are reported in the table below.

Indicator	Primary enrollment	Secondary enrollment	Life expectancy	Parliamentary representation
Per capita income	0.4176	0.9787	0.0597	−0.3163
	(5.461)	(7.296)	(2.643)	(−4.086)
Per capita income squared	−0.0224	−0.0528	−0.0031	0.0191
	(−5.013)	(−6.535)	(−2.387)	(3.897)
Average gender rights	0.0641	0.0934	0.0177	0.0970
	(5.262)	(5.673)	(6.730)	(7.745)
R^2	0.51	0.57	0.38	0.28
Number of observations	277	286	265	287
Years	1980, 1985, 1990, 1995	1980, 1985, 1990, 1995	1980, 1985, 1990, 1997	1975, 1985, 1990, 1995

Note: Numbers in parentheses are t-statistics based on robust standard errors.

Alternative Measures of Gender Equality Considered and Rejected

This report uses female to male ratios as measures of gender equality in education and health. Absolute differences between female and male achievement as indicators of gender equality could have been used, but ratios better capture gender inequality—especially if one is comparing countries with substantially different absolute levels of an indicator.

For example, if male enrollment in country A is 20 percent and female enrollment 10 percent, and in country B male enrollment is 100 percent and female enrollment 90 percent, the absolute difference in enrollment rates is identical—10 percentage points—in both countries. But in country A female enrollments are only half of male enrollments, whereas female enrollments are 90 percent of male enrollments in country B. These differences are reflected in the female to male ratios: 0.5 for country A and 0.9 for country B.

Although the graphical representations in the report use female to male ratios as the measure of gender equality, the basic results would not significantly differ if absolute female to male differences were used. The basic regression results are shown in the table below. In all cases, income and its quadratic are jointly significant at 1 percent.

Coefficient Estimates from Regressions on Gender Differences

Indicator	Primary enrollment	Secondary enrollment	Life expectancy	Parliamentary representation
Per capita income	28.2619	12.2932	4.8793	−4.238
	(3.794)	(1.982)	(4.357)	(−4.155)
Per capita income squared	−1.4343	−0.5476	−0.2399	0.0253
	(−3.284)	(−1.446)	(−3.592)	(3.945)
Average gender rights	4.7352	4.204	1.322	0.1411
	(4.899)	(5.194)	(8.359)	(8.431)
R^2	0.44	0.35	0.62	0.30
Number of observations	277	286	265	287
Years	1980, 1985, 1990, 1995	1980, 1985, 1990, 1995	1980, 1985, 1990, 1997	1975, 1985, 1990, 1995

Note: Numbers in parentheses are t-statistics based on robust standard errors.

Description of Key Figures Presenting Regression Results

Overview

Figure 8 predicts gender equality from the above regressions at various levels of rights, adjusting for income. The figure shows population-weighted averages for the latest available year for each indicator.

299

Figure 9 predicts gender equality from the secondary enrollment regression at various levels of income, adjusting for rights. The regression line is based on pooled cross-sectional time series data. The scatter plot depicts 1995 data for female to male secondary enrollment.

Figure 11 predicts gender equality from the secondary enrollment and parliamentary representation regressions at various levels of income and rights, and calculates population-weighted averages for the four-way classification by income and rights.

Chapter 3

Figure 3.1 predicts gender equality from the above regressions at various levels of rights, adjusting for income. The figure shows population-weighted averages for the latest available year for each indicator.

Chapter 5

Figures 5.3 and 5.4 predict gender equality from the above regressions at various levels of income, adjusting for rights. The regression line is based on pooled cross-sectional time series data. The scatter plots depict the latest available year for each indicator as well.

Chapter 6

Figure 6.1 predicts gender equality from the above regressions at various levels of income and rights, and calculates population-weighted averages for the four-way classification for each indicator.

Figures 6.2, 6.3, and 6.4 are based on the above regressions. Figure 6.2 predicts the indicator at the specified levels of rights, adjusting for income. Figure 6.3 predicts the indicator at the specified levels of income, adjusting for rights. Figure 6.4 adds on to the actual indicator first the increase predicted from specified levels of rights, adjusting for income, and then from specified levels of income, adjusting for rights. Population-weighted averages are shown.

APPENDIX 3

Relative Earnings of Women and Men Adjusted for Differences in Human Capital

Development group, economy, and year of data	Relative pay	Unexplained pay [a] (percent)	Source	Wage source/sample
Industrial countries				
Australia 1985	85	68	Miller and Rummery 1991	Hourly wage
Australia 1986, 1987, 1990, 1991, 1994[b]	74	87	Blau and Kahn 1999	National survey, hours controlled
Australia 1989	87	64	Miller 1994	Hourly wage
Australia 1990	85	61	Langford 1995	Hourly wage
Austria 1985–87, 1989, 1991–92, 1994[b]	75	87	Blau and Kahn 1999	National survey, hours controlled
Canada 1970	60	74	Baker and others 1995	Census, annual wage
Canada 1970	63	64	Gunderson 1998	Census, annual wage
Canada 1972	60	45	Gunderson 1975	Civilian workers
Canada 1980	64	73	Baker and others 1995	Census, annual wage
Canada 1980	67	67	Gunderson 1998	Census, annual wage
Canada 1985	66	75	Baker and others 1995	Census, annual wage
Canada 1986	64	79	Baker and others 1995	Survey of consumer finances, annual wage
Canada 1989	75	75	Kidd and Shannon 1996	National survey
Canada 1990	72	71	Gunderson 1998	Census, annual wage
Canada 1990	62	53	Gunderson 1998	Census, weekly wage
Canada 1991	67	84	Baker and others 1995	Census, annual wage
Canada 1992–94[b]	75	85	Blau and Kahn 1999	National survey, hours controlled
Denmark 1980	80	68	Rosholm and Smith 1996	Public sector, salaried, hourly wage
Denmark 1980	72	75	Rosholm and Smith 1996	Private sector, salaried, hourly wage
Denmark 1983	68	88	Gupta, Oaxaca, and Smith 1998	National survey, hourly wage
Denmark 1989	68	91	Gupta, Oaxaca, and Smith 1998	National survey, hourly wage
Denmark 1990	74	77	Rosholm and Smith 1996	Private sector, salaried, hourly wage

(table continues on following page)

Development group, economy, and year of data	Relative pay	Unexplained pay [a] (percent)	Source	Wage source/sample
Denmark 1990	83	81	Rosholm and Smith 1996	Public sector, salaried, hourly wage
Denmark 1990	74	77	Rosholm and Smith 1996	Private sector, salaried, hourly wage
Denmark 1994	67	88	Gupta, Oaxaca, and Smith 1998	National survey, hourly wage
Denmark 1995	87	55	Rice 1999	Monthly wage, hours controlled
France 1995	82	61	Rice 1999	Monthly wage, hours controlled
Germany 1985–93[b]	73	88	Blau and Kahn 1999	Monthly wage, hours controlled
Germany 1995	70	83	Rice 1999	Monthly wage, hours controlled
Greece 1995	80	59	Rice 1999	National survey, hours controlled
Ireland 1988–90, 1993–94[b]	80	96	Blau and Kahn 1999	National survey, hours controlled
Italy 1986, 1988, 1990, 1992–94[b]	80	83	Blau and Kahn 1999	Monthly wage, hours controlled
Italy 1991	79	104	Bonjour and Pacelli 1998	Private sector, daily wage
Italy 1995	84	94	Rice 1999	Hourly wage
Japan 1968	51	53	Horton 1996	Hourly wage
Japan 1978	57	55	Horton 1996	Hourly wage
Japan 1988	59	44	Horton 1996	National survey, hours controlled
Japan 1993–94[b]	43	93	Blau and Kahn 1999	National survey, hours controlled
Netherlands 1988–89[b]	76	62	Blau and Kahn 1999	National survey, hours controlled
New Zealand 1991–94[b]	83	104	Blau and Kahn 1999	National survey, hours controlled
Norway 1989–94[b]	76	93	Blau and Kahn 1999	Monthly wage, hours controlled
Portugal 1995	84	73	Rice 1999	Monthly wage, hours controlled
Spain 1995	82	83	Rice 1999	Private sector, white-collar workers
Sweden 1974	76	71	Edin and Richardson 1999	National survey, hourly wage
Sweden 1974	67	61	Gustafsson 1981	National survey, hourly wage
Sweden 1981	83	64	Edin and Richardson 1999	National survey, hourly wage
Sweden 1991	83	64	Edin and Richardson 1999	National survey, hours controlled
Sweden 1994	81	103	Blau and Kahn 1999	National survey, hours controlled

(table continues on following page)

Development group, economy, and year of data	Relative pay	Unexplained pay [a] (percent)	Source	Wage source/sample
Switzerland 1987	62	50	Blau and Kahn 1999	National survey, hours controlled
Switzerland 1991	79	75	Bonjour and Pacelli 1998	Private sector, hourly wage
United Kingdom 1985–94[b]	69	102	Blau and Kahn 1999	Hourly wage
United Kingdom 1991	84	93	Makepeace and others 1999	Monthly wage, hours controlled
United Kingdom 1994	83	53	Davies, Peronaci, and Joshi 1998	National survey, hourly wage
United Kingdom 1995	76	64	Rice 1999	National survey, hours controlled
United States 1980	61	57	Neumark 1988	National longitudinal survey, hourly wage
United States 1985–94[b]	67	97	Blau and Kahn 1999	Hourly wage
United States 1987	70	44	Blau and Kahn 1994	National survey, hours controlled
United States 1987	69	73	Gyimah-Brempong, Fichtenbaum, and Willis 1992	Hourly wage
Developing countries				
Argentina 1985	65	62	Psacharopoulos and Tzannatos 1992	Buenos Aires, monthly wage
Argentina 1989	89	*	Artecona and Cunningham 2000b	Hourly wage
Argentina 1995	98	*	Artecona and Cunningham 2000b	Hourly wage
Bolivia 1989	63	76	Psacharopoulos and Tzannatos 1992	Weekly wage
Brazil 1970	30	113	Birdsall and Behrman 1991	Census, formal workers, hours controlled
Brazil 1970	50	10	Birdsall and Fox 1991	Teachers, monthly wage
Brazil 1981	50	*	Tzannatos 1999	Hourly wage
Brazil 1989	70	89	Psacharopoulos and Tzannatos 1992	Hourly wage
Brazil 1989	63	*	Artecona and Cunningham 2000b	Hourly wage
Brazil 1990	54	*	Tzannatos 1999	Hourly wage
Brazil 1995	67	*	Artecona and Cunningham 2000b	Hourly wage
Bulgaria 1992–93[b]	84	121	Blau and Kahn 1999	National survey, hours controlled
Chile 1980	68	*	Tzannatos 1999	Hourly wage
Chile 1987	71	*	Tzannatos 1999	Hourly wage
Chile 1987	71	114	Psacharopoulos and Tzannatos 1992	Weekly wage

(table continues on following page)

Development group, economy, and year of data	Relative pay	Unexplained pay [a] (percent)	Source	Wage source/sample
Chile 1990	89	*	Montenegro 1999	Hourly wage
Chile 1996	101	*	Montenegro 1999	Hourly wage
Chile 1996	101	95	Montenegro 1999	National survey, hourly wage
China 1985	80	16	Meng and Kidd 1997	Rural industry
China 1985	80	112	Meng and Miller 1995	Rural industry
China 1987	88	47	Meng 1992	State workers
Colombia 1984	67	*	Tzannatos 1999	Hourly wage
Colombia 1988	84	85	Psacharopoulos and Tzannatos 1992	Weekly wage
Colombia 1990	70	*	Tzannatos 1999	Hourly wage
Costa Rica 1980	90	*	Tzannatos 1999	Hourly wage
Costa Rica 1989	97	*	Tzannatos 1999	Hourly wage
Costa Rica 1989	81	93	Psacharopoulos and Tzannatos 1992	Monthly wage
Costa Rica 1989	88	*	Artecona and Cunningham 2000b	Hourly wage
Costa Rica 1995	91	*	Artecona and Cunningham 2000b	Hourly wage
Côte d'Ivoire 1985	76	*	Tzannatos 1999	Hourly wage
Côte d'Ivoire 1988	81	*	Tzannatos 1999	Hourly wage
Czech Republic 1992, 1994[b]	73	97	Blau and Kahn 1999	National survey, hours controlled
Ecuador 1987	66	43	Psacharopoulos and Tzannatos 1992	Hourly wage
Ethiopia 1990	78	119	Appleton, Hoddinott, and Krishnan 1999	Urban workers
Germany, Dem. Rep. 1990–93[b]	84	97	Blau and Kahn 1999	National survey, hours controlled
Guatemala 1989	77	45	Psacharopoulos and Tzannatos 1992	Monthly wage
Guinea 1990	45	58	Glick and Sahn 1997	Hourly wage
Honduras 1986	65	*	Tzannatos 1999	Hourly wage
Honduras 1989	81	147	Psacharopoulos and Tzannatos 1992	Weekly wage
Honduras 1990	68	*	Tzannatos 1999	Hourly wage
Hungary 1988–94[b]	75	95	Blau and Kahn 1999	National survey, hours controlled
Hungary 1994	80	77	Rice 1999	Monthly wage, hours controlled
India 1987–88	56	74	Horton 1996	Urban workers
India 1987–88	51	66	Horton 1996	Rural workers
Indonesia 1980	39	66	Horton 1996	Urban workers
Indonesia 1980	39	78	Horton 1996	Rural workers
Indonesia 1986	56	*	Tzannatos 1999	Hourly wage
Indonesia 1990	54	62	Horton 1996	Urban workers

(table continues on following page)

Development group, economy, and year of data	Relative pay	Unexplained pay [a] (percent)	Source	Wage source/sample
Indonesia 1990	50	81	Horton 1996	Rural workers
Indonesia 1992	60	*	Tzannatos 1999	Hourly wage
Indonesia 1992	71	48	Manning 1998	National survey
Israel 1993–94[b]	73	109	Blau and Kahn 1999	National survey, hours controlled
Jamaica 1989	58	119	Psacharopoulos and Tzannatos 1992	Weekly wage
Jordan 1991	78	74	Psacharopoulos and Tzannatos 1992	Annual wage
Kenya 1986	63	60	Agesa 1999	Urban workers
Korea, Rep. of 1980	44	33	Berger, Groothuis, and Jeon 1997	National survey, hourly wage
Korea, Rep. of 1984	42	*	Tzannatos 1999	Hourly wage
Korea, Rep. of 1984	42	49	Horton 1996	Manufacturing workers
Korea, Rep. of 1988	51	*	Tzannatos 1999	Hourly wage
Korea, Rep. of 1988	51	53	Horton 1996	Manufacturing
Korea, Rep. of 1991	54	29	Berger, Groothuis, and Jeon 1997	National survey, hourly wage
Malaysia 1973	59	66	Chua 1984	Civilian workers
Malaysia 1973	57	*	Tzannatos 1999	Hourly wage
Malaysia 1973	57	88	Horton 1996	Annual earnings
Malaysia 1984	69	*	Tzannatos 1999	Hourly wage
Malaysia 1984	69	93	Horton 1996	Annual earnings
Mexico 1984	85	80	Psacharopoulos and Tzannatos 1992	Weekly wage
Nicaragua 1978	43	67	Psacharopoulos and Tzannatos 1992	Biweekly wage
Nicaragua 1991	43	71	Behrman and Wolfe 1991	National survey, hours controlled
Panama 1989	80	85	Psacharopoulos and Tzannatos 1992	Monthly wage
Peru 1990	84	85	Psacharopoulos and Tzannatos 1992	Hourly wage
Philippines 1978	71	*	Tzannatos 1999	Hourly wage
Philippines 1978	75	137	Horton 1996	Urban workers, hourly wage
Philippines 1988	80	*	Tzannatos 1999	Hourly wage
Philippines 1988	76	127	Horton 1996	Urban workers, hourly wage
Poland 1991–94[b]	75	118	Blau and Kahn 1999	National survey, hours controlled
Romania 1994	79	84	Paternostro and Sahn 1999	Hourly wage
Romania 1994	79	84	Paternostro and Sahn 1999	Hourly wage
Russian Federation 1991–94[b]	69	99	Blau and Kahn 1999	National survey, hours controlled
Russian Federation 1994	72	118	Glinskaya and Mroz 1996	Hourly wage

(table continues on following page)

305

Development group, economy, and year of data	Relative pay	Unexplained pay [a] (percent)	Source	Wage source/sample
Slovenia 1991–94[b]	87	104	Blau and Kahn 1999	National survey, hours controlled
Soviet Union 1989	73	85	Katz 1997	Taganrog City, hourly wage
Taiwan, China, 1982	64	56	Gannicott 1986	National survey
Taiwan, China, 1989	62	84	Kao, Polachek, and Wunnava 1994	National survey, monthly wage
Tanzania 1971	75	17	Knight and Sabot 1991	Manufacturing, monthly wage
Tanzania 1980	86	4	Psacharopoulos and Tzannatos 1992	Urban workers, manufacturing, monthly wage
Thailand 1980	74	*	Tzannatos 1999	Hourly wage
Thailand 1980	84	70	Horton 1996	Employees
Thailand 1989	90	85	Horton 1996	Employees
Thailand 1990	80	*	Tzannatos 1999	Hourly wage
Uganda 1992	72	74	Appleton, Hoddinott, and Krishnan 1999	Urban workers
Uruguay 1989	74	77	Psacharopoulos and Tzannatos 1992	Monthly wage, Monthly wage
Venezuela 1981	87	*	Tzannatos 1999	Hourly wage
Venezuela 1989	77	95	Psacharopoulos and Tzannatos 1992	Weekly wage
Venezuela 1990	93	*	Tzannatos 1999	Hourly wage
Zambia 1993	74	65	Nielsen 1998	National survey

Note: All studies control for education and potential experience unless marked with an asterisk (*)—these present only raw wage comparisons. Most studies that control for education and experience use the male wage as the reference wage structure. The basic decomposition methodology can be found in Oaxaca (1973).

a. Figures above 100 percent mean that working women are more qualified (say, in terms of education) than men. Without gender bias, women's wages would not only have been larger than their current wages but greater than men's wages.

b. Unweighted averages are reported across years.

Empirical Tests of the "Unitary" Household Model

Focus of study, source, countries	Approach	Key findings
Income pooling and consumption		
Quisumbing and Maluccio 1999 Bangladesh, Ethiopia, Indonesia, South Africa	Analyzes household survey data collected to understand intrahousehold resource allocation. Uses assets at marriage as an indicator of bargaining power to assess the impact on household spending patterns and education outcomes. Uses Engel's curve approach to estimate household spending shares for goods (food, education, health care, children's clothing). Uses two-stage least-squares regressions to control for possible endogeneity.	The unitary model is rejected as a description of household behavior in all four countries, but to different degrees. Results suggest that assets controlled by women have a positive and significant effect on spending allocations toward the next generation, such as children's education and children's clothing. Findings indicate that mothers and fathers do not have identical preferences toward sons and daughters.
Phipps and Burton 1998 Canada	Analyzes impact of male and female incomes on spending shares for 14 categories of goods using an Engel curve approach in families where both husbands and wives are full-time employees. Husband and wife labor incomes used to represent control of resources.	A test for the equality of the impact of husband and wife income is rejected for 8 of the 14 categories of goods. In particular, income controlled by women has a larger impact on such traditional "women's goods" as child care, children's clothing, and food, while income controlled by men is more important for transportation. Findings indicate that husbands and wives do not always have identical preferences on spending categories.
Lundberg, Pollak, and Wales 1997 United Kingdom	Based on a "natural experiment" (a policy change that transferred a substantial child allowance to wives in the late 1970s); analyzes its impact on household spending patterns.	The policy coincided with a shift toward higher spending on women's and children's clothing relative to men's clothing. Findings indicate that husbands and wives do not always have identical preferences on spending categories.

(table continues on following page)

Focus of study, source, countries	Approach	Key findings
Thomas 1997 Brazil	Examines impacts of male and female resource control on shares of the household budget spent on different commodities and considers household demand for nutrients. Special attention paid to the role of measurement error and unobserved heterogeneity, and robust tests developed that exploit comparisons of income effects among siblings in the same household.	Placing more resources in the hands of women results in greater spending on human capital goods (household services, health, education), leisure goods (recreation, ceremonies), and nutrients, and more positive effects on children's nutritional status.
Thomas, Contreras, and Frankenberg 1997 Indonesia	Analyzes impact of assets brought into marriage by husbands and wives on gender-differentiated child illnesses, including cough, fever, and diarrhea.	A test of the difference between the impact of maternal and paternal assets on morbidity of sons relative to daughters is significant for coughs. This suggests that sons of women with higher assets at marriage are less likely than their sisters to experience respiratory disorders.
Ward-Batts 1997 United Kingdom	Uses an exogenous source of variation in the distribution of household income, provided by a change in the United Kingdom family allowance policy, to examine whether the distribution of income affects demand. Uses least squares, Tobit, and purchase infrequency models to estimate spending shares for a wide range of goods and services.	Among 11 broad categories, the policy shift coincided with higher spending on durables, food (eaten in and out), fuel, clothing, and miscellaneous, and with lower spending on housing and tobacco. Among narrow categories, spending on pets and books went up, while spending on noncigarette tobacco declined. Findings indicate that husbands and wives do not always have identical preferences on spending categories.
Thomas, Schoeni, and Strauss 1996 Brazil	Analyzes the impact of paternal and maternal education on children's education. Also examines the different impacts on schooling of sons and daughters. Uses ordinary least-squares regressions.	Rejects income pooling for children's education because maternal education has a bigger effect than paternal education. Moreover, maternal education affects the schooling of daughters more, while paternal education affects the schooling of sons more. Findings indicate that mothers and fathers do not have identical preferences toward sons and daughters, or with regard to spending categories.

(table continues on following page)

Focus of study, source, countries	Approach	Key findings
Hoddinott and Haddad 1995 Côte d'Ivoire	Provides an econometric test of the proposition that changes in the gender-specific control of income translate into changes in spending patterns. Estimates household spending functions for 10 categories of goods with the share of household income accruing to the spouse(s) of the household head as indicator of bargaining strength. Uses two-stage least-squares regressions to address endogeneity problems.	Rejects income pooling for 6 of 10 spending categories. Wives' share of cash income has a positive significant effect on the budget share of food and a negative significant effect on the budget shares of meals eaten out, children's clothing, adults' clothing, alcohol, and cigarettes. Findings indicate that husbands and wives do not have identical preferences on spending categories.
Browning and others 1994 Canada	Analyzes how relative income and age affect allocations of household spending between husbands and wives.	Rejects income pooling and shows that a wife's share in household spending rises with age and her share in household income.
Haddad and Hoddinott 1994 Côte d'Ivoire	Analyzes the different impact on boys' and girls' height for age and weight for height of the share of cash income accruing to the wives of the male household head. Addresses the problem of endogeneity by using an instrumental variables technique.	Rejects income pooling for height for age. Boys do better than girls in terms of height for age as a result of increasing female income shares. Findings indicate that mothers and fathers do not have identical preferences toward sons and daughters.
Thomas 1994 Brazil, Ghana, United States	Analyzes the impact of parental education on child height in all three countries. Also examines the different impact of nonlabor income of fathers and mothers on child height in Brazil. Analyzes endogeneity in some countries.	In all three countries maternal education has a bigger impact on daughters' height, while paternal education has a bigger effect on sons' height. In Brazil women's nonlabor income has a positive effect on their daughters' health but not on their sons'. Findings indicate that mothers and fathers do not have identical preferences toward sons and daughters.
Bourguignon and others 1993 France	Analyzes the impact of gender-disaggregated labor earnings on nine categories of goods. Uses Engel's curve approach to estimate household spending shares for goods.	Rejects income pooling using test of the hypothesis that all coefficients on male and female labor earnings are equal. Findings indicate that mothers and fathers do not have identical preferences on spending categories.

(table continues on following page)

Focus of study, source, countries	Approach	Key findings
Thomas 1990 Brazil	Analyzes the different impact of nonlabor income—from pensions, social security, workers' compensation, rents, and incomes from assets and gifts—in the hands of women and men on child health indicators. Controls for endogeneity using two-stage least-squares regressions.	Rejects income pooling in the demand for per capita caloric and protein intakes, child survival, and weight-for-height for children under eight. The different impacts of female- and male-controlled income are particularly large for child survival probabilities. The marginal impact of female-controlled income on child survival is 20 times that of male-controlled income.
Labor supply Fortin and Lacroix 1997 Canada	Tests the unitary and collective models of labor supply for families where both spouses work. Analyzes whether variables like nonlabor income controlled by a spouse and the presence of children affect the labor supply decisions of spouses differently. No mention is made of endogeneity issues.	Rejects income-pooling restrictions on coefficients in labor supply estimates. For example, the presence of children affects women's labor supply negatively but affects men's labor supply positively. Cross-wage elasticities are not symmetric.
Alderman and Sahn 1993 Sri Lanka	Adapts the "almost ideal demand system" to include leisure in the same manner as commodities.	Explores the substitutability between goods, female leisure, and male leisure. Results indicate that the marginal propensity to consume leisure is quite high, especially in rural areas. Complementarity between male and female leisure is also observed. Cross-price elasticities of commodities with respect to male and female wages show no regular pattern.
Lundberg 1988 United States	Labor supply functions for married men and women formulated as a dynamic simultaneous equations system, which is estimated using panel data. Controlling for fixed individual effects allows marginal labor supply responses to be disentangled from permanent patterns in hours worked due to assortative mating.	Results suggest that the labor supply of husband and wives without preschool children is not jointly determined in the short run, while families with young children exhibit strong interactions in work hours and negative cross-earning effects. Neither the joint utility model of family labor supply nor an ad hoc "traditional family" model is supported by these results.

(table continues on following page)

Focus of study, source, countries	Approach	Key findings
Ashenfelter and Heckman 1974 United States	Estimates labor supply functions. Analyzes the formulation of theoretical restrictions on the labor supply functions of husbands and wives in a model of labor supply in a way that makes them amenable to testing. Analyzes the cross-effects of husbands' wages on wives' labor supply and vice versa.	An increase in husbands' wages decreases wives' leisure and an increase in wives' wages increases husbands' leisure.
Investment and production Menon 1999 Bangladesh	Analyzes the long-run benefits of participation in microfinance programs by studying the consumption-smoothing abilities of members of different durations.	The effect of female borrowing on consumption smoothing is greater than the effect of household borrowing, implying that female effects are greater than male effects.
Khandker 1998 Bangladesh	Analyzes the impact of male and female borrowing on different outcome variables (per capita spending, net worth, school enrollment, fertility, height for age, contraceptive use). Controls for program placement endogeneity and for self-selection into the programs using a quasi-experimental survey.	Microfinance has different effects on outcome variables when it is provided to women rather than men. The effect on household consumption of borrowing by women was about twice that of borrowing by men: it increases girls' enrollment, has a significant impact on boys' and girls' nutritional well-being, and smoothes household consumption.
Pitt and Khandker 1998 Bangladesh	Analyzes the impact of participation (measured by quantity of cumulative borrowing) in microfinance programs by gender on the labor supply of men and women, schooling of girls and boys, household per capita spending on consumption, and women's nonland assets. The method used corrects for the potential bias arising from unobserved individual-, household-, and village-level heterogeneity. The analysis also pays careful attention to endogeneity and self-selection issues.	Participation in microfinance programs is a significant determinant of many of these outcomes. Furthermore, credit provided to women often has different impacts than credit provided to men.
Udry 1996 Burkina Faso	Analyzes plot yield by gender. Also examines the impact of the gender of farmers on intensities of labor and manure use. Uses ordinary least-squares fixed effects, Tobit fixed effects, and nonlinear ordinary least-squares fixed effects.	Rejects pooling of productive resources. Plots controlled by women are not farmed as intensively as plots controlled by men, using less male, child, and hired labor and manure per hectare. Women's plots thus have lower yields than men's plots in the same household, planted with the same crop in the same year.

(table continues on following page)

Focus of study, source, countries	Approach	Key findings
Udry and others 1995 Burkina Faso	Analyzes Pareto efficiency for the allocation of resources across plots within a household. Uses detailed four-year agronomic panel data.	Reveals substantial inefficiencies in agricultural production. These may be indicative of a production system in which resources are neither pooled nor traded among household members.
Jones (1983, 1986) Cameroon	Analyzes household production decisions by gender under the SEMRY project, which allowed Massa farmers to cultivate irrigated rice. Uses ordinary least-squares regressions.	Rejects pooling of resources among married couples. Married women, who are compensated by husbands for working on rice fields controlled by men, prefer to cultivate sorghum, whose output they control.
Risk pooling Dercon and Krishnan 2000 Ethiopia	Using panel data on individual nutritional status, looks at the factors determining the intrahousehold allocation of nutrition. In particular, analyzes consumption smoothing over time and within households.	Poorer households are unable to smooth their nutritional status. Furthermore, poor southern households do not engage in complete risk-sharing; women in these households bear the brunt of adverse shocks. This result implies that the collective model of household organization, which imposes Pareto efficiency on allocations, is rejected for these households.
Goldstein 1999 Ghana	Building on recent empirical literature on consumption smoothing and risk sharing, analyzes household responses to agricultural and health shocks to examine whether spouses pool risks.	Households do not pool risk or respond to shocks as a single unit. Rather, women pool their risk with other women in the village. Men have a wider, less-defined risk pool.

Education Simulations

B OX 6.1 PRESENTS ESTIMATES OF THE POTENTIAL COSTS OF alternative policies to promote gender equality in primary education. The estimates focus on the Middle East and North Africa, South Asia, and Sub-Saharan Africa—the three regions with the largest gender inequalities in education—and draw on simulation analysis of two basic scenarios:

- A reduction in household costs for primary education sufficient to achieve universal primary education—a goal donors have supported since 1990.
- A reduction in household costs for primary education sufficient to achieve universal primary education, but targeted only to the poorest 40 percent of households.

For each scenario the cost estimates assume, first, that the policy is not targeted by gender and, second, that the price (cost) cuts are targeted only to girls (as in the Bangladesh secondary school stipend program; see chapter 4).

In addition to gender targeting, the simulations focus on targeting the poor because gender gaps in education tend to be widest among the poor. Moreover, by targeting interventions by gender and poverty status, countries can contain budget costs. To carry out the simulations that focus on children in the poorest 40 percent of households, survey data on enrollment rates by gender and income quintiles are used (Filmer 1999). Data on price elasticities of demand for boys and girls come from published estimates based on cross-country data analysis (Schultz 1987). Data on the implied public costs of different interventions are supported by published data on the share of private spending in total education spending in developing countries (World Bank 1996, 1997). For the simulations of targeted interventions, the estimates incorporate information on the typical administrative (and leakage-related) costs associated with gender and poverty targeting (Grosh 1994). The key steps and results are shown in the tables below.

General Data Used for Education Simulations

Region	Gross enrollment rate for poor males (percent)	Gross enrollment rate for poor females (percent)	Gross enrollment rate for all males (percent)	Gross enrollment rate for all females (percent)	Public spending on primary education (billions of dollars)[a]	Private spending on primary education (billions of dollars)[b]
Middle East and North Africa	66.2	44.0	91.4	79.8	25.7	1.1
South Asia	61.0	39.4	106.8	84.0	15.9	0.8
Sub-Saharan Africa	52.4	46.3	81.3	66.4	9.8	3.8

a. Calculated using data on GNP, share of GNP spent on education, and share of primary education in public education spending based on data from World Bank (1997, 1999d).

b. Calculated using data on private share of education spending from World Bank (1997).

Sources: Filmer (1999); World Bank (1997, 1999d).

d. Calculated as percentages of initial public spending on primary education.

Policy to Achieve Universal Primary Education (UPE) for All Students

Region	Price cut necessary to achieve UPE for males (percent)[a]	Price cut necessary to achieve UPE for females (percent)[a]	Increase in public primary education spending with untargeted policy (millions of dollars)[b]	Increase in public primary education spending with targeted policy (millions of dollars)[c]	Increase in public primary education spending with untargeted policy (percent)[d]	Increase in public primary education spending with targeted policy (percent)[d]
Middle East and North Africa	The gross enrollment rate for the nonpoor already exceeds 100 percent, so the policy to achieve universal					
South Asia	primary education for poor students (described in the table below) would be sufficient to achieve universal					
	primary education for all students. No separate policy would be required.					
Sub-Saharan Africa	29.7	44.3	1,394.3	851.4	33.3	20.4

a. Calculated using elasticity data from Schultz (1987) with a 100 percent enrollment target.

b. Calculated from the increase in public spending on primary education needed to compensate for the decline in private spending arising from the price cut for males shown in the second column and the price cut for females shown in the third column.

c. Calculated from the increase in public spending on primary education needed to compensate for the decline in private spending arising from the price cut for females shown in the third column.

d. Calculated as percentages of initial public spending on primary education.

Policy to Achieve Universal Primary Education (UPE) for Poor Students

Region	Price cut necessary to achieve UPE for males (percent) [a]	Price cut necessary to achieve UPE for females (percent) [a]	Increase in public primary education spending with untargeted policy (millions of dollars) [b]	Increase in public primary education spending with targeted policy (millions of dollars) [c]	Increase in public primary education spending with untargeted policy (percent) [d]	Increase in public primary education spending with targeted policy (percent) [d]
Middle East and North Africa	53.6	73.7	306.0	180.7	3.3	2.0
South Asia	61.9	79.7	218.3	125.3	3.3	1.9
Sub-Saharan Africa	75.6	70.7	1,278.1	630.1	30.6	15.1

a. Calculated using elasticity data from Schultz (1987) with a 100 percent enrollment target.

b. Calculated from the increase in public spending on primary education needed to compensate for the decline in private spending arising from the price cut for males shown in the second column and the price cut for females shown in the third column, along with a 9 percent increase in program costs due to targeting the poor.

c. Calculated from the increase in public spending on primary education needed to compensate for the decline in private spending arising from the price cut for females shown in the third column, a 9 percent increase in program costs due to targeting the poor, and a 2 percent increase in program costs due to targeting females.

d. Calculated as percentages of initial public spending on primary education.

Glossary of Terms in Figures

Average years of schooling: The mean years of schooling at all levels for the population age 15 and older.

Corruption Index: Based on data collected by the International Country Risk Guide, the index measures corruption within a political system. A value of 0 indicates low levels of corruption, a value of 10 indicates high levels. This index focuses on actual corruption and the risk of corruption associated with high levels of political patronage, nepotism, job reservations, secret party funding, and excessively close ties between politics and business.

Gross enrollment ratio: The total enrollment in a specific level of education (such as primary or secondary), regardless of students' ages, expressed as a percentage of the official school-age population corresponding to the same level of education in a given school year.

Gross enrollment ratio, female to male: The ratio of the female *gross enrollment ratio* to the male gross enrollment ratio.

High-income countries: In figure 3 countries whose gross national product (GNP) per capita in 1995 was US$9,386 or more as classified by the World Bank in 1997. In figures 5 and 6.1, high-income countries are those whose GNP per capita was greater than US$4,000 in 1995 prices.

Humana rights indexes: In figure 1.1 the indexes, based on data collected by Humana (1986, 1992), capture gender equality in political and legal rights, social and economic rights, and rights in marriage and divorce proceedings. In other figures an aggregate index is presented based on the average of these three rights indexes. Scaled from 1 to 4, a score of 1 represents a low degree of gender equality in rights; a score of 4 represents a high degree of equality in rights.

Income elasticity of demand: The responsiveness of the quantity demanded of a good or service to changes in income. It is generally expressed as the percentage change in demand for a good or service in response to a 1 percent change in income, and is generally computed at the mean values of these variables.

Informal sector: Production and distribution of goods and services that take place outside the reach of the regulatory framework, often in household-based and small-scale enterprises. These enterprises generally lack legal recognition and may not be subject to labor and other standards prescribed by the legal code. Employees in the informal sector commonly lack nonwage benefits, such as disability, severance, or pensions, which are often required by law for formal sector employees.

Life expectancy at birth: The number of years a newborn infant would be expected to live if prevailing patterns of age-specific mortality at the time of birth were to stay the same throughout life.

Life expectancy ratio, female to male: The ratio of female *life expectancy at birth* to male life expectancy at birth.

Low-income countries: In figure 3 countries whose GNP per capita in 1995 was US$765 or less as classified by the World Bank in 1997. In figures 5 and 6.1, low-income countries are those whose GNP per capita was US$4,000 or less in 1995 prices.

Market activities: The boundary between market-oriented (valued work) and nonmarket activities (unvalued work) corresponds roughly to the production boundary defined by the United Nations System of National Accounts (SNA 1968). Activities that are market-oriented qualify for entry into national accounts and include work outside the home and production of self-consumed products of subsistence agriculture because they could be marketed. (See also *nonmarket activities.*)

Middle-income countries: In figure 3 countries whose GNP per capita in 1995 was between US$766 and US$9,385 as classified by the World Bank in 1997.

Nonmarket activities: Productive activities that do not qualify for entry into national accounts. They include schooling, voluntary community work, and household maintenance and care. (See also *market activities.*)

Occupational representation ratio, female to male: The ratio of the number of women in an occupational group divided by the total female nonagricultural labor force to the number of men in that occupational group divided by the total male nonagricultural labor force, based on Anker (1998). A value greater than 1 indicates that women are overrepresented in that occupational category compared with men; a value lower than 1 indicates that women are underrepresented.

Parliamentary representation ratio, female to male: The ratio of elected seats in national parliaments (or other nationally elected assemblies) occupied by women to seats occupied by men.

Potential average time savings: The estimated savings in time spent on water and fuel collection by household members each year, on average, resulting from reduced distances to potable water sources and fuelwood lots. In figures 4.3 and 10 this refers specifically to time savings in five areas of rural Africa that resulted from ensuring that potable water sources were no more than 400 meters (about a six-minute walk) and fuel sources no more than a 30-minute walk from each household. Estimates are from Barwell (1996).

Price elasticity of demand: The responsiveness of the quantity demanded of a good to its own price. It is generally expressed as the percentage change in quantity demanded of a good or service resulting from a 1 percent change in its price, and is generally computed at the mean values of these variables.

Purchasing power parity conversion factor: The purchasing power parity (PPP) conversion factor shows how much of a country's currency is needed in that country to buy what one unit of the numeraire currency would buy in the numeraire country, typically the United States. Using the PPP conversion factor instead of the currency exchange rate means that a country's GNP per capita calculated in national currency units can be converted into GNP per capita in U.S. dollars, taking into account differences in domestic prices for the same goods. Because prices are usually lower in developing countries than in the United States, their GNP per capita expressed in PPP dollars tends to be higher than their GNP per capita expressed in standard U.S. dollars. In industrial countries the opposite is true. The PPP conversion factors used here are derived from the most recent round of price surveys conducted by the International Comparison Programme, a joint project of the World Bank and the regional economic commissions of the United Nations. This round of surveys, completed in 1996 and covering 118 countries, is based on a 1993 reference year.

Women's Economic and Social Human Rights (WESHR) Index: This index captures different dimensions of rights using female to male ratios for seven development indicators: the right to work, as measured by the rates of economic activity; the right to an adequate standard of living, as measured by anemia rates and total daily caloric intake; the right to health and well-being, as measured by mortality rates and sex ratios; and the right to an education, as measured by literacy rates and primary school enrollment rates. For each indicator, a ratio of 1 means parity between the sexes. Scores below 1 signify some degree of gender disparity favoring males; scores above 1 signify some degree of gender disparity favoring females. The seven female to male ratios are then added together to obtain the composite WESHR index. A score of 7 is interpreted as gender equality in the achievement of economic and social rights.

References

Abu, Katherine. 1983. "The Separateness of Spouses: Conjugal Resources in an Ashanti Town." In C. Oppong, ed., *Female and Male in West Africa.* London: Allen and Unwin.

Adnan, Shapan. 1993. "'Birds in a Cage': Institutional Change and Women's Position in Bangladesh." In Nora Federici, Karen Oppenheim Mason, and Solvi Sogner, eds., *Women's Position and Demographic Change.* Oxford: Clarendon Press.

Agarwal, Bina. 1994. *A Field of One's Own: Gender and Land Rights in South Asia.* Cambridge, England; New York: Cambridge University Press.

_____. 1997. "'Bargaining' and Gender Relations: Within and Beyond the Household." Food Consumption and Nutrition Division Discussion Paper 27. International Food Policy Research Institute, Washington, D.C. Available online at *http://www.ifpri.cgiar.org/index1.htm*

Agesa, Richard U. 1999. "The Urban Gender Wage Gap in an African Country: Findings from Kenya." *Canadian Journal of Development Studies* 20 (1): 59–76.

Agrawal, Nisha. 1996. "The Benefits of Growth for Indonesian Workers." Policy Research Working Paper 1637. World Bank, Development Research Group, Washington, D.C. Available online at *http://wbln0018.worldbank.org/research/workpapers.nsf/policyresearch?openform*

Ahikire, Josephine. 1994. "Women, Public Politics and Organization: Potentialities of Affirmative Action in Uganda." *Economic and Political Weekly* 29 (October 29): WS77–WS83.

Ahuja, Vinod, Benu Bidani, Francisco Ferreia, and Michael Walton. 1997. *Everyone's Miracle? Revisiting Poverty and Inequality in East Asia.* A Directions in Development book. Washington, D.C.: World Bank.

Alderman, Harold. 2000. "Anthropometry." In Margaret Grosh and Paul Glewwe, eds., *Designing Household Survey Questionnaires for Developing Countries: Lessons from Fifteen Years of the Living Standards Measurement Study.* Oxford and New York: Oxford University Press.

Alderman, Harold, and Paul Gertler. 1997. "Family Resources and Gender Differences in Human Capital Investments: The Demand for Children's Medical Care in Pakistan." In Lawrence Haddad, John Hoddinott, and Harold Alderman, eds., *Intrahousehold Resource Allocation in Developing Countries : Models,*

Methods, and Policy. Baltimore, Md. and London: The Johns Hopkins University Press.

Alderman, Harold, and Elizabeth M. King. 1998. "Gender Differences in Parental Investment in Education." *Structural Change and Economic Dynamics* 9: 453–68.

Alderman, Harold, and David E. Sahn. 1993. "Substitution between Goods and Leisure in a Developing Country." *American Journal of Agricultural Economics* 75: 875–83.

Alderman, Harold, Jere R. Behrman, David Ross, and Richard Sabot. 1996. "Decomposing the Gender Gap in Cognitive Skills in a Poor Rural Economy." *Journal of Human Resources* 31 (1): 229–54.

Alderman, Harold, Pierre-André Chiappori, Lawrence Haddad, John Hoddinott, and Ravi Kanbur. 1995. "Unitary versus Collective Models of the Household: Is it Time to Shift the Burden of Proof?" *The World Bank Research Observer* 10 (1): 1–19.

Allison, Christine, and Dena Ringold. 1996. *Labor Markets in Transition in Central and Eastern Europe 1989–1995.* World Bank Technical Paper 352. Social Challenges of Transition Series. Washington, D.C.

Altonji, Joseph G. 1991. "The Demand For and Return to Education When Education Outcomes are Uncertain." NBER Working Papers Series No. 3714. National Bureau for Economic Research, Cambridge, Mass. Available online at *http://papers.nber.org/papers/W3714*

Anderson, Joan B., and Denise Dimon. 1999. "Formal Sector Job Growth and Women's Labor Sector Participation: The Case of Mexico." *Quarterly Review of Economics and Finance* 39 (2): 169–91.

Anderson, Lisa R., Yana V. Rodgers, and Roger R. Rodriguez. 1998. "Risk Aversion and Gender: Some Cross-cultural Evidence from Bargaining Experiments." Department of Economics, The College of William and Mary, Williamsburg, Virginia.

Andreoni, James and Lise Vesterlund. Forthcoming. "Which is the Fair Sex? Gender Differences in Altruism." *Quarterly Journal of Economics.* Available online at *http://www.ssc.wisc.edu/~andreoni/WorkingPapers/fairsex.pdf*

Angrist, Joshua D., and William N. Evans. 1998. "Children and Their Parents' Labor Supply: Evidence from Exogenous Variation in Family Size." *American Economic Review* 88 (3): 450–77.

Angrist, Joshua D., Eric Bettinger, Erik Bloom, Elizabeth M. King, and Michael Kremer. 2000. "Vouchers for Private Schooling in Colombia: Evidence from a Randomized Natural Experiment." Massachusetts Institute of Technology, Cambridge, Mass.

Anker, Richard. 1998. *Gender and Jobs: Sex Segregation of Occupations in the World.* Geneva: International Labour Office.

Appleton, Simon. 1995. "Exam Determinants in Kenyan Primary School: Determinants and Gender Differences." World Bank, Economic Development Institute, Washington, D.C.

Appleton, Simon, and Paul Collier. 1995. "On Gender Targeting of Public Transfers." In Dominique van de Walle and Kimberly Nead, eds., *Public Spending and the Poor:*

Theory and Evidence. Baltimore, Md.: The Johns Hopkins University Press.

Appleton, Simon, John Hoddinott, and Pramila Krishnan. 1999. "The Gender Wage Gap in Three African Countries." *Economic Development and Cultural Change* 47: 289–312.

Artecona, Raquel, and Wendy Cunningham. 2000a. "The Effects of Trade Liberalization on the Gender Wage Gap." Background paper for *Engendering Development.* World Bank, Washington, D.C.

_____. 2000b. "Labor Market Outcomes: Recent Trends and the Role of Gender in Three LAC Countries." World Bank, Latin American and Caribbean Region, Poverty Reduction and Economic Management Unit, Washington, D.C.

Aryeetey, Ernest, Amoah Baah-Nuakoh, Tamara Duggleby, Hemamala Hettige, and William F. Steel. 1994. *Supply and Demand for Finance of Small Enterprises in Ghana.* World Bank Discussion Paper 251. Africa Technical Department Series. Washington, D.C.

Aryeetey, Ernest, Hemamala Hettige, Machiko Nissanke, and William F. Steel. 1997. *Financial Market Fragmentation and Reforms in Sub-Saharan Africa.* World Bank Technical Paper 356. Africa Region Series. Washington, D.C.

Ashenfelter, Orley, and James Heckman. 1974. "The Estimation of Income and Substitution Effects in a Model of Family Labor Supply." *Econometrica* 42 (1): 73–85.

Ashworth, J., and D. Ulph. 1981. "Household Models." In Charles V. Brown, ed., *Taxation and Labor Supply.* London: Allen and Unwin.

Baden, Sally, and Kirsty Milward. 1995. "Gender and Poverty." BRIDGE (Briefings on Development and Gender) Report 30. Institute of Development Studies, Brighton, U.K.

Baker, Michael, Benjamin Dwayne, Andree Desaulniers, and Mary Grant. 1995. "The Distribution of Male/Female Earnings Differential, 1970–1990." *Canadian Journal of Economics* 28 (3): 479–501.

Bangladesh, Government of. 1999. "Database on Food Situation in Bangladesh." Food Planning and Monitoring Unit, Dhaka.

Banister, Judith, and Ansley J. Coale. 1994. "Five Decades of Missing Females in China." *Demography* 31: 459–79.

Bardhan, Kalpana, and Stephan Klasen. 1998. "Women in Emerging Asia: Welfare, Employment, and Human Development." *Asian Development Review* 16 (1): 72–125.

Bardhan, Pranab. 1990. "Symposium on the State and Economic Development." *Journal of Economic Perspectives* 4 (3): 3–7.

Barrera, Albino. 1990. "The Role of Maternal Schooling and Its Interaction with Public Health Programs in Child Health Production." *Journal of Development Economics* 32: 69–91.

Barro, Robert J., and Jong-Wha Lee. 1994. "Sources of Economic Growth." *Carnegie-Rochester Conference on Public Policy* 40: 1–46.

Barwell, Ian. 1996. *Transport and the Village.* World Bank Discussion Paper 344. Africa Region Series. Washington, D.C.

Basu, Alaka M. 1992. *Culture, the Status of Women, and Demographic Behavior: Illustrated with the Case of India.* Oxford: Clarendon Press.

Basu, Ananya. 1997. "Sibling Rivalry, Resource Constraints, and Gender Bias in Education: Evidence from Rajasthan." Harvard University, Cambridge, Mass.

Becker, Gary. 1971. *The Economics of Discrimination.* 2nd ed. Chicago: University of Chicago Press.

_____. 1974. "A Theory of Social Interactions." *Journal of Political Economy* 82: 1063–93.

_____. 1981. *A Treatise on the Family.* Cambridge, Mass.: Harvard University Press.

Beegle, Kathleen, Elizabeth Frankenberg, Duncan Thomas, Wayan Suriastini, and Victoria Beard. 1999. "Indonesia's Economic Crisis and Its Effects on Health and Family Planning." RAND, Santa Monica, Calif.

Behrman, Jere R. 1988. "Intrahousehold Allocation of Nutrients in Rural India: Are Boys Favored? Do Parents Exhibit Inequality Aversion?" *Oxford Economic Papers* 40 (1): 32–54.

_____. 1997. "Intrahousehold Distribution and the Family." In Mark Rosenzweig and Oded Stark, eds., *Handbook of Population and Family Economics.* Amsterdam and New York: Elsevier.

Behrman, Jere R., and Anil B. Deolalikar. 1990. "The Intrahousehold Demand for Nutrients in Rural South India: Individual Estimates, Fixed Effects, and Permanent Income." *Journal of Human Resources* 25 (4): 665–96.

_____. 1995. "Are There Differential Returns to Schooling by Gender? The Case of Indonesian Labour Markets." *Oxford Bulletin of Economics and Statistics* 57 (February): 97–118.

Behrman, Jere R., and Elizabeth M. King. 2000. "Competition and Gender Gap in Wages: Evidence From 16 Countries." Background paper for *Engendering Development.* World Bank, Washington, D.C.

Behrman, Jere R., and James C. Knowles. 1999. "Household Income and Child Schooling in Vietnam." *The World Bank Economic Review* 13 (May): 211–56.

Behrman, Jere R., and Pranee Tinakorn. 1999. "The Impact of the Thai Financial Crisis on Thai Labor." Thailand Development Research Institute, Bangkok.

Behrman, Jere R., and Barbara L. Wolfe. 1991. "Earnings and Determinants of Labor Force Participation in a Developing Country: Are There Gender Differentials?" In Nancy Birdsall and Richard Sabot, eds., *Unfair Advantage: Labor Market Discrimination in Developing Countries.* A World Bank Regional and Sectoral Study. Washington, D.C.

Behrman, Jere, Suzanne Duryea, and Miguel Székely. 1999. "Intergenerational Schooling Mobility and Macro Conditions and Aggregate Schooling Policies in Latin America." In Nancy Birdsall and Carol Grahans, *New Markets, New Opportunities? Economic and Social Mobility in a Changing World.* Washington, D.C.: Brookings Institution and Carnegie Endowment for International Peace.

Behrman, Jere R., Andrew D. Foster, Mark R. Rosenzweig, and Prem Vashishtha. 1999. "Women's Schooling, Home Teaching, and Economic Growth." *Journal of Political Economy* 107 (4): 632–714.

Bellew, Rosemary T., and Elizabeth M. King. 1993. "Educating Women: Lessons from Experience." In Elizabeth M. King and Anne M.

Hill, eds., *Women's Education in Developing Countries: Barriers, Benefits, and Policies*. Baltimore, MD and London: The Johns Hopkins University Press.

Beneria, Lourdes. 1995. "Toward a Greater Integration of Gender in Economics." *World Development* 23 (11): 1839–50.

Berger, Mark C., Peter Groothuis, and B. Philip Jeon. 1997. "The Changing Gender Wage Gap in Korea." *Applied Economics Letters* 4 (9): 579–82.

Bertranou, Fabio. 1998. "Social Security-Pension Contributions as a Measure of Pension Coverage: Exploration of Gender Specific Factors in Argentina and Chile." University of Pittsburgh, Department of Economics.

Bevan, David, Paul Collier, and Jan W. Gunning. 1989. *Peasants and Governments*. Oxford: Clarendon Press.

Bhattacharya, Debapriya, and Mustafizur Rahman. 1998. "Female Employment under Export-Propelled Industrialization: Prospects for Internalizing Global Opportunities in Bangladesh's Apparel Sector." Occasional Paper 10. United Nations Research Institute for Social Development–United Nations Development Programme Study on Technical Cooperation and Women's Lives: Integrating Gender into Development Policy (phase II), Geneva and New York. Available online at *http://www.unrisd.org/engindex/publ/cat/p318.htm*

Bindlish, Vishva, and Robert Evenson. 1993. *Evaluation of the Performance of T and V Extension in Kenya*. World Bank Technical Paper 208. Washington, D.C.

Birdsall, Nancy, and Jere R. Behrman. 1991. "Why Do Males Earn More than Females in Urban Brazil: Earnings Discrimination or Job Discrimination?" In Nancy Birdsall and Richard Sabot, eds., *Unfair Advantage: Labor Market Discrimination in Developing Countries*. A World Bank Regional and Sectoral Study. Washington, D.C.

Birdsall, Nancy, and M. Louise Fox. 1991. "Why Males Earn More: Location and Training of Brazilian Schoolteachers." In Nancy Birdsall and Richard Sabot, eds., *Unfair Advantage: Labor Market Discrimination in Developing Countries*. A World Bank Regional and Sectoral Study. Washington, D.C.

Birdsall, Nancy, and Richard Sabot, eds. 1991. *Unfair Advantage: Labor Market Discrimination in Developing Countries*. A World Bank Regional and Sectoral Study. Washington, D.C.

Black, Sandra E., and Elizabeth Brainerd. 1999. "Importing Equality? The Effects of Increased Competition on the Gender Wage Gap." Federal Reserve Bank of New York and Williams College, Department of Economics, Williamstown, Mass. Available online at *http://www.ny.frb.org/rmaghome/staff_rp/sr74.pdf*

Black, Sandra E., and Philip E. Strahan. 1999. "Rent-Sharing and the Gender Wage Gap: The Effects of Banking Deregulation on the Labor Market." Federal Reserve Bank of New York, New York.

Blackden, C. Mark, and Chitra Bhanu. 1999. *Gender, Growth and Poverty Reduction: Special Program of Assistance for Africa*. World Bank Technical Paper 428. Washington, D.C.

Blau, David M., and Philip K. Robins. 1988. "Child-Care Costs and Family Labor Supply." *Review of Economics and Statistics* 70 (3): 374–81.

Blau, Francine, D. 1998. "Continuing Progress? Trends in Occupational Segregation in the United States Over the 1970s and 1980s." NBER Working Paper 6716. National Bureau for Economic Research, Cambridge, Mass. Available online at *http://papers.nber.org/papers/W6716*

Blau, Francine D., and Lawrence M. Kahn. 1992. "The Gender Earnings Gap: Learning from International Comparisons." *American Economic Review* 82 (2): 533–38.

_____. 1994. "Rising Wage Inequality and the U. S. Gender Gap." *American Economic Review Papers and Proceedings* 84: 23–28.

_____. 1997. "Swimming Upstream: Trends in the Gender Wage Differential in the 1980s." *Journal of Labor Economics* 15 (1, Part 1): 1–42.

_____. 1999. "Understanding International Differences in the Gender Pay Gap." Cornell University, School of Industrial Labor Relations, Department of Labor Economics, Ithaca, N.Y.

Bloch, Francis, and Vijayendra Rao. 2000. "Terror as a Bargaining Instrument: A Case Study of Dowry Violence in Rural India." Policy Research Working Paper 2347. World Bank, Development Research Group, Washington, D.C. Available online at *http://wbln0018.worldbank.org/research/workpapers.nsf/policyresearch?openform*

Blöndal, Sveinjörn, and Stefano Scarpetta,. 1997. "Early Retirement in OECD Countries: The Role of Social Security Systems." *OECD Economic Studies* 29:7–54.

Boeri, Tito, and Mark Keese. 1992. "Labour Markets and the Transition in Central and Eastern Europe." *OECD Economic Studies* 18 (Spring): 133–63.

Bolton, Gary E., and Elena Katok. 1995. "An Experimental Test for Gender Differences in Beneficent Behavior." *Economics Letters* 48 (3 June): 287–92.

Bonjour, Dorothe, and Lia Pacelli. 1998. "Wage Formation and the Gender Wage Gap: Do Institutions Matter? Italy and Switzerland Compared." Working Paper. Queen Mary and Westfield College, University of London, Department of Economics.

Boone, Peter. 1996. "Political and Gender Oppression as a Cause of Poverty." CEPR Discussion Paper 294. London School of Economics, Center for Economic Performance.

Boserup, Ester. 1970. *Women's Role in Economic Development*. New York: St. Martin's Press.

Bouis, Howarth. 1998. "Commercial Vegetable and Polyculture Fish Production in Bangladesh: Their Impacts on Income, Household Resource Allocation, and Nutrition." International Food Policy Research Institute, Washington, D.C.

Bourguignon, François, Martin Browning, Pierre-Andre Chiappori, and Valeire Lechene. 1993. "Intra Household Allocation of Consumption: A Model and Some Evidence from French Data." *Annales d'Economie et de Statistique* 29: 137–56.

Bradshaw, York, and Ana-Maria Wahl. 1991. "Foreign Debt Expansion, the International Monetary Fund, and Regional Variation in Third World Poverty." *International Studies Quarterly* 35: 251–72.

Brainerd, Elizabeth. 1998. "Winners and Losers in Russia's Economic Transition." *American Economic Review* 88 (5): 1094–1116.

BRIDGE (Briefings on Development and Gender). 1994. "Background Paper on Gender Issues in Ghana." Report prepared for the U.K. Overseas Development Administration's West and North Africa Department. Institute of Development Studies, Brighton.

Bronars, Stephen G., and Jeff Grogger. 1994. "The Economic Consequences of Unwed Motherhood: Using Twin Births as a Natural Experiment." *American Economic Review* 84 (5): 1141–56.

Brown, Lynn R., and Lawrence Haddad. 1995. "Time Allocation Patterns and Time Burdens: A Gendered Analysis of Seven Countries." International Food Policy Research Institute, Washington, D.C.

Browning, Martin, François Bourguignon, Pierre-Andre Chiappori, and Valeire Lechene. 1994. "Income and Outcomes: A Structural Model of Intrahousehold Allocation." *Journal of Political Economy* 102 (6): 1067–96.

Bruce, Judith, Cynthia B. Lloyd, and Ann Leonard. 1995. "Families in Focus: New Perspectives on Mothers, Fathers, and Children." Population Council, New York.

Budlender, Debbie. 1999. "The South African Women's Budget Initiative." Paper presented at the United Nations Development Programme–United Nations Development Fund for Women Workshop on Pro-Poor, Gender- and Environment-Sensitive Budgets, New York, June 28–30. Community Agency for Social Enquiry, South Africa.

Bureau of Labor Statistics. 1994. *Technology and Labor in Pulp, Paper, Paperboard and Selected Converting Industries.* BLS Bulletin 2443. Washington, D.C.: GPO.

Buvinič, Mayra, and Marguerite Berger. 1990. "Sex Differences in Access to a Small Enterprise Development Fund in Peru." *World Development* 18 (5): 695–705.

Buvinič, Mayra, and Geeta Rao Gupta. 1997. "Female-headed Households and Female Maintained Families: Are They Worth Targeting to Reduce Poverty in Developing Countries?" *Economic Development and Cultural Change* 45 (2): 259–80.

Buvinič, Mayra, Andrew Morrison, and Michael Shifter. 1999. *Violence in Latin America and the Caribbean: A Framework for Action.* Washington, D.C.: Inter-American Development Bank. Available online at *http://www.iadb.org/sds/doc/1073eng.pdf*

Cagatay, Nilufer, Diane Elson, and Caren Grown. 1995. "Gender, Adjustment and Macroeconomics: Introduction." *World Development* 23 (11): 1827–36.

Castel, Paulett, and Louise Fox. 1999. "Gender in Pension Reform in the Former Soviet Union." Paper prepared for a World Bank conference on New Ideas about Old Age Security, 14–15 September, Washington, D.C.

Charmes, Jacques. 1998. "Informal Sector, Poverty and Gender: A Review of Empirical Evidence." French Scientific Research Institute for Development and Cooperation and University of Versailles-St. Quentin, Yvelines, France.

Chen, Gregory. 2000. "Three Innovative Institutions in Bangladesh: BRAC, ASA, and Buro-Tangail." Consultative Group to Assist the Poorest Secretariat, Washington, D.C. *http://www.worldbank.org/html/cgap/newsltr5/bangla.htm*

Chen, Lincoln C., Emdadul Huq, and Stan D'Souza. 1981. "Sex Bias in the Family Allocation of Food and Health Care in Rural Bangladesh." *Population and Development Review* 7 (1): 55–70.

Chen, Martha. 1995. "A Matter of Survival: Women's Right to Employment in India and Bangladesh." In Martha Nussbaum and Jonathan Glover, ed., *Women, Culture and Development: A Study of Human Capabilities*. New York: Oxford University Press.

_____, ed. 1998. *Widows in India: Social Neglect and Public Action*. New Delhi and Thousand Oaks, California: Sage Publications.

Chi, Truong, Thi Ngoc, Lisa Leimar Price, and Mahabub M. Hossain. 1998. "Impact of IPM Training on Male and Female Farmers' Knowledge and Pest Control Behavior: A Case Study of Vietnam." Working Paper. International Rice Research Institute, Manila.

Chua, Yee Yen. 1984. "Wage Differentials in Peninsular Malaysia." Ph. D. diss. University of California at Santa Barbara.

CIDA (Canadian International Development Agency). 1999. *CIDA's Policy on Gender Equality*. Quebec, Canada. Available online at *http://www.acdi-cida.gc.ca*

Cleveland, Gordon, Morley Gunderson, and Douglas Hyatt. 1996. "Child Care Costs and the Employment Decisions of Women: The Canadian Experience." *Canadian Journal of Economics* 29 (1): 132–49.

Coale, Ansley J. 1991. "Excess Female Mortality and the Balance of the Sexes: An Estimate of the Number of 'Missing Females.'" *Population and Development Review* 17: 517–23.

Coleman, J. S. 1987. "Equality." In J. Eatwell, M. Milgate, and P. Newman, eds., *The New Palgrave: A Dictionary of Economics*, Vol. 2. London: The Macmillan Press Limited.

Collier, Paul. 1988. "Women in Development: Defining the Issues." Planning Research Working Paper 129. World Bank, Population and Human Resources Department, Washington, D.C.

Collier, Paul, and Jan Willem Gunning. 1999. "Explaining African Economic Performance." *Journal of Economic Literature* 37 (1): 64–111.

Collier, Paul, A.C. Edwards, and Kalpana Bardhan. 1994. "Gender Aspects of Labor Allocation during Structural Adjustment." In Susan Horton, Ravi Kanbur, and Dipak Mazumdar, eds., *Labor Markets in an Era of Adjustment*. Washington, D.C.: World Bank.

Collier, William L., Soentoro, Gunawan Wiradi, and Makili. 1974. "Agricultural Technology and Institutional Change in Java." *Food Research Institute Studies* 13: 169–194.

Commonwealth Secretariat. 1991. *Women and Structural Adjustment: Selected Case Studies Commissioned for a Commonwealth Group of Experts*. Commonwealth Economic Papers 22. Economic Affairs Division, London.

Connelly, Rachel, and Jean Kimmel. 2000. "Marital Status and Full-time/Part-time Work Status in Child Care Choices." W.E. Upjohn Institute for Employment Research, Staff Working Papers, Kalamazoo, Michigan. Available online at *http://www.upjohninst.org/publications/wp/99-58.pdf*

Connelly, Rachel, Deborah S. DeGraff, and Deborah Levison. 1996. "Women's Employment and Child Care in Brazil." *Economic Development and Cultural Change* 44 (3): 619–56.

Connelly, Rachel, Deborah S. DeGraff, Deborah Levison, and Brian McCall. 1999. "Tackling the Endogeneity of Fertility in the Study of Women's Employment: Alternative Estimation Strategies Using Data from Urban Brazil." Bowdoin College, Brunswick, Maine.

Cooke, Priscilla A. 1998. "Intrahousehold Labor Allocation Responses to Environmental Goods Scarcity: A Case Study from the Hills of Nepal." *Economic Development and Cultural Change* 46: 807–30.

Cost, Quality & Child Outcomes Study Team. 1995. *Cost, Quality, and Child Outcomes in Child Care Centers.* Public Report, 2nd ed. Denver, Colo.: University of Colorado at Denver, Department of Economics.

Cox, Donald, and Emmanuel Jimenez. 1998. "Risk Sharing and Private Transfers: What about Urban Households?" *Economic Development and Cultural Change* 46 (April): 621–37.

Cox-Edwards, Alejandra. 1999. "A Close Look at the Living Standards of Chilean Elderly Men and Women." Paper prepared for the World Bank research project on Gender and Social Security. World Bank, Washington, D.C.

_____. 2000. "Pension Projections for Chilean Men and Women: Estimates from Social Security Contributions." Background paper for *Engendering Development.* World Bank, Washington, D.C.

Cunningham, Wendy. 2000. "Breadwinner Versus Caregiver: Labor Force Participation and Sectoral Choice over the Mexican Business Cycle." World Bank, Latin America and the Caribbean Gender Sector, Washington, D.C.

Currie, Janet. 1999. "Is the Impact of Health Shocks Cushioned by Socioeconomic Status? The Case of Low Birthweight." *American Economic Review* 89 (2): 245–250.

DAC (Development Assistance Committee) 1998. "DAC Guidelines on Gender Equality and Women's Empowerment in Development Cooperation." OECD, Paris. Available online at *http://www.oecd.org/dac/htm/pubs/p-gender.htm*

Das, Manju Dutta. 1995. "Improving the Relevance and Effectiveness of Agricultural Extension Activities for Women Farmers: An Andre Mayer Research Study." United Nations Food and Agriculture Organization, Rome.

Das Gupta, Monica. 1987. "Selective Discrimination against Female Children in Rural Punjab, India." *Population and Development Review* 13 (1): 77–100.

_____. 1996. "Life Course Perspectives on Women's Autonomy and Health Outcomes." *Health Transition Review,* 6 (Supplement): 213–231.

Das Gupta, Monica, Sunhwa Lee, Patricia Uberoi, Danning Wang, Lihong Wang, and Xiaodan Zhang. 2000. "State Policy and Women's Autonomy in China, S. Korea and India, 1950–2000: Lessons From Contrasting Experiences." Background paper for *Engendering Development.* World Bank, Washington, D.C.

Davies, Hugh, Heather Joshi, and Romana Peronaci. 1998. "The Gender Wage Gap and Partnership." Working Paper. University of London, Department of Economics.

Davis, Rebecca Howard. 1997. *Women and Power in Parliamentary Democracies. Cabinet Appointments in Western Europe, 1968–1992.* Lincoln: University of Nebraska Press.

Davison, Jean, ed. 1988. *Agriculture, Women and Land: The African Experience.* Boulder, Colo.: Westview Press.

Day, T. 1995. "The Health-Related Costs of Violence against Women in Canada: The Tip of the Iceberg." Centre for Research on Violence Against Women and Children, University of Western Ontario, London, Ontario.

Deaton, Angus. 1997. *The Analysis of Household Surveys.* Baltimore, Md.: The Johns Hopkins University Press.

de Tray, Dennis. 1988. "Government Policy, Household Behavior, and the Distribution of Schooling: A Case Study of Malaysia." In T. Paul Schultz, ed., *Research in Population Economics* 6. Greenwich, Conn. and London: JAI Press.

Deere, Carmen Diana, and Magdalena Leon. 1997. "Women and Land Rights in the Latin American Neo-Liberal Counter Reforms." Women in International Development Working Paper 264. Michigan State University.

_____. 1999. "Institutional Reform of Agriculture under Neoliberalism: The Impact of the Women's and Indigenous Movements." Keynote address prepared for the CEDLA (Centre for Latin American Research and Documentation, CERES (Research School for Resource Studies for Development), and Wageningen Agricultural University conference on Land in Latin America: New Context, New Claims, New Concepts, 26–27 May, Amsterdam.

Deininger, Klaus, and Lyn Squire. 1996. "A New Data Set Measuring Income Inequality." *The World Bank Economic Review* 10 (3): 565–91.

Dercon, Stefan, and Pramila Krishnan. 2000. "Vulnerability, Seasonality and Poverty in Ethiopia." *Journal of Development Studies* 36 (6).

Desai, Sonalde. 1998. "Maternal Education and Child Health: Is There a Strong Causal Relationship?" *Demography* 35 (1): 71–81.

Desai, Sonalde, Vijayendra Rao, and B.L. Joshi. 2000. "The Social and Economic Context of Child Marriage in Rural North India." Department of Sociology, University of Maryland, College Park.

Deutsch, Ruthanne. 1998. "Does Child Care Pay? Labor Force Participation and the Earnings Effects of Access to Child Care in the Favelas of Rio de Janeiro." IDB Working Paper 384. Inter-American Development Bank, Washington, D.C. Available online at *http://www.iadb.org/ OCE/working_papers_list.cfm?CODE=WP-384*

Devereux, Stephen. 1998. "Conceptualizing Anti-Poverty Programmes and Targeting Women in Sub-Saharan Africa." Poverty Research Programme Working Paper. Institute of Development Studies, Sussex.

Dey Abbas, Jennie. 1997. "Gender Asymmetries in Intrahousehold Resource Allocation in Sub-Saharan Africa: Some Policy Implications for Land and Labor Productivity." In Lawrence Haddad, John Hoddinott, and Harold Alderman, eds., *Intrahousehold Resource Allocation in Developing Countries: Models, Methods, and Policy.* Baltimore, Md. and London: The Johns Hopkins University Press.

DFID (Department for International Development). 1998. *Breaking the Barriers: Women and the Elimination of World Poverty.* London, U.K.

Diamond, Ian, Margaret Newby, and Sarah Varle. 1999. "Female Education and Fertility: Examining the Links." In Caroline H. Bledsoe and others, eds., *Critical Perspectives on Schooling and Fertility in the Developing World.* Washington, D.C.: National Academy Press.

Dollar, David, and Roberta Gatti. 1999. "Gender Inequality, Income, and Growth: Are Good Times Good for Women?" Background paper for *Engendering Development.* World Bank, Washington, D.C. Available online at *http://www.worldbank.org/gender/prr/dg.pdf*

Dollar, David, Raymond Fisman, and Roberta Gatti. Forthcoming. "Are Women Really the 'Fairer' Sex? Corruption and Women in Government." *Journal of Economic Behavior and Organization.* Available online at *http://www.worldbank.org/gender/prr/dfgpaper.pdf*

Dollar, David, Paul Glewwe, and Jennie Litvack, eds. 1998. *Household Welfare and Vietnam's Transition.* A World Bank Regional and Sectoral Study. Washington, D.C.

Doss, Cheryl R. 1996. "Women's Bargaining Power in Household Economic Decisions: Evidence from Ghana." Staff Paper Series P96-11. University of Minnesota, College of Agricultural, Food, and Environmental Sciences, Department of Applied Economics. Available online at *http://agecon.lib.umn.edu/mn/p96-11.pdf*

Drèze, Jean. 1990. "Widows in Rural India." London School of Economics, Development Economics Research Programme DEP 26.

Drèze, Jean, and P.V. Srinivasan. 1998. "Widowhood and Poverty in Rural India: Some Inferences from Household Survey Data." In Martha A. Chen, ed., *Widows in India: Social Neglect and Public Action.* New Delhi: Sage Publications.

Due, Jean M., and Christina H. Gladwin. 1991. "Impacts of Structural Adjustment Programs on African Women Farmers and Female-headed Households." *American Journal of Agricultural Economics* 73 (5): 1431–39.

Duncan, Greg J., and Saul D. Hoffman. 1985. "A Reconsideration of the Economic Consequences of Marital Dissolution." *Demography* 22 (4): 485–98.

Duncan, Otis Dudley, and Beverly Duncan. 1955. "A Methodological Analysis of Segregation Indices." *American Sociological Review* 20(2):210-217.

Dyson, Tim, and Mick Moore. 1983. "On Kinship Structure, Female Autonomy and Demographic Behavior in India." *Population and Development Review* 9 (March): 35–60.

Easterly, William. 1999. "Life during Growth: International Evidence on Quality of Life and Per Capita Income." Policy Research Working Paper 2110. World Bank, Development Research Group, Washington, D.C. Available online at *http://wbln0018.worldbank.org/research/workpapers.nsf/policyresearch?openform*

Eckel, Catherine, and Philip Grossman. 1996. "The Relative Price of Fairness: Gender Differences in a Punishment Game." *Journal of Economic Behavior and Organization* 30 (2): 143–58.

_____. 1998. "Are Women Less Selfish Than Men? Evidence from Dictator Games." *The Economic Journal* 108: 726–35.

Edin, Per-Anders, and Katarina Richardson. 1999. "Swimming with the Tide: Solidarity Wage Policy and the Gender Earnings Gap." Working Paper. Uppsala Univesity, Department of Economics, Sweden.

Ehrenreich, Barbara. 1999. "Men Hate War Too." *Foreign Affairs* 78 (1): 118–22.

Elson, Diane. 1992. "Male Bias in Structural Adjustment." In H. Afshar and C. Dennis, eds., *Women and Adjustment Policies in the Third World.* New York: St. Martin's Press.

England, Paula. 1999. "The Case for Comparable Worth." *Quarterly Review of Economics and Finance* 39 (5): 743–55.

Estudillo, Jonna P., Agnes R. Quisumbing, and Keijiro Otsuka. 1999. "Gender Differences in Schooling and Land Inheritance in the Philippines." International Food Policy Research Institute, Washington, D.C.

Esteve-Volart, Berta. 2000. "Sex Discrimination and Growth." IMF Working Paper WP/00/84. International Monetary Fund, African Department, Washington, D.C. Available online at *http://www.imf.org/external/pubs/cat/longres.cfm?sk&sk=3559.0*

Esu-Williams, Eka. 1995. "Sexually Transmitted Diseases and Condom Interventions among Prostitutes and Their Clients in Cross River State." *Health Transition Review* 5 (Supplement): 223–28.

Fafchamps, Marcel. 2000. "Ethnicity and Credit in African Manufacturing." *Journal of Development Economics* 61 (1): 205–35.

Fairlamb, Cheryl D., and Wilhelmus L. Nieuwoudt. 1991. "Economic Factors Affecting Human Fertility in the Developing Areas of Southern Africa." *Agricultural Economics* 6 (2): 185–200.

Fajnzylber, Pablo. 2000. "A Note on Gender and Labor Demand in Colombia and Chile." Universidade Federal de Minas Gerais, Belo Horizonte, Brazil.

Fan, Wei, Marc Melitz, and Claudia Sever. 1996. "Firm Heterogeneity across Worker Gender and Skill Level: Evidence from Trade Liberalization in Chile." University of Michigan, Department of Economics, Ann Arbor.

Ferguson, Brian. 1999. "Perilous Positions." *Foreign Affairs* 78 (1): 125–27.

Fields, Judith, and Edward N. Wolff. 1997. "Gender Wage Differentials, Affirmative Action, and Employment Growth on the Industry Level." Working Paper 186. Bard College, Jerome Levy Economic Institute, Annandale-on-Hudson, N.Y.

Filmer, Deon. 1999. "The Structure of Social Disparities in Education: Gender and Wealth." Background paper for *Engendering Development.* World Bank, Washington, D.C. Available online at *http://www.worldbank.org/gender/prr/filmer.pdf*

Filmer, Deon, Elizabeth M. King, and Lant Pritchett. 1998. "Gender Disparity in South Asia: Comparisons between and within Countries." Policy Research Working Paper 1867. World Bank, Development Research Group, Washington, D.C. Available online at *http://wbln0018.worldbank.org/research/workpapers.nsf/policyresearch?openform*

Floro, Maria Sagrario. 1995. "Women's Well-Being, Poverty, and Work Intensity." *Feminist Economics* 1 (3): 1–25.

Folbre, Nancy. 1986. "Hearts and Spades: Paradigms of Household Economics." *World Development* 14 (2, special issue): 245–55.

_____. 1998. "The Neglect of Care-Giving." *Challenge* 41 (5): 45–58.

Fong, Monica, and Michael Lokshin. 2000. "Child Care and Women's Labor Force Participation in Romania." Policy Research Working Paper 2400. World Bank, Development Research Group, Washington, D.C. Available online at *http://wbln0018.worldbank.org/research/workpapers.nsf/policyresearch?openform*

Fong, Monica S., Wendy Wakeman, and Anjana Bhushan. 1996. "Toolkit on Gender in Water and Sanitation." Gender Toolkit Series 2. World Bank, Poverty and Social Policy Department, Washington, D.C.

Forsythe, Nancy, Roberto Patricio Korzeniewicz, and Valerie Durrant. 2000. "Gender Inequalities and Economic Growth." *Economic Development and Cultural Change* 48 (3): 573–618.

Fortin, Bernard, and Guy Lacroix. 1997. "A Test of the Unitary and Collective Models of Household Labor Supply." *The Economic Journal* 107: 933–55.

Foster, Andrew D., and Mark R. Rosenzweig. 1995. "Information, Learning, and Wage Rates in Low-Income Rural Areas." In T. Paul Schultz, ed., *Investment in Women's Human Capital*. Chicago and London: University of Chicago Press.

_____. 1996. "Technical Change and Human-Capital Returns and Investments: Evidence from the Green Revolution." *American Economic Review* 86 (4): 931-53.

_____. 1999. "Missing Women, the Marriage Market and Economic Growth." Brown University, Providence, R.I., and University of Pennsylvania, Phildelphia.

Frankenberg, Elizabeth, Duncan Thomas, and Kathleen Beegle. 1999. "The Real Costs of Indonesia's Economic Crisis: Preliminary Findings from the Indonesia Family Life Surveys." Labor and Population Program Working Paper 99-04. RAND, Santa Monica, Calif.

Fuess, Scott M., Jr., and Bun Song Lee. 1994. "Government Reforms, Economic Restructuring and the Employment of Women: South Korea, 1980–92." In Nahid Aslanbeigui, Steven Pressman, and Gale Summerfield, eds., *Women in the Age of Economic Transformation: Gender Impact of Reforms in Post-socialist and Developing Countries.*. London and New York: Routledge.

Fukuyama, Francis. 1995. *Trust.* New York: Free Press.

_____. 1998. "Women and the Evolution of World Politics." *Foreign Affairs* 77 (5): 24–40.

Gage, Anastasia J., A. Elisabeth Sommerfelt, and Andrea L. Piani. 1997. "Household Structure and Childhood Immunization in Niger and Nigeria." *Demography* 34 (2): 295–309.

Gannicott, Kenneth. 1986. "Women, Wages and Discrimination: Some Evidence from Taiwan." *Economic Development and Cultural Change* 34: 721–30.

Garg, Ashish, and Jonathan Morduch. 1996. "Sibling Rivalry, Resource Constraints, and the Health of Children." Harvard Institute of Economic Research Discussion Paper 1779. Harvard University, Cambridge, Massachusetts.

_____. 1998. "Sibling Rivalry and the Gender Gap: Evidence from Child Health Outcomes in Ghana." *Journal of Population Economics* 11 (4): 471–93.

Gatti, Roberta. 1999. "A Cross-country Analysis of Fertility Determinants." World Bank, Development Research Group, Washington, D.C.

Gavrilova, Natalia S., Victoria G. Semyonova, Galina N. Evdokushkina, and Leonid A. Gavrilov. 1999. "The Response of Violent Mortality to Economic Crisis in Russia." Paper presented at the Population Association of America 1999 Annual Meeting, 25–27 March, New York.

Geddes, Rick, and Dean Lueck. 1999. "The Gains from Self-Ownership and the Expansion of Women's Rights." Fordham University, Department of Economics, Bronx, New York and Montana Sate University, Department of Agricultural Economics, Bozeman, Montana.

Gertler, Paul, and Paul Glewwe. 1992. "The Willingness to Pay for Education for Daughters in Contrast to Sons: Evidence from Rural Peru." *The World Bank Economic Review* 6 (1): 171–88.

Gertler, Paul J., and John W. Molyneaux. 1994. "How Economic Development and Family Planning Programs Combined to Reduce Indonesian Fertility." *Demography* 31 (1): 33–63.

Gertler, Paul J., and John L. Newman. 1991. "Family Labour Supply Decisions in Rural Peru." In Marc Nerlove, ed., *Issues in Contemporary Economics: Proceedings of the Ninth World Congress of the International Economic Association.* New York: New York University Press.

Gindling, Tim H., and Maria Crummett. 1997. "Maternity Leave Legislation and the Work and Pay of Women in Costa Rica." University of Baltimore County, Department of Economics, Maryland.

Gladwin, Christina H., ed. 1991. *Structural Adjustment and African Women Farmers.* Gainesville: University of Florida Press.

Glewwe, Paul. 2000. "The Household Roster." In Margaret Grosh and Paul Glewwe, eds., *Designing Household Survey Questionnaires for Developing Countries: Lessons from Fifteen Years of the Living Standards Measurement Study.* Oxford and New York: Oxford University Press.

Glewwe, Paul, Hanan G. Jacoby, and Elizabeth M. King. Forthcoming. "Early Childhood Nutrition and Academic Achievement: A Longitudinal Analysis." *Journal of Public Economics.*

Glick, Peter, and David E. Sahn. 1997. "Gender and Education Impacts on Employment and Earnings in West Africa: Evidence from Guinea." *Economic Development and Cultural Change* 45: 793–823.

Glinskaya, Elena, and Thomas A. Mroz. 1996. "The Gender Gap in Wages in Russia from 1992 to 1995." University of North Carolina at Chapel Hill, Carolina Population Center.

Goetz, Anne Marie. 1998. "Women in Politics & Gender Equity in Policy: South Africa & Uganda." *Review of African Political Economy* 25 (76): 241–62.

_____. 1999. "Auditing Local Development Expenditure from a Gendered Perspective: Nascent Initiative in India." Paper prepared for the United Nations Development Programme–

United Nations Development Fund for Women Workshop on Pro-Poor, Gender- and Environment-Sensitive Budgets, New York, June 28–30. Institute of Development Studies, U.K.

Goetz, Anne Marie, and Rina Sen Gupta. 1996. "Who Takes the Credit? Gender, Power and Control over Loan Use in Rural Credit Programs in Bangladesh." *World Development* 24 (1): 45–63.

Goldblatt, Beth and Sheila Meintjes. 1998. "South African Women Demand the Truth." In Margaret Turshen, and Clotilde Twagiramariya, eds., *What Women Do in Wartime. Gender and Conflict in Africa.* London and New York: Zed Books.

Goldin, Claudia. 1988. "Maximum Hours Legislation and Female Employment: A Reassessment." *Journal of Political Economy* 96 (11): 189–205.

_____. 1990. *Understanding the Gender Gap.* New York: Oxford University Press.

Goldstein, Anne. 1999. "Thinking outside Pandora's Box." Background paper for *Engendering Development.* World Bank, Washington, D.C.

Goldstein, Markus. 1999. "Chop Time, No Friends: Intrahousehold and Individual Insurance Mechanisms in Southern Ghana." University of California at Berkeley, Department of Agricultural and Resource Economics, and Yale University, Economic Growth Center, New Haven, Conn.

Gopal, Gita, and Maryam Salim, eds. 1998. *Gender and Law: Eastern Africa Speaks.* Proceedings of a World Bank–Economic Commission for Africa conference. Washington, D.C.: World Bank.

Graham, Carol. 1996. "Gender Issues in Poverty Alleviation: Recent Experience with Demand-Based Programs in Latin America, Africa, and Eastern Europe." Issues in Development Discussion Paper 11. International Labour Organization, Geneva.

Granovetter, Mark. 1985. "Economic Action and Social Structure: The Problem of Embeddedness." *American Journal of Sociology* 91 (3): 481–510.

Gray, Leslie, and Michael Kevane. 1996. "Land Tenure Status of African Women." Background paper to the Project on Gender and Property Rights in Africa. World Bank, Washington, D.C.

Greenhalgh, Susan. 1985. "Sexual Stratification: The Other Side of Growth with Equity in East Asia." *Population and Development Review* 11 (2): 265–314.

Grootaert, Christian, and Harry Patrinos. 1999. *Policy Analysis of Child Labor: A Comparative Study.* New York: St. Martin's Press.

Grosh, Margaret E. 1994. *Administering Targeted Social Programs in Latin America: From Platitudes to Practice.* Washington, D.C.: World Bank.

Gruber, Jonathan. 1994. "The Incidence of Mandated Maternity Benefits." *American Economic Review* 84 (3): 622–41.

Gruber, Jonathan, and David A. Wise. 1998. "Social Security and Retirement: An International Comparison." *American Economic Review, Papers and Proceedings* 88:158–63.

Gunderson, Morley. 1975. "Male-Female Wage Differentials and the Impact of Equal Pay Legislation." *Restat* 57 (4): 462–69.

_____. 1998. *Women and the Canadian Labour Market: Transition Towards the Future.* Statistics Canada, Census Monograph Series, Catalogue Number 96-321-MPE No.2.

Gupta, Navanita Datta, Ronald L. Oaxaca, and Nina Smith. 1998. "Wage Dispersion, Public Sector and the Stagnating Danish Gender Wage Gap." Working Paper 98-18. University of Aarhus and Aarhus School of Business, Centre for Labour Market and Social Research, Denmark.

Gustafsson, Siv. 1981. "Male-Female Life Time Earnings Differentials and Labor Force History." In Gunnar Eliasson, Bertil Homlund, and Frank Stafford, eds., *Studies in Labor Market Behavior: Conference Report.* Stockholm: Industrial Institute for Economic and Social Research.

Gustafsson, Siv, and Frank Stafford. 1992. "Daycare Subsidies and Labor Supply in Sweden." *Journal of Human Resources* 27(2): 204–230.

Gutierrez, Leah C. 1998. "Infants' Illness and Mothers' Time Allocations." Syracuse University, Center for Policy Research, Syracuse, N.Y.

Gyimah-Brempong, Kwabena, Rudy Fichtenbaum, and Gregory Willis. 1992. "The Effects of College Education on the Male-Female Wage Differential." *Southern Economic Journal* 58: 790–804.

Haddad, Lawrence, and John Hoddinott. 1994. "Women's Income and Boy-Girl Anthropometric Status in Côte d'Ivoire." *World Development* 22 (4): 543–53.

Haddad, Lawrence, Lynn R. Brown, Andrea Richter, and Lisa Smith. 1995. "The Gender Dimension of Economic Adjustment Policies: Potential Interactions and Evidence to Date." *World Development* 23 (6): 881–96.

Haddad, Lawrence, Christine Pena, Chizuru Nishida, Agnes Quisumbing, and Alison Slack. 1996. "Food Security and Nutrition Implications of Intrahousehold Bias: A Review of Literature." Food Consumption and Nutrition Division Discussion Paper 19. International Food Policy Research Institute, Washington, D.C. Available online at *http://www.ifpri.cgiar.org/index1.htm*

Hammel, E.A., and Peter Laslett. 1974. "Comparing Household Structure over Time and between Cultures." *Comparative Studies in Society and History* 30: 95–115.

Handa, Sudhanshu. 2000. "The Impact of Education, Income, and Mortality on Fertility in Jamaica." *World Development* 28 (1): 173–86.

Hare, Denise. 1999. "Women's Economic Status in Rural China: Household Contributions to Male-Female Disparities in the Wage-Labor Market." *World Development* 27 (6): 1011–29.

Hashemi, Syed M., Sidney R. Schuler, and Ann P. Riley. 1996. "Rural Credit Programs and Women's Empowerment in Bangladesh." *World Development* 24 (4): 635–53.

Heide, Ingeborg. 1999. "Supranational Action Against Sex Discrimination: Equal Pay and Equal Treatment in the European Union." *International Labour Review* 138 (4): 381–410.

Heise, Lori, Mary Ellsberg, and Megan Gottemoeller. 1999. "Ending Violence against Women." *Population Reports* L (11). Johns Hopkins University, School of Public Health, Population Information Program, Baltimore, Md.

Available online at *http://www.jhuccp.org/pr/ l11edsum.stm*

Heise, Lori L., Jacqueline Pitanguy, and Adrienne Germain. 1994. *Violence against Women: The Hidden Health Burden.* World Bank Discussion Paper 255. Washington, D.C.

Hellerstein, Judith K., David Neumark, and Kenneth R. Troske. 1997. "Market Forces and Sex Discrimination." NBER Working Paper 6321. National Bureau for Economic Research, Cambridge, Mass. Available online at *http:// papers.nber.org/papers/w6321*

Hellum, Anne. 1998. "Women's Human Rights and African Customary Laws: Between Universalism and Relativism—Individuallism and Communitarianism." *European Journal of Development Research (U.K.)* 10 (2): 88–104.

Hill, M. Anne, and Elizabeth M. King. 1995. "Women's Education and Economic Well-being." *Feminist Economics* 1 (2): 1–26.

Hoddinott, John, and Christopher Adam. 1998. "Testing Nash Bargaining Household Models with Time Series Data: Divorce Law Reform and Female Suicide in Canada." Food Consumption and Nutrition Division Discussion Paper 52. International Food Policy Research Institute, Washington, D.C.

Hoddinott, John, and Lawrence Haddad. 1995. "Does Female Income Share Influence Household Expenditures? Evidence from Côte d'Ivoire." *Oxford Bulletin of Economics and Statistics* 57 (1): 77–96.

Hoddinott, John, and Bill Kinsey. 2000. "Adult Health at the Time of Drought." Food Consumption and Nutrition Division Discussion

Paper 79. International Food Policy Research Institute, Washington, D.C. Available online at *http://www.ifpri.cgiar.org/index1.htm*

Hoddinott, John, Harold Alderman, and Lawrence Haddad. 1997. "Testing Competing Models of Intrahousehold Allocation." In Lawrence Haddad, John Hoddinott, and Harold Alderman, eds., *Intrahousehold Resource Allocation in Developing Countries: Models, Methods, and Policy.* Baltimore, Md.: The Johns Hopkins University Press.

Holt, Sharon L., and Helena Ribe. 1991. *Developing Financial Institutions for the Poor and Reducing Barriers to Access for Women.* World Bank Discussion Paper 117. Washington, D.C.

Holzer, Harry J., and David Neumark. 1998. "What Does Affirmative Action Do?" NBER Working Paper 6605. National Bureau of Economic Research, Cambridge, Mass. Available online at *http://papers.nber.org/papers/w6605*

———. 1999. "Are Affirmative Action Hires Less Qualified? Evidence From Employer-Employee Data on New Hires." *Journal of Labor Economics* 17 (3): 535–69.

Honig, Benson. 1998. "Women in the Informal Sector of the Economy." In Nelly P. Stromquist, ed., *Women in the Third World. An Encyclopedia of Contemporary Issues.* New York: Garland Publishing, Inc.

Honig, Emily. 1985. "Socialist Revolution and Women's Liberation in China—A Review Article." *Journal of Asian Studies* 44: 328–36.

Hooper, Beverley. 1984. "China's Modernization. Are Young Women Going to Lose Out?" *Modern China* 10 (3): 317–343.

Horton, Susan. 1996. *Women and Industrialization in Asia.* London and New York: Routledge.

Horton, Susan, and Dipak Mazumdar. 1999. "Vulnerable Groups and the Labour Market: The Aftermath of the Asian Financial Crisis." Paper prepared for a World Bank–International Labour Organization–Japan Ministry of Labor–Japan Institute of Labor seminar on Economic Crisis, Employment and Labour Markets in East and South-East Asia, October, Tokyo.

Horton, Susan, Ravi Kanbur, and Dipak Mazumdar, eds. 1994. *Labor Markets in an Era of Adjustment.* Washington, D.C.: World Bank.

Humana, Charles. 1986. *World Human Rights Guide.* 2nd ed. London: Hodder and Stoughton.

_____. 1992. *World Human Rights Guide.* 3rd ed. New York: Oxford University Press.

ICRG (International Country Risk Guide). 1999. Syracuse, NY: Political Risk Services, Institutional Reform and Informational Sector.

Ilahi, Nadeem. 1999a. "Children's Work and Schooling: Does Gender Matter? Evidence from the Peru LSMS Panel Data." World Bank, Latin American and Caribbean Region, Poverty Reduction and Economic Management Unit, Washington, D.C.

_____. 1999b. "Gender and the Allocation of Adult Time: Evidence from the Peru LSMS Panel Data." Background paper for *Engendering Development.* World Bank, Washington, D.C.

_____. 2000. "Gender and the Allocation of Time and Tasks: What Have We Learnt from the Empirical Literature?" Background paper for *Engendering Development.* World Bank, Wash-ington, D.C. Available online at *http://www.worldbank.org/gender/prr/wp13.pdf*

Ilahi, Nadeem, and Franque Grimard. Forthcoming. "Public Infrastructure and Private Costs: Water Supply and Time Allocation of Women in Rural Pakistan." *Economic Development and Cultural Change.*

Ilahi, Nadeem, and Saqib Jafarey. 1999. "Guestworker Migration, Remittances, and the Extended Family: Evidence from Pakistan." *Journal of Development Economics* 58: 485–512.

ILO (International Labour Organization). 1997. "Breaking through the Glass Ceiling: Women in Management." Report prepared for discussion at the Tripartite Meeting on Breaking through the Glass Ceiling: Women in Management. Sectoral Activities Programme, Geneva.

_____. 2000. *Yearbook of Labour Statistics.* Geneva: International Labour Organization Bureau of Statistics.

Inglehart, Ronald. 1997. "Changing Gender Gaps." Paper presented at conference on *Representation and European Citizenship*, Rome, November. Institute for Social Research, University of Michigan.

Inglehart, Ronald, Miguel Basañez and Alejandro Moreno. 1998. *Human Values and Beliefs: A Cross-Cultural Sourcebook: Political, Religious, Sexual and Economic Norms in 43 Societies: Findings from the 1990-1993 World Values Survey.* Ann Arbor, MI: The University of Michigan Press.

Inglehart, Ronald, and others. 2000. "World Values Surveys and European Values Surveys, 1981–

1984, 1990–1993, and 1995–1997." Database. ICPSR version. Ann Arbor, Mich.: Inter-University Consortium for Political and Social Research.

Inoue, Shunichi. 1998. "Family Formation in Japan, South Korea, and the United States: An Overview." In Karen O. Mason, Noriko O. Tsuya, and Minja Kim Choe, eds., *The Changing Family in Comparative Perspective: Asia and the United States.* Honolulu, Hawaii: East-West Center.

IPU (Inter-Parliamentary Union). 2000. *Politics: Women's Insight.* Geneva.

Isham, Jonathan, Deepa Narayan, and Lant Pritchett. 1995. "Does Participation Improve Performance? Establishing Causality with Subjective Data." *The World Bank Economic Review* 9 (2): 175–200.

Jacobs, Susie. 1998. "Past Wrongs and Gender Rights: Issues and Conflicts in South Africa's Land Reform." *Journal of Development Research* 10 (2): 70–87.

Jacobsen, Joyce P., James Wishart Pearce III, and Joshua L Rosenbloom. 1999. "The Effects of Childbearing on Married Women's Labor Supply and Earnings: Using Twin Births as A Natural Experiment." *Journal of Human Resources* 34 (3): 449–74.

Jalan, Jyotsna, and Martin Ravallion. 1999. "Income Gains to the Poor from Workfare: Estimates for Argentina's Trabajar Program." Policy Research Working Paper 2149. World Bank, Development Research Group, Washington, D.C. Available online at *http://wbln0018.worldbank.org/research/workpapers.nsf/policyresearch?openform*

James, Estelle. 1999. "Gender, Old Age and Social Security: The Case of Mexico." Background paper for *Engendering Development.* World Bank, Washington, D.C.

Jayarajah, Carl, William Branson, and Binayak Sen. 1996. *Social Dimensions of Adjustment: World Bank Experience, 1980–93.* Washington, D.C.: World Bank.

Jejeebhoy, Shireen J. 1995. *Women's Education, Autonomy, and Reproductive Behavior: Experience from Developing Countries.* New York: Oxford University Press.

Johnson, Simon, Daniel Kaufmann, and Pablo Zoido-Lobaton. 1998. "Regulatory Discretion and the Unofficial Economy." *American Economic Review* 88(2): 387–392.

Jones, Christine. 1983. "The Mobilization of Women's Labor for Cash Crop Production: A Game Theoretic Approach." *American Journal of Agricultural Economics* 65 (5): 1049–54.

_____. 1986. "Intrahousehold Bargaining in Response to the Introduction of New Crops: A Case Study from Northern Cameroon." In Joyce Lewinger Moock, ed., *Understanding Africa's Rural Households and Farming Systems.* Boulder, Colo. and London: Westview Press.

Jones, Mark P. 1996. "Increasing Women's Representative via Gender Quotas: The Argentine Ley de Cupos." *Women and Politics* 16 (4): 75–96.

Juster, F. Thomas, and Frank P. Stafford. 1991. "The Allocation of Time: Empirical Findings, Behavioral Models, and Problems of Measurement." *Journal of Economic Literature* 29 (June): 471–522.

Kabeer, Naila. 1998. "'Money Can't Buy Me Love'? Re-evaluating Gender, Credit and Empowerment in Rural Bangladesh." IDS Discussion Paper 363. University of Sussex, Institute of Development Studies, Brighton.

_____. 2000. *The Power to Choose: Bangladeshi Women and Labour Market Decisions in London and Dhaka.* London and New York: Verso.

Kao, Charng, Solomon W. Polachek, and Phanindra V. Wunnava. 1994. "Male-Female Wage Differentials in Taiwan: A Human Capital Approach." *Economic Development and Cultural Change* 42 (2): 351–74.

Kapadia, Karin. 1999. "The Politics of Difference and the Formation of Rural Industrial Labour in South India Today." In Jonathan Parry, Jan Breman, and Karin Kapadia, eds., *The Worlds of Indian Industrial Labour.* New Delhi: Sage Publications.

Katz, Katarina. 1997. "Gender, Wages and Discrimination in the USSR: A Study of a Russian Industrial Town." *Cambridge Journal of Economics* 21: 431–52.

Kaufmann, Daniel. 1998. "Challenges in the Next Stage of Anti-corruption." In *New Perspectives on Combating Corruption.* Washington, D.C.: Transparency International and World Bank.

Kevane, Michael. Forthcoming. "Extra-household Norms and Intra-household Bargaining: Gender in Sudan and Burkina Faso." In Anita Spring, ed., *Women Farmers and Commercial Ventures: Increasing Food Security in Developing Countries.* Boulder, Colorado: Lynne Rienner Publishers. Available online at *http://www-acc.scu.edu/~mkevane/*

Kevane, Michael, and Leslie Gray. 1996. "'A Woman's Field is Made at Night': Gendered Land Rights in and Norms in Burkina Faso." Santa Clara University, Department of Economics, Santa Clara, CA.

_____. 1999. "'A Woman's Field Is Made at Night': Gendered Land Rights in and Norms in Burkina Faso." *Feminist Economics* 5 (3): 1-26. Available online at *http://www-acc.scu.edu/~mkevane/*

Khandker, Shahidur R. 1988. "Determinants of Women's Time Allocation in Rural Bangladesh." *Economic Development and Cultural Change* 37: 111–26.

_____. 1996. *Education Achievements and School Efficiency in Rural Bangladesh.* World Bank Discussion Paper 319. Washington, D.C.

_____. 1998. *Fighting Poverty with Microcredit: Experience in Bangladesh.* Washington, D.C.: World Bank.

Khandker, Shahidur R., Baqui Khalily, and Zahed Khan. 1995. *Grameen Bank: Performance and Sustainability.* World Bank Discussion Paper 306. Washington, D.C.

Khandker, Shahidur, Victor Lavy, and Deon Filmer. 1994. *Schooling and Cognitive Achievements of Children in Morocco: Can the Government Improve Outcomes?* World Bank Discussion Paper 264. Washington, D.C.

Kidd, Michael P., and Michael Shannon. 1996. "The Gender Wage Gap: A Comparison of Australia and Canada." *Canadian Journal of Economics* 29 (special issue, part 1): S121–25.

Kikuchi, Masao, and Yujiro Hayami. 1983. "New Rice Technology, Intrarural Migration, and Institutional Innovation in the Philippines."

Population and Development Review 9 (2): 247–57.

Killingsworth, Mark R. 1983. "Labour Supply." Cambridge: Cambridge University Press.

Kim, Jooseop, Harold Alderman, and Peter Orazem. 1998. "Can Cultural Barriers Be Overcome in Girls' Schooling? The Community Support Program in Rural Balochistan." Working Paper Series on Impact Evaluation of Education Reforms 10. World Bank, Development Research Group, Washington, D.C.

_____. 1999. "Can Private School Subsidies Increase Schooling for the Poor? The Quetta Urban Fellowship Program." *The World Bank Economic Review* 13 (3): 443–65.

King, Elizabeth M., and M. Anne Hill, eds. 1993. *Women's Education in Developing Countries*. Baltimore, Md.: The John Hopkins University Press.

King, Elizabeth M., and Lee A. Lillard. 1987. "Education Policy and Schooling Attainment in Malaysia and the Philippines." *Economics of Education Review* 6 (2): 167–81.

King, Elizabeth M., Peter F. Orazem, and Darin Wohlgemuth. 1999. "Central Mandates and Local Incentives: Colombia's Targeted Voucher Program." *World Bank Economic Review* 13 (3): 467–91.

Kingdon, Geeta G. 1998. "Does the Labour Market Explain Lower Female Schooling in India? *Journal of Development Studies* 35 (1): 39–65.

Kishor, Sunita. 1993. "'May God Give Sons to All'. Gender and Child Mortality in India." *American Sociological Review* 58: 247–65.

Klasen, Stephan. 1994. "'Missing Women' Reconsidered." *World Development* 22 (7): 1061–71.

_____. 1999a. "Does Gender Inequality Reduce Growth and Development? Evidence from Cross-country Regressions." Background paper for *Engendering Development*. World Bank, Washington, D.C. Available online at *http://www.worldbank.org/gender/prr/klasen.pdf*

_____. 1999b. "Malnourished and Surviving in South Asia, Better Nourished and Dying Young in Africa: What Can Explain This Puzzle?" Paper presented at the annual meeting of the European Society for Population Economics, University of Munich.

Knack, Stephen, and Philip Keefer. 1995. "Institutions and Economic Performance: Cross-country Tests Using Alternative Institutional Measures." *Economics and Politics* 7: 207–27.

Knight, J.B., and Richard H. Sabot. 1991. "Labor Market Discrimination in a Poor Urban Economy." In Nancy Birdsall and Richard Sabot, eds., *Unfair Advantage: Labor Market Discrimination in Developing Countries*. A World Bank Regional and Sectoral Study. Washington, D.C.

Knowles, Stephen, Paula K. Lorgelly and P. Dorian Owen. Forthcoming. "Are Educational Gender Gaps a Brake on Economic Development? Some Cross-country Empirical Evidence." *Oxford Economic Papers*.

Kooreman, Peter, and Arie Kapteyn. 1986. "On the Empirical Implementation of Some Game Theoretic Models of Household Labor Supply." *The Journal of Human Resources* 25 (4): 584–98.

Krueger, Alan B. 1993. "How Computers Have Changed the Wage Structure: Evidence from Microdata, 1984–1989." *Quarterly Journal of Economics* 108 (1): 33-60.

Krueger, Anne O. 1990. "Government Failures in Development." *Journal of Economic Perspectives* 4 (3): 9–23.

Kumar, Shubh K. 1994. "Adoption of Hybrid Maize in Zambia: Effects on Gender Roles, Food Consumption, and Nutrition." Research Report 100. International Food Policy Research Institute, Washington, D.C.

Kumar, Shubh K., and David Hotchkiss. 1988. "Consequences of Deforestation for Women's Time Allocation, Agricultural Production, and Nutrition in Hill Areas of Nepal." Research Report 69. International Food Policy Research Institute, Washington, D.C.

La Porta, Rafael, Florencio Lopez-de Silanes, Andrei Shleifer, and Robert W. Vishny. 1997. "Trust in Large Organizations." *American Economic Review* 87(2): 333–38.

Lampietti, Julian A., and Linda Stalker. 2000. "Consumption Expenditure and Female Poverty: A Review of the Evidence." Background paper for *Engendering Development*. World Bank, Washington, D.C. Available online at *http://www.worldbank.org/gender/prr/wp11.pdf*

Landes, Elisabeth M. 1980. "The Effect of State Maximum-Hours Laws on the Employment of Women in 1920." *Journal of Political Economy* 88 (3): 476–94.

Langford, Malcolm S. 1995. "The Gender Wage Gap in the 1990s." *Australian Economic Papers* 34: 62–85.

Lapidus, Gail W. 1992. "The Interaction of Women's Work and Family Roles in the Former USSR." In Hilda Kahne and Janet Z. Giele, eds., *Women's Work and Women's Lives.* Boulder, Colo.: Westview Press.

_____. 1993. "Gender and Restructuring: The Impact of Perestroika and Its Aftermath on Soviet Women." In Valentine M. Moghadam, ed., *Democratic Reform and the Position of Women in Transitional Economies.* Oxford: Clarendon Press.

Lastarria-Cornheil, Susana. 1997. "Impact of Privatization on Gender and Property Rights in Africa." *World Development* 25 (8): 1317–33.

Lavy, Victor. 1996. "School Supply Constraints and Children's Educational Outcomes in Rural Ghana." *Journal of Development Economics* 51 (2): 291–314.

Leonard, Jonathan. 1985. "Affirmative Action as Earnings Redistribution: The Targeting of Compliance Reviews." *Journal of Labor Economics* 3 (3): 363–84.

_____. 1990. "The Impact of Affirmative Action Regulation and Equal Employment Opportunity Law on Black Employment." *Journal of Economic Perspectives* 4 (4): 47–64.

_____. 1996. "Wage Disparities and Affirmative Action in the 1980s." *American Economic Review Papers and Proceedings* 86 (2): 285–301.

Levinsohn, James. 1999. "Employment Responses to International Liberalization in Chile." *Journal of International Economics* 47 (2): 321–44.

Li, Tianyou, and Junsen Zhang. 1998. "Returns to Education under Collective and Household Farming in China." *Journal of Development Economics* 56 (2): 307–35.

Lillard, Lee A., and Robert J. Willis. 1994. "Intergenerational Educational Mobility: Effects of Family and State in Malaysia." *Journal of Human Resources* 29 (4): 1126–66.

Lin, Vivian. 1985. "Women Factory Workers in Asian Export Processing Zones." In Ernst Utrecht, ed., *Transnational Corporations and Export-oriented Industrialization: Transnational Corporations in South-East Asia and the Pacific Series 7*. Sydney: University of Sydney, Transnational Corporations Research Project.

Lipton, Michael, and Martin Ravallion. 1995. "Poverty and Policy." In Jere Behrman and T.N. Srinivasan, eds., *Handbook of Development Economics* Vol. 3. Amsterdam, New York, and Oxford: Elsevier Science Publishers.

Liu, Pak-Wai, Xin Meng, and Junsen Zhang. Forthcoming. "The Impact of Economic Reform on Gender Wage Differentials and Discrimination in China." *Journal of Population Economics*.

Lloyd, Cynthia B., Barbara S. Mensch, and Wesley H. Clark. 1998. "The Effects of Primary School Quality on the Educational Participation and Attainment of Kenyan Girls and Boys." Working Paper 116. Population Council, New York.

Lokshin, Michael M. 2000. "Effects of Child Care Prices on Women's Labor Force Participation in Russia." Background paper for *Engendering Development*. World Bank, Washington, D.C. Available online at *http://www.worldbank.org/gender/prr/lokshin.pdf*

Lokshin, Michael M., Elena Glinskaya, and Marito Garcia. 2000. "Effect of Early Childhood Development Programs on Women's Labor Force Participation and Older Children's Schooling in Kenya." Background paper for *Engendering Development*. World Bank, Washington, D.C. Available online at *http://www.worldbank.org/gender/prr/wp15.pdf*

Lombard, Karen V. 1999. "Women's Rising Market Opportunities and Increased Labor Force Participation." *Economic Inquiry* 37 (2): 195–212.

Long, Lynellyn D., Le Ngoc Hung, Allison Truitt, Le Thi Phuong Mai, and Dang Nguyen Anh. 2000. "Changing Gender Relations in Vietnam's Post *Doi Moi* Era." Background paper for *Engendering Development*. World Bank, Washington D.C. Available online at *http://www.worldbank.org/gender/prr/wp14.pdf*

Lorgelly, Paula K., and P. Dorian Owen. 1999. "The Effect of Female and Male Schooling on Economic Growth in the Barro-Lee Model." *Empirical Economics* 24 (3): 537–57.

Lundberg, Shelly. 1988. "Labor Supply of Husbands and Wives: A Simultaneous Equations Approach." *Review of Economics and Statistics* 70 (2): 224–35.

Lundberg, Shelley, Robert A. Pollak, and Terence J. Wales. 1997. "Do Husbands and Wives Pool Their Resources? Evidence from the United Kingdom Child Benefit." *Journal of Human Resources* 32 (3): 463–80.

Makepeace, Gerald, Pierella Paci, Heather Joshi, and Peter Dolton. 1999. "How Unequally Has Equal Pay Progressed since the 1970s? A Study of Two British Cohorts." *Journal of Human Resources* 34: 534–56.

Malhotra, Anju, Reeve Vanneman, and Sunita Kishor. 1995. "Fertility, Dimensions of Patriarchy, and

Development in India." *Population and Development Review* 21 (2): 281–305.

Malmberg Calvo, Christina. 1994. "Case Study on the Role of Women in Rural Transport: Access of Women to Domestic Facilities." Sub-Saharan Africa Transport Policy Program Working Paper 11. World Bank and Economic Commission for Africa, Washington, D.C.

Manning, Chris. 1998. *Indonesia's Labour in Transition: An East Asian Success Story?* Cambridge, New York, and Melbourne: Cambridge University Press.

Marcoux, Alain. 1998. "The Feminization of Poverty: Claims, Facts, and Data Needs." *Population and Development Review* 24 (1): 131–39.

Martin, Doris M., and Fatuma Omar Hashi. 1992. "Women in Development: The Legal Issues in Sub-Saharan Africa Today." Working Paper 4. World Bank, Women in Development Unit, Washington, D.C.

Mason, Andrew D., and Shahidur R. Khandker. 1996. "Measuring the Opportunity Cost of Children's Time in a Developing Country: Implications for Education Sector Analysis and Interventions." Human Capital Development Working Paper 72. World Bank, Washington, D.C.

Mason, Karen O., Herbert L. Smith, and S. Philip Morgan. 1998. "Muslim Women in the Non-Islamic Countries of Asia: Do They Have Less Autonomy Than Their Non-Muslim Neighbors?" Paper presented at the annual meeting of the American Sociological Association, 21–25 August, San Francisco.

Matin, Nilufar, Hameeda Hossain, Sara Hossain, Tania Sultana, Nusrat Jahan, and Lubia

Begum. 2000. "Gender Violence and the Legal System: A Bangladesh Study." Background paper for *Engendering Development*. World Bank, Washington, D.C.

Maurer-Fazio, Margaret, and James Hughes. 1999. "The Effect of Institutional Change on the Relative Earnings of Chinese Women: Traditional Values vs. Market Forces." Bates College, Department of Economics, Lewiston, Maine.

Mauro, Paolo. 1995. "Corruption and Growth." *Quarterly Journal of Economics* 110: 681–712.

Mazumdar, Dipak. 1994. "Labor Markets in an Era of Adjustment: Malaysia." In Susan Horton, Ravi Kanbur, and Dipak Mazumdar, eds., *Labor Markets in an Era of Adjustment*. Washington, D.C.: World Bank.

McDonald, Peter. 1992. "Convergence or Compromise in Historical Family Change?" In Elza Berquo and Peter Xenos, eds., *Family Systems and Cultural Change*. Oxford: Clarendon Press.

Mencarini, Letizia. 1999. "An Analysis of Fertility and Infant Mortality in South Africa Based on 1993 LSDS Data." Paper presented at the Third African Population Conference, "African Population in the 21st Century," 6–10 December, Durban, South Africa. Available online at *http://www.ds.unifi.it/ricerche/poverty/conferences/mencarin/mencarin.htm*

Meng, Xin. 1992. "Individual Wage Determination in Township, Village and Private Enterprises in China." Ph.D. diss. Australian National University, Department of Economics, Canberra.

———. 1993. "The Economic Position of Women in Asia." *Asian-Pacific Economic Literature* 10: 23–41.

Meng, Xin, and Michael P. Kidd. 1997. "Labor Market Reform and the Changing Structure of Wage Determination in China's State Sector during the 1980s." *Journal of Comparative Economics* 25 (3): 403–21.

Meng, Xin, and Paul Miller. 1995. "Occupational Segregation and Its Impact on Gender Wage Description in China's Rural Industrial Sector." *Oxford Economic Papers* 47: 136–55.

Menon, Nidhiya. 1999. "Micro Credit, Consumption Smoothing and Impact on Repayment Behavior: An Euler Equation Approach." Brown University, Department of Economics, Providence, R.I.

Mensch, Barbara S., and Cynthia B. Lloyd. 1998. "Gender Differences in the Schooling Experiences of Adolescents in Low-income Countries: The Case of Kenya." *Studies in Family Planning* 29 (2): 167–84.

Migot-Adholla, Shem, Peter Hazell, Benoit Blarel, and Frank Place. 1991. "Indigenous Land Rights Systems in Sub-Saharan Africa: A Constraint on Productivity?" *The World Bank Economic Review* 5: 155–75.

Miller, Paul W. 1994. "Occupation Segregation and Wages in Australia." *Economics Letters* 45: 367–71.

Miller, Paul, and Sarah Rummery. 1991. "Male-Female Wage Differentials in Australia: A Reassessment." *Australian Economic Papers* 30: 50–69.

Mohiuddin, Yasmeen. 1996. "Country Rankings by the Status of Women Index." Paper presented at the 1996 conference of the International Association for Feminist Economists. The 1996 Conference of the International Association for Feminist Economics, American University, Washington, D.C., June 21–23. The University of the South, Sewanee, Tennessee. Available online at *http://coral.bucknell.edu/~jshackel/iaffe/*

Montenegro, Claudio. 1999. "Wage Distribution in Chile: Does Gender Matter? A Quantile Regression Approach." World Bank, Poverty Reduction and Economic Management Network, Washington, D.C. Available online at *http://www.itam.mx/lames/papers/contrses/monteneg.pdf*

Moock, Peter R. 1976. "The Efficiency of Women as Farm Managers: Kenya." *American Journal of Agricultural Economics* 58 (5): 831–35.

Moon, H., H. Lee, and G. Yoo. 1999. "Social Impact of the Financial Crisis in Korea." Asian Development Bank, Manila.

Morduch, Jonathan. 1999a. "Between the State and the Market: Can Informal Insurance Patch the Safety Net?" *The World Bank Research Observer* 14 (2):187–207.

_____. 1999b. "The Microfinance Promise." *Journal of Economic Literature* 37: 1569–1614.

Morrison, Andrew R., and María Beatríz Orlando. 1999. "Social and Economic Costs of Domestic Violence: Chile and Nicaragua." In Andrew Morrison and Loreto Biehl, eds. *Too Close to Home: Domestic Violence in the Americas.* Washington, D.C.: Inter-American Development Bank and Johns Hopkins Press.

Moser, Carolyn O. 1989. "Impact of Recession and Structural Adjustment on Women." *Society for International Development* 1: 75–83.

Mueser, Peter. 1987. "Discrimination." In John Eatwell, Murray Milgate, and Peter Newman, eds., *The New Palgrave: A Dictionary of Economics*. London and Basingstoke: Macmillan.

Muntemba, Shimwaayi. 1999. "Ghana: Financial Services for Women Entrepreneurs in the Informal Sector." Economic Management and Social Policy Findings 136. World Bank, Washington, D.C.

Murray, Christopher J.L., and Allan D. Lopez. 1996. *The Global Burden of Disease*. Cambridge, Mass.: Harvard University Press for the World Health Organization and the World Bank.

Murthi, Mamta, Anne-Catherine Guio, and Jean Drèze. 1996. "Mortality, Fertility, and Gender Bias in India: A District-Level Analysis." *Population and Development Review* 21: 745–82.

Nanda, Priya. 1999. "Women's Participation in Rural Credit Programmes in Bangladesh and Their Demand for Formal Health Care: Is There a Positive Impact?" *Health Economics and Econometrics* 8: 415–28.

Narayan, Deepa. 1995. "The Contribution of People's Participation: Evidence from 121 Rural Water Supply Projects." Environmentally Sustainable Development Occasional Paper 1. World Bank, Washington, D.C.

Narayan, Deepa, with Raj Patel, Kai Schafft, Anne Rademacher, and Sarah Koch-Shulte. 2000. *Voices of the Poor: Can Anyone Hear Us?* Oxford: Oxford University Press.

Nataraj, Sita, Yana van der Meulen Rodgers, and Joseph Zveglich, Jr. 1998. "Protecting Female Workers in Industrializing Countries." *International Review of Comparative Public Policy* 10: 197–221.

NCRFW (National Commission on the Role of Filipino Women). 1999. *Toward a Gender-Responsive Legislation*. Manila.

Neumark, David. 1988. "Employers' Discriminatory Behavior and the Estimation of Wage Discrimination." *Journal of Human Resources* 23 (3): 279–95.

Newman, Constance. 2000. "Gender, Time Use, and Change: Impacts of Agricultural Export Employment in Ecuador." World Bank, Development Research Group, Washington, D.C.

Newman, Constance, and Roy Sudarshan Canagarajah. 1999. "Non-Farm Employment, Poverty, and Gender Linkages: Evidence from Ghana and Uganda." World Bank, Development Research Group and Human Development Network, Washington, D.C.

Newman, John, Steen Jorgensen, and Menno Pradhan. 1991. "How Did Workers Benefit from Bolivia's Emergency Social Fund?" *The World Bank Economic Review* 5 (2): 367–93.

Nielsen, Helena Skyt. 1998. "Wage Discrimination in Zambia: An Extension of the Oaxaca-Blinder Decomposition." Centre for Labour Market and Social Research Working Paper 98-01. University of Aarhus, Department of Economics, Denmark.

Notzon, Francis, Yuri Komarov, Sergei P. Ermakov, Christopher T. Sempos, James S. Marks, and Elena V. Sempos. 1996. "Causes of Declining Life Expectancy in Russia." *Journal of the American Medical Association* 279 (10): 793–800.

Nua Internet Surveys. 2000. See *http://www.nua.ie/surveys/*

Oaxaca, Ronald. 1973. "Male-Female Wage Differentials in Urban Labor Markets." *International Economic Review* 14 (3): 693–709.

Olson, Mancur, Naveen Sarna, and Anand Swamy. Forthcoming. "Governance and Growth: A Simple Hypothesis Explaining Cross-country Differences in Productivity Growth." *Public Choice.*

Orazem, Peter F., and Milan Vodopivec. 1999. "Male-Female Differences in Labor Market Outcomes during the Early Transition to Market: The Case of Estonia and Slovenia." Policy Research Working Paper 2087. World Bank, Development Research Group, Washington, D.C. Available online at *http://wbln0018.worldbank.org/research/workpapers.nsf/policyresearch?openform*

Osmani, S. R. 1997. "Poverty and Nutrition in South Asia." In *Nutrition and Poverty.* Papers from the United Nations Administrative Committee on Coordination/Subcommittee on Nutrition 24th Session Symposium, Kathmandu, Nepal.

Osterberg, Christina, and Birgitta Hedman. 1997. "Women and Men in the Nordic Countries: Facts on Equal Opportunities Yesterday, Today and Tomorrow." The Nordic Council of Ministers. Copenhagen, Denmark.

Over, Mead. 1998. "The Effects of Societal Variables on Urban Rates of HIV Infection in Developing Countries: An Exploratory Analysis." In Martha Ainsworth, Lieve Fransen, and Mead Over, eds., *Confronting AIDS: Evidence from the Developing World.* Brussels and Washington, D.C.: European Commission and World Bank.

Pangestu, Mari, and Medelina K. Hendytio. 1997. "Survey Responses from Women Workers in Indonesia's Textile, Garment and Footwear Industries." Policy Research Working Paper 1755. World Bank, Development Research Group, Washington, D.C. Available online at *http://wbln0018.worldbank.org/research/workpapers.nsf/policyresearch?openform*

Parish, William L., Xiaoye Zhe, and Fang Li. 1995. "Nonfarm Work and Marketization of the Chinese Countryside." *The China Quarterly* 143:697–730.

Paternostro, Stefano, and David E. Sahn. 1999. "Wage Determination and Gender Discrimination in a Transition Economy: The Case of Romania." Policy Research Working Paper 2113. World Bank, Development Research Group, Washington, D.C. Available online at *http://wbln0018.worldbank.org/research/workpapers.nsf/policyresearch?openform*

Paul-Majumdar, Pratima, and Anwara Begum. 2000. "The Gender Imbalances in Export Oriented Industries: A Case of the Ready Made Garment Industry in Bangladesh." Background paper for *Engendering Development.* World Bank, Washington, D.C.

Pebley, Anne R., Noreen Goldman, and German Rodriguez. 1996. "Prenatal and Delivery Care and Childhood Immunization in Guatemala: Do Family and Community Matter?" *Demography* 33 (2): 231–47.

Phipps, Shelley A., and Peter S. Burton. 1998. "What's Mine Is Yours? The Influence of Male and Female Incomes on Patterns of Household Expenditure." *Economica* 65: 599–613.

Pitt, Mark M., and Shahidur R. Khandker. 1998. "The Impact of Group-based Credit Programs on Poor Households in Bangladesh: Does the

Gender of Participants Matter?" *Journal of Political Economy* 106: 958–96.

Pitt, Mark M., and Mark R. Rosenzweig. 1990. "Estimating the Intrahousehold Incidence of Illness: Child Health and Gender-Inequality in the Allocation of Time." *International Economic Review* 31 (4): 969–80.

Pitt, Mark M., Mark R. Rosenzweig, and M. Nazmul Hassan. 1990. "Productivity, Health, and Inequality in the Intrahousehold Distribution of Food in Low-Income Countries." *American Economic Review* 80 (5): 1139–56.

Pitt, Mark M., Shahidur R. Khandker, Signe-Mary McKernan, and M. Abdul Latif. 1999. "Credit Programs for the Poor and Reproductive Behavior in Low-income Countries: Are the Reported Causal Relationships the Result of Heterogeneity Bias?" *Demography.* 36 (1): 1–21.

Plantenga, Janneke, and Johan Hansen. 1999. "Assessing Equal Opportunities in the European Union." *International Labour Review* 138 (4): 351–79.

Pradhan, Sanjay. 1996. "Evaluating Public Spending: A Framework for Public Expenditure Reviews." World Bank Discussion Paper No. 323, World Bank, Washington, D.C.

Prügl, Elisabeth. 1999. *The Global Construction of Gender: Home-based Work in the Political Economy of the 20th Century.* New York: Columbia University Press.

Psacharopoulos, George, and Zafiris Tzannatos. 1992. *Women's Employment and Pay in Latin America: Overview and Methodology.* Washington, D.C.: World Bank.

Putnam, Robert. 1993. *Making Democracy Work: Civic Traditions in Modern Italy.* Princeton, NJ: Princeton University Press.

Pyne, Hnin Hnin. 1999. "Gender Dimensions of the East Asian Crisis: A Review of Social Impact Studies in Korea, Indonesia, the Philippines and Thailand." World Bank, South Asia Region, Health, Population and Nutrition Sector, Washington, D.C.

Quibiria, M.G. 1995. "Gender and Poverty: Issues and Policies with Special Reference to Asian Developing Countries." *Journal of Economic Surveys* 9 (4): 373–411.

Quisumbing, Agnes R. 1994. "Improving Women's Agricultural Productivity as Farmers and Workers." Education and Social Policy Department Discussion Paper 37. World Bank, Washington, D.C.

_____. 1996. "Male-Female Differences in Agricultural Productivity: Methodological Issues and Empirical Evidence." *World Development* 24: 1579–95.

Quisumbing, Agnes R., and John Maluccio. 1999. "Intrahousehold Allocation and Gender Relations: New Empirical Evidence." Background paper for *Engendering Development.* World Bank, Washington, D.C. Available online at *http://www.worldbank.org/gender/prr/qm.pdf*

Quisumbing, Agnes R., Lawrence Haddad, and Christine L. Pena. 2000. "Are Women Overrepresented Among the Poor? Poverty Measures and Dominance Analysis for Ten Developing Countries." International Food Policy Research Insititute, Washington, D.C.

Quisumbing, Agnes R., Ellen Payongayong, J.B. Aidoo, and Keijiro Otsuka. 1999. "Women's Land Rights in the Transition to Individualized Ownership: Implications for the Management of Tree Resources in Western Ghana." Food Consumption and Nutrition Division Discussion Paper 58. International Food Policy Research Institute, Washington, D.C. Available online at *http://www.ifpri.cgiar.org/index1.htm*

Rama, Martin, and Donna MacIssac. 1999. "Earnings and Welfare after Downsizing: Central Bank Employees in Ecuador." *The World Bank Economic Review* 13 (1): 89–116. Available online at *http://www.worldbank.org/research/journals/wber/revjan99/pdf/article4.pdf*

Ranis, Gustav. 1993. "Labor Markets, Human Capital and Development Performance in East Asia." Discussion Paper 697. Yale University, Economic Growth Center, New Haven, Conn.

Rao, Vijayendra. 1998. "Wife-Abuse, Its Causes and Its Impact on Intra-Household Resource Allocation in Rural Karnataka: A 'Participatory' Econometric Analysis." In Maithreyi Krishnaraj, Ratna M. Sudarshan, and Abusaleh Shariff, eds., *Gender, Population and Development*. Delhi, Oxford, and New York: Oxford University Press.

Ribero, Rocio. 1999. "Gender Dimensions of Non-Formal Employment in Colombia." Background paper for *Engendering Development*. World Bank, Washington, D.C.

Rice, Patricia. 1999. "Gender Earnings Differentials: The European Experience." Background paper for *Engendering Development*. World Bank, Washington, D.C. Available online at *http://www.worldbank.org/gender/prr/rice.pdf*

Rodgers, William, and William Spriggs. 1996. "The Effect of Federal Contractor Status on Racial Differences in Establishment-Level Employment Shares: 1979–1992." *American Economic Review* 86 (2): 290–93.

Rodgers, Yana van der Meulen. 1999. "Protecting Women and Promoting Equality in the Labor Market: Theory and Evidence." Background paper for *Engendering Development*. World Bank, Washington, D.C. Available online at *http://www.worldbank.org/gender/prr/rodgers.pdf*

Rose, Elaina. 1999. "Consumption Smoothing and Excess Female Mortality in Rural India." *Review of Economics and Statistics* 81 (February): 41–49.

Rosen, Sherwin. 1995. "Public Employment, Taxes and the Welfare State in Sweden." NBER Working Paper 5003. National Bureau of Economic Research, Cambridge, Mass. Available online at *http://papers.nber.org/papers/w5003*

_____. 1996. 'Public employment and the welfare state in Sweden." *Journal of Economic Literature* 34 (June): 729–40.

Rosenhouse, Sandra. 1989. "Identifying the Poor: Is 'Headship' a Useful Concept?" Living Standards Measurement Survey Working Paper 58. World Bank, Washington, D.C.

Rosenzweig, Mark R., and T. Paul Schultz. 1982. "Market Opportunities, Genetic Endowments, and Intrafamily Resource Distribution: Child Survival in Rural India." *American Economic Review* 72 (4): 803–15.

Rosenzweig, Mark R. and Kenneth I. Wolpin. 1994. "Are There Increasing Returns to the

Intergenerational Production of Human Capital? Maternal Schooling and Child Intellectual Achievement." *Journal of Human Resources* 29 (2): 670–93.

_____. 1980. "Testing the Quantity-Quality Fertility Model: The Use of Twins as a Natural Experiment." *Econometrica* 48 (1): 227–40.

Rosholm, Michael, and Nina Smith. 1996. "The Danish Gender Wage Gap in the 1980's: A Panel Data Study." *Oxford Economic Papers* 48: 254–79.

Rozelle, Scott, Xiao-yuan Dong, Linxiu Zhang, and Andrew D. Mason. 2000. "Opportunities and Barriers in Reform China: Gender, Work, and Wages in the Rural Economy." University of California at Davis, Department of Agricultural and Resource Economics.

Rubaclava, Luis, and Duncan Thomas. 1997. "Family Bargaining and Welfare." University of California at Los Angeles and RAND, Santa Monica, Calif.

Ruhm, Christopher J. 1998. "The Economic Consequences of Parental Leave Mandates: Lessons From Europe." *The Quarterly Journal of Economics* 113 (1): 285–317.

Sahn, David, and Lawrence Haddad. 1991. "The Gendered Impacts of Structural Adjustment Programs in Africa: Discussion." *American Journal of Agricultural Economics* 73 (5): 1448–51.

Saito, Katrine A., and Daphne Spurling. 1992. *Developing Agricultural Extension for Women Farmers.* World Bank Discussion Paper 156. Washington, D.C.

Saito, Katrine A., Hailu Mekonnen, and Daphne Spurling. 1994. *Raising the Productivity of Women Farmers in Sub-Saharan Africa.* World Bank Discussion Paper 230. Washington, D.C.

Salaff, Janet W. 1981. *Working Daughters of Hong Kong: Filial Piety or Power in the Family?* Cambridge: Cambridge University Press.

Samuelson, Paul. 1956. "Social Indifference Curves." *Quarterly Journal of Economics* 70 (1): 1–21.

Sanchez, Susana. 1998. "The Participation of Mexican Microenterprises in Credit Markets: Gender Differences." World Bank, Latin American and the Caribbean, Finance, Private Sector and Infrastructure, Washington, D.C.

Sara-Lafosse, Violeta. 1998. "Machismo in America Latina and the Caribbean." In Nelly P. Stromquist, ed., *Women in the Third World: An Encyclopedia of Contemporary Issues.* New York: Garland Publishing.

Schneider, Friedrich. 2000. "The Value Added of Underground Activities: Size and Measurement of the Shadow Economies and Shadow Economy Labor Force All Over the World." Faculty of Business, Economics and Social Sciences, Johannes Kepler University of Linz, Austria.

Schuler, Sidney Ruth, and Syed M. Hashemi. 1994. "Credit Programs, Women's Empowerment, and Contraceptive Use in Rural Bangladesh." *Studies in Family Planning* 25: 65–76.

Schuler, Sidney R., Syed M. Hashemi, and Ann P. Riley. 1997. "The Influence of Women's Changing Roles and Status in Bangladesh's Fertility and Contraceptive Use." *World Development* 25: 563–75.

Schuler, Sidney R., Syed M. Hashemi, Ann P. Riley, and Shireen Akhter. 1996. "Credit Programs,

Patriarchy and Men's Violence against Woman in Rural Bangladesh." *Social Science and Medicine* 43 (12): 1729–42.

Schultz, T. Paul. 1961. "Investment in Human Capital." *American Economic Review* 51 (1): 1–17.

_____. 1985. "School Expenditures and Enrollments, 1960-1980: The Effects of Income, Prices and Population Growth." Yale Economic Growth Center Discussion Paper: 487. Yale University, New Haven, Conn.

_____. 1987. "School Expenditures and Enrollments, 1960–1980: The Effects of Income, Prices and Population Growth." In D. Gale Johnson and R. Lee, eds., *Population Growth and Economic Development.* Madison: University of Wisconsin Press.

_____. 1990. "Testing the Neoclassical Model of Family Labor Supply and Fertility." *Journal of Human Resources* 25 (4): 599–634.

_____, ed. 1991. *Research in Population Economics* 7. Greenwich, Conn. and London: JAI Press.

_____. 1993. "Returns to Women's Schooling." In Elizabeth M. King and M. Anne Hill, eds., *Women's Education in Developing Countries: Barriers, Benefits and Policy.* Baltimore, Md.: The Johns Hopkins University Press.

_____. 1998. "Why Governments Should Invest More Educating Girls." Yale University, Department of Economics, New Haven, Conn.

Seguino, Stephanie. 1997. "Gender Wage Inequality and Export-Led Growth in South Korea." *Journal of Development Studies* 34 (2): 102–32.

_____. 2000. "Gender Inequality and Economic Growth: A Cross-Country Analysis." *World Development* 28 (7): 1211–30.

Sen, Amartya K. 1984. *Resources, Values and Development.* Cambridge, MA and London, UK: Harvard University Press.

_____. 1989. "Women's Survival as a Development Problem." *Bulletin of the American Academy of Arts and Sciences* 43: 14–29.

_____. 1992. "More than 100 Million Women Are Missing." *New York Review of Books* (December): 61–66.

_____. 1998. "Mortality as an Indicator of Economic Success and Failure." *Economic Journal* 28 (January): 1–25.

_____. 1999. *Development and Freedom.* New York: Knopf.

Sen, Gita, and Caren Grown. 1987. *Development, Crises, and Alternative Visions : Third World Women's Perspectives.* New York: Monthly Review Press.

Sen, Samita. 2000. "Toward a Feminist Politics? The Indian Women's Movement in Historical Perspective." Background paper for *Engendering Development.* World Bank, Washington, D.C.

Sethuraman, S.V. 1998. "Gender, Informality and Poverty: A Global Review: Gender Bias in Female Informal Employment and Incomes in Developing Countries." World Bank, Poverty Reduction and Economic Management, Washington, D.C. and Women in Informal Employment: Globalising and Organising, Geneva.

Singh, Inderjit, Lyn Squire, and John Strauss, eds. 1986. *Agricultural Household Models: Extensions, Applications and Policy.* Baltimore, Md.: The Johns Hopkins University Press.

Singh, Ram D. 1994. "Fertility-Mortality Variations across LDCs: Women's Education, Labor

Force Participation, and Contraceptive-Use." *KYKLOS* 47: 209–29.

Sipahimalani, Vandana. 1999. "Education in the Rural Indian Household: The Impact of Household and School Characteristics on Gender Differences." Working Paper 68. National Council of Applied Economic Research, New Delhi.

Skoufias, Emmanuel. 1993. "Labor Market Opportunities and Intrafamily Time Allocation in Rural Households in South Asia." *Journal of Development Economics* 40 (2): 277–310.

Smith, James P., and Michael Ward. 1989. "Women in the Labor Market and in the Family." *Journal of Economic Perspectives* 3 (1): 9–23.

Smith, James P., and Finis Welch. 1984. "Affirmative Action and Labor Markets." *Journal of Labor Economics* 2 (2): 269–301.

Smith, Lisa C., and Lawrence Haddad. 2000. "Explaining Child Malnutrition in Developing Countries: A Cross-country Analysis." Research Report 111. Washington D.C.: International Food Policy Research Institute. Available online at *http://www.ifpri.cgiar.org/index1.htm*

Sokoloff, Kenneth L. and Stanley L. Engerman. 2000. "Institutions, Factor Endowments, and Paths of Development in the New World." *Journal of Economic Perspectives* 14 (3): 217–232.

Squire, Lyn. 1989. "Project Evaluation in Theory and Practice." In Hollis Chenery and T.N. Srinivasn, eds., *Handbook of Development Economics*, Vol. 2. New York and Amsterdam: Elsevier Science Publishers.

State Committee of the CIS (Commonwealth of Independent States. 1999. *CIS Stat CD*. Moscow.

Staudt, Kathleen. 1978. "Agricultural Poverty Gaps: A Case Study of Male Preference in Government Policy Implementation." *Development and Change* 9(3): 439–57.

_____, ed., 1997. *Women, International Development, and Politics: The Bureaucratic Mire*. Philadelphia, PA: Temple University Press. Updated and expanded edition.

Steel, William F., and Ernest Aryeetey. 1994. "Informal Savings Collectors in Ghana: Can They Intermediate?" *Finance and Development* (March): 36–37.

Stokey, Nancy L. 1994. "Sources of Economic Growth: Comments on Barro and Lee." *Carnegie-Rochester Conference Series on Public Policy* 40 (0): 47–57.

Stotsky, Janet G. 1997. "Gender Bias in Tax Systems." *Tax Notes International* (June 9): 1913–23.

Summerfield, Gale and Nahid Aslanbeigui. 1998. "The Impact of Structural Adjustment and Economic Reform of Women." In Nelly P. Stromquist, ed. *Women in the Third World. An Encyclopedia of Contemporary Issues*. New York: Garland Publishing, Inc.

Summers, Lawrence H. 1992. "Investing in *All* the People." *The Pakistan Development Review* 31 (4, part I): 367–404.

_____. 1994. "Investing in All the People. Educating Women in Developing Countries." Seminar Paper 45. World Bank, Economic Development Institute, Washington, D.C.

Swamy, Anand, Steve Knack, Young Lee, and Omar Azfar. Forthcoming. "Gender and Corruption." *Journal of Development Economics*.

Swedish Institute. 1999. "The Care of the Elderly in Sweden." Stockholm. Available online at *http://www.si.se/eng/esverige/elderly.html*

Taggart, Nancy, and Chloe O'Gara. 2000. "Training Women for Leadership and Success in Information Technology." Academy for Educational Development, Washington, D.C.

Takayoshi, Kusago, and Zafiris Tzannatos. 1998. "Export Processing Zones: A Review in Need of Update." Discussion Paper 9802. World Bank, Human Development Network, Social Protection Group, Washington, D.C. Available online at *http://wbln0018.worldbank.org/HDNet/HD.nsf/SectorPages/SP?Opendocument*

Tansel, Aysit. 1998. "Determinants of School Attainment of Boys and Girls in Turkey." Discussion Paper 789. Yale University, Economic Growth Center, New Haven, Conn. Available online at *http://www.econ.yale.edu/growth_pdf/cdp789.pdf*

_____. 2000. "Wage Earners, Self Employed and Gender in the Informal Sector in Turkey." Background paper for *Engendering Development*. World Bank, Washington D.C.

TGNP (Tanzania Gender Networking Programme). 1999. *Budgeting with a Gender Focus*. Dar es Salaam.

Thomas, Duncan. 1990. "Intrahousehold Resource Allocation: An Inferential Approach." *Journal of Human Resources* 25: 635–64.

_____. 1994. "Like Father, Like Son; Like Mother, Like Daughter: Parental Resources and Child Height." *Journal of Human Resources* 29 (4): 950–88.

_____. 1997. "Incomes, Expenditures, and Health Outcomes: Evidence on Intrahousehold Resource Allocation." In Lawrence Haddad, John Hoddinott, and Harold Alderman, eds., *Intrahousehold Resource Allocation in Developing Countries : Models, Methods, and Policy*. Baltimore, Md.: The Johns Hopkins University Press.

Thomas, Duncan, and John Strauss. 1992. "Prices, Infrastructure, Household Characteristics and Child Height." *Journal of Development Economics* 39 (2): 301–31.

Thomas, Duncan, Dante Contreras, and Elizabeth Frankenberg. 1997. "Child Health and the Distribution of Household Resources at Marriage." RAND, Santa Monica, Calif., and University of California at Los Angeles, Department of Economics.

Thomas, Duncan, Robert F. Schoeni, and John Strauss. 1996. "Parental Investments in Schooling: The Roles of Gender and Resources in Urban Brazil." Working Paper Series, Labor and Population Program 96-02. RAND, Santa Monica, California.

Todd, Petra, Jere R. Behrman, and Yingmei Cheng. 2000. "Evaluating Preschool Programs When Length of Exposure to the Program Varies: A Nonparametric Approach." Department of Economics and Population Studies Center, University of Pennsylvania, Philadelphia, PA.

Transparency International. 1999. *Corruption Perceptions Index*. Berlin. Available online at *http://www.transparency.de/documents/cpi/2000/cpi2000.html*

Turshen, Margaret. 1998. "Women's War Stories." In Margaret Turshen, and Clotilde

ENGENDERING DEVELOPMENT

Twagiramariya, eds., *What Women Do in War-time. Gender and Conflict in Africa.* London and New York: Zed Books.

Tzannatos, Zafiris. 1998. "Women's Labor Incomes." In Nelly P. Stromquist, ed., *Women in the Third World: An Encyclopedia of Contemporary Issues.* New York and London: Garland Publishing.

_____. 1999. "Women and Labor Market Changes in the Global Economy: Growth Helps: Inequalities Hurt and Public Policy Matters." *World Development* 27 (3): 551–69.

Udry, Christopher. 1996. "Gender, Agricultural Production, and the Theory of the Household." *Journal of Political Economy* 104 (5): 1010–46.

Udry, Christopher, John Hoddinott, Harold Alderman, and Lawrence Haddad. 1995. "Gender Differentials in Farm Productivity: Implications for Household Efficiency and Agricultural Policy." *Food Policy* 20 (5): 407–23.

UN (United Nations). 1985. *The Nairobi Forward-looking Strategies for the Advancement of Women.* Adopted by the World Conference to review and appraise the achievements of the United Nations Decade for Women: Equality, Development and Peace, held in Nairobi, Kenya, 15–26 July 1985. Available online at *gopher://gopher.un.org/00/conf/fwcw/nfls/nfls.en%09%09%2B*

_____. 1989. "Household Income and Expenditure Surveys: A Technical Study." National Household Survey Capability Program. New York.

_____. 1995. *The Beijing Declaration and Platform for Action.* Adopted by the Fourth World Conference on Women, held in Beijing, China, 4–15 September 1995. Available online at *gopher://gopher.un.org/00/conf/fwcw/off/plateng/9520p1.en%09%09%2B*

_____. 1997. *Human Rights and Legal Status of Women in the Asian and Pacific Region.* New York: Economic and Social Commission for Asia and the Pacific, Studies on Women in Development.

_____. 2000. *Review and Appraisal of the Implementation of the Beijing Platform for Action.* Report of the Secretary General. Advance Unedited Version. E/CN.6/2000/PC/2.

UN ECLAC (United Nations Economic Commission for Latin America and the Caribbean). 1998. *Social Panorama of Latin America.* Santiago.

UNAIDS (Joint United Nations Programme on HIV/AIDS). 1999. *The UNAIDS Report.* Geneva. *http://www.unaids.org/publications/documents/responses/theme/repjuly99.doc*

UNDP (United Nations Development Programme). 1991. *Human Development Report 1991.* New York: Oxford University Press.

_____. 1995. *Human Development Report 1995.* New York: Oxford University Press.

_____. 2000. *Human Development Report 2000.* New York: Oxford University Press.

UNFPA (United Nations Population Fund). 1997. *The State of World Population.* New York. Available online at *http://www.unfpa.org/swp/1997/swpmain.htm*

UNICEF (United Nations Children's Fund). 1999a. *The State of the World's Children 2000.* New York: Oxford University Press.

_____. 1999b. "Women in Transition." Regional Monitoring Report No. 6 of the MONEE ("Central and Eastern Europe in Transition: Public Policy and Social Conditions") Project, Florence, Italy.

UNIFEM (United Nations Development Fund for Women). 1998. *Engendering Governance and Leadership: 1998 Annual Report.* New York.

U.S. Department of State. 1997. "China Country Report on Human Rights Practices for 1997." Available online at *http://www.state.gov/www/global/human_rights/1997_hrp_report/china.html*

Van de Walle, Dominique, and Kimberly Nead, eds. 1995. *Public Spending and the Poor: Theory and Evidence.* Baltimore, Md.: Johns Hopkins University Press.

van der Gaag, Jacques, and Jee-Peng Tan. 1998. *The Benefits of Early Child Development Programs: An Economic Analysis.* Washington, D.C.: World Bank.

Vijverberg, Wim. 1998. "Non-farm Household Enterprises in Vietnam." In David Dollar, Paul Glewwe, and Jennie Litvack, eds., *Household Welfare and Vietnam's Transition.* A World Bank Regional and Sectoral Study. Washington, D.C.

Viravong, Manivone. 1999. "Reforming Property Rights in Laos." In Irene Tinker and Gale Summerfield, eds., *Women's Rights to House and Land (China, Laos, Vietnam).* Boulder, CO: Lynne Reienner Publishers, Inc.

Vishwanath, Tara, Shahidur R. Khandker, Andrew D. Mason, and Anand V. Swamy. 1996. "Gender, Land Rights and Agricultural Productivity: A Survey of Issues and a Case Study of Burkina Faso." World Bank, Gender Analysis and Policy Group, Poverty and Social Policy Department, Washington, D.C.

von Braun, Joachim, and Patrick J. R. Webb. 1989. "The Impact of New Crop Technology on the Agricultural Division of Labor in a West African Setting." *Economic Development and Cultural Change* 37 (April): 513–34.

Waldfogel, Jane, Yoshio Higuchi, and Masahiro Abe. 1998. "Family Leave Policies and Women's Retention after Childbirth: Evidence from the United States, Britain and Japan." Columbia University, School of Social Work, New York.

Waldron, Ingrid. 1986. "What Do We Know about the Causes of Sex Differences in Mortality?" *Population Bulletin on the United Nations* 18: 59.

Ward-Batts, Jennifer. 1997. "Modeling Family Expenditures to Test Income Pooling." University of Washington, Department of Economics, Seattle.

Weinberg, Bruce A. 2000. "Computer Use and the Demand for Female Workers." *Industrial and Labor Relations Review* 53 (2): 290–308.

Westley, Sidney B., and Andrew Mason. 1998. "Women Are Key Players in the Economies of East and Southeast Asia." *Asia-Pacific Population & Policy* 44 (January). East-West Center Program on Population, Honolulu. Available online at *http://www.eastwestcenter.org/stored/pdfs/p&p044.pdf*

WHO (World Health Organization). 1998. "Gender and Health: A Technical Paper." Geneva. Available online at *http://www.who.int/frh-whd/GandH/GHreport/gendertech.htm*

_____. 2000. *The World Health Report 2000 Health Systems: Improving Performance.* Geneva. Available online at *http://www.who.int/whr/*

Whiting, B.B., and C.P. Edwards. 1988. *Children of Different Worlds: The Formation of Social Behavior.* Cambridge, Mass.: Harvard University Press.

Williamson, Oliver E. 1975. *Markets and Hierarchies: Analysis and Antitrust Implications.* New York: Free Press.

Wise, David A. 1997. "Retirement against the Demographic Trend: More Older People Living Longer, Working Less, and Saving Less." *Demography* 34 (1): 83–95.

WISTAT (Women's Indicators and Statistics Database). 1998. Version 3. Prepared by the United Nations Statistical Division. New York.

Wong, Rebeca, and Ruth E. Levine. 1992. "The Effect of Household Structure on Women's Economic Activity and Fertility: Evidence from Recent Mothers in Urban Mexico." *Economic Development and Cultural Change* 41 (1): 89–102.

Wong, Rebeca, and Susan W. Parker. 1999. "Welfare of the Elderly in Mexico: A Comparative Perspective." Background paper for *Engendering Development.* World Bank, Washington D.C.

Woolcock, Michael. 2000. "Managing Risk, Shocks, and Opportunity in Developing Economies: The Role of Social Capital." In Gustav Ranis, ed., *The Dimensions of Development.* New Haven, CT: Yale University Center for International and Area Studies.

World Bank. 1993. *The East Asian Miracle: Economic Growth and Public Policy: Summary.* A Policy Research Report. New York: Oxford University Press.

_____. 1994a. *Adjustment in Africa: Reforms, Results, and the Road Ahead.* Washington, D.C.

_____. 1994b. *Averting the Old Age Crisis: Policies to Protect the Old and Promote Growth.* A Policy Research Report. New York: Oxford University Press.

_____. 1994c. *Gender Discrimination in the Labor Market and the Role of the Law: Experiences in Six Latin American Countries.* Washington, D.C.

_____. 1994d. *World Development Report 1994: Infrastructure for Development.* New York: Oxford University Press.

_____. 1995a. *World Development Report 1995: Workers in an Integrating World.* New York: Oxford University Press.

_____. 1996. "Bangladesh: Public Expenditure Review." Resident Mission, Country Operations Division, Dhaka.

_____. 1997. "Bangladesh: Female Secondary School Assistance Project: Mid-term Review." South Asia Regional Office, Populations and Human Resources Division, Washington, D.C.

_____. 1998a. *Assessing Aid: What Works, What Doesn't, and Why.* A Policy Research Report. New York: Oxford University Press.

_____. 1998b. *East Asia: The Road to Recovery.* Washington, D.C.

_____. 1999a. *Confronting AIDS: Public Priorities in a Global Epidemic.* Revised ed. A Policy Research Report. New York: Oxford University Press.

_____. 1999b. *Population and the World Bank: Adapting to Change.* Health, Nutrition, and Population Team, Washington, D.C.

_____. 1999c. "Vietnam Development Report 2000: Attacking Poverty." Country Economic Memorandum, Poverty Reduction and Economic Management Unit, East Asia and Pacific Region, World Bank, Washington, D.C.

_____. 1999d. *World Development Indicators 1999.* Washington, D.C.

_____. 2000a. *World Development Report 1999/2000: Entering the 21st Century.* New York: Oxford University Press.

_____. 2000b. *World Development Report 2000/2001: Attacking Poverty.* New York: Oxford University Press.

Ye, Xiao. 1998. "Gender Analysis of Poverty and Education Issues in SSA: Household Data Sets." Background paper for the Special Program of Assistance to Africa Status Report. World Bank, Africa Region, Poverty Reduction and Social Development Group, Washington, D.C.

Young, Mary. 1996. *Early Child Development: Investing in the Future.* Washington, D.C.: World Bank.

Zabalza, Antoni, and Zafiris Tzannatos. 1985. *Women and Equal Pay: The Effects of Legislation on Female Employment and Wages in Britain.* Cambridge: Cambridge University Press.

Zaman, Hassan. 1999. "Assessing the Impact of Micro-Credit on Poverty and Vulnerability in Bangladesh." Policy Research Working Paper 2145. World Bank, Development Research Group, Washington, D.C. Available online at *http://wbln0018.worldbank.org/research/workpapers.nsf/policyresearch?openform*

Zulficar, Mona. 1999. "The Islamic Marriage Contract in Egypt." Shalakany Law Office, Cairo.

Zveglich, Joseph E., Jr., and Yana van der Meulen Rodgers. 1999. "The Impact of Protective Measures For Female Workers." Asian Development Bank, Manila.

Zveglich, Joseph E., Jr., Yana van der Meulen Rodgers, and William M. Rodgers, III. 1997. "The Persistence of Gender Earnings Inequality in Taiwan, 1978–1992." *Industrial and Labor Relations Review* 50 (4): 594–609.

Index

(Page numbers in italics indicate material in figures, tables, or boxes.)

359